AA

Britain's
Best

guest houses, inns,
farmhouses & other
interesting places to stay

AA **Lifestyle Guides**

Ordnance Survey® This product includes mapping data licensed from Ordnance Survey® with the permission of the Controller of Her Majesty's Stationery Office.

© Crown Copyright 2002. All rights reserved. Licence number 399221

Atlas prepared by the Cartographic Department of The Automobile Association   A00927

Typeset by Anton Graphics, Andover

Cover photograph: King Charles II Guest House, Rye, East Sussex

Printed and bound by Graficas estella, S.A., Navarra, Spain

Editorial contributors: Julia Hynard, Linda Edge & Denise Laing

A CIP catalogue record for this book is available from the British Library

ISBN 0749532572

Published by AA trading which is a trading name of Automobile Association Developments Limited, whose registered office is Millstream, Maidenhead Road, Windsor, Berkshire, SL4 5GD

Registered number 1878835

CONTENTS

*H*ow to use the guide

The guide is divided into countries: England, Scotland, and Wales. Channel Islands and the Isle of Man follow the England section.

Each country is listed in county order, and then in approximate alphabetical town/village location within each county.

There is a county map on page 12 to help you locate counties within Britain. In the England section, counties are indicated at the top left or right hand side of each page.

Finding the Town

If you know which town you are looking for, refer to the index at the back of the guide. Towns are listed alphabetically, with their county, page number and establishments in or closest to the town. Within a town or village, establishments are listed approximately alphabetically.

Map Reference

The map refers to the town/village. The map page number refers to the atlas at the front of the guide, and is followed by the National Grid Reference. To find the location, read the first figure across and the second figure vertically within the lettered square. Maps locating each establishment can also be found on the AA website, www.theAA.com

Contact Details

Telephone and fax numbers are given where available for the establishments. Please refer to page 10 for an explanation of telephone codes and international dialling. E -mail and website addresses are also given where appropriate.

www.theAA.com

The AA website gives details of all AA recommended accommodation including all the places to stay listed in this guide.

Address and Directions

The full postal address of each establishment is given, followed by brief directions.

Rooms

The number of rooms is shown in the heading box after the directions. Further

details of room facilities will appear in the main description, check when booking to ensure that all the facilities you require will be available.

AA Inspection and Diamond Classification ◆

All bed & breakfast accommodation in the guide has been inspected by the AA and belonged to the AA guest accommodation scheme at the time of going to press. Establishments are given the classification of between one and five Diamonds for quality. More details about Diamond Classification can be found on page 8.

Rosette Awards 🏵

The AA's food award. Further explanation can be found on page 8.

Prices

Prices are provided by the proprietors and are believed to be correct at the time of going to press. Prices may vary for different rooms or at peak times. Do check exactly what is included in the price when booking.

Smoking Restrictions

Restrictions for smokers are given in the heading box, see also page 7.

Description

The description of the establishment will include information about the range and type of facilities and special features.

Recommended in the Area

We asked the establishments to tell us about places to visit in their area which they recommend to their guests. At the beginning of each county section you will find details of AA recommended pubs and restaurants, taken from our database. The AA website may feature many other pubs and restaurants in the area you are visiting. You may also find some of our other guides useful - The Pub Guide, The Restaurant Guide and The Days Out Guide.

Hints for Booking Your Stay

The AA inspects and classifies small private hotels, guest houses, farmhouses and inns. Establishments applying for AA quality assessment are visited on a 'mystery guest' basis by one of the AA's team of qualified accommodation inspectors. Inspectors stay overnight to make a thorough test of the accommodation, food and hospitality offered. On settling the bill the following morning they identify themselves and ask to be shown round the premises. The inspector completes a full report, making a recommendation for the appropriate level of quality (see Diamond Classification on page 8). The establishments in this guide have been recommended by AA inspectors for their excellent hospitality, accommodation and food.

Guest Houses

Many guest houses include the word 'hotel' in their name which can lead to confusion. For AA purposes, small and private hotels are included in the guest accommodation category when they cannot offer all the services required for the AA hotel star scheme (for example evening meals). The establishments selected for this guide represent top of the range accommodation with many of the services and facilities you might expect of a hotel, however there may be restricted guest access to the house, particularly in the late morning and during the afternoon, so do ask about this when booking.

Farmhouses

Farmhouse accommodation generally represents good value for money and excellent home-cooking. Many farmhouses listed are on working farms, and while some farmers are happy to allow visitors to look around, or even to help feed the animals, others may discourage visitors from exploring the working land. Please note that modern farms are potentially dangerous places, especially where machinery and chemicals are concerned. Visitors should exercise care, in particular when accompanying children, and should never leave children unsupervised around the farm. Farmhouses may also be in remote locations so do ask for directions when booking to supplement the information provided in the guide.

Inns

Traditional inns provide a cosy bar, convivial atmosphere, good beer and pub food. Inns with accommodation entries in the guide will provide breakfast in a suitable room and should also serve light meals during licensing hours. Some small, fully licensed hotels may be classified as inns, and the character of the properties will vary according to whether they are traditional country inns or larger town establishments. Check

details before you book, including arrival times as these may be restricted to the opening hours.

Breakfast and evening meals

Guest houses usually offer a full, cooked breakfast in the British tradition, where this is advertised as not available, a substantial continental breakfast will be provided. Some guest houses offer bed and breakfast only, so guests must go out for the evening meal. Many guest houses do provide evening meals, ranging from a set meal to a full menu, some have their own restaurants. You may have to arrange dinner in advance, at breakfast or on the previous day, so ask about this when booking. If you book on bed, breakfast and evening meal terms, you may find that the tariff includes only the set menu, if there is a carte you may be able to order from this and pay a supplement. On Sundays, many establishments serve the main meal at midday, and provide only a cold supper in the evening. In some parts of Britain, particularly in Scotland, high tea (a savoury dish followed by bread and butter, scones, cake etc.) is sometimes served instead of dinner. Dinner may be available as an alternative.

Booking

Advance booking is strongly recommended to avoid disappointment. The peak holiday period in Great Britain is from the beginning of June to the end of September, Easter and public holidays are also busy times so bear this in mind when planning your stay. In some parts of Scotland the skiing season is a peak holiday period. Some establishments may only accept weekly bookings from Saturday. Some establishments will require a deposit on booking.

Further Details

We have tried to provide sufficient information about establishments in the guide but if you require more information, contact the establishment direct. Address, telephone, fax, e-mail and website details are given where known. Do please quote this publication in any enquiry. Although we try to publish accurate information, please bear in mind that all details, especially prices, may be subject to change without notice during the currency of the guide. If in any doubt confirm details with the establishment at the time of booking.

Cancellation

If you find that you must cancel a booking, let the proprietor know immediately. If the room you booked cannot be re-let you may be held legally responsible for partial payment. This may mean losing your deposit or being liable for compensation. You should consider taking out cancellation insurance.

Payment

Guest houses may not accept credit cards so do check when booking. VAT (Value Added Tax at 17·5%) is payable in the UK and in the Isle of Man, on both basic prices and any service. VAT does not apply in the Channel Islands. You should always confirm the current prices before making a booking. The prices in this guide must be accepted as indications rather than firm quotations. It is a good idea to confirm exactly what is included in the price when booking.

Smoking Regulations

No Smoking appears in the heading box when there is a total ban on smoking throughout all main areas of the premises. If only certain areas are restricted this will appear e.g. No smoking in bedrooms. Although we have tried to get accurate information about smoking restrictions, please be aware that the situation may change during the currency of the guide. If smoking regulations are of importance to you please make sure that you check the exact details with the establishment when booking.

AA Classification and Awards

When choosing a place to stay it is important to be sure that your chosen establishment offers comfortable, well-equipped accommodation and pleasant surroundings. But how can you be sure in advance that where you stay will satisfy your requirements?

◆ Diamond Classification

All places to stay in this guide are AA inspected and rated according to the Diamond Classification Scheme. These ratings ensure that your accommodation meets the AA's highest standards of cleanliness, with the emphasis on professionalism, proper booking procedures and a prompt and efficient service.

The AA's Diamond Awards cover bed and breakfast establishments (see page 6), reflecting guest accommodation at five grades of quality, with one Diamond indicating the simplest, and Five Diamonds at the top of the scale. The criteria for eligibility is guest care and quality rather than the choice of extra facilities. Establishments are visited by a team of qualified inspectors to ensure that the accommodation, food and hospitality meet the AA's own exacting standards. (All the establishments in this book have been rated either four or five Diamonds.)

Guests should receive a prompt, professional check in and check out, comfortable accommodation equipped to modern standards, regularly changed bedding and towels, a sufficient hot water supply at all times, good, well-prepared meals, and a full English or continental breakfast.

AA Rosette Awards

Some of the establishments in this guide have been awarded AA Rosettes for their food. Rosettes are awarded annually, on a rising scale of one to five, and are made solely on the basis of a meal visit or visits by one or more of our restaurant inspectors.

At the simplest level, one rosette, the chef should display a mastery of basic techniques, and be able to produce dishes of sound quality and clarity of flavours, using good, fresh ingredients.

To gain two rosettes, the chef must show great technical skill, more consistency and judgement in combining and balancing ingredients, and a clear ambition to achieve high standards.

The award of three rosettes takes a restaurant into the big league, and in a typical year fewer than 10% of the restaurants in our scheme achieve this distinction. Expectations of the kitchen are high, and there is little room for inconsistencies.

At the four rosette level, all technical skills should be exemplary, and there should also be daring ideas - which must work. There is no room for disappointment.

Five rosettes is the ultimate award, signifying cooking at the pinnacle of achievement. Technique should be of such perfection that flavours, combinations and textures show a faultless sense of balance.

It is important to remember that many places serve very enjoyable food but do not qualify for the AA Rosette Awards.

Useful Information

Licensed Premises

All inns hold a full licence but not all guest houses are licensed to sell alcohol. Some may have a full liquor licence, others may have a table licence and wine list so check when booking. Licensed premises are not obliged to remain open throughout the permitted hours, and they may do so only when they expect reasonable trade.

London

AA guest accommodation in London includes small hotels which may not be privately owned. London prices tend to be higher than outside the capital and usually only include bed and breakfast, check when booking.

Fire Precautions and Safety

Many of the establishments listed in the guide are subject to the requirements of the Fire Precautions Act of 1971. The Fire Precautions Act does not apply to the Channel Islands or the Isle of Man where their own rules are exercised. All establishments should display details of how to summon assistance in the event of an emergency at night.

Codes of Practice

The AA encourages the use of The Hotel Industry Voluntary Code of Booking Practice in appropriate establishments. Its prime objective is to ensure that the

customer is clear about the price and the exact services and facilities being purchased, before entering into a contractually binding agreement. If the price has not been previously confirmed in writing, the guest should be handed a card at the time of registration, stipulating the total obligatory charge.

The Tourism (Sleeping Accommodation Price Display) Order 1977 compels hotels, motels, guest houses, farmhouses, inns and self-catering accommodation with four or more letting bedrooms to display in entrance halls the minimum and maximum prices charged for each category of room. This order complements the Voluntary Code of Booking Practice.

Dogs

Some establishments which do not normally accept dogs may accept guide dogs. Some establishments that accept dogs may restrict the size and breed of dogs permitted and the rooms into which they may be taken. Check the conditions when booking.

Children

Restrictions for children may be mentioned in the description. Some establishments may offer free accommodation to children when they share their parents' room. Please note that this information may be subject to change without notice and it is essential to check when booking.

Complaints

Readers who have any cause to complain are urged to do so on the spot. This should provide an opportunity for the proprietor to correct matters. If a personal approach fails, readers should inform AA Hotel Services, Fanum House, Basingstoke, Hants RG21 4EA. The AA does not however undertake to obtain compensation for complaints.

*T*elephone codes & international dialling

Dialling the UK from Abroad

The telephone and fax numbers given for establishments in this guide are made up of a four digit area code followed by a local number. When dialling from abroad first dial the international network access code - 00- from Europe, -011- from the US. Next dial the country code (44 for the UK). Omit the first digit of the area code then dial the rest of the local number.

For example
0111 121212 becomes:
00 44 111 121212 from Europe, or
011 44 111 121212 from the US.

Dialling Abroad from the UK

When dialling abroad from the UK the same principles apply. First dial the international network access code, then the country code. Country codes are listed at the back of UK telephone directories. The first digit of the area code should be omitted (with the exception of calls to Russia). Further information can be obtained from International Directory Enquiries by dialling 153 from the UK, calls are charged.

Telephone and fax numbers given in the guide are believed correct at the time of going to press but changes may occur during the currency of the guide. The AA website is regularly updated, establishment details can be found on the accommodation pages at www.theAA.com/getaway

Telephones

Many guest houses have direct dial telephones in the rooms or guests may have use of a telephone by arrangement with the proprietor, check the rate that you will be charged before calling. Payphones may be available, these usually take cash or phonecards. Phonecards can generally be purchased from newsagents and post offices. Some payphones, usually in large cities, will also take credit cards. Some cell phones may be adaptable for use in Britain, check with your service provider.

International Information

Money

Establishments may not accept travellers cheques or credit cards so ask about payment methods when you book. Make sure you have enough currency for your everyday needs, particularly in rural areas, as there may be little opportunity to exchange currency. There are exchange offices at airports and usually at high street banks where the current exchange rates will be displayed. Some European and American credit and debit cards will allow you to withdraw cash from British ATMs, check with your bank before travelling.

Medical Treatment and Health Insurance

Travellers who normally take certain medicines should ensure that they have sufficient supply for their stay before travelling. Travellers who for health reasons carry drugs or appliances e.g. a hypodermic syringe, may experience difficulties in entering the UK without a letter from their doctor describing the condition and treatment required. Before travelling to the UK from abroad make sure that you are covered by insurance for emergency medical and dental treatment as a minimum. Before taking out additional insurance check whether your homeowner or health insurance policy covers you for travel abroad. Many European countries have reciprocal agreements for medical treatment and will require EU citizens to obtain a validated E111 certificate of entitlement before travel. You should not rely exclusively on these arrangements and are strongly advised to take out personal travel insurance.

Electrical appliances

These may require an adapter for the plug, as well as an electrical voltage converter that will allow for example a normal 110-volt American appliance to take 220-240-volt British current. Two-in-one adapter/converters are available at some hardware stores.

Trains

There is an extensive rail network in Britain. Check with a travel agent before travelling to find out about special offers or passes. It may be advisable to book more popular routes (e.g. London to Edinburgh) well in advance. When booking accommodation check that it is accessible by train if this is your main method of transport.

Ferries

Ferries operate regularly between the Isle of Wight, Isle of Man, Scottish Islands, Channel Islands and mainland Britain. Services operate for foot passengers as well as cars and it may be necessary to book in advance. Ferry services are subject to seasonal variations so check with a travel agent in advance.

Air

Heathrow, Gatwick, Birmingham, Manchester and Glasgow are the major international airports in the UK. There are airports in many cities and internal flights can be a relatively cheap option for longer distances. Ask your travel agent or browse the internet, often the best prices are limited to a small number of seats available only through advance booking.

Car Rental & Driving

You will need your drivers licence and preferably an International Driving Permit (a document with a photograph which confirms you as the holder of a valid driving licence in your own country), you may also be asked to show your passport. You may be required to produce an additional credit card or further proof of identity when renting more expensive cars. It is advisable to book in advance and check that you have the appropriate insurance coverage, mileage allowance and transmission (you'll pay more for an automatic). When collecting your car check whether it takes diesel, unleaded or leaded petrol. Drive on the left and overtake on the right in the UK. Ensure that seatbelts are worn by every occupant of your car, whether they sit in the front or the rear. Observe the speed limits, displayed in miles per hour.

County Index

The county map shown here will help you identify the counties within each country. The England section of the guide has the county names in the panel at the edge of each page. To find towns featured in the guide use the atlas pages which follow, and the index at the back of the book.

England

1	Bedfordshire
2	Berkshire
3	Bristol
4	Buckinghamshire
5	Cambridgeshire
6	Greater Manchester
7	Herefordshire
8	Hertfordshire
9	Leicestershire
10	Northamptonshire
11	Nottinghamshire
12	Rutland
13	Staffordshire
14	Warwickshire
15	West Midlands
16	Worcestershire

Scotland

17	City of Glasgow
18	Clackmananshire
19	East Ayrshire
20	East Dunbartonshire
21	East Renfrewshire
22	Perth & Kinross
23	Renfrewshire
24	South Lanarkshire
25	West Dunbartonshire

Wales

26	Blaenau Gwent
27	Bridgend
28	Caerphilly
29	Denbighshire
30	Flintshire
31	Merthyr Tydfil
32	Monmouthshire
33	Neath Port Talbot
34	Newport
35	Rhondda Cynon Taff
36	Torfaen
37	Vale of Glamorgan
38	Wrexham

County Map

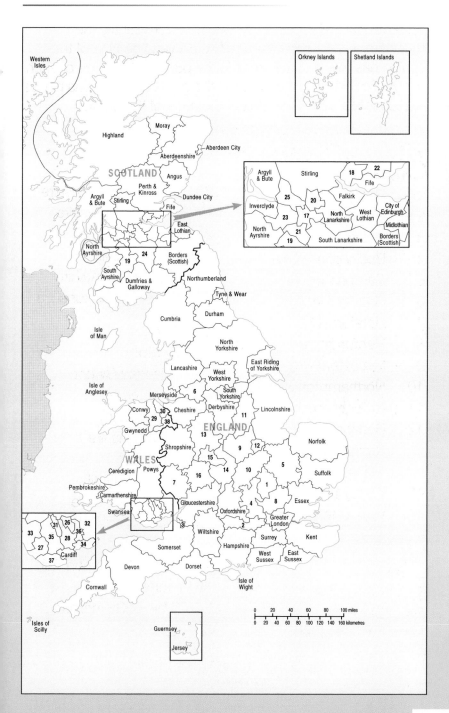

*C*ounty & Country Index

KEY TO ATLAS PAGES

13 Shetland Islands

Orkney Islands

11 **12**
• Inverness
Aberdeen•
Fort William•

○ Town Names
● Bed & Breakfast
◎ Motorway junction
◉ Restricted motorway junction

Perth•
9 **10**
Glasgow• Edinburgh•

Stranraer• Newcastle•
Carlisle•
Kendal• Middlesbrough•
5 **6** **7** York• **8**
Leeds• Hull•
Liverpool• Manchester•
Holyhead• •Sheffield
Lincoln•

•Nottingham Norwich•
Aberystwyth•
Birmingham•
•Cambridge
Carmarthen• Gloucester•
Oxford• Colchester•
Cardiff• •Bristol **3** LONDON **4**
1 **2** Guildford•
Barnstaple• •Taunton Southampton• Maidstone• •Dover
Exeter • Dorchester• Brighton•
•Plymouth
•Penzance
Isles of Scilly

13
Channel Islands

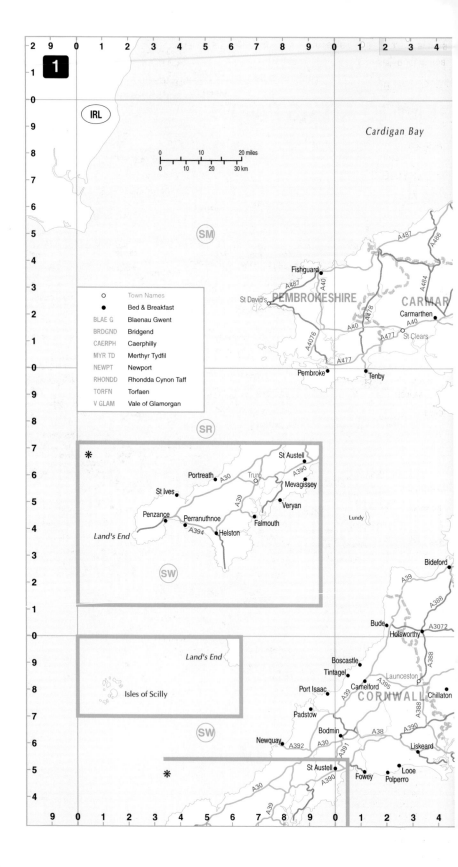

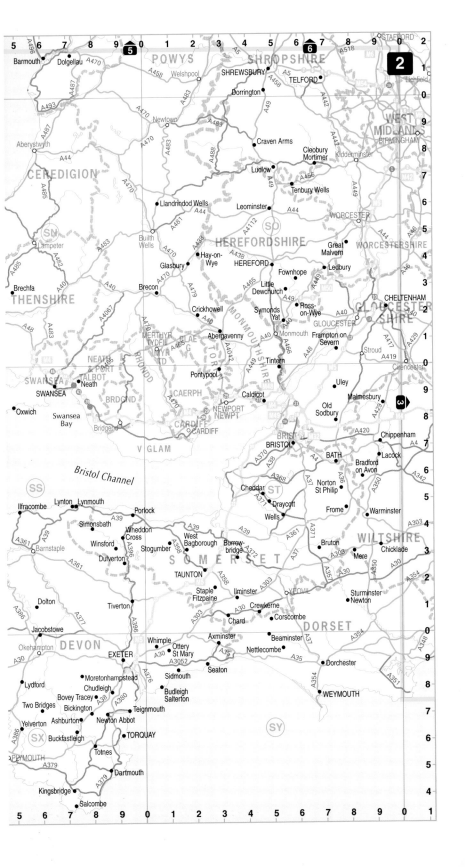

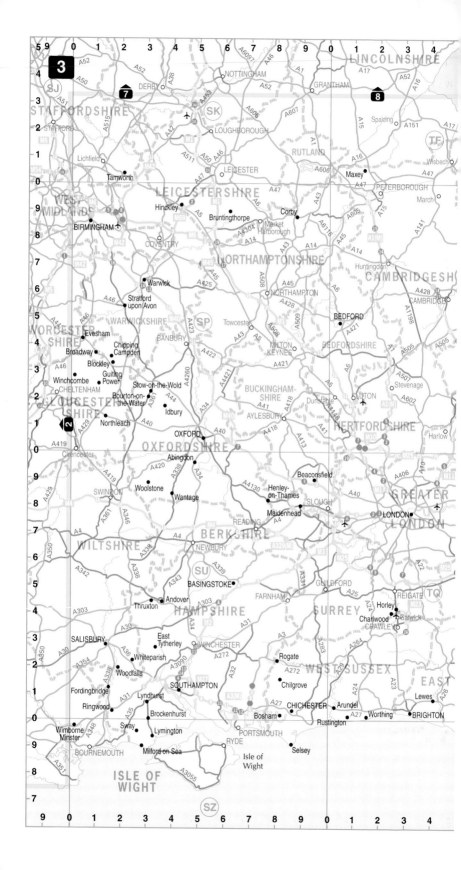

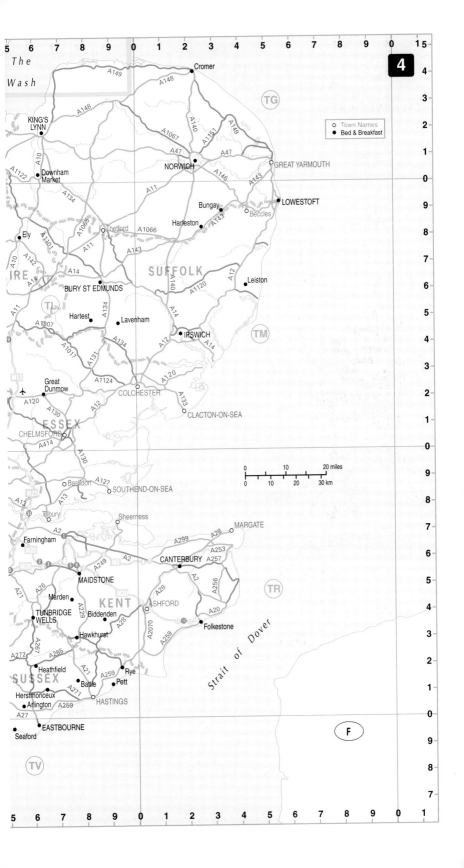

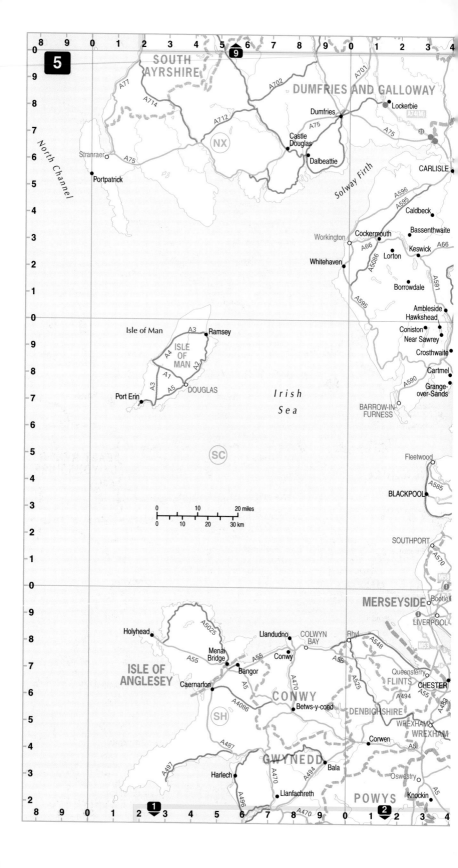

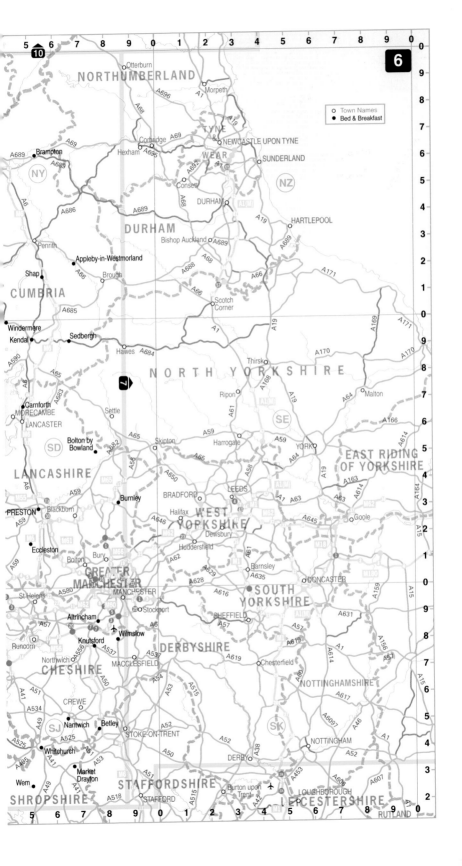

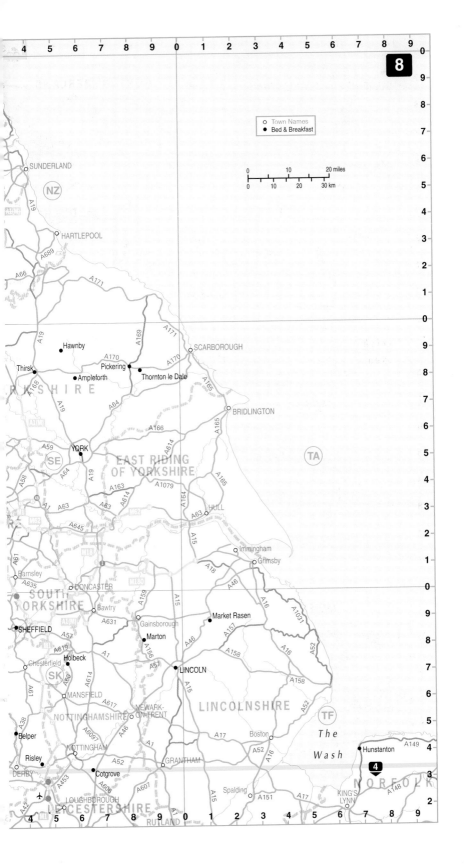

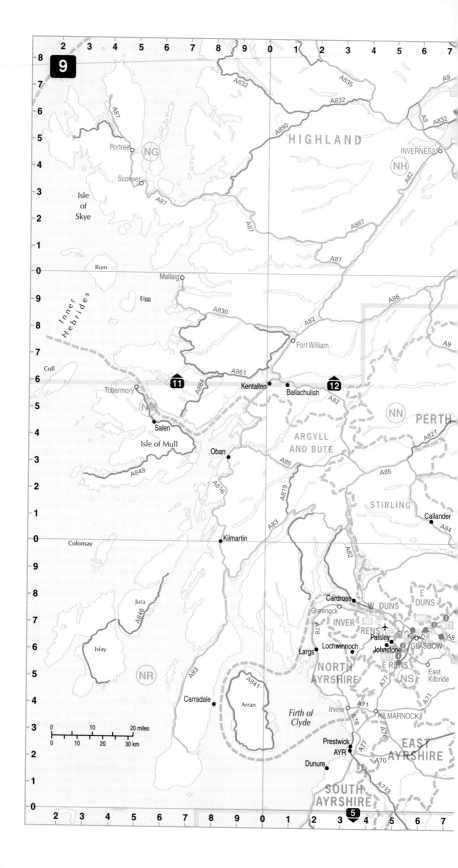

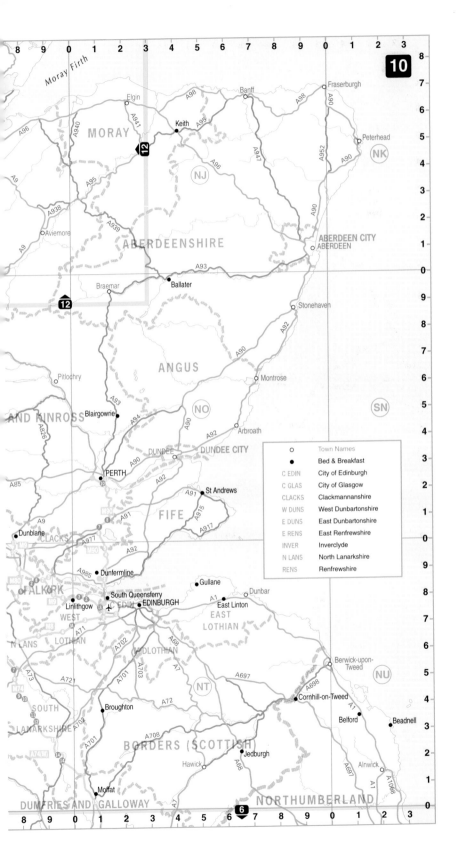

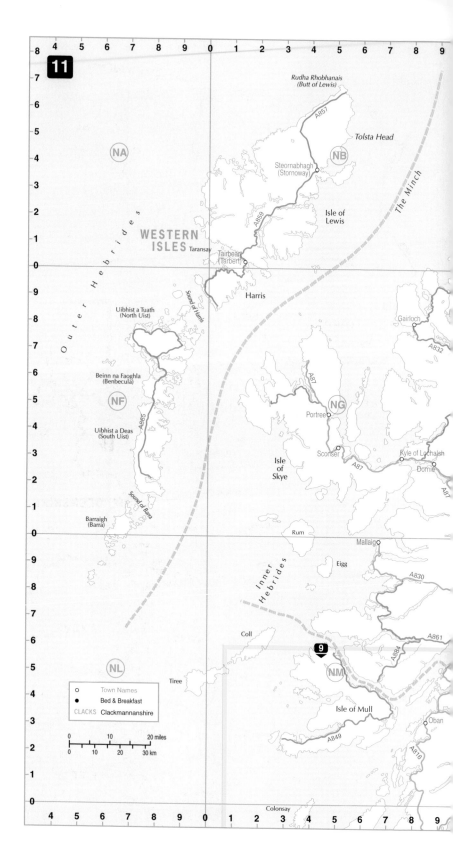

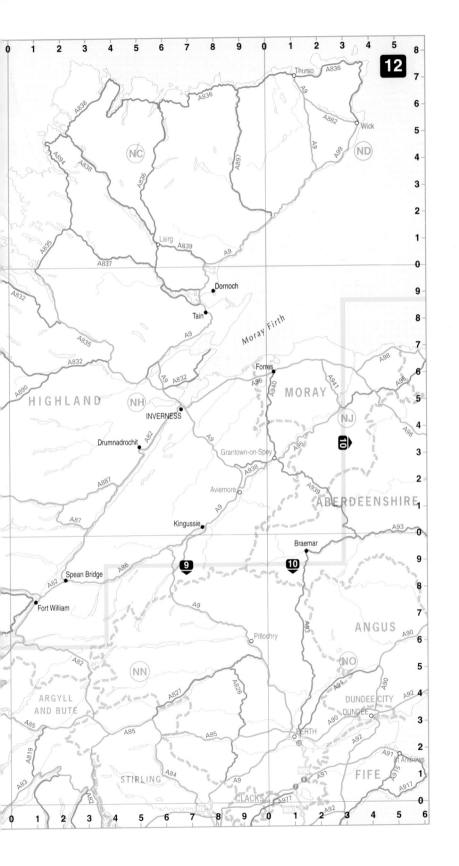

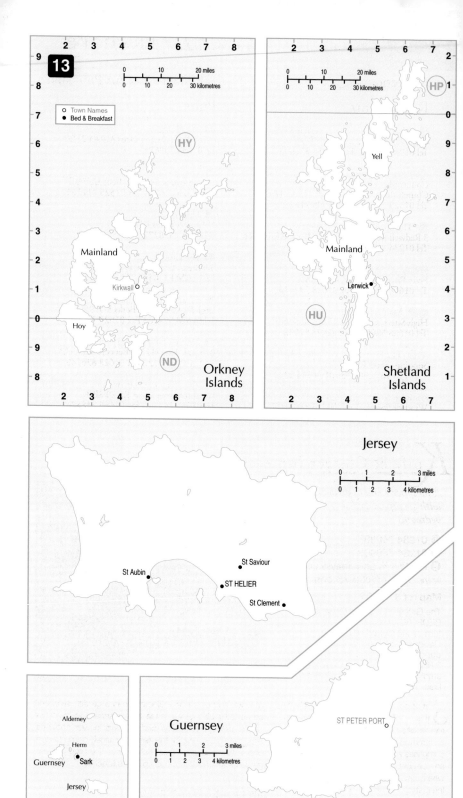

Bedfordshire/Berkshire

A selection of places to eat from the AA Restaurant & AA Pub Guides

Restaurants

◎ Woodlands Manor (Traditional French)
Clapham, Bedford MK41 6EP
Tel 01234 363281 Fax 01234 272390

◎◎ Menzies Flitwick Manor (Traditional, Country-house)
Church Road, Flitwick, Beds MK45 1AE
Tel 01525 712242 Fax 01525 718753

◎ The Strawberry Tree (Modern)
3 Radwell Rd, Milton Ernest, Beds MK44 1RY
Tel 01234 823633 Fax 01234 825976

◎◎◎◎ Waterside Inn (Classic)
Ferry Road, Bray, Berks SL6 2AT
Tel 01628 620691 Fax 01628 784710

◎◎ Malik's (Classic Country-house)
High Street, Cookham, Berks SL6 9SF
Tel 01628 520085 Fax 01628 529321

◎◎ The French Horn (Formal, French)
Sonning, Berks RG4 6TN
Tel 0118 969 2204 Fax 0118 944 2210

◎ Rose & Crown (Traditional)
Windsor Forest, Winkfield, Berks SL4 2DP
Tel 01344 882051 Fax 01344 885346

Pubs

◖ The Chequers
Brook End, Keysoe, Beds MK44 2HR
Tel 01234 708678

◖ The Five Bells
Station Rd, Stanbridge, Beds LU7 9JF
Tel 01525 210224 Fax 01525 211164

◖ The Bell Inn
Aldworth, Berks RG8 9SE
Tel 01635 578272

◖ The Crown
Burchett's Green, Berks SL6 6QZ
Tel 01628 822844

◖ Bel and The Dragon
High St, Cookham, Berks SL6 9SQ
Tel 01628 521263 Fax 01628 851008

◖ Bird in Hand Country Inn
Bath Rd, Knowl Hill, Berks RG10 9UP
Tel 01628 826622 Fax 01628 826748

◖ The Winterbourne Arms
Winterbourne, Berks RG20 8BB
Tel 01635 248200 Fax 01635 248824

Knife & Cleaver Inn ♦♦♦♦ ◎

Atmospheric inn of great character with good food and some luxurious bedrooms

☏ 01234 740387
🖷 01234 740900
✉ info@knifeandcleaver.com
www.knifeandcleaver.com

Map ref 3 - TL04

The Grove, Houghton Conquest,
BEDFORD, MK45 3LA
turn off A6 signed Houghton
Conquest, 5m S of Bedford. Inn
opposite church in village
9 Rooms, S £45-£59 D £49-£74, No
smoking in dining room, Closed 27-30
Dec

Set opposite the medieval parish church, this 17th-century restaurant-with-rooms offers real character and delightful accommodation. The fine period inn comprises an oak-panelled bar/lounge, and an elegant Victorian-style conservatory where award-winning food is served. Interesting, freshly-prepared dishes complemented by a good wine list are served in these intimate surroundings both at lunch and dinnertime. Bedrooms in a garden wing and converted stable block range from standard to executive rooms of superb quality, and all have power showers, refrigerators and satellite television. Genuinely caring owners offer a friendly but professional service. The pretty flowery garden with terrace is a lovely place to linger in.

RECOMMENDED IN THE AREA

Woburn Abbey and Safari Park; RSPB Nature Reserve at Sandy

Beehive Manor ◆◆◆◆

Medieval manor house just 15 minutes from Heathrow Airport

☎ 01628 620980
📠 01628 621840
✉ beehivemanor@cs.com

Map ref 3 - SU88

Cox Green Lane, MAIDENHEAD, SL6 3ET
M4 J8/9, follow Cox Green signs and at 2nd rdbt turn into Cox Green Rd, then left at Forresters pub
3 Rooms, S £55 D £70, No smoking, Closed Xmas/New Year

For over four hundred years this lovely manor house has provided a comfortable family home, and now offers a peaceful retreat close to many places of interest. These include historic Windsor (10 minutes by car), and the Thameside towns of Marlow and Henley renowned for their annual regattas. Day trips could take in Blenheim Palace, Hampton Court, the Cotswolds, Oxford and Stratford-upon-Avon. The capital is 30 minutes by train from Maidenhead Railway Station, itself just a mile and a half from the manor.

The house is full of character, with wooden beams, a large stone fireplace, and fine period furniture in the breakfast room, where guests eat at a shared table.

RECOMMENDED IN THE AREA

Ascot Races including 'Royal Ascot'; Marlow Regatta; Henley Regatta

Bristol

A selection of places to eat from the AA Restaurant & AA Pub Guides

Restaurants

◉ Blue Goose Restaurant (Informal, Modern)
344 Gloucester Road, Horfield BS7 8TP
Tel 0117 942 0940 Fax 0117 944 4033

◉ Glass Boat Restaurant (Classic)
Welsh Back BS1 4SB
Tel 0117 929 0704 Fax 0117 929 7338

◉◉◉ Harveys Restaurant (Contemporary)
12 Denmark Street BS1 5DQ
Tel 0117 927 5034 Fax 0117 927 5001

◉ Hotel du Vin & Bistro (Traditional, Bistro-style)
The Sugar House, Narrow Lewins Mead BS1 2NU
Tel 0117 925 5577 Fax 0117 925 1199

◉◉ Howards Restaurant (Traditional, French)
1a-2a Avon Crescent, Hotwells BS11 6XQ
Tel 0117 926 2921 Fax 0117 925 5585

◉◉ Markwicks (Classic, Chic)
43 Corn Street BS1 1HT
Tel 0117 926 2658 Fax 0117 926 2658

◉ Red Snapper Restaurant (Chic, Minimalist)
1 Chandos Road, Redland BS6 6PG
Tel 0117 973 7999 Fax 0117 923 7999

Pubs

🍺 Brewery Tap
Upper Maudlin Street BS1 5BD
Tel 0117 921 3668

🍺 Highbury Vaults
164 St Michaels Hill, Cotham BS2 8DE
Tel 0117 973 3203 Fax 0117 974 4828

🍺 The Hunters Rest
King Lane, Clutton Hill, Clutton BS39 5QL
Tel 01761 452303 Fax 01761 452308

$\mathcal{D}$ownlands House ♦♦♦♦

An elegant townhouse on the edge of Durdham Downs, with pleasing accommodation

☎ 0117 962 1639 📠 0117 962 1639
📧 mjdownlands@compuserve.com
www.downlandshouse.com

Map ref 2 - ST57

33 Henleaze Gardens, Henleaze, BRISTOL, BS9 4HH
M5 J17 (Westbury on Trym/City Centre), past private girls' schools, Henleaze Gdns on L
10 Rooms, S £32-£45 D £46-£58, No smoking

*O*ffering all the charm and warmth of a family home, Downlands is a well-maintained and hospitable guest house handily located for visiting Clifton village and Bristol Zoo. This elegant Victorian town house offers a wide choice of bedrooms, including doubles, twins and singles, and a large ground-floor room. Most benefit from en suite facilities, and all are equipped with colour televisions, hospitality trays, reading material and quality toiletries. A delightful conservatory has been well furnished as a breakfast room, and the very friendly owners are keen to make sure that all of their guests enjoy a relaxing stay.

RECOMMENDED IN THE AREA

Clifton Suspension Bridge; Brunel's SS Great Britain; @ Bristol Exploration Centre & Imax Theatre

$\mathcal{D}$owns Edge ♦♦♦♦

A country location in the heart of the city

☎ 0117 968 3264
📠 0117 9683264
📧 welcome@
downsedge.com

Map ref 2 - ST57

Saville Road, Stoke Bishop, BRISTOL, BS9 1JA
M5 take J17 onto A4018. At 4th rdbt R into Parrys Lane B4054. 1st L Saville Rd, 3rd R Hollybush Ln, after 2nd speed ramp, L into drive
6 Rooms, S £39-£49 D £59-£65, No smoking, Closed Xmas/New Year

*R*ight on the edge of Durdham Downs, Bristol's 450-acre park, this substantial property is quietly located with all the amenities of the city close to hand. Parking is provided in the impressive grounds, which open directly on to the park. Inside, the house is carefully appointed with period furnishings, fine paintings and a library with many books on the history of Bristol. Six of the bedrooms have en suite facilities and all are equipped with colour televisions, hairdryers, hospitality trays and a basket of little essentials. Breakfast is served family-style at one large table, and the menu offers a wide variety of hot and cold dishes alongside the morning papers.

RECOMMENDED IN THE AREA

The Avon Gorge (5/10 minutes' walk); Clifton Suspension Bridge (20 minutes' walk/5 minutes' drive); Bristol Zoo (10 minutes' walk, 5 minutes' drive)

Westbury Park Hotel ◆◆◆◆

Lovely Victorian house close to the Durdham Downs

☎ 0117 962 0465
🖷 0117 962 8607
✉ reception@
   westburypark-hotel.co.uk
www.westburypark-hotel.co.uk

Map ref 2 - ST57

37 Westbury Road, Westbury-on-Trym, BRISTOL, BS9 3AU
M5 J17, follow A4018 for 4.5m, hotel is on the left
8 Rooms, S £40-£46 D £55-£60, No smoking in bedrooms or dining room

*I*deal accommodation for tourists or business guests is offered at this attractive hotel, conveniently situated on the edge of the Durdham Downs, with easy access to the motorways, city centre and shopping mall. The atmosphere is relaxed and staff are friendly.

The bedrooms have been decorated with taste and style and modern comforts are provided, including en suite facilities, colour televisions, direct dial telephones, hair dryers and hospitality trays in every room.

There is a comfortable lounge bar area where guests can relax. Breakfast is served in the spacious dining room. Parking is easy and there is also limited private parking available.

RECOMMENDED IN THE AREA

Bristol Zoo; SS Great Britain; @ Bristol

Buckinghamshire

A selection of places to eat from the AA Restaurant & AA Pub Guides

Restaurants

⊛⊛ La Chouette (Country-house)
Westlinton Green, Dinton, Nr Aylesbury
HP17 8UW
Tel 01296 747422 Fax 01296 747422

⊛ Bert's Restaurant (Modern, Mediterranean)
Chesham Road, Hyde End, Great Missenden
HP16 0QT
Tel 01494 865625 Fax 01494 866406

⊛⊛ Green Dragon (Classic, Bistro-style)
8 Churchway, Haddenham HP17 8AA
Tel 01844 291403 Fax 01844 299532

⊛ The King's Head (Chic & Traditional)
Ivinghoe LU7 9EB
Tel 01296 668264 Fax 01296 668107

⊛⊛ The Angel Restaurant (Chic)
47 Bicester Road, Long Crendon HP18 9EE
Tel 01844 208268 Fax 01844 202497

⊛⊛ The Compleat Angler (Classic, Formal)
Marlow Bridge, Marlow SL7 1RG
Tel 0870 400 8100 Fax 01628 485388

⊛⊛⊛ Cliveden, Waldo's Restaurant
Cliveden Estate, Taplow SL6 0JF
Tel 01628 668561 Fax 01628 661837

Pubs

🍺 The Royal Standard of England
Brindle Lane, Forty Green, Beaconsfield HP9 1XT
Tel 01494 673382 Fax 01494 523332

🍺 Ivy House
London Road, Chalfont St Giles HP8 4RS
Tel 01494 872184 Fax 01494 872840

🍺 The Polecat Inn
170 Wycombe Road, Prestwood,
Great Missenden HP16 0HJ
Tel 01494 862253 Fax 01494 868393

🍺 The Rising Sun
Little Hampden, Great Missenden HP16 9PS
Tel 01494 488393 Fax 01494 488788

🍺 The Green Dragon
8 Churchway, Haddenham HP17 8AA
Tel 01844 291403

🍺 The Frog
Skirmett RG9 6TG
Tel 01491 638996 Fax 01491 638045

🍺 The Bull & Butcher
Turville RG9 6QU
Tel 01491 638283 Fax 01491 638283

The George Hotel •••••

Grade II listed inn located in the old town area of Beaconsfield

☎ 01494 673086
📠 01494 674034
✉ info@
thegeorgehotel.com
www.thegeorgehotel
beaconsfield.com

Map ref 3 - SU99

Wycombe End, Old
Town, BEACONSFIELD,
HP9 1LX
Exit M40 J2, 0.5m into
Beaconsfield. Hotel
over main rdbt on R
10 Rooms,

*I*mpeccable standards are maintained at this privately owned hotel, an award-winning 15th-century coaching inn right at the historic centre of the old town. Local shops and restaurants are conveniently close by, and the M40 is easy to get to. The quality of the furnishings and decor is exceptional throughout, traditional in style and sympathetic to the Tudor character of the property. The accommodation takes the form of suites, both in the main building and in the garden cottages developed from the old stable block. The latter are designed in an open plan style over two floors. Self-catering accommodation is offered in the Courtyard Suite, which is available for short or long-term lets. All the suites and cottages have en suite bathrooms with a power shower as well as a bath, and other in-room facilities include colour televisions and microwave ovens. Tea and coffee trays and bottled water are thoughtful touches.

RECOMMENDED IN THE AREA

Visit Windsor Castle or the City of London; Wycombe Swan (theatre)

Cambridgeshire

A selection of places to eat from the AA Restaurant & AA Pub Guides

Restaurants

◉ Cambridge Quy Mill (Rustic)
Newmarket Road, Stow Cum Quy, Cambridge
CB5 9AG
Tel 01223 293383 Fax 01223 293770

◉◉ Duxford Lodge (Traditional, Country-house)
Ickleton Road, Duxford CB2 4RU
Tel 01223 836444 Fax 01223 832271

◉ Old Fire Engine House (Traditional, Rustic)
25 Saint Mary's Street, Ely CB7 4ER
Tel 01353 662582 Fax 01353 668364

◉ Sycamore House (Traditional French-style)
1 Church Street, Little Shelford CB2 5HG
Tel 01223 843396

◉◉◉ Pink Geranium (Traditional)
Station Road, Melbourn SG8 6DX
Tel 01763 260215 Fax 01763 262110

◉◉ Sheene Mill (Modern, Chic)
Station Road, Melbourn SG8 6DX
Tel 01763 261393 Fax 01763 261376

◉ Orton Hall (Classic Country-house)
Orton Longueville, Peterborough PE2 7DN
Tel 01733 391111 Fax 01733 231912

Pubs

◖ The Fitzwilliam Arms
34 Peterborough Road, Castor PE5 7AX
Tel 01733 380251 Fax 01733 380116

◖ The Anchor Inn
Sutton Gault, Ely CB6 2BD
Tel 01353 778537 Fax 01353 776180

◖ White Pheasant
Fordham CB7 5LQ
Tel 01638 720414 Fax 01638 720447

◖ The Chequers
High Street, Fowlmere SG8 7SR
Tel 01763 208369 Fax 01763 208944

◖ The Old Bridge House
1 High Street, Huntingdon PE29 3TQ
Tel 01480 424300 Fax 01480 411017

◖ The Three Horseshoes
High Street, Madingley CB3 8AB
Tel 01956 210221 Fax 01954 212043

◖ The Bell Inn
Great North Road, Stilton PE7 3RA
Tel 01733 241066 Fax 01733 245173

The Anchor Inn ♦♦♦♦ ◉

Fenland inn with a riverside setting

☎ 01353 778537
🖷 01353 776180
✉ AnchorInnSG@aol.com
www.anchor-inn-restaurant.co.uk

Map ref 4 - TL47

Sutton Gault, ELY, CB6 2BD
Sutton Gault signposted off B1381 at
southern end of Sutton village (6m W
of Ely)
2 Rooms, S £50-£65 D £66.50-£95,
No smoking in bedrooms or lounge,
Closed 26 Dec

The Anchor is a 17th-century inn on the bank of the New Bedford River with stunning views over the surrounding countryside.

Public rooms are full of character, with scrubbed pine tables and old-fashioned gaslights. An imaginative menu is offered in the restaurant, which has an AA rosette award for its food, and the discerning guest will also appreciate real ale straight from the cask and a minimum of 8 wines available by the glass from the 100-bin wine list.

En suite accommodation is available in a twin room or a spacious suite (which can sleep three), each with remote control television, direct dial telephone and complimentary tea and coffee.

RECOMMENDED IN THE AREA

Ely Cathedral (15 minutes away); Cambridge and the colleges (25 minutes away); Welney Wildfowl Reserve (15 minutes away)

Springfields .....

A charming, elegant bungalow situated just a short drive from Ely

☎ 01353 663637
🖶 01353 663130
✉ springfields@talk21.com

Map ref 4 - TL57

Ely Road, Little Thetford, ELY, CB6 3HJ
on A10, 10m N of Cambridge
3 Rooms, S £35 D £50, No smoking, Closed Dec

RECOMMENDED IN THE AREA

Ely Cathedral; Welney Wildfowl Trust; Oliver Cromwell's House

Springfields is set in an acre of landscaped gardens and orchard, surrounded by mature trees. It is just a mile from Ely Cathedral and 11 miles from the city of Cambridge, so there is much to see and do in the area. Ample floodlit parking is provided, and the friendly Bailey family offer tea and home-made pastries to guests on arrival. The bedrooms, comprising two doubles and one twin, are located on the ground floor overlooking the rear garden, where a great variety of birds come to feed.

You might also see rabbits, squirrels or even deer stealing in to the garden, where over 500 roses bloom in the summer months. The rooms are lavishly furnished and all have en suite facilities, colour televisions, clock radios. Other welcoming touches include tea trays, confectionary, toiletries and fresh flowers. Breakfast is served from Minton china at one large table in the elegant dining room, and vegetarians can be catered for. Pets and children under 12 cannot be accommodated.

Hill House Farm ♦♦♦♦

Victorian farmhouse in a delightful village setting

☎ 01353 778369
📠 01353 778369
✉ Hill_house@madasafish.com

Map ref 4 - TL58

9 Main Street, Coveney, ELY, CB6 2DJ
off A142 3m W of Ely
3 Rooms, S £30-£41 D £46-£50,
No smoking, Closed Xmas

This charming farmhouse is situated in the village of Coveney, about three miles west of Ely. Guests can expect a warm welcome from the caring proprietor Mrs Nix.

Although the bedrooms are part of the main house, each room has the unique advantage of its own separate entrance. The bedrooms are immaculately kept with a fresh, bright appearance. The pleasant decor and co-ordinated fabrics are enhanced by modern en suite facilities and a range of useful extras.

Public rooms comprise a comfortably furnished sitting room and a separate dining room, where guests are served a freshly cooked breakfast at the highly polished communal table. The house is not suitable for children under twelve or pets, and is entirely non-smoking.

RECOMMENDED IN THE AREA

Ely Cathedral; Oliver Cromwell's House; and Welney Wildfowl Trust

---

Abbey House ♦♦♦♦

Historic stone-built property in a village setting

☎ 01778 344642 📠 01778 342706
✉ info@abbeyhouse.co.uk
abbeyhouse.co.uk

Map ref 3 - TF10

West End Road, MAXEY, Peterborough, PE6 9EJ
from rdbt on A15, 1m S of Market Deeping, turn L into Maxey. 1st R (Castle End Rd), 1st L (West End Rd), Abbey House 400 yrds on L
10 Rooms, S £26-£43 D £42-£66, No smoking

Convenient for the A1, Abbey House is a mellow stone building set in the conservation village of Maxey, between Stamford and Peterborough. It is surrounded by fine gardens, including an 800-year-old yew tree. Parts of the house date from the 12th century, but it has been sympathetically renovated over the years to provide modern facilities while retaining original features.

The bedrooms all have en suite facilities, colour TV and complimentary tea and coffee. There is a comfortable lounge, and breakfast is served in the elegant dining room overlooking the garden. For dinner, there is a good choice of pubs and restaurants in the area. Children are welcome but not pets.

RECOMMENDED IN THE AREA

Peterborough Cathedral; Burghley House, Deene Park, Belvoir Castle and Grimsthorpe Castle

Cheshire & Greater Manchester

A selection of places to eat from the AA Restaurant & AA Pub Guides

Restaurants

Mauro's Restaurant (Classic Italian)
88 Palmerston Street, Bollington SK10 5PW
Tel 01625 573898 Fax 01625 572800

Crewe Hall (Modern)
Weston Road, Crewe CW1 6UZ
Tel 01270 253333 Fax 01270 253322

Belfry House (Classic, French)
Stanley Road, Handworth SK9 3LD
Tel 0161 437 0511 Fax 0161 499 0597

Cottons Hotel (Traditional)
Manchester Road, Knutsford WA16 0SU
Tel 01565 650333 Fax 01565 755351

Rookery Hall (Classic Country-house)
Main Road, Worleston, Nantwich CW5 6DQ
Tel 01270 610016 Fax 01270 626027

Juniper (Classic, Bistro-style)
21 The Downs, Altrincham WA14 2QD
Tel 0161 929 4008 Fax 0161 929 4009

Moss Nook (Modern)
Ringway Road, Moss Nook, Manchester
M22 5WD
Tel 0161 437 4778 Fax 0161 498 8089

Pubs

The Grosvenor Arms
Chester Road, Aldford CH3 6HJ
Tel 01244 620228 Fax 01244 620247

The Bhurtpore Inn
Wrenbury Road, Aston CW5 8DQ
Tel 01270 780917 Fax 01270 780170

The Pheasant Inn
Burwardsley CH3 9PF
Tel 01829 770434 Fax 01829 771097

The Cholmondeley Arms
Cholmondeley SY14 8HN
Tel 01829 720300 Fax 01829 720123

Plough Inn Hotel
Macclesfield Road, Eaton, Congleton CW12 2NR
Tel 01260 280207 Fax 01260 280207

The Dog Inn
Well Bank Lane, Over Peover, Knutsford
WA16 8UP
Tel 01625 861421 Fax 01625 864800

The Oddfellows Arms
73 Moor End Road, Mellor SK6 5PT
Tel 0161 449 7826

Ash Farm Country Guest House ♦♦♦♦♦

Situated in the quiet village of Little Bollington in the heart of National Trust countryside

☎ 0161 929 9290 📠 0161 928 5002
📧 jan@ashfarm97.fsnet.co.uk
www.ashfarm.co.uk

Map ref 6 - SJ78

Park Lane, Little Bollington, ALTRINCHAM,
Greater Manchester, WA14 4TJ
turn off A56 beside Stamford Arms
3 Rooms, S £45-£52 D £58-£70, No smoking,
Closed 22 Dec-5 Jan

*T*his beautiful country guest house is just a short walk from Dunham Massey Hall and Park, formerly the home of the Earl of Stamford, and yet conveniently situated from M56 (2 miles), M6 (3 miles), Manchester Airport (6 miles) and Manchester City Centre (10 miles). The luxury double bedrooms offer en suite facilities, telephone, colour television and video.

Thoughtful extras include fresh fruit, tea and coffee making facilities, mints and towelling robes. Guests can enjoy exploring the surrounding countryside and canal and come home to a welcoming fire.

RECOMMENDED IN THE AREA

Dunham Massey Stately Home and Park (5 minutes' walk); Tatton Park Stately Home (4 miles); Shopping at The Trafford Centre (5 miles)

Redland Private Hotel ♦♦♦♦♦

Elegant Victorian villa with original features

☎ 01244 671024 ✆ 01244 681309

Map ref 5 - SJ36

64 Hough Green, CHESTER, Cheshire, CH4 8JY
from Chester on A483 Wrexham rd, 1m, take A5104
Saltney rd for 200yds, opp Westminster Park
13 Rooms, S £45 D £65-£80, No smoking in dining
room

The Redland Hotel, a handsome property dating from 1850, has been beautifully restored by the resident proprietors. Rich wood panelling, suits of armour and antique four-poster beds all contribute to the general atmosphere of period splendour.

The bedrooms, including four honeymoon suites, have been individually designed and equipped with thoughtful extras. All the rooms have luxurious en suite facilities and feature some fine pieces of antique and period furniture. There is a delightful drawing room, and for further enjoyment and relaxation there is a solarium, sauna and honesty bar. An additional convenience is the guests' laundry.

The hotel is located just a mile from Chester city centre and provides ample parking.

RECOMMENDED IN THE AREA

Chester Zoo; Dewa Roman Experience;
Chester Cathedral

The Hinton Guest House ♦♦♦♦

A comfortable guest house with attractive gardens, handily located for Manchester Airport. The owners are clearly dedicated to providing an enjoyable experience for their guests, and there are plenty of homely touches throughout the house.

All bedrooms offer en suite facilities, beverage bar, television, trouser press and many other useful extras, and there is a two-bedroom suite which is ideal for families.

Evening meals can be cooked by prior arrangement, and both dinner and breakfast are served in the spacious dining room. Guests can also use the lounge (and play on the organ if they wish), and a conservatory which leads onto a patio.

Welcoming guest house with modern bedrooms and lots of homely touches

☎ 01565 873484 ✆ 01565 873484

Map ref 6 - SJ77

Town Lane, Mobberley, KNUTSFORD, Cheshire,
WA16 7HH
on B5085. From Knutsford, Hinton on R just past
shops. From Wilmslow, Hinton just past car
showroom
5 Rooms, S £44 D £58, No smoking

RECOMMENDED IN THE AREA

Tatton Park (5 minutes away); explore
Cheshire, Derbyshire Peak District and North
Wales

Matteo's Bar & Country Hotel ••••

Friendly restaurant/country hotel specialising in fresh fish, with comfortable, well-equipped bedrooms

☎ 01457 852418
🖷 01457 852418

Map ref 7 - SJ98

Rock Tavern, Glossop Road, Marple Bridge, MARPLE, Stockport, Greater Manchester, SK6 5RX
on A626
5 Rooms, S £49.50 D £75, No smoking in bedrooms or dining room

Located high on the borders of Cheshire and Derbyshire, this family-run restaurant offers a number of quality bedrooms for the discerning guest. There is a warm welcome and a friendly atmosphere which go hand in hand with a cosy, relaxed ambience to make for a very pleasant stay. Panoramic views of the delightful surrounding countryside can be enjoyed from the thoughtfully-equipped bedrooms, all of which are pleasantly decorated and furnished. Each room has a bathroom fitted with quality fixtures and a range of useful facilities. Guests can unwind in the comfort of the lounge bar or the popular main bar, and after a drink can move into the adjoining restaurant, a spacious room where a good range of popular dishes is available. The regularly-changing menus feature fresh fish as a speciality, and cheerful, competent serving staff are happy to oblige.

RECOMMENDED IN THE AREA

Lyme Park; Bramhall Hall and Park; museums and shopping in Manchester

The Limes ♦♦♦♦♦

An elegant period property, convenient for the M6

☎ 01270 624081
🖷 01270 624081

Map ref 6 - SJ65

5 Park Road, NANTWICH, Cheshire, CW5 7AQ
M6 J16 follow signs for Nantwich & Stapeley Water Gdns, continue into Nantwich, follow signs for A530 Whitchurch
3 Rooms, S £40-£45 D £50-£60, No smoking, Closed Nov-Jan

An impressive Victorian house, The Limes is set in a leafy residential area of Nantwich, just a short walk from the centre of town. It is well located for exploring the many and varied centres of interest in the area.

The house is impeccably maintained and the owners, Judy and Keith Chesters, extend a warm and friendly welcome to their guests. Three spacious and well equipped bedrooms are available. All have en suite facilities and one has a four-poster bed, ideal for special occasions. The lounge is elegantly furnished, and there is a delightful dining room where breakfast is served. The house has pleasant lawns and gardens to the rear, and private parking is provided at the front.

RECOMMENDED IN THE AREA

Chester and the Potteries (30 minute drive); Stapeley Water Gardens and Bridgemere; Historic Market Town of Nantwich

Oaklands House ♦♦♦♦♦

A warm welcome awaits you at Oakland

☎ 01270 567134
www.smoothhound.co.uk/hotels/oaqkland.html

Map ref 6 - SJ65

252 Newcastle Road, Blakelow, Shavington, NANTWICH, Cheshire, CW5 7ET
on A500 5m from M6 junct 16, and 2m from Nantwich
9 Rooms, S £30-£34 D £45-£49, No smoking

Sandra and Michael Groom are the friendly hosts in this family run guest house. In a semi-rural situation, conveniently located for both the M6 and various local attractions, Oaklands provides open views to the front and rear. En suite bedrooms, some in an adjacent building, are attractively furnished and well equipped with television, hair dryer, tea and coffee-making facilities.

There is a spacious sitting room and modern conservatory, overlooking the pretty garden and beyond into the Cheshire countryside. Hearty full English breakfasts, or simpler alternatives, can be enjoyed in a relaxed, friendly atmosphere around a large family table.

RECOMMENDED IN THE AREA

Bridgemere Nurseries and Stapeley Water Gardens (1 mile); canal systems (2 miles); Cholmondley, Peckforton and Beeston Castles (10 miles)

*P*ear Tree Cottage Country Guest House ◆◆◆◆◆

Delightful well-furnished accommodation offering luxurious home comforts

☎ / ✆ **0161 439 5755**
📧 P-T-cottage@fsbdial.co.uk
www.u-net.com/mbp/pcott

Map ref 6 - SJ88

Church Lane, Woodford,
WILMSLOW, Cheshire, SK7 1PQ
A34/B5094, opposite Bramhall
Cricket Club
3 Rooms, S £40-£45 D £55-£75,
No smoking

*T*his beautiful thatched cottage is just 15 minutes' drive from Manchester Airport and makes an ideal base or stopover point for the holiday or business traveller. Dating back to 1520, the property combines olde worlde charm with luxury modern comforts. The bedrooms are exceptionally well equipped and tastefully furnished, and enjoy delightful views over open countryside. A farmhouse or continental breakfast is served in the traditional beamed dining room and tasty home-cooked evening meals are provided by prior arrangement on weekdays. You can be assured of a warm welcome from the friendly owners and will find their lovely cottage home a genuine haven of peace and tranquility, parking and return courtesy transport to the airport is available.

RECOMMENDED IN THE AREA

Bramall Hall (3 miles); Quarry Bank Mill, Lyme Park and Tatton Park; shopping at the Trafford Centre (easy driving distance)

County *D*urham

A selection of places to eat from the AA Restaurant & AA Pub Guides

Restaurants

⊚ Austins Bar & Bistro
Durham County Cricket Club, Chester-le-Street
DH3 3QR
Tel 0191 388 3335 Fax 0191 387 4697

⊚⊚ Hall Garth Hotel (Country-house)
Coatham Mundeville, Darlington DL1 3LU
Tel 01325 300400 Fax 01325 310083

⊚ Bistro 21 (Classic, Bistro-style)
Aykley Heads House, Aykley Heads, Durham
DH1 5TS
Tel 0191 384 4354 Fax 0191 384 1149

⊚⊚ Kings Lodge Hotel
Flass Vale, Durham DH1 4BG
Tel 0191 370 9977 Fax 0191 370 9988

⊚ Swallow Eden Arms (Traditional, Classic)
Rushyford DL17 0LL
Tel 01388 720541 Fax 01388 721871

⊚ Parkmore Hotel (Traditional)
636 Yarm Road, Eaglescliffe, Stockton-on-Tees
TS16 0DH
Tel 01642 786815 Fax 01642 790485

⊚ Manor House (Country-house, Formal)
The Green, West Auckland DL14 9HW
Tel 01388 834834 Fax 01388 833566

Pubs

🍺 The County
Aycliffe Village Green, Darlington DL5 6LX
Tel 01325 312273 Fax 01325 308780

🍺 Countryman Inn
Bolam DL2 2UP
Tel 01388 834577 Fax 01388 834577

🍺 Duke of York Country Inn
Fir Tree, Crook DL15 8DG
Tel 01388 762848 Fax 01388 767055

🍺 Seven Stars Inn
High Street North, Shincliffe Village, Durham
DH1 2NU
Tel 0191 384 8454 Fax 0191 386 0640

🍺 Rose & Crown
Romaldkirk, Barnard Castle DL12 9EB
Tel 01833 650213 Fax 01833 650828

41

Clow Beck House •••••

Luxurious rooms with superb furnishings in the beautiful gardens of a working farm

☎ 01325 721075
📠 01325 720419
📧 heather@
clowbeckhouse.co.uk
www.clowbeckhouse.
co.uk

Map ref 7 - NZ21

Monk End Farm, Croft on Tees, DARLINGTON, DL2 2SW
A167 to Northallerton for 2m into Croft, over bridge, follow 3 brown signs to Clowbeck House
13 Rooms, S £50 D £80, No smoking in dining room

Clow-Beck House gets its name from the beck which winds its way through the grounds of the farm to meet the River Tees, providing a perfect opportunity for some trout fishing.

The bedrooms are in a cottage and in separate chalets in the gardens. Each one has been decorated with great expertise to give a real sense of period style. The beamed dining room is light and airy. There is a good wine list, and an à la carte menu that is imaginative in its diversity. The inviting lounge with its attractive blue upholstery is in the house itself.

Heather and David Armstrong are dedicated to making you feel at home, and they are keen to help you plan your route for an outing through the rolling North Yorkshire countryside.

RECOMMENDED IN THE AREA

Raby Castle (10 minute drive); Beamish Museum (30 minute drive); Yorkshire Dales & Moors (15 minute drive)

Hillrise Guest House ♦♦♦♦

Just a short detour off junction 61 of the A1(M), Hillrise is only two miles from the centre of Durham and close to other places of interest, such as Hadrian's Wall and the Beamish Open Air Museum.

The house is personally run by the hospitable proprietor and guests are assured of a friendly welcome. Bedrooms come in a variety of sizes, all with en suite or private facilities, televisions and hospitality trays. Attractive public areas include a lounge with chunky leather chairs and a spacious dining room were delicious home-cooked breakfasts are served.

Though the house is completely no smoking, smokers can use the small patio area outside the dining room.

Family-run guest house in a convenient location

☎ 0191 377 0302 📠 0191 377 0898
www.hill-rise.com

Map ref 7 - NZ33

13 Durham Road West, Bowburn, DURHAM, DH6 5AU
A1 junct 61, Hillrise approx 200yds on left
5 Rooms, S £20-£25 D £45-£50, No smoking

RECOMMENDED IN THE AREA

Beamish Open Air Museum (15 minute drive); Durham Cathedral and Castle (10 minute drive); Metro Centre, Gateshead (20 minute drive)

Greenhead Country House Hotel ♦♦♦♦

Converted traditional Dales longhouse and blacksmith's workshop

☎ 01388 763143 📠 01388 763143
✉ info@thegreenheadhotel.co.uk
www.thegreenheadhotel.co.uk

Map ref 7 - NZ13

FIR TREE, Crook, DL15 8BL
on A68, turn right at Fir Tree Inn
8 Rooms, S £45-£55 D £65-£75, No smoking in bedrooms or dining room

Greenhead is an extended early 18th-century property, just 500 yards from the A68, set in well tended gardens at the foot of the Weardale Valley. The location is convenient for visiting Durham, the Beamish Open Air Museum, and the Durham Dales. It is a smartly presented establishment with spacious modern en suite bedrooms. One room has a four-poster bed, all have colour television, tea and coffee making facilities, and clock radios. Accommodation is provided in a quiet and reserved atmosphere.

The central stone arched lounge provides a relaxed centre for planning future outings. There are three restaurants in Fir Trees, all serving dinner from 7 to 9pm, two are within easy walking distance. Menus are available to view in the house, no advance booking is required.

RECOMMENDED IN THE AREA

Durham Cathedral (10 minutes); the highest road, waterfall and market town in England, & Hadrian's Wall (all within half an hour's drive)

Cornwall & Isles of Scilly

A selection of places to eat from the AA Restaurant & AA Pub Guides

Restaurants

Atlantic House (Traditional)
17-18 Summerleaze Crescent, Bude EX23 8HJ
Tel 01288 352451 Fax 01288 356666

Thyme & Plaice (Modern, Chic)
3 Church Street, Callington PL17 7RE
Tel 01579 384933 Fax 01579 384933

Food for Thought
The Quay, Fowey PL23 1AT
Tel 01726 832221 Fax 01726 832077

Well House Hotel (Modern)
St Keyne, Liskeard PL14 4RN
Tel 01579 342001 Fax 01579 343891

Cornish Range (Modern Chic)
6 Chapel Street, Mousehole TR19 6SB
Tel 01736 731488 Fax 01736 732255

Mullion Cove (Traditional)
Mullion, near Helston TR12 7EP
Tel 01326 240328 Fax 01326 240998

Brocks (Classic, French)
The Strand, Padstow PL28 8AJ
Tel 01841 532565

The Seafood Restaurant (Modern)
Riverside, Padstow PL28 8BY
Tel 01841 532700 Fax 533574

Harris' Restaurant
46 New Street, Penzance TR18 2LZ
Tel 01736 364408 Fax 01736 333273

Critchards Seafood Restaurant
(Traditional, Spanish)
The Harbour Head, Porthleven TR13 9JA
Tel 01326 562407 Fax 01326 564444

The Castle Rock Hotel (Afro-Mediterranean)
4 New Road, Port Isaac PL29 3SB
Tel 01208 880300 Fax 01208 880219

Tabb's Restaurant (Classic, Rustic)
Railway Terrace, Portreath TR16 4LD
Tel 01209 842488 Fax 01209 842488

Porthminster Beach Restaurant
(Modern, Mediterranean)
Porthminster, St Ives TR26 2EB
Tel 01736 795352 Fax 01736 795352

The Old Rectory
(Traditional Country-house)
St Keyne, near Liskeard PL14 4RL
Tel 01579 342617 Fax 01579 342293

St Martin's on the Isle
Lower Town, St Martin's TR25 0QW
Tel 01720 422092 Fax 01720 422298

Pubs

The Maltsters Arms
Chapel Amble PL27 6EU
Tel 01208 812473

Trengilly Wartha Inn
Nancenoy, Constantine TR11 5RP
Tel 01326 340332 Fax 01326 340332

Ye Olde Plough House Inn
Duloe PL14 4PN
Tel 01503 262050 Fax 01503 264089

The Hazlephron Inn
Gunwalloe, near Helston TR12 7QB
Tel 01326 240406 Fax 01326 241442

The Halfway House Inn
Fore Street, Kingsand PL10 1NA
Tel 01752 822279 Fax 01752 823146

Royal Oak Inn
Duke Street, Lostwithiel PL22 0AQ
Tel 01208 872552 Fax 01208 872552

The Old Coastguard Hotel
The Parade, Mousehole TR19 6PR
Tel 01736 731222 Fax 01736 731720

Pandora Inn
Restronguet Creek, Mylor Bridge TR11 5ST
Tel 01326 372678 Fax 01326 372678

The Roseland Inn
Philleigh, TR2 5NB
Tel 01872 580254 Fax 01872 501528

Turks Head
St Agnes (Isles of Scilly) TR22 0PL
Tel 01720 422434 Fax 01720 423331

The Sloop Inn
The Wharf, St Ives TR26 1LP
Tel 01736 796584 Fax 01736 793322

The Rising Sun
The Square, St Mawes TR2 5DJ
Tel 01326 270233 Fax 01326 270198

The Springer Spaniel
Treburley, PL15 9NS
Tel 01579 370424 Fax 01579 370113

The New Inn
New Grimsby, Tresco TR24 0QQ
Tel 01720 422844 Fax 01720 423200

The Gurnards Head Hotel
Treen, Zennor TR26 3DE
Tel 01736 796928 Fax 01736 795313

Mount Pleasant ◆◆◆

Enjoy good home cooking, splendid views and a highly attentive service in the Cornish countryside

☎ 01208 821342
✆ colette@
capper61.fsnet.co.uk
www.peacefulholiday.co.uk

Map ref 1 - SX16

Mount, BODMIN, PL30 4EX
from Bodmin follow A30 signed
Launceston for 4m, then turn R
signed Millpool, continue for 3m
6 Rooms, S £30-£45 D £60-£90, No
smoking, Closed Oct-Etr

Set on the edge of Bodmin Moor, this 17th-century converted farmhouse enjoys a beautiful, peaceful location with splendid views and plenty of interesting places to visit in all directions. The Eden Project, the Lost Gardens of Heligan, and the beaches at Looe, Polperro and Rock are all a short drive away. The house is particularly well equipped, with a games room and a heated indoor swimming pool. The cosy bedrooms are furnished to a good standard, and all come complete with en suites and colour television. Many also have wonderful country views. An indoor garden, including hanging grapes, is a feature of the spacious sun lounge, and there is also a guests' bar and an attractive dining room. Breakfast (and dinner by arrangement) are delicious, made from good local produce. A friendly personal service from owners Jeremy and Colette is guaranteed.

RECOMMENDED IN THE AREA

The Eden Project (15 miles); Lanhydrock House and Gardens (6 miles); Camel Trail Cycle Way (6 miles)

Tolcarne House Hotel & Restaurant ♦♦♦♦

Large Victorian property with superb coastal and rural views

☎ 01840 250654
🖷 01840 250654
✉ crowntolhouse@eclipse.co.uk
www.milford.co.uk/go/
tolcarne.html

Map ref 1 - SX09

Tintagel Road, BOSCASTLE,
PL35 0AS
at junct of B3266/B3263 in Boscastle
8 Rooms, S £30-£32 D £50-£65, No
smoking in dining room

*I*n an elevated position 800 yards from the sea, this substantial house is quietly located in delightful grounds with expansive lawns and mature trees. A short walk through the old village takes you to the Elizabethan harbour, now a National Trust property. Bedrooms, each named after a local beauty spot, are individually decorated and some have sea and valley views. All have en suite facilities, colour television, beverage making equipment, clock radios and hairdryers. No-smoking rooms are also available. Guests eat at individual tables in the dining room, where a home-cooked dinner is served from a menu that always offers a choice of meat or fish dishes.

RECOMMENDED IN THE AREA

Lanhydrock House and Pencarrow House; Eden Project (30 miles); Tintagel Castle

Downlands ♦♦♦♦

Chalet-style bungalow overlooking the golf course

☎ 01288 355545

Map ref 1 - SS20

1 Flexbury Avenue, BUDE, EX23 8RE
turn R off A39 to Bude, through one-way system, past PO, take R fork but
L lane. Downlands approx 200yds
7 Rooms, S £26-£32 , No smoking in
dining room, Closed Jan

A warm welcome awaits guests at Yvonne Phillip's delightful detached property. The comfortably furnished bedrooms include two on the ground floor, all have en suite facilities, colour televisions and hospitality trays. Family suites, double, twin and single rooms are available.

A spacious guests' lounge is provided, and a dining room with a polished wooden floor. Breakfast is a feast beginning with fresh fruits, yoghurts and fruit juices. There follows a choice of freshly cooked breakfasts, including traditional English choices such as smoked salmon and scrambled eggs, or warm croissants and pain au chocolat, served with fresh coffee or one of a range of teas. For your evening meal there are plenty of restaurants within easy reach.

Downlands overlooks the golf course and is within walking distance of the lovely sandy beaches and the town centre. The house has its own large private car park.

RECOMMENDED IN THE AREA

Swimming and surfing on Bude's beaches; explore Dartmoor, Exmoor and Bodmin Moor; National Trust beaches at Sandymouth, Duckpool and Northcott Mouth

*P*endragon House ♦♦♦♦

Victorian rectory with extensive moorland views

☎ 01840 261131 📠 01840 261131
✉ john1pendragonho@aol.com
www.pendragonhouse.co.uk

Map ref 1 - SX18

Davidstow, CAMELFORD, PL32 9XR
Turn off A30 onto A395 Pendragon House is 9.5m on right
4 Rooms, S £23 D £46, No smoking

A substantially built property, this former rectory stands in an acre and a half of gardens with glorious views across Bodmin Moor and Dartmoor. The house is easily accessible from all the main routes through Cornwall and is conveniently located for the resorts of Bude, Boscastle and Tintagel, and the historic town of Launceston.

The bedrooms are generously proportioned, stylishly furnished and well equipped, with en suite facilities, full central heating, colour television, and tea and coffee-making provisions. The breakfast menu offers a wide choice including vegetarian options.

Parking for six cars is available in the grounds. Children under 10 years are not accepted; neither are pets.

RECOMMENDED IN THE AREA

The Arthurian Centre at Slaughterbridge (2 miles); Brown Willie and Rough Tor – walking on Bodmin Moor; picturesque harbours of Boscastle, Trebarwith and Port Isaac

*C*otswold House Hotel ♦♦♦♦

Tempting cuisine and relaxing surroundings in an ideal holiday location

☎ 01326 312077
📠 01326 319181
✉ ellis@
cotswoldhousehotel.fsnet.co.uk
www.bedbreakfastCornwall.
com/bb

Map ref 1 - SW82

Melvill Road, FALMOUTH, TR11 4DF
A39 into Falmouth, follow signs for docks, beaches & Princess Pavillion. Hotel on R.
10 Rooms, S £26-£30 D £52-£60, No smoking in dining room or lounge

*T*astefully appointed and elegant but appealingly comfortable, this small hotel is perfect for either a short or long getaway break. With many of its rooms enjoying lovely views of the sea or Falmouth harbour, it is just the place to relax and unwind. The smart lounge opens onto a small secluded patio which is ideal for basking in the sun, and freshly cooked evening meals and excellent breakfasts are served in the stylish dining room.

The hotel also has a bar offering beers, wines and spirits. En suite bedrooms are beautifully furnished and decorated, in keeping with the rest of this superior hotel.

RECOMMENDED IN THE AREA

New Maritime Museum (opens June 2002); Eden Project; Trebah and Glendurgan Gardens

*T*he Dolvean Hotel ·····

Traditional Victorian hotel retaining its original character while offering modern facilities

☎ 01326 313658
📠 01326 313995
✉ reservations@dolvean.freeserve.co.uk
www.dolvean.co.uk

Map ref 1 - SW83

50 Melvill Road, FALMOUTH, TR11 4DQ
on main road to Pendennis Castle & docks
10 Rooms, S £30-£40 D £70-£80, No smoking, Closed Xmas

RECOMMENDED IN THE AREA

Pendennis & St Mawes Castles; Trebah, Trelissick and Glendurgan Gardens; National Maritime Museum Cornwall

*T*he Dolvean is a Victorian gentleman's residence ideally situated between the beach and Falmouth's internationally renowned harbour, where everything from tall ships to cruise liners can be seen. With its outstanding natural beauty and splendid Tudor castle, the area is one of Cornwall's finest locations for exploring the far South-West of England. Carol and Paul have carefully chosen interesting antiques, fine china, and fascinating books to create an ambience where you can relax and feel at home. Each bedroom has its own individual character with pretty pictures, and lots of ribbon and lace to create an atmosphere that makes every occasion special. All bedrooms enjoy full en suite facilities, fluffy white towels, and a range of luxury toiletries. Thoughtful extras include hospitality tray, Cornish mineral water, and chocolates by your bedside. The traditional breakfast menu is quintessentially English and uses only the finest Cornish produce available. There is an enclosed car park.

Prospect House ◆◆◆◆◆

Historically interesting property offering smartly presented accommodation

☎ 01326 373198
📠 01326 373198
✉ prospecthouse@
　cornwall-selectively.co.uk
www.cornwall-selectively.co.uk

Map ref 1 - SW73

1 Church Road, Penryn, FALMOUTH,
TR10 8DA
Leave A39 at Treluswell rdbt, onto
B3292, past pub & through lights,
after 50m turn R through white gates
next to phone box
4 Rooms, S £30-£35 D £60-£65, No
smoking in bedrooms or dining room

Prospect House is a Grade II listed Packet Ship Captain's house, situated at the top of the Penryn River and set in a traditional Cornish walled plantsman's garden with Victorian conservatory.

Spacious and beautifully appointed accommodation is offered in three en suite bedrooms (twin, King and Queen size beds).

An elegant and comfortable drawing room is provided, with a log fire on cold evenings, and a traditional English breakfast is served in the dining room around a large antique Flemish dining table.

RECOMMENDED IN THE AREA

Eden Project (30 minutes); National Maritime Museum (5 minutes); Helford River Gardens – Trebah and Glendurgan (5 minutes)

Rosemullion Private Hotel ◆◆◆◆

Friendly, pleasant hotel offering quality accommodation by the sea

☎ 01326 314690 📠 01326 210098
✉ gail@rosemullionhotel.demon.uk

Map ref 1 - SW83

Gyllyngvase Hill, FALMOUTH, TR11 4DF
13 Rooms, S £25.50-£27.50 D £47-£53, No
smoking, Closed 23-27 Dec

Built as a gentleman's residence towards the end of the 19th century, this striking mock-Tudor hotel still caters for the discerning guest. Hospitality and customer care are high on the owners' list of priorities, and the peaceful atmosphere draws people back again and again. Bedrooms are beautifully decorated and furnished, and some enjoy glorious views over the bay; two have their own balconies. Breakfast is served in a smart wood-panelled dining room, and the lovely drawing room with its tranquil colour scheme and flower arrangements is a delightful place for relaxing. Rosemullion is a few short steps to Falmouth's main beach, and handy for the town and harbour.

RECOMMENDED IN THE AREA

Gyllyngvase Beach and Pendennis Castle (3 minutes' walk to beach); Helford River and Trebah Gardens (20 minutes' drive); Eden Project (50 minutes' drive)

Carnethic House ♦♦♦♦

Regency family home and beautiful gardens with excellent facilities

☎ 01726 833336
🖷 01726 833296
📧 carnethic@btinternet.com
www.carnethic.co.uk

Map ref 1 - SX15

Lambs Barn, FOWEY, PL23 1HQ
off A3082, directly opposite 'Welcome to Fowey' sign
8 Rooms, S £45 D £60-£80, No smoking in bedrooms or dining room, Closed Dec-Jan

The warmth and exuberance of Paul and Marion Allison's hospitality makes guests feel very welcome. Their home, with its covered veranda and large windows, looks across an award-winning garden with well tended lawns, mature trees and shrubs, as well as an outdoor heated swimming pool, putting green, golf practice net and a grass tennis court. At the end of the garden, there is a leafy lane leading to the beach. There is ample parking for cars and boats.

The bedrooms are light, with a clean, modern look and very good beds; five rooms are en suite. Traditional breakfast is served in the dining room, where you can also choose to have dinner from the changing menu, fresh local fish is a speciality. There is a licensed lounge bar.

RECOMMENDED IN THE AREA

The hotel enjoys a close relationship with both the Eden Project (10 minutes away) and the Heligan Gardens and regularly organises visits to both; port of Charlestown

Trevanion Guest House ♦♦♦♦

Character property in the heart of Daphne du Maurier country

☎ 01726 832602 🖷 01726 832602
📧 trefoy@globalnet.co.uk
www.users.globalnet.co.uk/
~trefoy/fowey.htm

Map ref 1 - SX15

70 Lostwithiel Street, FOWEY, PL23 1BQ
exit A390 onto B3269 signposted for Fowey, on descending the hill premises situated 200mtrs past turning for main car park
3 Rooms, D £45-£50, No smoking, Closed Nov-Feb

Trevanion is a Grade II listed building, dating in part from the 16th century, conveniently situated for exploring the whole of the historic town on foot. It offers comfortable accommodation, with colour televisions and tea and coffee making equipment. Two of the three bedrooms have en suite facilities and all the rooms are attractively decorated with co-ordinated fabrics.

The charming dining room retains many original features, and in addition to the hearty cooked breakfast, a good selection of alternatives is offered. Car parking is provided, and the house is an ideal base from which to explore the area. Children under twelve cannot be accommodated, and neither can dogs (except guide dogs).

RECOMMENDED IN THE AREA

The Eden Project (15 minute drive); The Lost Garden Of Heligan (25 minute drive); Coastal Path and walks around Fowey River estuary

Colvennor Farmhouse ◆◆◆◆

*17th-century former farmhouse
with later additions and high
comfort levels*

☎ 01326 241208
✉ colvennor@aol.com
Map ref 1 - SW62

Cury, HELSTON, TR12 7BJ
A3083 Helston-Lizard, across rdbt at
end of Airfield, next right to
Cury/Poldhu Cove, follow road for
1.4m, farm on right at top of hill
3 Rooms, S £26-£30 D £40-£50, No
smoking, Closed Dec-Jan

A long driveway leads to this Grade II listed building which stands in an acre of gardens surrounded by open countryside. Views of the nearby Mounts Bay can be enjoyed from the garden. This former farmhouse has a striking granite frontage which hides a warm and hospitable interior, a place that guests love to return to. The bedrooms are part of the reason, furnished and equipped with their comfort in mind, and each with en suite facilities and daily fresh towels. A beamed lounge with plenty of maps and books is inviting, and breakfast is a memorable experience. The nearest beach is a mile and a half away.

RECOMMENDED IN THE AREA

*National Trust gardens of Glendurgan and Trelissick; walk the
Coastal Path to Poldhu, Mullion and Kynance Coves; visit the
Lizard's unspoilt villages and harbours*

Tregondale Farm ◆◆◆◆

*A lovely location near the coast
and close to the A38 and A390*

☎ 01579 342407
🖷 01579 342407
**✉ tregondale@
connectfree.co.uk**
www.tregondalefarm.co.uk

Map ref 1 - SX26

Menheniot, LISKEARD, PL14 3RG
E of Liskeard. Exit A38 for Menheriot
at Hayloft Rest. 1.5m through village,
1m L at junct. Signs on R. From A390
follow signs to Menheniot
3 Rooms, S £25-£27 D £41-£46, No
smoking in bedrooms, dining room or
lounge

This lovely farmhouse stands in an old walled garden, surrounded by 200 acres of farmland and convenient for the many National Trust properties in the area. Mervyn and Stephanie offer a warm welcome to their home, where the attractive en suite rooms reflect Stephanie's flair for interior design. There is a log fire in the cosy guest lounge, and home-cooked meals, making use of local produce, are a speciality. Explore the farm trail through a wooded valley, with wildflowers and lambs in spring. The farm is home to an award-winning herd of pedigree cattle, and is a bird-watchers' paradise.

RECOMMENDED IN THE AREA

*Eden Project; Lost Gardens of Heligan;
Cotehele (oldest National Trust house in
Cornwall)*

51

*B*ucklawren Farm ◆◆◆◆

Farmhouse set amid 500 acres just a mile from the beach

☎ 01503 240738
🖷 01503 240481
✉ bucklawren@
   compuserve.com
www.bucklawren.co.uk

Map ref 1 - SX25

St Martin-by-Looe, LOOE, PL13 1NZ
from Looe take B3253 to Plymouth.
After 2m turn R to Monkey Sanctuary.
After 1m turn R to Bucklawren. White
farmhouse 0.5m on L
6 Rooms, S £25-£30 D £46-£50, No
smoking in bedrooms or dining room,
Closed Dec-Feb

*H*igh quality guest accommodation is offered in the 19th-century farmhouse of this working farm, set deep in beautiful countryside, a mile from the beach and three miles from the historic port of Looe. The bedrooms are well equipped, tastefully furnished and all have en suite facilities. Front-facing rooms offer spectacular views across the fields to the sea. Other facilities within the house are the dining room, lounge and conservatory. A recent barn conversion has provided the delightful Granary Restaurant, bar and function facilities next door, where guests can enjoy an evening meal from the carte or set menu for residents. Five self-contained cottages have also been created from farm buildings.

RECOMMENDED IN THE AREA

The Eden Project (20 miles); fishing villages of Looe and Polperro (3 miles); Lanhydrock (National Trust) (10 miles)

*C*oombe Farm Hotel ◆◆◆◆

Superbly-situated country house with plenty of space and peace

☎ 01503 240223 🖷 01503 240895
✉ coombe_farm@hotmail.com

Map ref 1 - SX25

Widegates, LOOE, PL13 1QN
on B3253 just S of Widegates village,
3.5m E of Looe
10 Rooms, D £74, No smoking,
Closed Nov-14 Feb

*G*uests are very well looked after at this idyllically located country house, and offered plenty of activities to entertain themselves. A heated swimming pool and croquet in the 10-acre grounds, a cosy games room in a converted barn with snooker and table tennis, and more games in the sitting room are some of the options. The en suite bedrooms are comfortable and spacious, and there are magnificent views down an unspoilt wooded valley to the sea. Delicious four-course evening meals by prior arrangement are a great strength. The warm family atmosphere and the peaceful setting are most attractive, and nearby are the Eden Project, National Trust properties, the coastal footpath and various beaches.

RECOMMENDED IN THE AREA

The Eden Project and Lost Gardens of Heligan (30 minutes); Lanhydrock, Cotehele, Antony (National Trust houses) (20-30 minutes); Coastal Path, beaches at Looe, Fowey and Polperro (25 minutes)

St Aubyn's Guest House ◆◆◆◆◆

Impressive Victorian house with superb sea views

☎ 01503 264351
📠 01503 263670
✉ welcome@staubyns.co.uk
www.staubyns.co.uk

Map ref 1 - SX25

Marine Drive, Hannafore, LOOE, PL13 2DH
from Looe Bridge take West Quay road signed Hannafore 0.75m, carry onto Marine Drive, house on R facing sea
8 Rooms, S £26-£28 D £46-£70, No smoking, Closed Nov-Etr

St Aubyn's is a substantial family house set in attractive gardens at the headland of Hannafore looking out to sea towards Rame Head and Looe Island. The spacious rooms are typically Victorian, with some fine pieces of furniture, tapestries and paintings. A pot of tea is offered in the lounge on arrival, and breakfast is served in the relaxed atmosphere of the dining room. In the afternoon you might enjoy a cream tea on the veranda. The bedrooms, six of them en suite, are named after places in the Chilterns. Most have sea views, three have balconies, and all have colour televisions and hospitality trays. No children under five or pets.

RECOMMENDED IN THE AREA

The Eden Project (40 minute drive);
Lanhydrock and Antony (30 minute drive);
Coastal Path and walks in the Looe Valley

Woodlands ◆◆◆◆

Beautifully refurbished guest house overlooking the river estuary

☎ 01503 264405

Map ref 1 - SX25

St Martins Road, LOOE, PL13 1LP
on B3253, 1m from St Martins Church
5 Rooms, S from £20 D from £40, No smoking, Closed Dec-Jan

A lovely Victorian country house with stunning views over the peaceful Looe river estuary and the surrounding Looe valley. An attractive wood sits along one side of the property, and the harbour and beaches are both within walking distance. Bedrooms are comfortable and well equipped, including double, twin and single rooms, with en suite facilities. Two rooms are easily adapted into family accommodation.

Local produce wherever possible goes into the enjoyable breakfasts which are served at a relaxed pace in the elegant dining room. Delicious three-course dinners are available by prior arrangement. Woodlands offers on-site parking.

RECOMMENDED IN THE AREA

The Eden Project (easy driving distance);
coastal walks (e.g. Looe – Polperro);
Lanhydrock and other National Trust houses (easy driving distance)

Kerryanna Country House ♦♦♦♦

Peacefully located farmhouse eight minutes from the harbour

☎ 01726 843558
📠 01726 843558
✉ linda.hennah@btinternet.com
www.kerryanna.co.uk

Map ref 1 - SX04

Treleaven Farm, Valley Road,
MEVAGISSEY, PL26 6SA
off B3273 on entrance to village, turn
right by tennis courts
6 Rooms, S D £52-£56, No smoking in
bedrooms or dining room, Closed
Nov-Feb

Linda Hennah has been welcoming guests to her delightful home for 30 years. It is set in two acres of gardens with fabulous views of Mevagissey, the surrounding countryside and the sea.

The farm is mostly arable, though there is a pets' corner with a donkey, ponies, goats and chickens. Good home cooking is served at breakfast, at separate tables in the beamed dining room. The bedrooms all have en suite facilities, hospitality trays, remote control televisions, toiletries and easy chairs. One room is on the ground floor, and there is a family room sleeping three. Three lounge areas and a coin-operated laundry room are provided for guests.

RECOMMENDED IN THE AREA

The Eden Project (12 miles); Lost Gardens of Heligan (2 miles); Mevagissey harbour and Coastal Path (10 minute walk)

Colan Barton ♦♦♦♦

Perfect place to relax, well away from the outside world !

☎ 01637 874395
📠 01637 881388
✉ colanbarton@yahoo.co.uk

Map ref 1 - SW86

Colan, NEWQUAY, TR8 4NB
take A392 to Newquay. At hamlet of
Mountjoy 2nd R signed Lady Nance &
follow track for 1m, white-washed
house on L
3 Rooms, S £21-£26 D £32-£48, No
smoking, Closed Oct-Mar

The lush Cornish countryside and eleven acres of private land surround this peaceful 17th-century farmhouse, sited well off the beaten track. Renovated to keep the best of its original features, the Grade II listed building nevertheless offers high standards of comfort and amenities. Bedrooms are fitted with pine furniture and comfortable beds, and all come with quality en suite showers or bathrooms. Breakfast is a delight not to be missed, and guests can enjoy plenty of woodland walks afterwards, or a stroll to the nearby Norman church. This non-working farm has plenty of animals to visit, including horses, chickens, ducks and geese.

RECOMMENDED IN THE AREA

National Trust houses – Trerice Manor (2 miles); Lanhydrock (easy driving distance); the Eden Project (short drive); wonderful coastal walks along the Cornish coast (3 miles)

Degembris Farmhouse ◆◆◆◆

Traditional farmhouse in a beautiful countryside setting close to the sea

☎ 01872 510555
📠 01872 510230
✉ kathy@degembris.co.uk
www.degembris.co.uk

Map ref 1 - SW85

St Newlyn East, NEWQUAY, TR8 5HY
from A30, L for Summercourt village, at x-rds turn R towards Newquay on A3058, take 3rd L to St Newlyn East, & 2nd L
5 Rooms, S £22-£25 D £44-£50, No smoking, Closed Xmas

Degembris is a Grade II listed farmhouse, dating from the 16th to early 17th century with 18th-century additions. It is a stone construction with an unusual slate-hung exterior. The Woodley family first had the farm in 1893 and these days it is in the capable hands of Roger and Kathy Woodley. The farm overlooks a wooded valley, through which they have established a country trail, to help preserve the wildlife and the bluebell walks in spring. A good choice of accommodation is offered in single, double, twin and family rooms, three with en suite facilities. Bedrooms are individually decorated and each one offers colour television, a hairdryer, complimentary tea and coffee, electric blanket and heating. A comfortable sitting room is provided, with books, games and colour television, and traditional farmhouse cooking is served at separate tables in the beamed dining room at breakfast and dinner. Numerous attractions are within easy reach: the coastline, National Trust properties and famous Cornish gardens.

RECOMMENDED IN THE AREA

The Eden Project (20 minute drive); Trerice Manor (5 minute drive); Lost Gardens of Heligan (30 minute drive)

Melancoose Mill ♦♦♦♦

Mentioned in the Domesday Book, a historic watermill in a delightful rural setting

☎ 01637 872811 📠 01637 854254
✉ westmore@
   melancoose.freeserve.co.uk
www.melancoose.freeserve.co.uk

Map ref 1 - SW82

Colan, NEWQUAY, TR8 4JS
A30/A392. At Mountjoy turn right to Colan, at T-junct turn left, follow lane for 2m and take first right. Pass entrance to reservoir, bottom of hill
2 Rooms, S £25 D £50, No smoking, Closed Xmas

A picturesque old watermill tucked away in the tranquil Porth Valley, yet only a few miles from the busy resort of Newquay. Dating back to the Domesday Book, this restored property borders on a reservoir, making it ideal for anglers. There is also a nature reserve and bird sanctuary, and lovely gardens to enjoy. Nothing is too much trouble for the friendly owners, who keep horses on the property and offer informal, comfortable accommodation in en suite bedrooms. A hearty English breakfast using fresh local produce where possible ensures a great start to the day, and places to visit include the Eden Project and plenty of nearby beaches.

RECOMMENDED IN THE AREA

The Eden Project (20 minute drive); easy access to Coastal Path and beaches; National Trust houses

Newquay

Cross House Hotel ♦♦♦♦♦

Comfortable accommodation in a relaxed environment where guests can readily unwind

☎ 01841 532391
🖷 01841 533633
✉ info@crosshouse.co.uk
www.crosshouse.co.uk

Map ref 1 - SW97

Church Street, PADSTOW, PL28 8BG
turn off A30 onto B3274. Follow signs
to Padstow, on reaching town take
3rd right. Follow one way street past
church for 50 yds and sharp L
9 Rooms, S £50-£120 D £60-£120, No
smoking in bedrooms or dining room

*J*ust a short stroll from Padstow's historic harbour, this charming Georgian house is an ideal place to stay in any season. The Grade II listed building offers high levels of comfort and hospitality in both the main and adjacent house, with bedrooms in the latter offering more spacious en suite facilities. Rooms are well decorated and furnished, and equipped with extras like video recorders, air conditioning and telephones. There are two cosy lounges to relax in, and breakfast offers a choice of cooked dishes or lighter alternatives including a variety of pastries. There is a good range of eating places just a short walk from this friendly hotel.

RECOMMENDED IN THE AREA

Prideaux Place (5 minute walk); Camel Trail (Cycle Path) and Coastal Path (5 minute walk); the Eden Project

Blue Seas Hotel ♦♦♦♦

Attractive Regency house with excellent sea views

☎ 01736 364744 🖷 01736 330701

Map ref 1 - SW49

13 Regent Terrace, PENZANCE, TR18 4DW
A30, then at Penzance station follow road
along harbour in direction of Promenade.
Opp Jubilee Bathing Pool, Regent Terrace
2nd R
9 Rooms, S £21-£25 D £46-£60, No smoking

*O*ffering lovely views of Mounts Bay towards Mousehole, this comfortable hotel is located in a south facing terrace overlooking the promenade, convenient for the ferry and Scillies Heliport. The town centre is close by and ample private parking is provided. Guests can relax in the spacious lounge, or outside in the sheltered garden. Most of the bedrooms have sea views and all are en suite except for one room with a private bathroom. In-room comforts include crisp cotton bedding, colour television, and tea and coffee-making facilities. Breakfast is a real treat - a feast of local and home-made produce, freshly prepared and attractively presented. Children of all ages are welcome.

RECOMMENDED IN THE AREA

Land's End (7 miles); Isles of Scilly (by helicopter or ferry); Minack Theatre (15 minutes away)

Camilla House Hotel ◆◆◆◆

Comfortable 'no-smoking' hotel with friendly proprietors and splendid sea views

☎ 01736 363771 📠 01736 363771
📧 visitus@camillahouse-hotel.co.uk
www.camillahouse-hotel.co.uk

Map ref 1 - SW42

12 Regent Terrace, PENZANCE, TR18 4DW
take seafront road to Promenade, Regent
Terrace approx 30yds W of Jubilee Pool
8 Rooms, S £20-£25 D £40-£60, No smoking
Closed Nov-Feb (usually)

Welcoming and attentive hosts Rosemary and Bill Wooldridge really do want guests to feel at home in their lovely house, which was built for a Master Mariner in 1836. Rooms, many with en suite facilities, are furnished to a high standard and are very well equipped with guests' comfort in mind. Delightfully situated in a quiet terrace overlooking Mount's Bay, (and just off the only Promenade in Cornwall) Camilla House offers bed and breakfast with private parking and is an ideal base from which to explore this part of the West Country. All front rooms have wonderful sea views, and breakfast, served in the spacious dining room, features the

'Camilla Special', a tempting, healthy alternative to full English breakfast.

RECOMMENDED IN THE AREA

St Michael's Mount (National Trust) (3 miles); the Eden Project (easy driving distance); Land's End (10 miles)

Ennys ◆◆◆◆◆

Complete tranquillity at a beautiful Cornish manor house

☎ 01736 740262
📠 01736 740055
📧 ennys@zetnet.co.uk
www.ennys.co.uk

Map ref 1 - SW53

Trewhella Lane, St Hilary, PENZANCE,
TR20 9BZ
1m N of B3280, Leedstown to
Goldsithney road
5 Rooms, S £40-£50 D £60-£75, No
smoking in bedrooms or dining room,
Closed 1Nov-13 Feb

Guests return time after time to soak up the comfortable country house atmosphere at this beautiful 17th-century manor in the valley of the River Hayle. It has large, sheltered, landscaped gardens, with beautiful lawns and beds of colourful flowers and shrubs, and there is an outdoor heated swimming pool and a grass tennis court within the grounds.

The bedrooms are stylish and furnished with artefacts from the owner's extensive travels. There are three in the main house, all with en suite bathroom facilities, two with four-

poster beds. The family suites are in a converted barn adjoining the house. Children under two years and dogs cannot be accommodated.

RECOMMENDED IN THE AREA

Visit St Michael's Mount by boat; explore the artists' colony of St Ives; walk the most beautiful part of the Coastal Path to Land's End.

Chy-an-Mor •••••

A Grade II listed Georgian building in a prime seafront position

☎ 01736 363441 📠 01736 363441
📧 mikeandjan@chyanmor.co.uk
www.chyanmor.co.uk

Map ref 1 - SW42

15 Regent Terrace, PENZANCE, TR18 4DW
A30-Penzance. Follow road to rail station in L
lane to Newlyn. Pass harbour, onto promenade,
pass Jubilee Pool on L, R at Stanley Hotel
10 Rooms, S £32-£35 D £53-£62, No smoking,
Closed Dec-Jan

RECOMMENDED IN THE AREA

St Michael's Mount (3 miles); Land's End (10 miles); St Ives (10 miles)

Owners Mike and Jan Russell have sympathetically restored this lovely seaside property to its former glory. The bedrooms, most of which have sea views, are individually styled and beautifully decorated, with quality co-ordinated fabrics and furnishings.

Rooms come in a variety of sizes and some are located on the ground floor. Each has an en suite shower room, colour television, radio alarm, hairdryer, central heating and tea and coffee making facilities. The smart dining room has an art deco theme, and breakfast is served at separate tables. Guests can relax in the elegant ground floor lounge which offers fine views over Mounts Bay.

The town centre, harbour, promenade and gardens are just a short walk away, and there are plenty of places to eat in the locality. Ample private parking is provided.

Ednovean Farm ♦♦♦♦♦

Tranquil country property in an idyllic setting, with first-class accommodation

☎ 01736 711883
🖷 01736 710480
✉ info@ednoveanfarm.co.uk
www.ednoveanfarm.co.uk

Map ref 1 - SW52

PERRANUTHNOE, TR20 9LZ
from A394 Penzance/Helston turn off
for Perranuthnoe at Dynasty
Cantonese Restaurant, farm drive on
L on bend by post box
3 Rooms, S £55-£60 D £60-£70, No
smoking, Closed 24 Dec-2 Jan

Spectacular sea views over St Michael's Mount and Mount's Bay are a delightful feature of this restored and converted 17th-century farmhouse.

The impressive property stands high above the village in beautiful grounds which include an Italianate garden.

Three stylish bedrooms are furnished with comfortable beds and quality pieces, chintz fabrics, and plenty of thoughtful extras like flowers, magazines and fruit. Guests can relax in the elegant sitting room, the garden room and several sunny patios, and breakfast is served at a magnificent oak table in the dining room. The coastal footpath and the beach are just three minutes away.

RECOMMENDED IN THE AREA

St Michael's Mount and Gardens; Godolphin House (English Heritage restoration); Penlee House Gallery (Newlyn School paintings) (2 miles)

The Corn Mill ♦♦♦♦

The epitome of a delightful country cottage

☎ 01208 851079

Map ref 1 - SW09

Port Isaac Road, Trelill, PORT ISAAC,
PL30 3HZ
between villages of Pendoggett and
Trelill
3 Rooms, D £53, No smoking in
bedrooms, Closed 24 Dec-5 Jan

Dating from the 18th century, this former mill has been lovingly restored to provide a beautiful home, packed with character. The delightful garden and charming hostess add to the pleasure of a stay here. Bedrooms are individually styled, and many personal touches contribute to a wonderfully relaxed and homely atmosphere. Most rooms have their own shower room, while the twin room uses a bathroom with an enormous Victorian bathtub, and plenty of hot water. Luxury extras such as huge towels and pure cotton bed linen are welcome touches.

Delicious breakfasts with home-made nutty bread are served in the farmhouse kitchen. The Eden Project is only a half-hour drive away.

RECOMMENDED IN THE AREA

Spectacular coastal walks round the National Trust Coastal Path; beautiful beaches for swimming and surfing; historic houses, both National Trust and privately owned

*T*renderway Farm •••••

16th-century farmhouse set on the gentle slopes at the head of the Polperro valley

☎ 01503 272214 📠 01503 272991 📧 trenderwayfarm@hotmail.com
www.trenderwayfarm.co.uk

Map ref 1 - SX25

Pelynt, POLPERRO, PL13 2LY
from Looe take A387 to Polperro, farm is signposted on main road
4 Rooms, S £25-£45 D £60-£70, No smoking, Closed Xmas & New Year

RECOMMENDED IN THE AREA

Eden Project (30 minute drive); Lanhydrock House and other National Trust houses (easy driving distance); National Trust Coastal Path (10 minute drive)

*T*he farm comprises a group of local stone buildings set on a working mixed farm surrounded by stunning Cornish countryside. The perfect situation for a relaxed and peaceful stay. Talland Bay beach is just a mile away and there are miles of National Trust cliff paths to explore. The accommodation is stylishly presented, and includes a twin or king-size double room in the main house, or a king-size or four-poster room in the adjacent converted barn. All the rooms have en suite facilities with a bath and shower, central heating, colour television, and tea and coffee making equipment. Electric blankets are also provided in cooler weather. The four-course breakfast sets guests up for the day, though a lighter continental option is available. For dinner, the proprietors are happy to advise on local restaurants, and in the evening guests can relax by the open fire in the large sitting room.

Benson's ....

Modern purpose built guest house overlooking the village, harbour, valley and sea

☎ 01209 842534
🖶 01209 843578
✉ bensons@
   portreath.
   fsbusiness.co.uk

Map ref 1 - SW64

1 The Hillside,
PORTREATH, Redruth,
TR16 4LL
exit A30 for Portreath onto
B3300 and turn left by
Portreath school. Fork left
by Glenfeadon Castle
4 Rooms, S £25 D £40,
No smoking, Closed Oct-
14 Apr & 25 Apr-9 Jun

RECOMMENDED IN THE AREA

North and south coast beaches; the Eden Project; Tate Gallery St Ives

Many of Cornwall's favourite attractions are accessible from this attractive bed and breakfast establishment: the beaches of the north and south coasts as well as the Eden Project, Tate Gallery, and the famous Cornish gardens. Proprietors Christine and Peter Smythe's aim is to provide total quality and comfort, and their warm hospitality and genuine friendliness are exemplary. Benson's was designed as a guest house and built in the late 1980s, occupying an elevated position affording panoramic views over the bay. Bedrooms are spacious and comfortably furnished, and a choice of twin rooms or doubles with king size beds is offered, all with en suite facilities, colour televisions, trouser presses and tea and coffee-making materials. A full English breakfast is served in the centrally heated conservatory, with alternatives by arrangement. Parking is provided, and guests can enjoy the sandy beach, National Trust walks and the local pubs and restaurants. Pets and children under 12 cannot be accommodated.

The Lodge at Carlyon Bay ◆◆◆◆

Superbly situated guest house above the sea at Carlyon Bay

📞 01726 815543 📠 01726 810070
✉ thelodge@carlyonbay.demon.co.uk
www.thelodgeatcarlyonbay.co.uk

Map ref 1 - SX05
91 Sea Road, Carlyon Bay, ST AUSTELL, PL25 3SH
6 Rooms, S £50-£60 D £80-£90, No smoking

The warm hospitality at this charming house has guests returning time after time to enjoy the wonderful care and comfort. The Lodge offers excellent accommodation in ground floor rooms overlooking beautiful lawns and gardens. All the bedrooms have en suite facilities and are equipped with remote control colour televisions, radio alarms, hairdryers and hospitality trays.

Public rooms include a residents' lounge and a well-spaced, bright and airy dining room with a licensed bar. Ample safe car parking with CCTV is provided in the grounds. Close to the Eden Project, with the golf course, cliff top and coastal path just across the road, and the quaint harbour villages of Fowey, Charlestown and Mevagissey only short drives away.

RECOMMENDED IN THE AREA

The Eden Project (5 miles); Lost Gardens of Heligan (6 miles); Lanhydrock House (12 miles)

Chy-Garth ◆◆◆◆

Quality and value at the 'garden house by the sea'

📞 01736 795677
✉ ann@
chy-garth.demon.co.uk
www.stives-cornwall.co.uk/
members/chy-garth.html

Map ref 1 - SW58
Sea View Meadows, St Ives Road, Carbis Bay, ST IVES, TR26 2JX
A30/A3074 follow signs to St Ives through Lelant and into Carbis Bay. Establishment on right opposite Post Office and Methodist Church
8 Rooms, S £22-£26 D £40-£60, No smoking

Sea views and close proximity to lovely beaches are offered at this detached guest house, situated in sub-tropical gardens overlooking a bay ranked as one of the 40 most beautiful in the world. A good range of accommodation is offered, including single, twin, double, double coronet and triple rooms, and one room with a king-size four-poster. Some rooms are located on the ground floor, most of them are en suite and all have central heating, double-glazing, remote control television, hairdryers and hospitality trays. There is a comfortable residents' lounge and a separate dining room where full English, vegetarian or continental breakfast is served. Private parking on the premises

RECOMMENDED IN THE AREA

Tate Gallery; St Michael's Mount; Land's End; Porthcorno; lovely beaches for surfing, swimming and diving

Kynance Guest House ♦♦♦♦

19th-century tin miner's cottage in a conservation area

☏ 01736 796636
✉ enquiries@kynance24.co.uk
www.kynance24.co.uk

Map ref 1 - SW54

The Warren, ST IVES, TR26 2EA
A3074 into town centre, sharp R
before bus/coach terminus, into
station approach rd. Kynance 20yds
on L
6 Rooms, D £44-£52, No smoking,
Closed mid Nov-mid Mar

K ynance is a charming old property in the heart of the village, a short level walk from the picturesque harbour and sandy Porthminster beach. The bedrooms have either private or en suite facilities and are equipped with colour televisions and hospitality trays. Some have stunning views of the harbour and bay. The lounge and dining room have been cleverly altered, and the decor reflects the St Ives' heritage, featuring work by local artists. Guests are offered a choice at breakfast, including a vegetarian option. There is a south facing patio garden from where a short flight of steps takes you to within 50 yards of the coach terminus and railway station car park. (Guests' parking available.)

Dawn and Simon Norris are welcoming hosts, happy to advise guests on the local attractions and restaurants for evening meals. Children under seven and pets cannot be accommodated.

RECOMMENDED IN THE AREA

The Tate Gallery (8 minute walk); St Michael's Mount (10 miles); Land's End (23 miles)

Port William Inn ♦♦♦♦

Delicious food and pleasant bedrooms in a welcoming cliffside inn

☏ 01840 770230 ☏ 01840 770936
✉ william@eurobell.co.uk

Map ref 1 - SX08

Trebarwith Strand, TINTAGEL, PL34 0HB
off B3263 from Camelford to Tintagel
5 Rooms, S £52-£60 D £69-£83, No smoking in bedrooms

T he views from this inn are spectacular, perched, as it is, on the side of a cliff just a short distance from Tintagel. All bedrooms share the same awesome views of the Atlantic Ocean, and each one offers comfortable, well-equipped accommodation with a high standard of decoration.

The traditional bar is furnished with old church pews and large wooden tables, and the highlight of a visit is the food served here. Menus offer a wide range of dishes, with the emphasis on locally caught fish, and the results are delicious and praiseworthy.

Hospitality is another strength, and the owners and staff provide a very good service.

RECOMMENDED IN THE AREA

Tintagel Castle; Launceston Castle; Bodmin Moor and North Cornish Coast

$\mathcal{E}$lerkey
Guest House ....

Exemplary hospitality at this village property, ideally located for exploring the beguiling Roseland peninsula

☎ 01872 501261
🖷 01872 501354
✉ anne.squire@btinternet.com
www.elerkey-guest-house.co.uk

Map ref 1 - SW93

Elerkey House, VERYAN, Truro,
TR2 5QA
A30 Exeter to St Austell, left fork
B3287 to Tregary & St Mawes.
Signposted Veryan after Esso garage
(bear left to Veryan). Follow brown
signs into village, Elerkey is 1st left
after church & water gardens
4 Rooms, S £22.50-£33.50 D £45-£47,
No smoking in bedrooms or dining
room, Closed Xmas/New Year

RECOMMENDED IN THE AREA

The Eden Project; the Lost Gardens of Heligan; Coastal Path and beaches (1 mile)

The village of Veryan is renowned for its round houses, and this friendly, family-run (though rectangular) guest house is situated right at the centre surrounded by attractive gardens. The bedrooms are furnished to a high standard and equipped with en suite facilities, hairdryers, radios, and complimentary tea and coffee. The proprietors, Margaret and Harvey Graver, can arrange discounted green fees for golfers and no-queue tickets for the Eden Project. Ample parking is provided, and for a small charge, guests can be collected from rail or coach terminals at Truro and St Austell. Tennis and bowls can be played at the village sports centre, and horse riding is available nearby. Harvey's original paintings and prints are available for sale in the adjoining Art Gallery & Gift Shop, along with an extensive display of silk and dried flowers. Also part of the establishment is the Tregarthen Coffee Shop, serving morning coffees, light lunches and afternoon teas, which can be enjoyed in the garden and patio area.

Cumbria

A selection of places to eat from the AA Restaurant & AA Pub Guides

Restaurants

◉ Appleby Manor Country House (Country-house)
Roman Road, Appleby-in-Westmorland
CA16 6JB
Tel 017683 51571 Fax 01768352888

◉◉ Borrowdale Gates Country House (Country-house)
Borrowdale CA12 5UQ
Tel 017687 77204 Fax 017687 77254

◉◉ Magenta's (Minimalist, Modern)
18 Fisher Street, Carlisle CA3 8RH
Tel 01228 546363 Fax 01228 546363

◉ Clare House (Classic)
Park Road, Grange-over-Sands LA11 7HQ
Tel 015395 33026

◉ The Jumble Room Café (Bistro, Italian)
Langdale Road, Grasmere LA22 0QF
Tel 015394 35188 Fax 015394 36088

◉◉◉◉ Michael's Nook Country House Hotel (Classic)
Grasmere, LA22 9RP
Tel 015394 35496 Fax 015394 35645

◉ Highfield House (Modern, Country-house)
Hawkshead Hill, Hawkshead LA22 0PN
Tel 015394 36344 Fax 015394 36793

◉◉◉ Sharrow Bay (Classic, Country-house)
Sharrow Bay, Howtown CA10 2LZ
Tel 017684 86301 Fax 017684 86349

◉ The Mill Hotel (Country-house)
Mungrisdale CA11 0XR
Tel 017687 79659 Fax 017687 79155

◉◉ Sawrey House Country Hotel (Country-house)
Near Sawrey, LA22 0LF
Tel 015394 36387 Fax 015394 36010

◉ Lakeside Hotel (Classic Country-house)
Lakeside, Newby Bridge LA12 8AT
Tel 015395 31207 Fax 015395 31699

◉ Leeming House (Country-house, Traditional)
Watermillock CA11 0JJ
Tel 0870 400 8131 Fax 017684 86443

◉◉ Fayrer Garden House (Modern, Country-house)
Lyth Valley Road, Bowness on Windermere
LA23 3JP
Tel 015394 88185 Fax 015394 45986

◉◉◉ Holbeck Ghyll (French, Country-house)
Holbeck Lane, Windermere LA23 1LU
Tel 015394 32375 Fax 015394 34743

◉◉ Miller Howe (Country-house)
Rayrigg Road, Windermere LA23 1EY
Tel 015394 42536 Fax 015394 45664

Pubs

🍺 The Royal Oak Inn
Bongate, Applebury-in-Westmorland CA16 6UN
Tel 017683 51463 Fax 017683 52300

🍺 Tufton Arms Hotel
Market Square, Applebury-in-Westmorland
CA16 6XA
Tel 017683 Fax 017683 52761

🍺 The Pheasant
Bassenthwaite CA13 9YE
Tel 017687 76234 Fax 01768776002

🍺 The Wheatsheaf Hotel
Beetham LA7 7AL
Tel 015395 62123 Fax 015395 64840

🍺 Blacksmiths Arms
Talkin Village, Brampton CA8 1LE
Tel 016977 3452 Fax 016977 3396

🍺 Masons Arms
Strawberry Bank, Cartmell LA11 6HW
Tel 015395 68486 Fax 015395 68780

🍺 Black Bull Inn & Hotel
1 Yewdale Road, Coniston LA21 8DU
Tel 015394 41335 Fax 015394 41668

🍺 The Britannia Inn
Elterwater LA22 9HP
Tel 015394 37210 Fax 015394 37311

🍺 Bower House Inn
Eskdale Green CA19 1TD
Tel 019467 23244 Fax 019467 23308

🍺 The Sun Inn
Main Street, Hawkshead LA22 0NT
Tel 015394 36236 Fax 015394 36155

🍺 The Horse & Farrier Inn
Threlkeld Village, Keswick CA12 4SQ
Tel 017687 79688

🍺 Pheasant Inn
Casterton, Kirkby Lonsdale LA6 2RX
Tel 015242 71230 Fax 015242 71230

🍺 Tower Banks Hotel
Near Sawrey LA22 0LF
Tel 015394 36334 Fax 015394 36334

🍺 Black Swan Hotel
Ravenstonedale CA17 4NG
Tel 015396 23104 Fax 015396 23604

🍺 Queens Head Hotel
Townhead, Troutbeck LA23 1PW
Tel 015394 32174 Fax 015394 31938

🍺 The Brackenrigg Inn
Watermillock CA11 0LP
Tel 017684 86206 Fax 017684 86945

🍺 Oddfellows Arms
Caldbeck, Wigton CA7 8EA
Tel 016974 78227 Fax 017684 86945

$\mathcal{D}$runken Duck Inn ♦♦♦♦ ◉

Traditional pub offering contemporary food

☎ 015394 36347 ✆ 015394 36781
✉ info@drunkenduckinn. demon.co.uk
www.drunkenduckinn.co.uk

Map ref 5 - NY30

Barngates, AMBLESIDE, LA22 0NG
from Ambleside go towards Hawkshead, turn L on B5285, follow for 2.5m, turn R signed Drunken Duck Inn, 0.5m up hill
11 Rooms, S £50-£100 D £70-£140, No smoking in bedrooms or dining room

$\mathcal{W}$inner of the 2002 AA Pub of the Year Award for England, the Drunken Duck continues to go from strength to strength. The warm, inviting interior of this traditional 400-year-old Lakeland pub is in stark contrast to the wild landscape of this isolated spot between Ambleside and Tarn Hows. Log fires and oak settles create a cosy feel in the bar, while the intimate candle-lit restaurant is the place for the imaginative cooking for which the place is renowned. Smartly-furnished bedrooms include two luxury suites housed in a separate building and one with a period four-poster. The pub has its own brewery, producing popular award-winning beers.

RECOMMENDED IN THE AREA

Lake Windermere; Ruskin Museum; Dove Cottage and the Wordsworth Museum

$\mathcal{K}$ent House ♦♦♦♦

Delicious cooking and generous hospitality in a Lakeland townhouse

☎ 015394 33279 ✆ 015394 31667
✉ info@kent-house.com
www.kent-house.com

Map ref 5 - NY30

Lake Road, AMBLESIDE, LA22 0AD
from town centre, by post office in one way system 300yds on left on terrace above main road
6 Rooms, D £48-£64, No smoking

$\mathcal{A}$ charming stone-built townhouse offering a warm, friendly welcome and delightful accommodation. Guests are encouraged to relax on the terrace in fine weather, or in front of a blazing fire in the inviting lounge when it is cooler. Tea with cake or muffins is served in the afternoon. Bedrooms are spacious and comfortable, and all offer en suite or private facilities, plus telephones, televisions and courtesy trays. Plenty of extras including plasters for sore feet are supplied. Home-baked bread is part of the lavish Lakeland breakfast served in the dining room, and home-cooked evening meals are also available by prior arrangement.

RECOMMENDED IN THE AREA

Magnificent walks – Laughrigg, Rydal and Wansfell; cruises on Lake Windermere (10 minute walk); Ambleside – shops etc

$\mathcal{E}$den Grove Farmhouse ◆◆◆◆

Peaceful, welcoming guest house offering excellent food

☎ 017683 62321
✉ edengrovecumbria@aol.com
www.ukworld.net/edengrove

Map ref 6 - NY62

Bolton, APPLEBY-IN-WESTMORLAND, CA16 6AX
off A66 1.5 miles into villiage, pass villiage hall, ist right 0.4 miles Edengrove right
3 Rooms, S £25 D £44-£50, No smoking, Closed Xmas/New Year

$\mathcal{T}$his friendly Victorian house offers quality accommodation and a warm welcome. The lovely garden enjoys views towards the Pennines. The well equipped en suite bedrooms benefit from luxurious towels and toiletries, as well as extras such as fruit and sweets.

There is a guests' lounge and a small conservatory dining room, where Jeanette Atkinson's Aga-cooked breakfasts and three-course dinners are served. Meals make the best of local produce, including local cured bacon, and home-made bread and preserves. An ideal location for walkers, cyclists, and lovers of peace and quiet.

RECOMMENDED IN THE AREA

Rheged; Carlisle/Settle railway; many beautiful country houses nearby

$\mathcal{L}$ink House ◆◆◆◆

Interesting, inviting late Victorian house enjoying lovely views

☎ 017687 76291
📠 017687 76670
✉ gfkerr@lineone.net
www.link-house.co.uk

Map ref 5 - NY13

BASSENTHWAITE LAKE,
Cockermouth, CA13 9YD
A66 through Keswick & keep W of lake to N end then turn R onto B5291. Follow road to L.
9 Rooms, S £22-£29 D £54-£57, No smoking in bedrooms, dining room or lounge

$\mathcal{S}$et in a quiet rural location midway between Keswick and Cockermouth, this well-maintained house offers spotlessly clean and comfortable accommodation. Traditionally built in the late Victorian age, the country house enjoys stunning views of the forests and surrounding fells including the 3,054ft Skiddaw. Bedrooms of varying sizes also have the advantage of the lovely views, and are equipped with en suite showers or baths. Many original features lend a gracious feel to the comfortable lounge, and there is also a bright conservatory with a residents' bar which benefits from the afternoon sun. A homely atmosphere is maintained by friendly, helpful hosts.

RECOMMENDED IN THE AREA

Wordsworth's birthplace, Cockermouth (10 minute drive); walking in Sale Fell and Wythop Forest (5 minutes); boat trips on Derwentwater (12 minute drive)

Greenbank Countryhouse Hotel ♦♦♦♦

Victorian property peacefully located in the heart of Borrowdale

☎ 017687 77215 ✉ jeanwwood@lineone.net

Map ref 5 - NY21

BORROWDALE, Keswick, CA12 5UY
3m S of Keswick on B5289
10 Rooms, S £28 D £50-£60, No smoking in
bedrooms or dining room, Closed Xmas & Jan

Greenbank is a delightful establishment, set in its own grounds, affording breathtaking views across the valley to Derwentwater and northwards towards Skiddaw. It is the perfect place from which to enjoy some excellent walking.

Jean Wood offers a warm welcome to all her guests, and provides comfortable accommodation in thoughtfully equipped bedrooms, with full en suite facilities, hospitality trays, hairdryers and clock radios. Two lounges and an honesty bar are available for guests' use, both with log fires and lovely views, and one with a television.

Guests are greeted with a tray of tea on arrival, and a four-course dinner of imaginatively presented dishes can be taken in the tastefully appointed dining room. Here too a substantial Cumbrian breakfast is served. The perfect setting for a peaceful holiday.

RECOMMENDED IN THE AREA

Slate quarry and shop; Cars of the Stars; Lakes Theatre

Hazel Bank Country House ♦♦♦♦♦

Award winning Victorian residence in the beautiful Borrowdale Valley

☎ 017687 77248
🖷 017687 77373
✉ enquiries@
　hazelbankhotel.co.uk
www.hazelbankhotel.co.uk

Map ref 5 - NY21

Rosthwaite, BORROWDALE,
Keswick, CA12 5XB
on B5289 Seatoller road, turn left at
sign just before Rosthwaite
8 Rooms, S £50-£73.50 D £100-£147,
No smoking, No pets

Set in four acres of grounds in the Borrowdale Valley, one of the Lake District's loveliest spots, Hazel Bank commands magnificent views of the central Lakeland peaks, including Great Gable. Many of the peaks are within walking distance. The house has been carefully renovated to provide modern facilities and high quality furnishings, while retaining its Victorian character. Bedrooms, including two with four-poster beds, are well proportioned, individually furnished and thoughtfully equipped. All have en suite facilities, colour television, hospitality trays, hairdryers, and, of course, wonderful views. The room price includes a full breakfast freshly cooked to your taste, and a set four-course dinner of award-winning standards using the best of local produce. Meals are served in the attractive dining room, and the house has a restaurant and residential licence.

RECOMMENDED IN THE AREA

The central Lakeland fells (walking distance); Derwentwater (3 miles); Keswick Pencil Museum (6 miles)

Cracrop Farm ◆◆◆◆

Friendly atmosphere at this smart 19th-century farmhouse on working farm

☎ **016977 48245**
🖷 **016977 48333**
✉ **cracrop@aol.com**
www.cracrop.co.uk

Map ref 6 - NY56

Kirkcambeck, BRAMPTON, CA8 2BW
At Brampton take A6071 (Longtown Rd) for 2m. After bridge, turn R, signed Walton/Roadhead. At Kirkeambeck over bridge, L at B&B sign, 1m on R.
4 Rooms, S £25-£30 D £50-£55, No smoking

*T*his delightful, south-facing property built in 1847 retains much of its original character. Peacefully set in open countryside, but just 13 miles from the M6, Cracrop is easily accessible. Enjoy the beautifully landscaped gardens or the summer- house and patio in fine weather. Indoors you will find spacious public areas: a fitness room and sauna and a smart, inviting lounge. Adjacent lies the traditional dining room where farmhouse breakfasts are served. Home-made supper trays or other meals may be arranged in advance. Large comfortable en suite bedrooms have colour co-ordinated furnishings and linen. Each is thoughtfully equipped. Ample parking space. No children under 10; no pets indoors.

RECOMMENDED IN THE AREA

Hadrian's Wall World Heritage Site – Birdoswald (5 miles); Cracrop Farm Trail; Talkin Tarn Country Park

Swaledale Watch Farm House ◆◆◆◆

Friendly atmosphere on a working sheep farm by a stream

☎ **016974 78409**
🖷 **016974 78409**
✉ **nan.savage@talk21.com**

Map ref 5 - NY33

Whelpo, CALDBECK, CA7 8HQ
1m SW on B5299
4 Rooms, S £20-£24 D £38-£42, No smoking, Closed 24-26 Dec

*T*his busy farm is set in idyllic surroundings, with open views of the fells and mountains. Guests are welcome to look round, a very special treat at lambing time. Just a mile away is the picturesque village of Caldbeck, once renowned for its milling and mining. Take a memorable walk through 'The Howk', a beautiful wooded limestone gorge with waterfalls. Nan and Arnold Savage work hard to make their hospitality seem effortless and to put their guests at ease.

The recently converted farmhouse, is enhanced by open stonework and has log fires for colder evenings. The lounges have TV, books and games. The bedrooms are tastefully furnished in pine, beautifully decorated and have bath and shower en suite. Two bedrooms and a lounge are in the converted cowshed, ideal for a group of four. Nan's homecooked dinners and hearty Cumbrian breakfasts are delicious.

RECOMMENDED IN THE AREA

Explore Swaledale Watch's own 100 acre nature reserve; discover Caldbeck village's mining and milling industries, long since gone; absorb the atmosphere of ancient settlements on Carrock Fell and Aughertree Fell.

$\mathscr{A}$ngus Hotel & Almonds Bistro ♦♦♦♦

Family-run hotel with its foundations, literally, on Hadrian's Wall

☎ 01228 523546 **℉** 01228 531895
📧 angus@hadrians-wall.fsnet.co.uk
www.angus-hotel.fsnet.co.uk

Map ref 5 - NY45

14 Scotland Road, CARLISLE, CA3 9DG
Exit M6 at junct 44, on A7 at 7th set of traffic lights
11 Rooms, S £45-£48 D £55-£60

$\mathscr{E}$laine and Geoff Webster's town house hotel is located in a Victorian terrace just north of the city. Eleven bedrooms have en suite facilities and are equipped with remote control televisions, radio alarms, direct dial telephones with laptop points, hairdryers and hospitality trays. Secure parking is provided, and cyclists will be interested to know that the hotel is on three established cycle routes.

Geoff is the chef, offering a full menu from Monday to Saturday in Almonds Bistro, including vegetarian options. From 5.30pm, an 'Early Bird' menu features alongside the main menu – ideal for pre-theatre suppers. You can also check your e-mails or surf the net, as the bistro operates as an Internet café.

RECOMMENDED IN THE AREA

Hadrian's Wall World Heritage Site; Carlisle Cathedral, Castle and Museum; Settle/Carlisle Railway

---

$\mathscr{U}$plands Hotel ♦♦♦♦♦ ◎◎

$\mathscr{T}$om and Di Peter's country hotel is located just outside the village, near Grange-over-Sands, on the southern edge of the Lake District. It is set in two acres of gardens with fine views, just three miles from Lake Windermere. Pre-dinner drinks and coffee are served in the bright lounge, where board games, books and magazines are also provided for guests' enjoyment.

The spacious restaurant has two AA Rosettes for Tom's ambitious cooking. Bedrooms, named after Cumbrian rivers, are all en suite, with colour televisions, direct dial telephones, radios, reading materials and toiletries. Also in residence are a couple of cats and a friendly Jack Russell.

Country house overlooking the Leven estuary on Morecambe Bay

☎ 015395 36248 **℉** 015395 36848
📧 uplands@kencomp.net
www.uplands.uk.com

Map ref 5 - SD37

Haggs Lane, CARTMEL, LA11 6HD
5 Rooms, S £66-£86 D £112-£154, No smoking in dining room, Closed Jan-Feb

RECOMMENDED IN THE AREA

Pretty village of Cartmel – antique shops and 12th century priory; boating on Lake Windermere (3 miles); walking in the Lake District and Yorkshire Dales

Sundawn ♦♦♦♦

Victorian property with panoramic views of Lakeland fells

☎ 01900 822384
🖷 01900 822885
✉ robert.hodge1@virgin.net
www.sundawn-guesthouse.co.uk

Map ref 5 - NY13

Carlisle Road, Bridekirk,
COCKERMOUTH, CA13 0PA
1.5m from Cockermouth N on A595
towards Carlisle
3 Rooms, D £35, No smoking,
Closed 20 Dec-5 Jan

*T*his substantial family home, with its own garden and paddock, offers wonderful views towards Skiddaw and the Lorton Valley, which can be enjoyed in comfort from the sun lounge. It is an ideal base for touring the Lake District, the coast, and the nearby town of Cockermouth, or for outdoor pursuits like walking or fishing.

Pauline and Bob Hodge offer sincere hospitality, and the house has a friendly and relaxed atmosphere. The stylishly decorated bedrooms are comfortably furnished with fine pieces of traditional furniture. Two rooms are en suite and the third has private facilities. Breakfast is served in the combined lounge and breakfast room.

RECOMMENDED IN THE AREA

Cockermouth – birthplace of William Wordsworth; Ambleside and Windermere (within an hour's drive); coastal towns of Maryport and Whitehaven

Arrowfield Country Guest House ♦♦♦♦

A Victorian house with beautiful views of the surrounding countryside

☎ 015394 41741

Map ref 5 - SD29

Little Arrow, Torver, CONISTON,
LA21 8AU
1.5m from Coniston on A593
5 Rooms, S £23-£26 D £46-£52, No smoking, Closed Dec-Feb

*T*he house is set back from the road in its own attractive gardens, in a quiet and peaceful location outside Coniston village. There is access to the fells, with walks to suit all tastes in the immediate vicinity. Other activities - riding, sailing, windsurfing - are not much further away. There is ample private parking. The bedrooms are bright and well equipped, four have en suite bathroom facilities. There is a spacious, luxurious guest lounge with deep, comfortable sofas and an open fire. The dining room has a fireplace made of local stone, and always a fire in cold weather it is a cosy place to sample the delicious breakfast, which includes an extensive buffet. Packed lunches can also be provided on request. With some help from the hens and the bees, eggs and honey, as well as bread, preserves, chutney and cakes are home produced.

RECOMMENDED IN THE AREA

Holker Hall, Sizergh Castle and Levens Hall, all with superb gardens, (easy driving distance); Wordsworth's Dove Cottage, Grasmere (12 miles); Beatrix Potter's Hill Top Farm, Near Sawrey (7 miles)

Coniston Lodge Hotel ◆◆◆◆◆

Excellent accommodation in a beautiful lakeland setting

☎ 015394 41201
📠 015394 41201
✉ info@coniston-lodge.com
www.coniston-lodge.com

Map ref 5 - SD39

Station Road, CONISTON, LA21 8HH
at x-rds on A593 (close to filling
station), turn up hill - Station Rd)
6 Rooms, D £65-£94, No smoking

This small private hotel, reminiscent of a Swiss chalet has stunning views. It makes an ideal base for touring the southern lakes and lakeland towns. Visitors will receive a warm welcome from hosts Anthony and Elizabeth Robinson. A special feature in the lounge is the commissioned relief in local slate depicting former guest Donald Campbell, with his famous Bluebird racing boat. Bedrooms are all en suite and furnished in modern style, they are well equipped with direct dial telephones, tea and coffee making facilities and colour television. Dinner can be taken in the co-ordinated dining room, the adventurous home cooking features local game and fresh fish. Children under ten can be accommodated by arrangement. No dogs, (with the exception of guide dogs).

RECOMMENDED IN THE AREA

Cruises on Coniston Water; Brantwood (home of John Ruskin); beautiful walks to suit everyone

Wheelgate Country Guest House ◆◆◆◆◆

17th-century former farmhouse in a beautiful Lakeland setting

☎ 015394 41418
📠 015394 41114
✉ wheelgate@
conistoncottages.co.uk
www.wheelgate.co.uk

Map ref 5 - SD29

Little Arrow, CONISTON, LA21 8AU
1.5m S of Coniston, on W side of road
5 Rooms, S £29-£32 D £50-£64, No
smoking in bedrooms, dining room or
lounge, Closed Jan-Feb

Full of character, with beams, oak panelling and beautiful furnishings, the Luptons' country home is set in award-winning gardens in one of the loveliest parts of England. This is magnificent walking country with stunning scenery and opportunities for other outdoor pursuits, particularly water sports, cycling and pony trekking. Guests are greeted with complimentary sherry and shortbread on arrival, and will enjoy the cosy bar, excellent breakfasts and free use of the health club (a short drive away). The range of en suite bedrooms includes one with a four-poster bed, one kingsize and one twin. All the rooms have colour televisions, tea and coffee-making facilities, hairdryers and radio alarms.

RECOMMENDED IN THE AREA

Brantwood – John Ruskin's house; cruises on Coniston Water; Ruskin Museum

Crosthwaite House ◆◆◆◆

Peace and quiet in unspoilt corner of the Lake District

☎ 01539 568264
📠 01539 568264
✉ bookings@
  crosthwaitehouse.co.uk
www.crosthwaitehouse.co.uk

Map ref 5 - SD49

CROSTHWAITE, Kendal, LA8 8BP
M6 J36, A591 (Kendal), A590
(Barrow), R onto A5074, 4m take small
through-road for Crosthwaite, 0.5m
turn L
6 Rooms, S £22-£25 D £44-£50, No
smoking, Closed mid Nov-Dec

*I*n a sturdy house from the middle of the 18th century, this establishment stands in the village of Crosthwaite, at the northern end of the Lyth Valley, famous for its damson orchards. You can see across the valley from the spacious lounge, and from the light and airy dining room, where an imaginative menu of traditional home cooking is served, all freshly prepared on the Aga. There is plenty of room in the bedrooms, and all have en suite showers and toilets, colour TV, and tea and coffee making facilities.

The owners have been looking after guests in Lakeland for many years now, and they create a relaxed atmosphere in which it is easy to feel at home. They know the local surroundings extremely well, and will be happy to provide you with any information.

RECOMMENDED IN THE AREA

Lake Windermere (4 miles); historic houses (Blackwell, Levens, Sizergh); 3 golf courses within 4 miles

Mayfields ◆◆◆◆

Quietly located guest house overlooking the bay

☎ 015395 34730
www.accomodata.co.uk/
010699.htm

Map ref 5 - SD47

3 Mayfield Terrace, Kents Bank Road,
GRANGE-OVER-SANDS, LA11 7DW
M6 J36, take A590 to Meathop rdbt,
turn for Lindale. L in Lindale at small
rdbt to Grange, 1m S past rail station
& fire station
3 Rooms, S £25 D £50, Dinner £12.50,
No smoking, Closed 21 Dec- 6 Jan

*M*ayfields is a friendly establishment situated to the south of Grange-over-Sands, close to open countryside and with splendid views across Morecambe Bay. Hearty breakfasts and imaginative dinners are served in the attractive dining room. Lunches are also available and the house has a table license with wines available on request. Non-residents are welcome for morning coffee

and lunch Tuesday-Saturday, traditional lunch on Sunday and for dinner each evening. The spacious guests' lounge is comfortably furnished and equipped with a piano as well as a colour television and video recorder. Bedrooms are individually decorated and offer many thoughtful extras. Two have en suite facilities.

RECOMMENDED IN THE AREA

Cartmel with its 12th century priory church; Lake Windermere (6 miles); lovely countryside for walking

Sawrey Ground ....

A 17th century farmhouse with a welcoming atmosphere

☎ 015394 36683 📠 015394 36683
✉ sawrey.ground@which.net 🌐 http://homepages.which.net/~gillian.oconnell/

Map ref 5 - SD39

Hawkshead Hill, HAWKSHEAD, LA22 0PP
from Hawkshead take Coniston rd 1m to Hawkshead Hill (B5285). Turn R immediately after Baptist Church and follow signs for 0.25m. Sawrey Ground on R
3 Rooms, S £30-£34 D £50-£60, No smoking

RECOMMENDED IN THE AREA

Great walks from the front door and easy access to most of the main fells, villages and towns of the central Lake District (10-25 minutes' drive); Blackwell House (Arts & Crafts Movement), Brantwood (Ruskin's home) (easy driving distance)

𝓑uilt by Anthony Sawrey in 1627, this picture-book oak-beamed farmhouse has a magical setting on the edge of the Tarn Hows Forest. Situated in a quiet and peaceful location, yet in the centre of the Lake District just above Hawkshead village. Mike and Gill O'Connell offer a warm welcome to their home, with its friendly, relaxed atmosphere and popular home-made bread and cakes. They will do all they can to make your stay enjoyable and memorable. Around the house there are many historical features, and the centuries have created a comfortable and lived-in feeling, from the entrance hall, lounge and dining room, to the attractive south-facing bedrooms. Many walks are possible from the front door, extending to Coniston, Windermere and Langdale, and including the beautiful lake of Tarn Hows. The area is good for bird-watching and wildlife, and also for cycling and fishing. The central location is ideal for touring the major lakes and centres of the region, and there are some excellent places to eat within easy driving distance.

The lake at Tarn Hows, photograph by Jon Sparks

Burrow Hall Country Guest House ♦♦♦♦

Restored 17th-century Lakeland farmhouse between Kendal and Windermere

☎ 01539 821711
www.burrowhall.co.uk

Map ref 6 - SD49

Plantation Bridge, KENDAL, LA8 9JR on A591, between Kendal and Windermere, 1.5m after Crook rdbt on right
3 Rooms, S £28-£30 D £48-£50, No smoking, Closed 23 Dec-9 Jan

Burrow Hall is set in large gardens on the fringes of the Lake District National Park, just 10 minutes' drive from the M6. The house dates from 1648 and has been sympathetically restored with bedrooms located in a modern addition. These provide spacious accommodation with en suite facilities, colour televisions, radio alarms, hairdryers and complimentary tea and coffee. Guests have access to their rooms at all times through a separate entrance. Public rooms in the original building are particularly appealing, and the friendly hosts create a relaxing home-from-home atmosphere. Breakfast is a substantial meal served at individual tables in the dining room. Dogs cannot be accommodated.

RECOMMENDED IN THE AREA

Kendal Castle; the Quaker Tapestry; Museum of Lakeland Life

Badgers Wood ♦♦♦♦

Comfortable bedrooms with fell views and plenty of home-from-home comforts

☎ 017687 72621 📠 017687 72621
✉ enquiries@badgers-wood.co.uk
http://badgers-wood.co.uk

Map ref 5 - NY22

30 Stanger Street, KESWICK, CA12 5JU
M6 J40, left for Keswick. Past 1st Keswick turn off. Exit at rdbt for Keswick. Turn left. At T junct left. Over rdbt & left into Stanger St
6 Rooms, S £18 D £36-£44, No smoking Closed Xmas & New Year

Ideally placed for hiking, cycling, touring or just pottering around the town, this delightful Victorian guest house offers a quiet retreat in a beautiful part of the Lake District. The house has been extensively restored to offer smartly decorated and furnished bedrooms, all enjoying views of the Cumbrian mountains. Most rooms are en suite, and all offer the same soft towels and crisp white sheets. Picturesque views of the fells can be seen from the attractive breakfast room, where full English breakfasts are served with lighter options. Vegetarians are welcome and well catered for, and the house is entirely non-smoking.

RECOMMENDED IN THE AREA

Derwentwater (a few minutes' walk); Carlisle (easy driving distance); walking and climbing in the Cumbrian mountains

Dalegarth House Country Hotel ♦♦♦♦

Super views of lakes and fells, with a great choice at dinner

☎ / 🖷 017687 72817
✆ john@dalegarth-house.co.uk
www.dalegarth-house.co.uk

Map ref 5 - NY22

Portinscale, KESWICK, CA12 5RQ
approach Portinscale from A66 pass
Farmers Arms approx 100yds on left
to hotel
10 Rooms, S £31-£33 D £62-£66,
No smoking

*I*n the small lakeside village of Portinscale, just one mile from Keswick, this roomy Edwardian house sits in a sunny elevated position. It has landscaped gardens and superb views towards Derwentwater and the surrounding mountains. There is a private car park. Children under five and dogs cannot be accommodated. Fresh, traditional food, carefully prepared, is served in the restaurant: full English breakfast, and a six-course table d'hôte dinner menu that changes daily, accompanied by an extensive wine list. Packed lunches are available on request. Bedrooms vary in size but all have en suite bathrooms and colour TV. There are two spacious lounges and a bar serving draught beer and lager which has over 100 malt whiskies for the connoisseur. The house is neatly furnished in a modern style. You can expect good value for money.

RECOMMENDED IN THE AREA

Cars of the Stars Motor Museum (Keswick); Rheged Discovery Centre (15 miles); Ravenglass Railway

Derwent Cottage ♦♦♦♦♦

Quietly located property with mature Lakeland gardens

☎ 017687 74838
**✆ enquiries@
dercott.demon.co.uk**
www.dercott.demon.co.uk

Map ref 5 - NY22

Portinscale, KESWICK, CA12 5RF
A66 to Portinscale, pass Farmers
Arms, 200mtrs turn R after L bend
4 Rooms, S £37-£46 D £54-£84, No
smoking, Closed Nov-Feb

*D*erwent Cottage is set in idyllic grounds set back from the village road. Enthusiastically run by Mr and Mrs Newman, the house is comfortably furnished and offers cosy lounges and a small, well-stocked bar. The dining room is the venue for freshly prepared, home-cooked meals in traditional English style, and hearty Cumbrian breakfasts to set you up for the day.

Bedrooms are spacious and well furnished with many personal touches. All the rooms have en suite facilities, colour televisions, and tea and coffee making equipment. Car parking is provided. This is an excellent location for easy access to the whole of the northern, central and eastern Lake District. Children under 12 years cannot be accommodated, neither can dogs (except guide dogs).

RECOMMENDED IN THE AREA

Boating on Derwentwater; Skiddaw Range for walking and views; Keswick town

The Grange Country House ◆◆◆◆◆

Elegant Lakeland house with panoramic views and relaxed hospitality

☎ 017687 72500
📠 017687 72500
✉ duncan.miller@
btconnect.com

Map ref 5 - NY22

Manor Brow, Ambleside Road,
KESWICK, CA12 4BA
leave M6 at J40 & take A66 into
Keswick, then L on A591 towards
Windermere for 0.5m. Take 1st R &
house 200 mtrs on R
10 Rooms, S £28-£37.50 D £56-£75,
No smoking, Closed mid Nov-mid Feb

Set in beautifully tended gardens, within walking distance of Keswick, this lovely Victorian residence boasts stunning views of the distant fells. Immaculately kept, the quality and comfort of the spacious lounges and en suite bedrooms speaks for itself. Relax by an open log fire in the lounge bar, or simply admire the grandeur of the place: the high ceilings, the long velvet curtains, that intricate ceiling rose. The individually decorated bedrooms are attractive and well equipped. Some rooms feature exposed beams, while a half-tester bed in one offers the appeal of luxury and romance. Although dinner is not available at The Grange, a full English breakfast is served in the stylish dining room.

RECOMMENDED IN THE AREA

Theatre by the Lake (1 mile); numerous National Trust properties (including Wordsworth's house); fell-walking

---

Greystones Hotel ◆◆◆◆

Attractive stone-built property close to the market square

☎ 017687 73108
✉ greystones@keslakes.freeserve.co.uk

Map ref 5 - NY22

Ambleside Road, KESWICK, Cumbria, CA12 4DP
opposite St John's Church
8 Rooms, S £23-£26 D £46-£52, No smoking,
Closed Dec

Ideally located for the glories of the Lake District, Greystones offers splendid views of Skiddaw and Blencathra, and is just a short walk from Keswick's Market Square, Derwentwater and the new Theatre by the Lake. Fell views are a feature of the individually decorated bedrooms. These are thoughtfully equipped with colour televisions, radios, hairdryers, and tea and coffee-making materials. Double and twin rooms are all en suite while the one single has private facilities nearby. Breakfasts are freshly cooked on the Aga and served at individual tables in the dining room. For other meals, there are plenty of good pubs and restaurants to choose from in the vicinity.

RECOMMENDED IN THE AREA

Evening cruises on Derwentwater (7 minute walk); majestic mountain scenery; Wordsworth's Dove Cottage (15 minute drive)

*H*owe Keld Lakeland Hotel ♦♦♦♦

Lakeland hotel close to the town and Derwentwater

☎ 017687 72417
📠 017687 72417
📧 david@howekeld.co.uk
www.howekeld.co.uk

Map ref 5 - NY22

5/7 The Heads, KESWICK, CA12 5ES
from town centre take rd to
Borrowdale. Turn R opp main car
park, first on L
15 Rooms, S £28-£30 D £50-£60, No
smoking in bedrooms or dining room ,
Closed Xmas

*M*odern accommodation in recently refurbished bedrooms is offered at this attractive Lakeland hotel. Howe Keld is conveniently located for the major attractions - Keswick, Lake Derwentwater and the fells, and the first floor lounge affords spectacular scenic views. Breakfast is a special occasion with a wide-ranging choice including a popular veggie fry-up. Home-made produce features, including bread and granola, otherwise options range from fruit compotes or freshly made pancakes with maple syrup to home-made fishcakes or a traditional ensemble of Cumbrian sausage with tomatoes, mushrooms, eggs and fried bread. Candlelit evening meals are available by arrangement, though there are plenty of good pubs and restaurants within strolling distance.

RECOMMENDED IN THE AREA

Rheged Centre, Penrith; boat trips on Derwentwater; Theatre by the Lake (4 minute walk)

*N*ew House Farm ♦♦♦♦♦

17th-century Lakeland farmhouse with warm hospitality and good cuisine

☎ 01900 85404 📠 01900 85404
📧 hazel@newhouse-farm.co.uk
www.newhouse-farm.co.uk

Map ref 5 - NY12

LORTON, CA13 9UU
6m S of Cockermouth, on B5289
between Lorton and Loweswater
5 Rooms, S £40-£55 D £80-£88,
No smoking

*D*espite its name, the farmhouse dates back to 1650. The old oak beams and rafters, flagged floors and stone open fireplaces remain unspoilt. These features and the bold decorative colour schemes create a cosy, traditional atmosphere. The property lies in 15 acres of open fields, woods, streams and ponds, in the picturesque Lorton Vale, with lakes and fells all around. There are spectacular views of the countryside from every window. The bedrooms, with large beds, antique furniture and thoughtful extras such as fresh fruit, biscuits and flowers, all have en suite

bathroom facilities. There are two separate sitting rooms on the ground floor, with deep sofas, books and magazines, both with original stone fireplaces where log fires crackle on colder days. Breakfast makes extensive use of local produce, and is served in the cosy dining room. Traditional five-course English dinners are also served, main courses are usually roasts, and puddings are a speciality.

RECOMMENDED IN THE AREA

Keswick (9 miles); Loweswater; Buttermere (3 miles)

The Old Vicarage ♦♦♦♦

Lakeland property in the peaceful Lorton Valley

☎ 01900 85656 📠 01900 85656
✉ enquiries@oldvicarage.co.uk
www.oldvicarage.co.uk

Map ref 5 - NY12

Church Lane, LORTON, CA13 9UN
turn off B5292 Whinlatter Rd onto
B5289 N of Lorton. Take 1st L signed
Church, house 1st on R
8 Rooms, S £28-£38 D £56-£76, No
smoking, Closed 2-31 Jan

Spacious accommodation is afforded at this delightful Victorian house, located in the Lorton Valley at the heart of the National Park. The hall with its mahogany staircase and galleried landing makes a stunning first impression. Guests also have use of a lounge overlooking the garden, and a dining room with views of Kirk Fell and Whinlatter, where hearty breakfasts and candlelit dinners are served. Bedrooms with distant mountain views are available in the main house, while a converted coach house offers two rooms ideal for family occupation. All have televisions, alarms and morning tea and coffee trays. Ground floor and four-poster rooms are available.

RECOMMENDED IN THE AREA

Wordsworth's birthplace in Cockermouth; shopping in Keswick and Cockermouth; many wonderful walks from the door

Ees Wyke Country House ♦♦♦♦♦

Georgian country house set in the Esthwaite valley

☎ 015394 36393
📠 015394 36393
✉ eeswyke@aol.com
www.smoothhound.uk/hotel/ees
wyke

Map ref 5 - SD39

NEAR SAWREY, Ambleside, LA22 0JZ
1.5m outside Hawkshead on B5285.
On the road to the ferry across
Windermere
8 Rooms, S £65 D £130, No smoking
in dining room, Closed Jan-Feb

A handsome property with lovely views over Esthwaite, Ees Wyke was once the holiday home of Lakeland writer Beatrix Potter. The garden provides colour all year round, and the terrace is a pleasant place to relax after a day's activities. Owners John and Margaret Williams create a friendly, relaxed atmosphere in the comfortable lounges and the spacious dining room, which overlooks the lake. Delightful five-course dinners are served, featuring the finest local produce. Breakfast offers a choice of a full English breakfast, smoked fish, or a lighter continental selection with porridge, cereals, fresh fruits and yoghurts, plus a wide range of preserves. Bedrooms are attractively furnished and comfortable. All of them have either en suite or private facilities, televisions, hairdryers, and tea and coffee making equipment.

RECOMMENDED IN THE AREA

Hill Top – Beatrix Potter's house (5 minute walk); Blackwell Arts and Crafts House (20 minute drive); Brantwood - John Ruskin's house (20 minute drive)

Sawrey House
Country Hotel & Restaurant ◆◆◆◆◆ ◎◎

A quality country house with spectacular views of Esthwaite Water and Grizedale Forest

☎ 015394 36387
🖷 015394 36010
📧 enquiries@
sawrey-house.com
www.sawrey-house.com

Map ref 5 - SO39

NEAR SAWREY, Ambleside,
LA22 0LF
From Ambleside take B5286
towards Hawkshead, L onto B5285.
Hotel is on R
11 Rooms, S £45-£65 D £90-£120,
No smoking, Closed Jan

*T*he house was built around 1830 of Lakeland stone. It has retained many original features and has been lovingly restored, with interesting details, notably a stained glass window in the spacious hall, and the interior has been stylishly decorated. There is an elegant lounge with deep sofas, and a log fire burns on chilly nights. Bedrooms are en suite, some are larger than others, and many have views of the lake. Sawrey House has been awarded two AA rosettes for its food, which is imaginatively and stylishly presented, helped along with a varied contemporary larder. Breakfast is in the traditional style with a choice of lighter alternatives, such as smoked haddock, or perhaps field mushrooms on brioche.

Centrally situated in the Southern Lakes, Sawrey House is an ideal base for touring the area. Beatrix Potter's house is just a stroll away in the village, with many gentle walks immediately accessible from the hotel. Lake Windermere and the village of Hawkshead are both just a mile and a half away. Fishing on Esthwaite waters, mountain biking in Grizedale Forest, and many places of historic interest are within easy reach by car.

RECOMMENDED
IN THE AREA

Hill Top – Beatrix Potter's house (in the village); Lake Windermere (5 minute drive); many walks directly from the hotel

Cross Keys Temperance Inn ....

A 400 year old National Trust Temperance Inn

☎ 015396 20284
📠 015396 21966
✉ clowes@freeuk.com

Map ref 6 - SD69

Cautley, SEDBERGH, LA10 5NE
M6 J37 to A683 through
Sedbergh. Hotel 4m north of
Sedbergh on L
2 Rooms, S £32.50 D £65, No
smoking

Nestling beneath the Howgill Fells, The Cross Keys was a coaching inn in the 1700s, and it is rich with character. The parlour has flagstones on the floor and a low beamed ceiling, 18th-century settle, old copper scales, lots of books, comfy chairs and a wind-up gramophone. The dining room has wooden floors and a glassed veranda, with spectacular views of the Cautley Spout waterfall. Dinner is served here (also for non-residents) Wednesday to Saturday. Superb traditional and modern British cooking is the norm, using only the finest local produce. The property was left to the National Trust by Edith Bunney in 1948, on the condition that alcohol never be sold here again, but you can bring your own drinks! Meals and snacks are availbale all day including Sunday lunch, and packed lunches can be provided. A library and sitting room adjoin the two bedrooms, each have en suite facilities; the double room also has a bed-settee, useful for families.

RECOMMENDED IN THE AREA

Farfield Mill Heritage & Arts Centre; Settle-Carlisle scenic railway; Quaker Tapestry Exhibition

$\mathscr{B}$rookfield Guest House ◆◆◆◆

A welcoming guest house run by caring and attentive owners

☎ / ℱ 01931 716397

Map ref 6 - NY51

SHAP, Penrith, CA10 3PZ
M6 J39, turn R onto A6 towards Shap
4 Rooms, S £19-£25 D £38-£46, No
smoking in bedrooms or dining room

$\mathscr{A}$ smart, well-maintained guest house offering warm hospitality and attentive service.

This inviting property is set in a lovely, peaceful location, and benefits from a delightful garden.

Bedrooms are comfortable and homely, and there is a relaxing lounge and a small bar where guests can while away the evenings. Both the substantial dinners and breakfasts are freshly prepared and nicely cooked, and served in the smart dining room. Despite its quiet country setting, this welcoming guest house is within just a few minutes drive of the M6.

RECOMMENDED IN THE AREA

Hawswater and the Lakes; Shap Abbey; Rheged

$\mathscr{C}$orkickle Guest House ◆◆◆◆

Beautifully maintained guest house with appealing accommodation and good hosts

☎ 01946 692073 ℱ 01946 692073
ℰ corkickle@tinyworld.co.uk

Map ref 5 - NX91

1 Corkickle, WHITEHAVEN, CA28 8AA
take Southern Access rd into Whitehaven
from A595 at bottom of hill, L at lights by
Esso garage, 1st L onto Corkickle, 1st house
on L
6 Rooms, S £22.50-£30 D £45-£50, No
smoking

$\mathscr{D}$ elightful end-of-terrace Regency house that is beautifully presented and inviting. Set in an elevated position in the town, it offers comfortable accommodation in well-equipped bedrooms, each of which has been individually styled and smartly decorated. Guests are invited to relax in the appealing lounge, and in the smart dining room delicious breakfasts and well-cooked evening meals (by prior appointment) are served around a large communal table. The very professional owner maintains high standards of hospitality and cleanliness.

RECOMMENDED IN THE AREA

Whitehaven's Georgian buildings, including St James' Church; Whitehaven to Ennerdale Cycle Path; Haig Colliery Mining Museum

The Fairfield ◆◆◆◆

Welcoming hotel within walking distance of Lake Windermere

☎ 015394 46565
🖷 015394 46565
✉ Ray&barb@the-fairfield.co.uk
www.the-fairfield.co.uk

Map ref 5 - SD49

Brantfell Road, Bowness-on-Windermere, WINDERMERE, LA23 3AE
follow Bowness signs. At mini rdbt take rd to lake, turn L opp church & L again in front of Spinnery Restaurant, house up hill on R
9 Rooms, S £26-£33 D £52-£66, No smoking, Closed Dec-Jan

A small Lakeland hotel, Fairfield dates back 200 years and was once owned by Annie Garnet, the water colourist, gardener, designer and weaver of textiles. The house is quietly located in mature gardens a short distance from Bowness village and Lake Windermere, and is right at the end of the Dales Way, a long distance walk between Ilkley and Bowness. Accommodation is offered in a choice of single, twin, double and family bedrooms. All have en suite or private facilities and are equipped with colour televisions, hairdryers and hospitality trays. Public rooms include an inviting lounge, a residents' bar and an attractive dining room. On site parking is provided. No pets.

RECOMMENDED IN THE AREA

Lake Windermere; The World of Beatrix Potter; Blackwell – the Arts & Crafts House

Howbeck ◆◆◆◆◆

Professionally run establishment where customer care comes first

☎ 015394 44739
🖷 015394 44739
✉ enquiries@howbeck.co.uk
www.howbeck.co.uk

Map ref 5 - SD49

New Road, WINDERMERE, LA23 2LA
L off A591 through Windermere town centre 300yds on L. Main road to Bowness
10 Rooms, D £50-£90, No smoking

Howbeck is conveniently situated on the main road close to the town centre and within easy reach of the lake. The proprietors are professional hoteliers and are proudly committed to providing caring service to their guests. They also have a wealth of local knowledge to assist guests with the planning of their itineraries.

Bedrooms are spacious and smartly appointed with quality fabrics and furniture. Some rooms offer four-poster beds, which are popular for special occasions. A good range of facilities is provided, including full en suites in each room. A full English or vegetarian breakfast is served in the relaxed atmosphere of the charming dining room. Howbeck also holds a residential licence.

RECOMMENDED IN THE AREA

Tarn Howes; The World of Beatrix Potter; Orrest Head viewpoint (30 minutes' walk)

Glencree Private Hotel ••••

Charming Lakeland stone building with stylish bedrooms and stunning en suites

☎ 015394 45822
📠 015394 45822
📧 h.butterworth@
   btinternet.com

Map ref 5 - SD49

Lake Road, WINDERMERE,
LA23 2EQ
0.5m from town centre. Follow
signs for Bowness & The Lake.
Glencree is 1st hotel on R after
large wooded area
5 Rooms, S £20-£35 D £40-
£65, No smoking

Set midway between Bowness and Windermere and not far from the lake, this beautifully-restored Lakeland stone guest house has plenty to offer visitors. The owner is happy to provide information on local attractions, as well as maps covering the many walks in the area. Bedrooms are delightfully furnished with warm colours, and each has its own superb bathroom or shower; one large room is handily located on the ground floor for those with difficulty climbing stairs. All bedrooms come equipped with tea/coffee-making facilities, radio alarms, hair dryers, toiletries, and remote-control television. Dinner (by prior arrangement) and breakfast are cooked with fresh local produce, and served in the charming dining room where tranquil views of the woodland and a pretty brook can be enjoyed. There is also a comfortable lounge, which makes a pleasant place in which to relax after a day's walking or touring. The 18-hole Windermere Golf Club is less than a mile away.

RECOMMENDED IN THE AREA

Windermere Steamboat Centre; Townend (National Trust property); Hill Top (Beatrix Potter's house)

Lakeshore House ♦♦♦♦♦

Luxurious accommodation on the shore of Lake Windermere

☎ 015394 33202
📠 015394 33213
📧 lakeshore@
lakedistrict.uk.com
www.lakedistrict.uk.com

Map ref 5 - SD30

Ecclerigg, WINDERMERE, LA23 1LJ
A591 - 1m after Windermere signs for
Brockhole Visitors Centre, the
driveway for the house is the 2nd
entrance on L. Take R fork to green
gate
3 Rooms, S £75-£112.50 D £130-
£170, No smoking

*E*very aspect of guests comfort has been considered at this stunning modern property - the perfect place to relax and indulge oneself in beautiful surroundings. The spacious en suite bedrooms offer every conceivable extra, including leather armchairs, television with video, bathrobes, direct dial telephones, flowers and a decanter of sherry. Two rooms on the first floor have private balconies, while the ground floor suite has its own sitting room and patio, all with wonderful Lakeland views. The Lakeshore breakfast, prepared from the best local produce, is served in the huge carpeted conservatory with its magnificent swimming pool and waterfall, overlooking Lake Windermere. No pets or children under 12.

RECOMMENDED IN THE AREA

Boating on Lake Windermere; The World of Beatrix Potter and Hill Top; Wordsworth's Cottage and National Trust walks

Newstead ♦♦♦♦♦

Elegant Victorian house with hospitable owners and pleasant gardens

☎ 015394 44485
📧 info@
    newstead-guesthouse.co.uk
www.newstead-
guesthouse.co.uk

Map ref 5 - SD49

New Road, WINDERMERE, LA23 2EE
0.5m from A591 between
Windermere/Bowness
7 Rooms, D £46-£55, No smoking

*A*beautiful detached Victorian guest house located midway between Bowness and Windermere, and set in attractive gardens. Guests are made to feel at home by relaxed, welcoming owners, and are free to wander in the garden, or unwind in the stylish sitting room. Many original features have been retained in the house, which is furnished with antiques and hand-crafted pieces. All seven bedrooms are en suite and fitted out with pine furniture; four-poster beds are available for special occasions, and there are hospitality trays and television in all rooms. Tasty breakfasts are served in the smart dining room, including vegetarian options.

RECOMMENDED IN THE AREA

Boating on Lake Windermere; Blackwell Arts and Crafts House; Hill Top (Beatrix Potter's House)

Derbyshire

A selection of places to eat from the AA Restaurant & AA Pub Guides

Restaurants

⊛⊛ Callow Hall (Classic, Country-house)
Mappleton Road, Ashbourne DE6 2AA
Tel 01335 300900 Fax 01335 300512

⊛ Renaissance Restaurant (Chic, French)
Bath Street, Bakewell DE45 1BX
Tel 01629 812687

⊛ Makeney Hall (Traditional, Country-house)
Makeney, Milford, Belper DE56 0RS
Tel 01332 842999 Fax 01332 842777

⊛⊛ Darleys Restaurant (Minimalist)
Darley Abbey Mill, Darley Abbey DE22 1DZ
Tel 01332 364987 Fax 01332 541356

⊛⊛ The George at Hathersage (Modern, Country-house)
Main Road, Hathersage S32 1BB
Tel 01433 650436 Fax 01433 650099

⊛⊛ Riber Hall (Traditional, Country-house)
Tansley, Matlock DE4 5JU
Tel 01629 582795 Fax 01629 580475

⊛⊛⊛ The Old Vicarage
Ridgeway Moor, Ridgeway S12 3XW
Tel 0114 247 5814 Fax 0114 247 7079

Pubs

◀ The Chequers Inn
Frogatt Edge, Calver, Bakewell S32 3ZJ
Tel 01433 630231 Fax 01433 631072

◀ The Lathkil Hotel
Over Haddon, Bakewell DE45 1JE
Tel 01629 812501 Fax 01629 812501

◀ The Monsal Head Hotel
Monsal Head, Bakewell DE45 1NL
Tel 01629 640250 Fax 01629 640815

◀ The Devonshire Arms
The Square, Beeley DE4 2NR
Tel 01629 733259 Fax 01629 733259

◀ The Druid Inn
Main Street, Birchover DE4 2BL
Tel 01629 650302 Fax 01629 650559

◀ The Waltzing Weasel Inn
New Mills Road, Birch Vale SK22 1BT
Tel 01663 743402 Fax 01663 743402

◀ The Red Lion Inn
Main Street, Hognaston DE6 1PR
Tel 01335 370396 Fax 01335 370961

Lichfield Guest House ♦♦♦♦

Handsome Georgian property with river views

☎ 01335 344422
🖷 01335 344422
✉ brionybull@ukonline.co.uk

Map ref 7 - SK14

Bridge View, Mayfield, ASHBOURNE, DE6 2HN
from town take A52 for Leek, after 1.25m, at Queens Arms L onto B5032 for Mayfield/Uttoxeter, 200yds up hill on L
3 Rooms, S £30-£37.50 D £45-£55, No smoking, Closed 25 & 26 Dec

The Lichfield is superbly located in landscaped gardens overlooking the River Dove, on the edge of the village of Mayfield and a mile and a half from Ashbourne. From here guests can take in all the sights of the Peak District and an abundance of stately homes. The house, which retains many period features, provides a guests' lounge supplied with books of local interest. Bedrooms are homely and well equipped with colour televisions and hospitality trays; all of them have the benefit of modern en suite shower rooms. A substantial breakfast is served, and for your evening meal there is a good choice of pubs and restaurants.

RECOMMENDED IN THE AREA

Walking in the Peak District National Park; Chatsworth House; many National Trust properties

*T*he Courtyard ....

Delightfully-converted Victorian cow sheds and milking area providing quality country accommodation

☎ 01335 330187
🖷 01335 330187
✉ andy@
dairyhousefarm.force9.co.uk
www.digitalpagesco.uk/
courtyard

Map ref 7 - SK13

Dairy House Farm, ALKMONTON,
Ashbourne, DE6 3DG
off A50 at Foston, approx 3.5m
up Woodyard Lane
7 Rooms, S £25-£30 D £48-£50,
No smoking, Closed Xmas

A collection of early Victorian cowsheds has been caringly converted into six luxury bedrooms and a family suite offering accommodation of a very high specification. Surrounded by the tranquil open countryside of the southern Derbyshire dales, The Courtyard is handily placed for visiting many local places of interest. Dovedale is only minutes away, and Chatsworth House, Calke Abbey, Sudbury Hall and Alton towers are all within easy reach. The former milking area has been turned into a large dining room for guests, and in here a hearty breakfast is served, as well as dinner by prior arrangement. The tastefully decorated and furnished bedrooms are all on the ground floor (two are particularly suitable for wheelchair access), equipped with smart en suite facilities, and kitted out with hospitality trays, television and radio. The family suite has separate bedrooms for parents and children, and everyone is treated to the same warm welcome.

RECOMMENDED IN THE AREA

The Peak District and the Derbyshire Dales; historic houses; Alton Towers

Omnia Somnia .....

Peacefully located and delightfully furnished, with unusual 'upside-down' layout offering guests convenient ground floor accommodation

☎ 01335 300145
✆ 01335 300958
✉ alan@omniasomnia.co.uk
www.omniasomnia.co.uk

Map ref 7 - SK14

The Coach House, The Firs, ASHBOURNE, DE6 1HF
From A52 Derby rd, descend hill into Ashbourne. At lights sharp L into Old Hill. Turn first L into The Firs & follow for Omnia Somnia
3 Rooms, S £50 D £70-£80, No smoking

RECOMMENDED IN THE AREA

Peak District National Park; Chatsworth, Haddon Hall, Kedleston Hall; Alton Towers (8 miles)

Situated within easy walking distance of the town, this beautifully furnished house offers guests every comfort. The quality of hospitality is very special, with intricate and unexpected attention to detail. No 'help yourself' service here; your hosts are determined to pamper you. The ground floor en suite guest rooms are all different in layout and design, from Meridies, with its fully-draped four-poster bed and sumptuous panelling to the little suite, Occidens, from whose sitting room you can climb your own stairs to a romantic hideaway bedroom and shower room. Home-made dinners - three courses plus coffee – and substantial breakfasts are served in the upstairs dining room, overlooking the garden and hillside beyond. Enjoy the fine quality of the white linen, silver cutlery, cut glass and bone china. And if you are less mobile, breakfast can be brought to you in your room. Retire, perhaps, to the cosy lounge and browse the ample reading material provided. Omnia Somnia indeed - 'everything is a dream'.

Dannah Farm
Country Guest House ♦♦♦♦♦

Beautifully furnished 18th-century farmhouse set in peaceful countryside just below Alport Heights, which stand at 1,034 feet offering superb views of five counties

☎ 01773 550273 🖷 01773 550590 ✉ reservations@dannah.demon.co.uk
www.dannah.co.uk

Map ref 8 - SK35

Bowmans Lane, Shottle, BELPER, DE56 2DR
from Belper A517 Ashbourne rd for approx 1.5m. After Hanging Gate pub on R, R to Shottle.
1m to village over x-rds turn R
8 Rooms, S £54-£65 D £75-£120, No smoking in bedrooms or dining room , Closed 24-26 Dec

RECOMMENDED IN THE AREA

Chatsworth House (25 minutes' drive); Crich National Tramway Museum (15 minutes' drive); Alton Towers & Dovedale (30 minutes' drive)

The house is full of character and beautifully furnished. Single, double and twin rooms are offered, all with en suite facilities and some with whirlpool baths or Japanese tubs. Colour televisions, direct dial telephones, radios, and hospitality trays are all provided. Two of the bedrooms are split-level, offering a private lounge on the ground floor leading via a spiral staircase to the upper floor with its canopied four-poster bed. There are two guests' sitting rooms and large gardens for peaceful relaxation. Good farmhouse cooking is served in The Mixing Place, and fresh local produce is a feature of the menu – and at breakfast you can expect home-made bread, organic sausages, and free range eggs.

Vegetarian and other special diets can also be catered for. Dannah is midway between Wirksworth and Belper, and convenient for Dovedale. There are plenty of places of interest in the vicinity, and some good shopping opportunities in the local factory shops. Ample safe car parking is provided.

FRI 6/9
A38
43 nnns
~~⊖~~ 13 nnns

Grendon Guest House ♦♦♦♦♦

Handsome Edwardian house on the outskirts of Buxton

☎ 01298 78831 📠 01298 79257
✉ parkerh1@talk21.com
www.grendonguesthouse.co.uk

Map ref 8 - SK07

Bishops Lane, BUXTON, SK17 6UN
0.75m from Buxton centre, just off A53, St John's Rd, behind Burbage Parish Church
3 Rooms, D £48-£66, No smoking

Supreme spaciousness is a distinguishing feature of this detached property, set in attractive gardens with views over the golf course to the hills of the Peak District. The house stands in a country lane within easy walking distance of the centre of Buxton, so guests can enjoy the best of town and country life. Co-ordinated design and antique furnishings characterise the interior, and the all-en suite accommodation comprises a twin, a double and a suite with a fine four-poster bed. All the rooms have televisions, easy chairs, hospitality trays and tourist information. Memorable breakfasts, including home-baked bread, are served in the elegant lounge/dining room, which open onto a large balcony.

RECOMMENDED IN THE AREA

Beautiful walks to the Goyt Valley from the door; Chatsworth House (30 minutes); Castleton Caverns (20 minutes)

The Bulls Head Inn ♦♦♦♦

RECOMMENDED IN THE AREA

Chatsworth House (10 minute drive); Castleton Caverns; Haddon Hall

Good food and quality accommodation in a village inn

☎ 01433 630873
📠 01433 631738

Map ref 7 - SK17

FOOLOW, Eyam, S32 5QR
from J29 M1 follow signs to Bakewell.
At Baslow take A623 Foolow is 3m after Stoney Middleton
3 Rooms, S £38 D £58, No smoking in bedrooms or dining room

This quiet pub in a peaceful village is a popular haunt with both locals and the many walkers who enjoy the splendid countryside of the Peak District. Many of the inn's original features have been retained, and it offers comfortable, well-equipped bedrooms with quality fittings and furnishings.

A very good range of food is served in the traditional dining room or the cosy bar areas, with a choice of imaginative bar meals as well as more formal dishes. Local and guest ales are also a feature of the bar. Breakfast is a comprehensive selection of hot and cold alternatives.

91

*H*ighlow Hall ♦♦♦♦

Peaceful 16th-century manor house overlooking the moors

☎ 01433 650393
📠 01433 650393

Map ref 7 - SK28

HATHERSAGE, Hope Valley, S32 1AX
B6001 from Hathersage (signed
Bakewell), after 0.5m turn R opp
Plough Inn signed Abney, house 1m
on L
3 Rooms, S £40 D £60-£65, No
smoking, Closed Xmas & New Year

A fine Tudor Manor House with many claims to fame. The original seat of the Eyre family. Charlotte Brontë wrote *Jane Eyre* whilst stayng in Hathersage and Highlow is reputed to be the most haunted house in Derbyshire. The house boasts a Great Hall with Tudor inglenook fireplace and staircase and is a perfect place to walk from as it is on the moors with incredible views. Bedrooms are of course en suite, one having a Tudor four-poster bed. There is a panelled dining room for the superb breakfasts and a Regency Style sitting room with TV. There are no televisions or phones in the bedrooms and your mobile will not work here. No children under 12.

RECOMMENDED IN THE AREA

Chatsworth House, seat of the Duke of Devonshire;
Haddon Hall, a gorgeous unspoiled mediaeval manor house;
The Blue John Caves at Castleton

*P*olly's B+B ♦♦♦♦

Lovingly renovated cottage in a pretty village setting

☎ 01433 650110

Map ref 7 - SK28

Moor View Cottage, Cannonfields,
Jaggers Lane , HATHERSAGE,
S32 1AG
enter village on A625 & take 1st R
after George Hotel into Jaggers Lane,
then 1st L
3 Rooms, S £35 D £42, No smoking

M oor View Cottage is located on one of the old tracks used by the 'jaggers' or travelling drapers who sold goods to all the villagers in the area in the days (pre-18th century) when there were few proper roads. The cottage offers three spacious guest rooms with modern en suite facilities and plenty of extras to make you feel at home, including television and tea and coffee-making facilities. An imaginative and varied breakfast menu is served at a shared table in the elegant dining room, and a second-floor guest room with superb views is also provided. For those interested in sporting pursuits, climbing, swimming, golf, cycling and walking are available locally.

RECOMMENDED IN THE AREA

Chatsworth House; Eyam (famous Plague village); many walks with breathtaking views

The Scotsman's Pack Inn ◆◆◆◆

Friendly inn on the edge of the picturesque village

☎ 01433 650253
📠 01433 650253

Map ref 7 - SK28

School Lane, HATHERSAGE, Hope Valley, S32 1BZ
from A625 turn into School Ln, Inn 50yds, follow signs to church
5 Rooms, S £32-£35 D £58-£61, No smoking in dining room, Closed 25 Dec

The unusual name harks back to an era when 'packmen' travelled from Scotland to sell tweeds to the farms in the area and would put up at the inn for food and rest. Although traces of the original building remain, the current inn dates from 1900. A good range of well-prepared food is served, including hearty breakfasts in the separate dining room. The bedrooms are thoughtfully furnished and all have en suite facilities and complimentary tea and coffee. The locality is ideal for outdoor pursuits - particularly walking, climbing, cycling, angling and golf - and a variety of attractions, including stately homes, the Blue John Caves and the plague village of Eyam.

RECOMMENDED IN THE AREA

Chatsworth House (9 miles); Chestnut Centre Conservation Park (6 miles); Blue John Caves (3 miles)

Underleigh House ◆◆◆◆◆

Cottage and barn conversion set amid glorious scenery

☎ 01433 621372
📠 01433 621324
📧 underleigh.house@btinternet.com
www.underleighhouse.co.uk

Map ref 7 - SK18

Off Edale Road, HOPE, Hope Valley, S33 6RF
from village church on A6187 (formerly A625) take Edale Road for 1m then L into lane
6 Rooms, S £33-£46 D £60-£66, No smoking, Closed Xmas & New Year

Underleigh House is surrounded by great walking country and is an ideal base for exploring the Peak National Park, historic Derbyshire towns, and village well dressings in summer. The bedrooms are thoughtfully furnished, with en suite facilities, colour television, radio alarms, hairdryers, and tea and coffee-making equipment. One room has a private lounge and others have direct access to the gardens. Guests can enjoy a drink on the terrace or by the log fire in the lounge. Breakfast, featuring home-made and local specialities, is served at one large table in the dining room. No children under 12 or animals are accepted (except by prior arrangement – owners' pets in residence). Packed lunches and maps available.

RECOMMENDED IN THE AREA

Walk in the Peak District National Park (from the front door); Chatsworth House, Haddon Hall and Lyme Park (easy driving distance); Castleton Caverns and Peveril Castle (3 miles)

*H*odgkinsons Hotel ♦♦♦♦

Stylish spa-town hotel dating from the 17th century

☎ 01629 582170 📠 01629 584891
✉ enquiries@hodgkinsons-hotel.co.uk
www.hodgkinsons-hotel.co.uk

Map ref 7 - SK25

150 South Parade, Matlock Bath, MATLOCK, DE4 3NR
on A6 in centre of village
7 Rooms, S £35-£38 D £65-£95, No smoking in dining room , Closed 24-26 Dec

*T*his is the first hotel established to serve the spa in Matlock Bath, built in 1698 and extended in the 1770s, when it took its name from then proprietor Job Hodgkinson. These days it is owned by Antonio and Dianne Carrieri; Antonio is a chef, so food is a highlight of any stay. The interior is filled with antiques and fascinating original fixtures and fittings. Bedrooms are individually designed and the elegant reception rooms include a bar and drawing room, where you can check out the menu before dinner, and an attractive dining room set out restaurant-style with separate tables. The provision of private parking is a bonus.

RECOMMENDED IN THE AREA

Peak District National Park (2 miles); Chatsworth House (6 miles); High Peak Trail and Cromford Canal Tow Path

---

*L*ittlemoor Wood Farm ♦♦♦♦

Rarebreed smallholding in a lovely village setting

☎ 01629 534302
📠 01629 534008
✉ groommatlock@
      compuserve.com
www.aplaceinthecountry.co.uk

Map ref 7 - SK35

Littlemoor Lane, Riber, MATLOCK, DE4 5JS
A615 to Tansley. Take rd opposite Royal Oak (Alders Lane) signed Riber. After 1m, turn L signed Lea/Holloway. Farm on R after 500yds
2 Rooms, S £30-£40 D £50, No smoking, Closed Xmas/New Year

*R*are breed enthusiasts Simon and Gilly Groom welcome guests to their attractive stone-built farmhouse and encourage them to get to know their Gloucester Old Spot pigs and Charolais sheep. Gilly's hearty breakfasts - award-winning - feature bacon and sausages produced from home-reared meat. The house is surrounded by 20 acres of fields and hay meadows farmed in traditional style. Apart from the walking, well dressings and stately homes the area has to offer, visitors might also pick up a bargain at one of the numerous factory outlets nearby. Accommodation comprises a kingsize/twin bedded room and a large double. Both have private bathrooms, televisions, hairdryers and hospitality trays.

RECOMMENDED IN THE AREA

High Peak Trail; Peak District National Park; Chatsworth and other stately homes

The Smithy ◆◆◆◆◆

Excellent hospitality and tasteful bedrooms in peaceful countryside

☎ 01298 84548
✉ thesmithy@newhaven
   derbyshire.freeserve.co.uk

Map ref 7 - SK16

NEWHAVEN, Buxton, SK17 0DT
on A515, 10m S of Buxton, 10m N of
Ashbourne. Adjacent to Biggin Lane,
entrance via private driveway opp Ivy
House
4 Rooms, S £39 D £58, No smoking

A carefully renovated, Grade II listed blacksmith's workshop and 17th-century drovers' inn house this delightfully upmarket guest house. The rolling countryside of the Peak National Park is the peaceful setting, where a converted barn houses the tastefully-decorated bedrooms. The family-size rooms are all en suite and well equipped, and the owners offer a highly personalised service to their guests. Tasty breakfasts including free range eggs and home-made preserves are served in the forge, where the vast open hearth and original bellows and tools have been kept. There is also a comfortable lounge, and pleasant gardens with a wildlife pond and terrace.

RECOMMENDED IN THE AREA

Chatsworth (10 miles); Tissington and High Peak Trails (walking distance); centrally located in Peak District National Park for Buxton, Ashbourne, Bakewell and Leek

---

Braeside Guest House ◆◆◆◆

Delightful property in beautiful country surroundings

☎ 0115 9395885
www.braeside.cjb.net

Map ref 8 - SK43

113 Derby Road, RISLEY, DE72 3SS
M1 J25, take 1st exit after A52, signed
Risley, past Post House Hotel on R, at
x-roads turn L into Risley, 2nd cottage
on L past pub
4 Rooms, D £48-£55, No smoking,
Closed Dec-Feb

Braeside offers a quiet country location eight miles from either Derby or Nottingham, and is popular with both business and leisure guests. Within visiting distance are the great Derbyshire houses, Dovedale, the American Adventure theme park and Alton Towers. There are also some lovely walks in the vicinity.

Bedrooms are divided between the main building and converted barns. They are all attractively appointed, with en suite shower rooms, colour televisions, hairdryers and tea and coffee making facilities. Breakfast is served in the conservatory, overlooking the garden and fields. Ample parking is provided with a locked gate for added security. Dinner can be taken at the hotel five minutes' walk away.

RECOMMENDED IN THE AREA

Chatsworth House; Calke Abbey; Peak District National Park

Devon

A selection of places to eat from the AA Restaurant & AA Pub Guides

Restaurants

◉ Agaric (Modern Chic)
30 North Street, Ashburton TQ13 7QD
Tel 01364 654478

◉◉ 22 Mill Street
22 Mill Street, Chagford TQ13 8AW
Tel 01647 432244 Fax 01647 433101

◉ Red Lion Hotel (Traditional, Rustic)
The Quay, Clovelly EX39 5TF
Tel 01237 431237 Fax 01237 431044

◉ Hotel Barcelona (Modern, Chic)
Magdalen Street, Exeter EX2 4HY
Tel 01392 281010 Fax 01392 281001

◉◉ Buckland-Tout-Saints (Classic, Country-house)
Goveton, Kingsbridge TQ7 2DS
Tel 01548 853055 Fax 01548 856261

◉ Pitt House Restaurant (Traditional)
2 Church End Road, Kingkerswell TQ12 5DS
Tel 01803 873374

◉ Tinhay Mill Restaurant (Classic, Country-house)
Tinhay, Lifton PL16 0AJ
Tel 01566 784201

◉ Manor House (Classic, Traditional)
Moretonhampstead TQ13 8RE
Tel 01647 440355 Fax 01647 440961

◉◉ Chez Nous (French)
13 Frankfort Gate, Plymouth PL1 1QA
Tel 01752 266793 Fax 01752 266793

◉◉ Tanners Restaurant (Traditional)
Prysten House, Finewell Street, Plymouth PL1 2AE
Tel 01752 252001 Fax 01752 252105

◉ Preston House (Traditional)
Saunton Ex33 1LG
Tel 01271 890472 Fax 01271 890555

◉ Mulberry House (Traditional, Country-house)
1 Scarborough Road, Torquay TQ2 5UJ
Tel 01803 213639

◉◉ Percy's Country Hotel (Country-house, Modern)
Coombeshead Estate, Virginstow, Nr Okehampton EX21 5EA
Tel 01409 211236 Fax 01409 211275

◉◉◉ Pophams (Bistro-style)
Castle Street, Winkleigh EX19 8HQ
Tel 01837 83767

Pubs

🍺 The Rising Sun
Woodland, Ashburton TQ13 7JT
Tel 01364 652544 Fax 01364 654202

🍺 Drewe Arms
Broadhembury EX14 3NF
Tel 01404 841267

🍺 The New Inn
Coleford, Crediton EX17 5BZ
Tel 01363 84242 Fax 01363 85044

🍺 The Nobody Inn
Doddiscombsleigh EX6 7PS
Tel 01647 252394 Fax 01647 252978

🍺 The Union Inn
Fore Street, Dolton EX19 8QH
Tel 01805 804633 Fax 01805 804633

🍺 The Rock Inn
Haytor Vale TQ13 9XP
Tel 01364 661305 Fax 01364 661242

🍺 Masons Arms Inn
Knowstone EX36 4RY
Tel 01398 341231

🍺 Dartmoor Inn
Lydford EX20 4AY
Tel 01822 820221 Fax 01822 820494

🍺 Rising Sun Hotel
Harbourside, Lynmouth EX35 6EG
Tel 01598 753223 Fax 01598 753480

🍺 Jack in the Green Inn
London Road, Rockbeare EX5 2EE
Tel 01404 822240 Fax 01404 823445

🍺 The Tower Inn
Church Road, Slapton TQ7 2PN
Tel 01548 580216 Fax 01548 580140

🍺 The Sea Trout
Staverton TQ9 6PA
Tel 01803 762274 Fax 01803 762506

🍺 Kings Arms
Stockland EX14 9BS
Tel 01404 881361 Fax 01404 881732

🍺 The White Hart Bar
Dartington Hall, Totnes TQ9 6EL
Tel 01803 847111

🍺 The Rising Sun Inn
Umberleigh EX37 9DU
Tel 01769 560447 Fax 01769 564764

$\mathcal{G}$reencott ◆◆◆◆

Attractive house with a secluded location amid beautiful countryside

☎ 01803 762649

Map ref 2 - SX76

Landscove, ASHBURTON, TQ13 7LZ
take A38 to Plymouth, then 2nd exit
signed Landscove. At top of slip rd
turn L, follow for 2m, keep village
green on R, opp village hall
2 Rooms, D £38, No smoking in
bedrooms or dining room ,
Closed 25-26 Dec

$\mathcal{M}$odern facilities in an old world atmosphere are offered at this totally renovated house in the village of Landscove, which is just two and a half miles from Ashburton. Greencott is set in its own garden with lovely country views. The guest bedrooms are carefully furnished and well equipped with en suite baths and showers, central heating and tea and coffee making amenities. Television, books, maps and information about the area are provided in the comfortable guest' sitting room, and traditional country cooking is served around the oak dining table. The full English breakfast includes home-made bread, and dinner is available on request. Older children are welcome, but pets cannot be accommodated, with the exception of guide dogs. Tarmac off-road parking is provided.

RECOMMENDED IN THE AREA

Cider press at Dartington; Steam railway at Staverton

$\mathcal{S}$hamwari ◆◆◆◆

Hospitable house with panoramic views of the Axe Valley

☎ 01297 32838 🖷 01297 34465

Map ref 2 - SY26

Musbury Road, Abbey Gate,
AXMINSTER, EX13 8TT
A35/A358 towards Musbury/Seaton,
under bridge past large white house
on L. Shamwari next on L around L
bend next to layby
3 Rooms, S £20-£22 D £40-£44,
No smoking

$\mathcal{S}$hamwari means 'my friend' and guests are assured of a friendly welcome at this easily accessible comfortable private house, set in three acres of gardens and meadowland surrounded by open countryside. This is ideal walking and cycling country, and the house is just a mile from historic Axminster and five miles from Lyme Regis and the coast. Hearty breakfasts are served in the cosy dining room and suppers by arrangement. All diets can be catered for - one of the owners is vegetarian. Double, twin or single en suite rooms are available. All have colour televisions and complimentary tea and coffee. Children cannot be accommodated.

RECOMMENDED IN THE AREA

Countryside and coastal walks, including several Nature Reserves and the "Jurassic Coast" (within 5 miles); Ford Abbey; National Trust properties – Killerton House, Shute Barton, Seaton Tramway

Chipley Farm ◆◆◆◆

Modern farmhouse with stunning views near both moor and sea

☎ 01626 821486
📠 01626 821486
✉ louisa@
   chipleyfarmholidays.co.uk
www.chipleyfarmholidays.co.uk

Map ref 2 - SX77

BICKINGTON, Newton Abbot,
TQ12 6JW
From A38 take junct signed Newton Abbot. At Drum Bridges rdbt take 3rd exit (Bickington) & continue until the Toby Jug pub. Turn L, R, L and fork L. Follow lane past traditional Dutch Barn & Chipley Farm is 1st on R
3 Rooms, S £25-£35 D £40-£50,
No smoking

*D*elightful hospitality is a highlight at Fred and Louisa Westcott's farmhouse - in fact Louisa was a recent finalist in the AA Landlady of the Year Awards. The modern split-level house is set in large, rambling gardens overlooking a south Devon valley, close to some lovely beaches and the wild beauty of Dartmoor. There is a double room and a twin room sharing an adjacent bathroom, and an en suite family room, the latter with a canopied four-poster bed and patio doors. All the rooms have remote control colour television and tea and coffee-making equipment. Farmhouse suppers are available in addition to the Aga-cooked breakfasts, featuring farm-fresh eggs and home-made preserves.

RECOMMENDED IN THE AREA

Dartmoor National Park; lovely beaches nearby; English Riviera and many tourist attractions

East Burne Farm ◆◆◆◆

Grade II listed medieval hall house with a cobbled courtyard

☎ 01626 821496
📠 01626 821105
✉ info@
   eastburnefarm.screaming.net
www.eastburnefarm.8k.com

Map ref 2 - SX77

BICKINGTON, TQ12 6PA
1.5m from A38 off A383
3 Rooms, S £22-£26 D £44-£52,
No smoking

*A*warm welcome is assured at this lovely old 15th century farmhouse from owners Mike and Emma Pallett. The house is very well kept and superbly located along a narrow winding lane in a quiet valley just a mile from the A38. Three guest bedrooms are provided, two twins with en suite facilities and a double with a four-poster bed and en suite bathroom. The rooms have electric night storage heating, electric blankets and tea and coffee making facilities. There is a beamed sitting room where an open fire burns in cooler weather.

In the morning a full English breakfast is served. Guests are free to explore the open farmland, which is rich in flora and fauna. There is a heated swimming pool in the garden with gentle steps at the shallow end. Some of the farm buildings around the cobbled yard have been converted into self-catering holiday accommodation.

RECOMMENDED IN THE AREA

Walking and horseriding on Dartmoor (10 minute drive); South Devon Coastal Walks; 10 National Trust properties nearby

The Pines at Eastleigh ◆◆◆◆

Listed farmhouse overlooking open countryside

☎ 01271 860561
📠 01271 861248
✉ barry@
  thepinesateastleigh.co.uk
www.thepinesateastleigh.co.uk

Map ref 1 - SS42

Old Barnstaple Road, Eastleigh,
BIDEFORD, EX39 4PA
turn off A39 Barnstaple/Bideford rd
onto A386 signed Torrington. After
0.75m turn L signed Eastleigh, 2m to
village, house on R
6 Rooms, S £35-£45 D £70-£90, No
smoking

The Pines is a Georgian farmhouse set in seven acres of gardens surrounded by beautiful North Devon countryside. Farmhouse-style meals are served in the dining room, including dinner by arrangement, freshly prepared from the best local ingredients, some from the garden. All diets can be catered for - vegetarian, vegan and gluten-free. Guests can relax in the licensed bar-lounge. Most of the bedrooms are on the ground floor overlooking the courtyard with its fishpond and fountain. There is a single, twin and four king size rooms, all en suite, with Teletext television, hospitality trays, hairdryers, telephones and central heating. Children and pets are welcome.

RECOMMENDED IN THE AREA

Coastal resorts of Instow (3 miles) and Westward Ho! (5 miles); gardens – RHS Rosemoor (12 miles) and Marwood Hill (15 miles); Tarka Trail (2 miles)

Front House Lodge ◆◆◆◆◆

Pretty 16th-century house with a sense of the past

☎ 01626 832202 📠 832202
✉ fronthouselodge@aol.com

Map ref 2 - SX87

East Street, BOVEY TRACEY,
TQ13 9EL
turn off A38 onto A382 into Bovey
Tracey, through town centre, Front
House Lodge is past the Town Hall
on R
6 Rooms, S £25-£35 D £48-£52,
No smoking

Front House Lodge is a charming property dating back to 1540 with interesting connections to the Civil War. Bovey Tracey is a little Dartmoor town featuring the River Bovey, Devon Guild of Crafts, with small shops, restaurants, pubs and tea shops. Three miles from Haytor rocks, on the edge of Dartmoor National Park it makes an ideal location for touring the South West.

The interior is enchanting throughout in English country style with a varied collection of antiques and china. The bedrooms are traditionally furnished, pretty beds with cushions and canopies all with shower or bath en-suite, CTV and many thoughtful extras.

Breakfasts are a delicious treat beautifully presented using lovely china and served in the beamed dining room. A relaxed friendly atmosphere plus secluded garden and private parking.

RECOMMENDED IN THE AREA

Dartmoor National Park; National Trust properties (Castle Drogo, Coleton Fishacre)

Kilbury Manor ◆◆◆◆

Delicious breakfasts and dinners in a beautifully-restored farmhouse

☎ 01364 644079
🖷 01364 644059
✉ accommodation@
   kilbury.co.uk
www.kilbury.co.uk

Map ref 2 - SX75

Colston Road, BUCKFASTLEIGH, TQ11 0LN
off A38 at Dart Bridge junct onto B3380 (Buckfastleigh), L after 0.5m (Old Totnes Rd), R at bottom, Kilbury Manor sign on wall on L
4 Rooms, S £30-£35 D £50-£60, No smoking

Idyllically set in delightful grounds including a well-stocked trout pond is this restored 17th-century South Devon farmhouse. The owners offer superb hospitality to their guests, who are invited to make themselves at home in this lovely property. Attractive bedrooms are very comfortably furnished, with en suite bathroom or shower, colour television and courtesy tray. Breakfasts are excellent, with fish, home-made muffins, scones and preserves adding to the choice on offer. Delicious award-winning dinners are also served using quality local ingredients, and unique cookery courses are available, which are geared to the needs of the individual and can be part of a special holiday package.

RECOMMENDED IN THE AREA

South Devon Steam Railway; Dartington Hall; Buckfast Abbey

The Long Range Hotel ◆◆◆◆

Delightful hotel close to the town centre and beach

☎ 01395 443321
🖷 01395 442132
✉ info@thelongrangehotel.co.uk
www.thelongrangehotel.co.uk

Map ref 2 - SY08

5 Vales Road, BUDLEIGH SALTERTON, EX9 6HS
Turn off East Budleigh Road (on NE access to Budleigh Salterton) into Raleigh Rd, after 20yds turn R into Vales Rd. Hotel on L
7 Rooms, S £30-£40 D £55-£65, No smoking

Located in a quiet residential area, this comfortable hotel is just a few minutes' walk from the seafront and the shops. It offers six en suite double bedrooms and a single with private facilities. Each room has a colour television and a well-stocked hospitality tray. Comfy sofas and daily papers make the sitting room an inviting spot. This opens onto the conservatory with its small bar area and dining room overlooking the garden.

Dinner is served Monday to Saturday, and lunch on Sundays. A good choice is available at every meal, with home-made breads and jams featuring at breakfast. Vegetarian and special diets catered for.

RECOMMENDED IN THE AREA

Bicton Park Botanical Gardens; coastal and country walks; Exeter Cathedral

Tor Cottage •••••

A very special place where everything is quality and luxury; a piece of heaven on earth

☎ 01822 860248 📠 01822 860126
📧 info@torcottage.co.uk
www.torcottage.co.uk

Map ref 1 - SX48

CHILLATON, Tavistock, PL16 0JE
from A30 exit Lewdown through Chillaton towards Tavistock. R 300mtrs after Post Office signed 'Bridlepath No Public Vehicular access' to end
4 Rooms, S £89.30 D £115, No smoking, Closed 17 Dec-7 Jan

RECOMMENDED IN THE AREA

The Eden Project (50 minute drive); various National Trust properties; Dartmoor (10 minute drive) and Devon/Cornish coasts (40 minute drive)

This attractive cottage, hidden in its own private valley, won AA Guest Accommodation of the Year for England 2001-2002. A romantic retreat offering tranquillity and seclusion in the 18 acres of grounds, Tor Cottage invites you to escape from the outside world. The beautiful en suite bed-sitting rooms, one in the cottage wing and the others lovingly restored former barns, have private terraces/gardens and their own log fires. Each is individually designed, from the warmth and style of The Art Deco room to the blue and cream elegance of The Craftsman's Room, and nothing is too much trouble for Maureen Rowlatt, who has equipped the bedrooms and bathrooms with everything you could desire. Breakfast, with its imaginative range of dishes, can be taken in the conservatory-style dining room or on the terrace in fine weather. The interesting gardens are a feature in their own right with many private corners, a stream and in summer, a heated swimming pool. Children cannot be accepted. No dogs. Autumn/spring breaks are available – 3 nights for the price of 2.

Broome Court .....

An attractive stone-built property set in an area of outstanding natural beauty

☎ 01803 834275
☎ 833260

Map ref 2 - SX84

Broomhill,
DARTMOUTH,
TQ6 0LD
A38 to A384, at Totnes right onto A381, L at Halwell onto A3122 to Dartmouth. At Sportsmans Arms turn right, then 3rd R
3 Rooms, S £40-£50 D £70-£90, No smoking in bedrooms or dining room

RECOMMENDED IN THE AREA

Britannia Royal Naval College Dartmouth (5 minutes, regular guided tours); Coleton Fishacre (National Trust House & Garden); Slapton Ley Nature Reserve (15 minutes)

*B*roome Court is situated at the end of a long winding lane, deep in glorious countryside. The atmosphere is that of a country house, friendly, relaxed and inclusive, with a warm welcome from owners Jan Bird and Tom Boughton. There is a charming paved courtyard, abundant with plants and shrubs, with a fountain at its centre. The bedrooms, including twins and doubles, are beautifully decorated and three have en suite facilities. All the rooms have tea-making equipment and colour television. Breakfast is served in the old farmhouse kitchen and guests also have the option of dinner. For relaxation guests have the use of the terrace, summer lounge and conservatory, and the winter lounge in cooler weather. Self-catering accommodation is also available in the Granary and 'Eeyore's Tail'.

Farmborough House ◆◆◆◆

Idylically located property close to Dartmoor

☎ 01626 853258
📠 01626 853258
✉ holidays@
farmborough-house.com
www.farmborough-house.com

Map ref 2 - SX88

Old Exeter Road, CHUDLEIGH,
TQ13 0DR
B3344 to Chudleigh. At war memorial,
turn into Old Exeter St, proceed for
1m. After bridge crossing A38, house
on L
3 Rooms, D £45-£52, No smoking

Guests can unwind completely in this large Edwardian house, confident in the knowledge that the welcoming owners are there to look after their needs. A warm welcome and personal attention go with the territory, and this peaceful, secluded spot near Dartmoor is ideal for country lovers. The bedrooms (two double and one twin) are all en suite and comfortably furnished, including one large luxury room overlooking the garden. On chilly evenings there's a log fire burning in the lounge, and both breakfast and supper (by prior arrangement) are served in an airy dining room. Expect quality ingredients like pork and apple sausages and dry-cured bacon, and local preserves.

RECOMMENDED IN THE AREA

Walks on Dartmoor (15 minute drive); Castle Drogo, Killerton House; Exeter (10 minute drive)

The Union Inn ◆◆◆◆

Country inn at the heart of the village

☎ 01805 804633
📠 01805 804633
✉ union.inn@eclipse.co.uk

Map ref 2 - SS51

Fore Street, DOLTON, EX19 8QH
from A3124 turn off at Beacon garage
onto B3217 to Dolton 1m on R in
village
3 Rooms, S £35 D £50, No smoking in
dining room, Closed 1st 2wks Feb

An original Devon longhouse, this delightful village inn is full of character, with beams, flagstone floors and an inglenook fireplace, where an open fire burns in cooler weather. The friendly personal attention of owners Ian and Irene Fisher and their staff make for an enjoyable stay, along with the good food, real ales and comfortable accommodation. Meals are served in either the cosy bar or restaurant; Ian is the chef, and his menus are based on locally sourced and produced ingredients. There are three individually furnished guest rooms, one with a four-poster bed and all with en suite facilities.

RECOMMENDED IN THE AREA

RHS Rosemoor; walking on Dartmoor (20 minute drive); Torrington 1646 Visitor Centre

103

Mill Farm ◆◆◆◆

Tranquil, welcoming working farm in attractive countryside setting

☎ 01392 832471

Map ref 2 - SX98

Kenton, EXETER, EX6 8JR
from Exeter take A379 towards Dawlish, and bypassing Exminster, across mini rdbt by Swans Nest. Farm 1.5m on R
5 Rooms, S £25 D £40,
No smoking in dining room or lounge, Closed Xmas

Just a short drive from the Powderham estate and outside the pretty village of Kenton, this charming working farmhouse is peacefully surrounded by pastureland and streams. Inside the décor is carefully co-ordinated, with stencilling on the walls and lots of antique furniture. Bedrooms are comfortable and sunny, with spacious en suites and wide countryside views. In the bright dining room hearty farmhouse breakfasts offer an appetising start to the day, and there are plenty of local places serving evening meals. There is also a visitors' lounge. The owner is very friendly, and keen to welcome guests to her well-managed home.

RECOMMENDED IN THE AREA

Powderham Castle (1.5 miles); explore Dartmoor (20 minute drive); walking and birdwatching in the Exe Estuary Nature Reserve (3 miles)

Clawford Vineyard ◆◆◆◆

Comfortable accommodation uniquely located on a working vineyard

☎ 01409 254177
🖷 01409 254177
✉ john.ray@clawford.co.uk
www.clawford.co.uk

Map ref 1 - SX30

Clawton, HOLSWORTHY, EX22 6PN
A388 Holsworth to Launceston road, turn L at Clawton x-rds, 1.5m to T-junct, turn L, then in 0.5m L again
11 Rooms, S £33-£36 D £55, No smoking

Situated in the peaceful Claw Valley, Clawford Vineyard, as its name suggests, is a working vineyard. It also has a cider orchard, and guests can enjoy sampling the produce. Extensive course fishing is also available, with some monster carp awaiting anglers in several well stocked lakes.

The spacious en suite bedrooms are a recent addition, all of them are exceedingly well furnished and equipped. Public areas, overlooking the lakes, include a comfortable lounge, spacious bar and games room. Meals are served in the conservatory, which allows each party to enjoy the views and observe the abundant wildlife.

The vineyard is centrally situated for the southwest tourist attractions and golf courses.

RECOMMENDED IN THE AREA

Famous village of Clovelly; rugged coastline for spectacular walks; RHS Rosemoor

$\mathcal{S}$trathmore Hotel ♦♦♦♦

Centrally-located hotel with delightful owners and welcoming accommodation

☎ 01271 862248 🖷 01271 862243
📧 strathmore@ukhotels.com
www.strathmore.ukhotels.com

Map ref 2 - SS54

57 St Brannocks Road, ILFRACOMBE, EX34 8EQ
on A361 approach into Ilfracombe, 0.5m from Mullacot Cross rdbt
9 Rooms, S £25-£33 D £40-£56,
No smoking in bedrooms or dining room

$\mathcal{R}$ooms filled with paintings and antiques bring a certain style to this delightful Victorian hotel. Set within walking distance of the centre of Ilfracombe, and near to Bicclescombe Park and Cairn Nature Reserve, it is also handily placed for the beach. The very dedicated owners offer a friendly welcome to their guests, and their interest in interior design is evident from the smartly furnished and decorated rooms. All bedrooms have an en suite shower or bathroom, and are thoughtfully fitted out and comfortable. Food is a special feature of this hotel, and delicious dinners and breakfasts cooked from fresh produce are served in the elegant dining room.

RECOMMENDED IN THE AREA

Beautiful walks on Exmoor (12-15 minute drive); Dunster Castle; Dartington Glass Factory

$\mathcal{V}$arley House ♦♦♦♦

Restful property with lovely views and spacious bedrooms

☎ 01271 863927
🖷 01271 879299
📧 info@varleyhouse.co.uk
www.varleyhouse.co.uk

Map ref 2 - SS54

Chambercombe Park, ILFRACOMBE, EX34 9QW
A399 Combe Martin Rd, R at swimming pool, round L corner, on the inside of the R hand bend
8 Rooms, S £24-£25 D £50-£52, No smoking in bedrooms or dining room, Closed Nov-Mar

$\mathcal{B}$uilt in the late 1890s to revitalise and refresh officers returning from the Boer War, this elegant Victorian house is gracious and welcoming, with generously proportioned rooms and a charming atmosphere. Guests will feel at home immediately, whether looking for a really active few days or simply enjoying a restful break. Overlooking Hillsborough Nature Reserve, and the beautiful North Devon coast, all rooms enjoy either sea or country views. The friendly proprietors make every effort to ensure an enjoyable stay in their delightful home. In addition, there is a private car park and the sunny garden overlooks the harbour.

RECOMMENDED IN THE AREA

South West Coastal Path; Ilfracombe town; Chambercombe Manor

Waterloo House Hotel ••••

A listed Georgian building right in the heart of old Ilfracombe

☎ 01271 863060 📠 01271 863060
✉ info@waterloohousehotel.co.uk
waterloohousehotel.co.uk

Map ref 2 - SS54

Waterloo Terrace, Fore Street, ILFRACOMBE, EX34 9DJ
exit M5 J27, to A361 to Ilfracombe, along High St, after Cinema, filter L into Fore St, through No Entry signs, 1st terrace on R
9 Rooms, S £35 D £50-£80, No smoking in bedrooms or dining room

RECOMMENDED IN THE AREA

Ilfracombe Golf Club (2 minutes' drive); Exmoor (5 minutes' drive); Woolacombe Beach (10 minutes' drive)

*T*his charming period property is within easy walking distance of the harbour and all the amenities of the town. Originally three cottages, the building has retained many of its original features, providing accommodation of character. Each of the rooms is themed after someone from the period; most have en suite facilities, and some have harbour views. All the rooms are equipped with hospitality trays, remote control colour televisions, individually controlled central heating and many other individual touches. Guests can relax in either the Wellington lounge bar or the elegant tented lounge based on Napoleons campaign tent. Smoking is only permitted in the bar. A good choice is available at breakfast, served up to 11 am. Gourmet meals are served in the evening in Bonapartes restaurant, which is also open to the public at weekends. Bar meals are also available. Children under 12 cannot be accommodated, making the hotel ideal for romantic breaks, weddings or group bookings. Special rates apply for house parties of 12 or more. Licensed for civil weddings.

Higher Cadham Farm ♦♦♦♦

Farmhouse accommodation with a riverside setting in rural Devon

☎ 01837 851647
📠 01837 851410
📧 kingscadham@
   btopenworld.com
www.highercadham.co.uk

Map ref 2 - SS50
JACOBSTOWE, Okehampton,
EX20 3RB
from Jacobstowe take A3216 towards
Hatherleigh/Bude, after church sharp R
in front of Cottage Farm, cont for 0.5m.
9 Rooms, S £19-£25 D £37-£50, No
smoking in dining room, Closed Dec

John and Jenny King have been welcoming guests to their lovely farmhouse for more than 25 years. The bedrooms are divided between rooms in the original farmhouse and those in converted farm buildings. Each is thoughtfully equipped, neatly decorated and furnished in modern pine. Five rooms have en suite facilities and one has a four-poster bed. The restaurant is open to the public for morning coffees, lunches and cream teas. For residents, there is a choice between continental and full English breakfast, and a set evening meal of Jenny's traditional

home cooking is available. The Kings farm on 100 acres and as supporters of green tourism, they are proud of the wildlife on their land, including a family of otters (the farm is located on the Tarka Trail). Well behaved dogs are welcome.

RECOMMENDED IN THE AREA

National Trust properties, (Castle Drogo, Lydford Gorge); RHS Rosemoor (30 minutes' drive); Dartmoor nearby

Staunton Lodge ♦♦♦♦

Waterside Edwardian property in the heart of the South Hams

☎ 01548 854542
📠 01548 854421
📧 miketreleaven@msn.com
www.stauntonlodge.co.uk

Map ref 2 - SX74
Embankment Road, KINGSBRIDGE,
TQ7 1JZ
from Kingsbridge town centre take
A381 along side the estuary,
signposted Dartmouth, Lodge approx
0.25m on left.
2 Rooms, S £35-£45 D £40-£50,
No smoking, Closed 20 Dec-10 Jan

Friendly but unobtrusive personal service is provided at this delightful house overlooking the Kingsbridge estuary. The town centre is just a short walk away, and ample off road parking is provided. Visitors will enjoy the local scenery, fine beaches and attractions such as the Eden Project, within easy driving distance. Stylish accommodation is offered in a choice of en suite room or double room or twin with private bathroom, equipped with colour

televisions, radios, tea/coffee and hairdryers. An award-winning breakfast menu is taken in the dining room, or a continental breakfast tray can be served to your room. Guests may relax in the lounge or the garden fronting the estuary.

RECOMMENDED IN THE AREA

Beautiful coastal and moorland walks; Dartmouth, Totnes and Plymouth within easy reach; 3 golf courses within 30 minutes' drive; National Trust properties – Saltram, Castle Drogo, Lanhydrock etc.

Moor View House ◆◆◆◆◆

Substantial Victorian house set in two acres of gardens with direct access to Dartmoor

☎ 01822 820220
📠 01822 820220

Map ref 2 - SX38

Vale Down, LYDFORD,
EX20 4BB
turn off A30 at Sourton Cross onto
A386 Tavistock rd, hotel drive
approx 4m on R
4 Rooms, S £40-£50 D £55-£75,
No smoking

RECOMMENDED IN THE AREA

The Garden House; Buckland Abbey, Lydford Gorge, Cothele and Castle Drogo; walking on Dartmoor

Comfortable accommodation and good food are offered at this hospitable establishment, now owned by David and Wendy Sharples but reputed once to have changed hands over a game of cards. The house was built in 1869 to face Dartmoor, while from the back there are magnificent views over Devon and Cornwall. Many original features have been retained and the rooms are stylishly furnished with interesting family pieces. Dinner is available by prior arrangement, and Wendy's four-course menu is based on traditional country recipes. Only the best of local meat, fish and game are used to create the appealing dishes. Quality is evident too in the exquisite table settings in the dining room, where dinner is served house party style at a large oak table, or, if preferred, an individual table. The sitting room is bright and inviting, with an open fire in winter and family photos atop the grand piano. The all en suite bedrooms have a Victorian decorative theme.

Rock House ····

Set magically beside the water's edge at the harbour entrance, a hotel full of character with comfortable bedrooms

☎ 01598 753508 📠 01598 753508
✉ enquiries@rock-house.co.uk
www.rock-house.co.uk

Map ref 2 - SS74

Manor Grounds, LYNMOUTH, EX35 6EN
on A39, at the foot of Countisbury Hill
6 Rooms, S £30 D £60-£80, No smoking in
bedrooms or dining room

RECOMMENDED IN THE AREA

Beautiful waterfalls in the Lyn Valley; Valley of the Rocks; scenic railway to Lynton (3 minute walk)

Set right at the harbour entrance between a river and the sea, this Grade II listed hotel has stunning views whichever way you look. The charming property is partly thatched, with a Gothic appearance and plenty of historical associations. All of the bedrooms enjoy a breathtaking outlook, including those on the ground floor, and even when the weather is stormy - and Lynmouth has the second highest tides in the world - they are cosy and warm. Each room is comfortably equipped with an en suite bathroom, television and alarm clock, as well as hospitality tray. The hotel's seafood restaurant looks out over the harbour, and freshly-cooked meals are served either here or in the fully-licensed bar. Lynmouth is handy for touring this interesting area which includes Exmoor and Lynton. Regular boat trips also leave the harbour to explore the high cliffs with their colonies of sea birds including razorbills, guillemots and kittiwakes.

Highcliffe House •••••

A beautifully-restored hotel standing high above sea level, with similarly elevated standards of hospitality

☎ 01598 752235
📠 01598 752235
✉ highcliffe.hotel@
  lycos.co.uk
www.highcliffehouse.co.uk
Map ref 2 - SS74
Sinai Hill, LYNTON, EX35 6AR
from A39 into Lynton 'Old Village'
direction and turn R from Lydiate
Lane.
6 Rooms, D £52-£76, No smoking,
Closed 21 Dec-13 Jan

 RECOMMENDED IN THE AREA

Many lovely walks in the area; gardens – RHS Rosemoor, Marwood and Arlington; 'Lorna Doone' country

Spectacular views over the Exmoor Hills and Lynmouth Bay towards the Bristol Channel and South Wales can be enjoyed to the full here. All six spacious bedrooms and most of the public rooms at this Victorian gentleman's summer residence make the most of the stunning setting and face out towards the sea. The lovely house makes an ideal location for a short break or longer holiday, with its elegant en suite bedrooms and plenty of extras including sherry decanter. Guests will linger long in the comfortable lounge and candle-lit conservatory restaurant, drawn by the panoramic view as much as the peace of the setting, and the imaginative cooking. Brian and Pam Howard are very pleasant hosts who welcome guests to their home with offers of refreshments and help with luggage. Their hospitable presence ensures a comfortable stay. Highcliffe House is also just the place for those wishing to explore this interesting area, and it is fortunate in the many lovely walks that begin right at the front door.

The Heatherville ◆◆◆◆

Cosy hotel with superb views over River Lyn and Lynmouth

☎ 01598 752327 📠 01598 752634

Map ref 2 - SS74

Tors Park, LYNMOUTH, EX35 6NB
1st left fork in Tors Rd
7 Rooms, S £25 D £50-£64, No smoking,
Closed Nov-Feb

From its elevated position The Heatherville enables you to enjoy the natural beauty of the local area. Many rooms - and outdoors both terrace and patio - afford picturesque views of the surrounding woodland. Visit the National Trust's Watersmeet, or enjoy a spectacular coastal walk, both within easy reach of the hotel. Most of the comfortable bedrooms offer en suite shower or bath and all are equipped with televisions, hairdryers and tea/coffee-making facilities. The cosy residential bar and charmingly furnished lounge are ideal places for unwinding. Breakfasts and evening meals are served in the spacious and well appointed dining room. Private parking is available for guests and pets are welcome free of charge.

RECOMMENDED IN THE AREA

Arlington Court (National Trust house); RHS Rosemoor (easy driving distance); Exmoor National Park

Blackaller Hotel & Restaurant ◆◆◆◆◆ ❀

17th-century woollen mill on the Bovey River

☎ 01647 440322
📠 01647 441131
✉ peter@
   blackaller.fsbusiness.co.uk
www.blackaller.co.uk

Map ref 2 - SX78

North Bovey, MORETONHAMPSTEAD,
TQ13 8QY
A382 to M'tonh'stead, then B3212 to
North Bovey
6 Rooms, S £32-£34 D £39-£40, No
smoking in bedrooms or dining room
Closed Jan

Blackaller is the West Country name for the Black Alder tree which grows along the river banks by this lovely former mill. Peter Hunt and Hazel Phillips run the hotel on very relaxed and friendly lines. Bedrooms are pleasing for their simplicity - comfortable and understated. All the rooms have en suite facilities, colour television, and tea and coffee making equipment. Public areas include a charming old sitting room, a well stocked bar, and an attractive dining room with an inglenook fireplace and exposed granite walls. A four-course dinner is served to residents and visitors, except on Sunday and Monday nights, and vegetarian meals can be provided on request. Fresh produce is a feature of the menus, all sourced from within the county, including organic Jacobs' lamb and fish from Brixham. Home-produced bread, honey and muesli are a real treat at breakfast.

RECOMMENDED IN THE AREA

Castle Drago; The Garden House; RHS Rosemoor

Gate House •••••

Thatched medieval hall house, Grade II listed, in a conservation village setting

☎ **01647 440479**
📠 **01647 440479**
✉ **gatehouseon**
    dartmoor@talk21.com

Map ref 2 - SX78

North Bovey,
MORETONHAMPSTEAD,
TQ13 8RB
take A30, A382 to
Moretonhampstead then
B3212 to North Bovey
3 Rooms, S £34-£36 D £58,
No smoking

A pot of tea and a slice of scrumptious home-made cake, what better way to welcome guests to this idyllic 15th-century hideaway? Hospitable hosts, John and Sheila Williams, are justly proud of their home, which is full of charm and character. Guests can relax beside the wood-burning stove, framed in the huge granite fireplace, and contemplate all that has taken place beneath this thatch during the last five centuries. Bedrooms are tastefully decorated in a country style and offer views of the garden or the moors. A hearty breakfast is served featuring local produce, and candlelit dinners are available by prior arrangement, providing the opportunity for Sheila to indulge her culinary skills.

There is a large garden with an outdoor swimming pool in a sheltered corner, where guests may like to relax in fine weather. Nearby, there are beautiful walks, historic houses and lovely gardens to visit.

RECOMMENDED IN THE AREA

Moorland & coastal walks; 6 National Trust properties within easy reach; golf & horseriding nearby

Bulleigh Park Farm ····

Farmhouse accommodation with spectacular country views

☎ 01803 872254
📠 01803 872254
✉ bulleigh@
   lineone.net

Map ref 2 - SX86

Ipplepen, NEWTON ABBOT, TQ12 5UA
turn off A381 for Compton at Jet garage
follow for approx 1m. Signed
3 Rooms, S £22.50-£25
D £40-£50, No smoking in bedrooms or dining room , Closed Xmas

The friendly Dallyn family welcome guests to their spacious farmhouse, which is set in rural surroundings just four miles from the coast. It is a working farm with prize-winning Aberdeen Angus cattle and Devon close wool sheep. The bedrooms, one en suite and another with private facilities, are equipped with televisions, hairdryers, generous hospitality trays and toiletries. One bedroom has a balcony where guests can relax and admire the fabulous scenery, and similarly pleasant views are afforded from the lounge, conservatory and dining room. The award-winning breakfasts are prepared from fresh local produce including home-made

RECOMMENDED IN THE AREA

Dartmoor; National Trust properties; Saltern Cove

preserves and speciality porridges laced with alcohol. For dinner the local pub is just a stroll away. Typically, guests enjoy visiting nearby beaches, gardens, antique centres and Agatha Christie's house, the newly opened National Trust property. Less well known is Britain's only underwater nature reserve at Saltern Cove, boasting the best coral in the country.

*M*oorcote Country Guest House ♦♦♦♦

*Small town Victorian property
with views over Dartmoor*

☎ 01647 440966
✉ moorcote@smartone.co.uk

Map ref 2 - SX78

Chagford Cross,
MORETONHAMPSTEAD, TQ13 8LS
A382 Chagford & Okehampton rd
from Moretonhampstead for 350mtrs.
Past hospital, Moorcote on R
5 Rooms, D £38-£42, No smoking in
dining room or lounge, Closed Nov-
Feb

*M*oorcote is ideally located for exploring Dartmoor and the glories of Devon, and has an attractive mature garden where guests can sit and relax. Despite this tranquil setting, the house is little more than a stroll from the centre of town and a good choice of pubs serving food and ales. Plenty of parking is provided at the house, so guests can have an enjoyable evening and leave the car behind. Most of the bedrooms offer country views and four have en suite facilities. Tea and coffee-making equipment, television, clock radios and hairdryers are provided in all rooms for guests' comfort.

RECOMMENDED IN THE AREA

Beautiful walks on Dartmoor (from the house); National Trust properties including Castle Drogo (3 miles) and Buckland Abbey

*P*itt Farm ♦♦♦♦

*A historic Devonshire farmhouse
with pretty gardens and
welcoming owners*

☎ 01404 812439
🖷 01404 812439
www.smoothhound.co.uk/hotels
/pittfarm.html

Map ref 2 - SY09

Fairmile, OTTERY ST MARY,
EX11 1NL
from A30 follow signs for Fairmile, L at
bottom of hill (B3176) signed Cadhay
House/Coombelake, 0.5m farm on L
5 Rooms, S £20-£22 D £40-£44, No
smoking in bedrooms and dining
room, Closed Xmas & New year

*T*here's plenty of character to this thatched 16th-century farmhouse, where traditional hospitality and pleasing home comforts go hand in hand. Set in the picturesque Otter Valley on a 185-acre livestock and arable farm, it offers guests the chance to relax and listen to the sounds of the countryside. In this friendly atmosphere, good hearty Devon breakfasts are an excellent way to start the day, and there is plenty to see nearby. Bedrooms are equipped with some thoughtful extras, and there is a choice of double, twin and family rooms with en suite, private or shared facilities. In the evening an open fire makes the lounge an inviting retreat.

RECOMMENDED IN THE AREA

Cadhay House (0.25 mile); Otter Nurseries (garden centre) (1.5 miles); Honiton (5 miles)

The Lodge ♦♦♦♦

A warm welcome is assured at this village guest house

☎ 01548 561405
🖷 01548 561766
✉ info@thelodge.uk.com
www.thelodge.uk.com

Map ref 2 - SX73

Higher Town, Malborough,
Kingsbridge, SALCOMBE, TQ7 3RN
A381 from Kingsbridge to Salcombe.
On reaching Malborough turn sharp
R into Higher Town. The Lodge is
100yds on L
10 Rooms, S £25-£30 D £50-£60,
No smoking

The Lodge is a small, friendly guest house set in a picturesque village conveniently located between Salcombe, Kingsbridge and Hope Cove in the heart of the South Hams. Bedrooms, including some ground floor rooms, are stylishly decorated and every one has en suite facilities, central heating with individual thermostats, remote control television, hairdryer and a hospitality tray. Guests can relax in the lounge or pleasant garden, and breakfast is prepared from best quality local produce. The guest house has a residential license, and off-street parking is provided for guests. Residential Artbreak painting holidays are available, taking advantage of the inspirational locality.

RECOMMENDED IN THE AREA

Overbecks Museum and Garden (10 minute drive); Sharpham Vineyard (30 minute drive); some of the country's finest beaches (3 mile radius)

Beach End at Seaton ♦♦♦♦

Lovely Edwardian guest house enjoying glorious views and sunsets

☎ 01297 23388
🖷 01297 625604
✉ beachendatseaton@aol.com

Map ref 2 - SY28

8 Trevelyan Road, SEATON,
EX12 2NL
turn off for Seaton from A3052 at
eastern end of seafront near yacht
club and harbour
3 Rooms, D £50, No smoking in
dining room or lounge,
Closed Nov-Mar

A delightful house located at the end of the sea front with beautiful views across Seaton bay. The Edwardian property was built on the site of an old coastguard cottage, and is sheltered from behind by cliffs.

All of the welcoming bedrooms are en suite, individually decorated and have sea views, hospitality trays, colour TV and hairdryer.

Breakfast can be full English or a choice from the menu. The unspoilt town of Seaton has a fine pebble beach and some interesting shops.

RECOMMENDED IN THE AREA

Seaton Tramway – unique narrow gauge electric tramway from Seaton to Colyton; Pecorama at Beer

*T*he Old Farmhouse •••••

Thatched 16th-century farmhouse, close to the sea and town centre

☎ 01395 512284

Map ref 2 - SY18

Hillside Road, SIDMOUTH, EX10 8JG from Exeter A3052 to Sidmouth, Bowd x-rds turn R, 2m, L at rdbt, L at mini-rdbt, next R, over humpback bridge, bear R on the corner
7 Rooms, S £23-£28 D £46-£56, No smoking, Closed Nov-Jan

*T*his charming farmhouse, in a quiet residential area, dates back to 1569, it gets a mention in the Doomsday Book. Some of the bedrooms are in the cottage across the patio which once housed the local cider mill. All of them have en suite bathrooms and they are decorated with pretty floral wallpaper. Beams, curtained alcoves and twisty hallways are enhanced by prints and dried flowers to give the place a traditional look.

The dining room has an inglenook fireplace and old china plates decorate the walls, the tables are set with royal blue cloths with lace, and linen napkins. Food is freshly prepared from the best local produce, with old-fashioned recipes forming the base of the varied menus. There is a TV lounge and an intimate Inglenook bar.

Recommended in the area

Sidmouth Donkey Sanctuary (3 miles); Bicton Park and Botanical Gardens (15 minute drive); National Trust Killerton House and Knightshayes Court

Thomas Luny House ♦♦♦♦♦

Georgian house quietly situated in the old quarter

☎ 01626 772976
✉ alisonandjohn@
thomas-luny-house.co.uk
www.thomas-luny-house.co.uk

Map ref 2 - SX97

Teign Street, TEIGNMOUTH, TQ14 8EG
A381 to Teignmouth, 3rd lights turn R to
quay, 50yds L to Teign St, 60yds, R thro arch
4 Rooms, S £45-£55 D £55-£75, No smoking

*A*lison and John Allan's delightful home was built in the late 18th century by the marine artist Thomas Luny. It is situated in the old part of town not far from the fish quay. The house is approached through an impressive archway leading into the courtyard, which provides ample parking space. The bedrooms vary in size and are individually designed, all with bath or shower en suite. Direct dial telephones, remote control colour televisions and tea/coffee making facilities are provided in the rooms along with welcoming extras such as fresh flowers, bottled water and toiletries. Public rooms include a large drawing room and dining room, beautifully furnished and both with open fires. French doors open onto a lovely walled garden. A selection of home-made dishes and a full cooked breakfast are served, attentive but unobtrusive service is assured.

RECOMMENDED IN THE AREA

Dartmoor; Totnes, Dartmouth & South Hams area; National Trust houses & gardens

Lower Collipriest Farm ♦♦♦♦

Thatched farmhouse with courtyard garden and delicious home cooking

☎ 01884 252321
🖷 01884 252321
✉ linda@lowercollipriest.co.uk
www.lowercollipriest.co.uk

Map ref 2 - SS91

TIVERTON, EX16 4PT
off Great Western Way, approx 1m
3 Rooms, S £25-£36 , No smoking,
Closed Nov-Etr

*L*ocated in the Exe Valley near Tiverton, with wonderful views of Exmoor and Dartmoor when walking, this attractive dairy farm is within easy reach of the Devon coasts and their lovely beaches. The spacious en suite bedrooms are tastefully decorated and have a number of thoughtful extras - electric blankets, a clock radio, tea and coffee making facilities and so on. Linda Olive offers genuine, warm hospitality. She prides herself on her home cooking, using fresh local produce - prize-winning cheeses and cream. Enjoy a hearty farmhouse breakfast and, by prior arrangement, delicious home-cooked dinners around a large communal table. Guests have use of the lounge with inglenook fireplace. No dogs.

RECOMMENDED IN THE AREA

Knightshayes Court (20 minute drive) and Killerton House (40 minute drive) (both National Trust); Grand Western Canal (10 minute drive)

Colindale Hotel ♦♦♦♦

RECOMMENDED IN THE AREA

Riviera Centre – pool with flume ride and waves; Cockington thatched village (1 mile); Brixham (6 miles); 17th century Torre Abbey & grounds

Delightful Victorian property set close to the beach

☎ 01803 293947

Map ref 2 - SX96

20 Rathmore Road, Chelston, TORQUAY, TQ2 6NY
From Torquay station 200mtr on left in Rathmore Rd
8 Rooms, S £22-£25 D £44-£50, No smoking in bedrooms or dining room or lounge

Hospitality and service are high on the agenda at this delightful hotel set close to the sea front. Outside, well-tended sub-tropical gardens are a pleasure to walk in, while indoors the stylish public rooms, including a licensed bar and extremely elegant lounge stocked with plenty of books and videos, offer a chance to relax. Many bedrooms enjoy views over Torbay, and all rooms are smartly comfortable and homely. Food is a strong feature, with excellent dinners cooked from fresh produce by prior arrangement, and delicious breakfasts, served in a beautifully-appointed dining room. The hotel sits beside Torre Abbey grounds, with its lakes, gardens and walks.

Norwood Hotel ♦♦♦♦

Welcoming hotel serving good food in pleasant surroundings

☎ 01803 294236
🖷 01803 294236
✉ enquiries@norwood-hotel.co.uk
www.norwood-hotel.co.uk

Map ref 2 - SX94

60 Belgrave Road, TORQUAY, TQ2 5HY
M5, follow signs to Torquay. At Torr station follow signs for Seafront which leads to Belgrave Rd, premises on R by traffic lights
11 Rooms, D £40-£50, No smoking in dining room, Closed Nov-Feb

Prize-winning floral displays adorn the front of this hotel, creating an inviting appearance, especially in summer. Indoors it is just as welcoming, with comfortable accommodation and spacious, well-furnished public rooms. Bedrooms offer home from home comforts, with television, radio and courtesy tray, and the en suite bathrooms are well equipped with good quality towels and toiletries. Freshly-prepared dinners from an excellent range of dishes are served in the smart dining room, and the premises benefit from a licencese. The Norwood is ideally located just a few minutes walk from the beach, the town centre, the Riviera Centre, and the bowling greens.

RECOMMENDED IN THE AREA

Kents Cavern; Babbacombe Model Village; Torre Abbey Historic House and Gallery

The Durant Arms ◆◆◆◆ ⬡

An 18th-century inn set in the centre of a picturesque village

☎ 01803 732240
📠 01803 732471
www.thedurantarms
.com

Map ref 2 - SX85

Ashprington, TOTNES,
TQ9 7UP
from A38 take A384 or
A385 to Totnes, at
traffic lights take A381
for Kingsbridge. 1m
turn L for Ashprington
3 Rooms, S £30-£35 D
£55-£60, No smoking in
bedrooms, Closed
Xmas & Boxing Day
evenings

The Durant Arms is a charming feature of the quiet village of Ashprington. The inn embodies traditional standards with fine ales, selected wines (including some from the nearby Sharpham Estate), and excellent food prepared by the creative kitchen team. The blackboard menu offers a good choice ranging from light lunches to full meals with delicious home-made soups and desserts. The beautifully furnished en suite bedrooms have their own private entrance. The views from the rooms are of the village and the countryside beyond, which invites exploration. This is the valley of the River Dart, with its rolling hills and enchanting lanes. The old town of Totnes, a centre of art and craft, is just three miles away. Proprietors Graham and Eileen Ellis extend a warm welcome to guests and make every effort to make their stay a memorable one.

RECOMMENDED IN THE AREA

Elizabethan town of Totnes (3 miles); Sharpham Vineyard (half a mile away); The Eden Project (64 miles)

The Old Forge at Totnes ◆◆◆◆

Historic creeper-clad building with generous guest accommodation

☎ 01803 862174
📠 01803 865385

Map ref 2 - SX86

Seymour Place, TOTNES, TQ9 5AY
turn off A38 towards Totnes. From
town centre cross river bridge and
take 2nd R
10 Rooms, S £42-£52 D £54-£74,
No smoking

Not many hotels boast a prison cell, but part of the Old Forge complex includes the old court room, and this curiosity remains. The historic 600-year-old stone building is covered in creeper, with a cobbled drive and coach arch. Within this historic building the cottage-style bedrooms are thoroughly modern and equipped with en suite facilities. Guests can relax in the spacious conservatory-style leisure lounge with its whirlpool spa, or sit in the delightful gardens and order a cream tea. A huge breakfast menu can be considered in the airy dining room, where vegetarians and special diets are willingly catered for.

RECOMMENDED IN THE AREA

Easy access to Dartmoor and coastal walks of South Devon; The Eden Project and Lost Gardens of Heligan (90 minute drive); river trips to Dartmouth, steam trains close by

Cherrybrook Hotel ◆◆◆◆

The highest hotel in England promising the warmest of welcomes

☎ 01822 880260
📠 01822 880260

Map ref 2 - SX67

TWO BRIDGES, Yelverton, PL20 6SP
on B3212
7 Rooms, S £46-£50 D £92-£100,
No smoking in dining room ,
Closed 24 Dec-2 Jan

Located on the High Moor, between Postbridge and Two Bridges in the centre of the Dartmoor National Park, this family-run, 19th-century hotel offers magnificent views over the surrounding countryside. It is an ideal base for walking and, for trips out, the north and south coasts of Devon and Cornwall are both within easy reach. Formerly a farmhouse, Cherrybrook has been extended over the years to provide a range of comfortable well-equipped bedrooms, all with en suite or private facilities. The building's original character has been retained, however, with beamed ceilings and slate floors in the lounge and bar. Delicious home-cooked four-course dinners are available by prior arrangement.

RECOMMENDED IN THE AREA

Walking on Dartmoor; visit Widecombe; climb Haytor

Woodhayes Country House and Cottage ♦♦♦♦♦

Small, friendly Georgian house in picturesque rural setting

☎ 01404 822237
📠 01404 822337
📧 info@woodhayes-hotel.co.uk
www.woodhayes-hotel.co.uk

Map ref 2 - SY07

WHIMPLE, EX5 2TD
Leave A30 Honiton/Exeter Road at
Junct named Daisymount and follow
the brown Woodhayes signs
6 Rooms, S £40-£65 D £60-£90,
No smoking in bedrooms or dining
room

Nestling in four acres of grounds bordering the pretty village of Whimple, Woodhayes is ideally positioned - near the M5 and A30/A303 - for touring Devon. Lynda and Eddie Katz provide a warm welcome to the relaxed, family atmosphere of their lovely home. The tastefully decorated dining room, lounge and country style bar with flagstone floor, all have open fires in winter, whilst the spacious grounds and sun terrace offer alternative venues to unwind. The en suite bedrooms enjoy attractive views. Spacious and comfortable, each is individually decorated, with a number of additional touches adding an air of luxury. Gourmet breakfasts served here are worth waking up for.

RECOMMENDED IN THE AREA

Devon coast (11 miles); Exeter (8 miles); Dartmoor and Exmoor National Parks (less than 30 minute drive)

Harrabeer Country House Hotel ♦♦♦♦

Historic Devon longhouse situated on the edge of Dartmoor

☎ 01822 853302
📠 01822 853302
📧 reception@harrabeer.co.uk
www.harrabeer.co.uk

Map ref 2 - SX56

Harrowbeer Lane, YELVERTON,
PL20 6EA
From Plymouth, A386 to Tavistock,
1st L on rdbt to Tavistock, 1st R into
Grange Rd, turn R. The Harrabeer is
on L
6 Rooms, S £30-£37 D £50-£57, No
smoking in bedrooms or dining room ,
Closed 14 Dec 2002–5 Jan 2003

A former Devon longhouse has been converted to provide attractive accommodation conveniently located for the Dartmoor National Park. It is a good area for walking, and you may come across wild moorland ponies. There is a large lounge, a cosy residents' bar with a log fire, and a dining room overlooking the garden.

Evening meals are provided and special diets can be catered for by prior request. All bedrooms have en suite or private bathrooms, and are equipped with colour television, telephones, hairdryers, and tea and coffee-making facilities. Pets are welcome by arrangement, and picnics can be prepared on request.

RECOMMENDED IN THE AREA

Walks on Dartmoor (walking distance or short drive); The Eden Project (90 minute drive); National Trust houses including Buckland Abbey

Dorset

A selection of places to eat from the AA Restaurant & AA Pub Guides

Restaurants

◉ Bridge House Hotel (Country House)
3 Prout Bridge, Beaminster DT8 3AY
Tel 01308 862200 Fax 01308 863700

◉◉ Bistro on the Bridge (Modern, Minimalist)
3-5 Bridge Street, Christchurch BH23 1DY
Tel 01202 482522 Fax 01202 470048

◉ The Mock Turtle (Traditional)
34 High West Street, Dorchester DT1 1UP
Tel 01305 264011

◉ Le Petit Canard (Classic/Simple Traditional)
Dorchester Road, Maiden Newton DT2 0BE
Tel 01300 320536 Fax 01300 321286

◉◉ Perry's Restaurant (Bistro-style)
4 Trinity Road, The Old Harbour, Weymouth
DT4 8TJ
Tel 01305 785799 Fax 01305 787002

◉◉ Les Bouviers (French)
Oakley Hill, Merley, Wimborne Minster
BH21 1RJ
Tel 01202 889555 Fax 01202 889555

Pubs

◖ The Anchor Inn
Seatown, Bridport DT6 6JU
Tel 01297 489215

◖ The Gaggle of Geese
Buckland Newton DT2 7BS
Tel 01300 345249

◖ The Cock & Bottle
East Morden BH20 7DL
Tel 01929 459238

◖ The Acorn Inn
Evershot DT2 0JW
Tel 01935 83228 Fax 01935 83707

◖ The Museum Arms
Farnham DT11 8DE
Tel 01725 516261

◖ The Bottle Inn
Marshwood DT6 5QJ
Tel 01297 678254 Fax 01297 678739

◖ The Brace of Pheasants
Plush DT2 7RQ
Tel 01300 348357

Watermeadow House ◆◆◆◆

Overlooking a river and unspoilt farmland, a peaceful Georgian-style house

☎ 01308 862619
🖷 01308 862619
✉ enquiries@
watermeadowhouse.co.uk
www.watermeadowhouse.co.uk

Map ref 2 - ST50

Bridge Farm, Hooke, BEAMINSTER,
DT8 3PD
turn off A356 approx 4m W of Maiden
Newton signed Hooke. Turn L at x-rds
signed Kingcombe. House 300yds
on R
2 Rooms, S £25-£26 D £44-£48,
No smoking, Closed Nov-Feb

A genuinely relaxed and friendly guest house on the edge of the village of Hooke, where peace and tranquility are assured. This Georgian-style country house is set on a working dairy farm, and views of the countryside and the river can be enjoyed from all of the rooms. Both bedrooms are particularly well equipped, featuring a fridge, colour television and hospitality tray. The large family/twin/double room has an en suite shower, and the double room has its own private bathroom. Guests can relax in the comfortable sitting room and the fully-glazed sunroom, where delicious farm breakfasts made from fresh local produce are served.

RECOMMENDED IN THE AREA

Mapperton House and Gardens (4 miles);
Broadwindsor Craft Centre (20 minute drive);
lovely walks in Hooke Woods (10 minute walk)

The Fox Inn ◆◆◆◆

A wonderful welcome, terrific food and atmosphere, and excellent en suite accommodation in an authentic country setting

☎ 01935 891330
🖷 01935 891330
✉ dine@fox-inn.co.uk
www.fox-inn.co.uk

Map ref 2 - ST50

CORSCOMBE, DT2 0NS
1 mile off A356, Crewkerne-Maiden Newton road or 5 miles off A37, Yeovil-Dorchester road
4 Rooms, S £70-£77 D £80-£100, No smoking in bedrooms, Closed 25 Dec

RECOMMENDED IN THE AREA

Fantastic walks with beautiful scenery (from the Fox); West Dorset Coast World Heritage Site (10 minute drive); historic houses and gardens including Forde Abbey and Athelhampton House (within 30 minute drive)

The very epitome of an English country inn, the 17th-century Fox can be found down winding lanes in the heart of rural Dorset. Popular with locals and tourists alike, it offers an authentic atmosphere and style with its thatched roof, inglenook fireplace and exposed beams. Good food is at the centre of the operation here, with fresh local ingredients going into an imaginative range of meals. All discerning tastes are catered for, and the cooking can be sampled in the cosy atmosphere of several dining areas. The inn also offers charming accommodation in the form of four spacious and well-equipped en suite bedrooms, each furnished with antiques in keeping with the building.

Breakfast is served in the attractive conservatory in the summer, and in the owners kitchen/dining room in the winter. The many returning visitors praise the warm welcome and unspoilt atmosphere which make this inn a special place.

*T*he Casterbridge Hotel ♦♦♦♦♦

An elegant Georgian residence in the town centre of Dorchester

☎ 01305 264043
🖷 01305 260884
✉ reception@
casterbridgehotel.co.uk
www.casterbridgehotel.co.uk

Map ref 2 - SY60

49 High East Street, DORCHESTER, DT1 1HU
in town centre 75mtrs from town clock
14 Rooms, S £40-£52 D £60-£85,
No smoking in dining room,
Closed 25-26 Dec

*T*his well run hotel maintains high standards of accommodation, enhanced with antiques and tasteful furnishings. The hotel provides a traditional English welcome with cheerful attentive staff. The public rooms include an elegant dining room, gracious drawing room and an intimate bar/library. Breakfast is served in the conservatory, providing an extensive buffet as well as individually cooked breakfasts. All bedrooms are ensuite with either bath or shower, one room is suitable for families and three are suitable for the less able. Children are welcome, cots and high chairs are available. All rooms have colour television, tea and coffee making facilities and direct dial telephones. The hotel also offers special short breaks.

RECOMMENDED IN THE AREA

Thomas Hardy Museum; Abbotsbury Swannery; Lulworth Cove

---

*Y*albury Cottage Hotel & Restaurant ♦♦♦♦♦ ◎◎

Thatched cottage offering excellent food and comfortable accommodation

☎ 01305 262382
🖷 01305 266412
✉ yalburycottage@aol.com
www.smoothhound.co.uk/
hotels/yalbury

Map ref 2 - SY79

Lower Bockhampton, DORCHESTER, DT2 8PZ
off A35 past Hardy's cottage, straight over x-rds, 400yds on L, past red phone box, opp village pump
8 Rooms, S £55 D £86, No smoking in bedrooms or dining room

*N*estling amid winding rivers and peaceful fields, Yalbury Cottage was originally the home of the local shepherd and keeper of the water meadows. It is a thatched property dating from the 17th century with attractive gardens, where teas and pre-dinner drinks are served in the summer. The pretty restaurant offers Head Chef Darren Gransbury's award winning food, in an atmosphere enhanced by oak beams and inglenook fireplaces. The cosy lounge, the only part of the building where smoking is permitted, is also in the old part of the building. The spacious cottage-style bedrooms all have en suite bathrooms, remote control television, hairdryers and tea and coffee making equipment. Ample parking is provided in the grounds.

RECOMMENDED IN THE AREA

Thomas Hardy's birthplace (1 mile);
Athelhampton House (10 minutes' drive);
beautiful walks in a conservation area

Yellowham Farmhouse ♦♦♦♦

Idyllic rural surroundings and spacious well-appointed accommodation

☎ 01305 262892
✆ 01305 257707
✉ b&b@
   yellowham.freeserve.co.uk
www.yellowham.freeserve.co.uk

Map ref 2 - SY73

Yellowham Wood, DORCHESTER,
DT2 8RW
1.5m E of Dorchester, turn off A35. Farm
situated on edge of Yellowham Wood
4 Rooms, S £30-£45 D £50-£60,
No smoking

Right in the heart of Hardy country nestling on the edge of Yellowham Wood is this peaceful farmhouse. A long drive through 120 acres of farmland and 130 acres of woodland leads to the mature gardens with tennis court where guests can easily while away the time. Inside it is warm and spacious, with a bright sitting/garden room and separate licensed dining room where well-cooked evening meals are served, as well as delicious breakfasts. Afternoon tea and pre-dinner drinks can be enjoyed in the garden. All bedrooms are on the ground floor, and combine solid home comforts with tasteful decorations and modern en suites.

RECOMMENDED IN THE AREA

Hardy's Cottage (1 mile); Abbotsbury – swannery, sub-tropical gardens, terracotta warriors (15 minute drive); beautiful heritage coastline walks (20 minute drive)

The Marquis of Lorne ♦♦♦♦

A 16th-century country inn with good food

☎ 01308 485236
✆ 01308 485666
✉ julie.woodroffe@
   btinternet.com
www.marquisoflorne.com

Map ref 2 - SY59

NETTLECOMBE, Bridport, DT6 3SY
N from Bridport on A3066, after 1.5m
after mini-rdbt turn R, through West
Milton, straight over at junct, premises
up hill
6 Rooms, S £45 D £70

This hostelry is found in the unspoilt Dorset hills, in the shadow of Eggardon hill, the ancient earth fort, and close to Powerstock common, with its ancient oaks, fallow deer and rare butterflies, making it great for country walks. It has a large car park and well kept gardens. Children under 10, and pets are not accepted in the rooms. The inn maintains its original character with exposed stone walls and wooden beams. It has two bars, a non-smoking area and a small games room, and has earned a fine reputation for its food, serving a menu that changes regularly, with home cooked favourites, some foreign dishes, vegetarian options and excellent fresh fish from the nearby coast. The menu is supported by an extensive wine list, a range of lagers and local Real Ales. The bedrooms are comfortable and simply furnished, all with en suite showers and colour TV.

RECOMMENDED IN THE AREA

Visit Charmouth and Lyme Regis; Abbotsbury Swannery and Sub-tropical Gardens; many lovely walks

Stourcastle Lodge ◆◆◆◆

Charming 18th-century house with a warm, friendly welcome

☎ 01258 472320
📠 01258 473381
✉ enquiries@
stourcastle-lodge.co.uk
www.stourcastle-lodge.co.uk

Map ref 2 - ST71

Goughs Close, STURMINSTER NEWTON, DT10 1BU
small lane off town square opposite cross
5 Rooms, S £41-£48 D £63-£77, No smoking in bedrooms or dining room

Tucked away down a quaint stone walled close in Sturminster Newton, you will enjoy this comfortable house and its lovely garden setting. Look out for some fascinating sculptures. Start the day with an award-winning farmhouse breakfast - free-range eggs, crusty home-made bread and local preserves. You may also like to end it with one of Jill Hookham-Basset's equally fine dinners, painstakingly prepared on the old-fashioned Aga. Enjoy the gentle aroma of dried flowers and spices in the spacious bedrooms, some with whirlpool baths, and all with en suite facilities. Elegantly decorated, the rooms feature brass bedsteads and many useful extra touches. Jill and Ken are excellent hosts.

RECOMMENDED IN THE AREA

National Trust properties – Stourhead and Kingston Lacey; wonderful Dorset country walks

Bay Lodge ◆◆◆◆◆

Cosy log fires and gorgeous views make it easy to relax here

☎ 01305 782419
📠 01305 782828
✉ barbara@baylodge.co.uk
www.baylodge.co.uk

Map ref 2 - SY60

27 Greenhill, WEYMOUTH, DT4 7SW
follow brown & white tourist signs to Sea Life Park. Hotel 200yds on town centre side of entrance on A353
12 Rooms, S £49.50-£59.50 D £64-£72, No smoking in dining room

Very friendly, hospitable owners create a pleasant, relaxing atmosphere at this well-placed seaside guest house. With panoramic views out over the bay from the public rooms, guests are likely to linger over breakfast, or sit by the windows in the oak-panelled lounge where a log fire burns on cold days. Several of the en suite bedrooms also share the view, and many of these are equipped with spa bath for extra luxury. Some rooms are located in an annexe which is easily accessible to less mobile guests. Pretty gardens with a pergola to shelter from the sun add to the attractions of this delightful property.

RECOMMENDED IN THE AREA

16th century fishing harbour and 'Time Walk'; Coastal Path and Dorset Downs; Abbotsbury Swannery

*A*shton Lodge ◆◆◆◆

A spacious family house with a pretty garden

☎ 01202 883423
🖷 01202 886180
✉ ashtonlodge@ukgateway.net
www.ashtonlodge.ukgateway.net

Map ref 3 - SU09

10 Oakley Hill, WIMBORNE
MINSTER, BH21 1QH
from A31 S of Wimborne take A349
towards Poole, exit L at next rdbt
signed Wimborne/Canford Magna.
House on R after 200yds
5 Rooms, S £24 D £48-£52, No
smoking

*A*shton Lodge is a smart, modern brick house with big bay windows, decorated with boxes of flowers. The owners give their guests a warm welcome, and they are very happy for you to enjoy their garden, which has two ponds. There is plenty of parking space. The bedrooms are very comfortable with attractive co-ordinated decor and fabrics, equipped with colour TV, clock radio, tea and coffee facilities, and hairdryer; two have en suite bathrooms. With your own key, you have free access to your room. There is a delicious freshly cooked full English breakfast, with a vegetarian option, and local marmalades and jams, which you can enjoy in the spacious dining room that overlooks the garden. A full colour brochure is available on request.

RECOMMENDED IN THE AREA

Castles & National Trust properties; beaches & coastal walks; display gardens & garden centres

$\mathcal{E}$ssex

A selection of places to eat from the AA Restaurant & AA Pub Guides

Restaurants

⊚⊚ Le Talbooth Restaurant (Classic, Country-house)
Dedham CO7 6HP
Tel 01206 323150 Fax 01206 322309

⊚ Reeves Restaurant (Traditional, Country-house)
Rumbles Cottage, Braintree Road, Felstead CM6 3DJ
Tel 01371 820996 Fax 01371 820100

⊚⊚ The Pier at Harwich (Classic, Formal)
The Quay, Harwich CO12 3HH
Tel 01255 241212 Fax 01255 551922

⊚ Francine's Restaurant (Classic, Country-house)
1a High Street, Maldon CM9 7PB
Tel 01621 856605 Fax 01621 856605

⊚ Stour Bay Café (Modern, Bistro-style)
39-43 High Street, Manningtree CO11 1AH
Tel 01206 396687 Fax 01206 395462

⊚ The Olive Branch Brasserie (Modern)
High Street, Thorpe-le-Soken CO16 0EA
Tel 01255 861199 Fax 01255 860758

Pubs

♣ Axe & Compass
High Street, Arkesden CB11 4EX
Tel 01799 550272 Fax 01799 550906

♣ The Bull Inn
Blackmore End CM7 4DD
Tel 01371 851037 Fax 01371 851037

♣ The Green Dragon at Young's End
Upper London Road, Young's End, Braintree CM7 8QN
Tel 01245 361030 Fax 01245 362575

♣ The Cricketers
Clavering CB11 4QT
Tel 01799 550442 Fax 01799 550882

♣ Bell Inn & Hill House
High Road, Horndon on the Hill SS17 8LD
Tel 01375 642463 Fax 01375 361611

♣ The Black Buoy Inn
Black Buoy Hill, Wivenhoe CO7 9BS
Tel 01206 822425 Fax 01206 827834

Homelye Farm ♦♦♦♦

Rural setting for accommodation seven miles from Stansted Airport

☎ 01371 872127
✆ 01371 876428
✉ homelye@supanet.com
www.homelyefarm.com

Map ref 4 - TL62

Homelye Chase, Braintree Road, GREAT DUNMOW, CM6 3AW
follow A120 E from Dunmow for 1m. Turn L off main road at large water tower. Farm at bottom of Homelye Chase
9 Rooms, S £30-£35 D £55-£60,
No smoking, Closed 24-27 Dec

Motel-style bedrooms are offered in sympathetically converted outbuildings at this former livestock farm. Guests can come and go at all hours - ideal for early morning flight departures from nearby Stansted Airport. Doubles, twins, family and single rooms are all available, and each one offers a colour television, hospitality tray, alarm clock and hairdryer. Homelye is a friendly, family-run establishment, and the owners have a good knowledge of the local area. A choice of full English or continental breakfast is served in the cosy dining room, located in the original farmhouse, and there is a good range of pubs and restaurants nearby. Pets are not permitted in the rooms.

RECOMMENDED IN THE AREA

Freeport (designer outlet village) (15 minute drive); pretty villages of Stebbing, Finchingfield, Thaxted (15 minute drive); Hatfield Forest, Hedingham Castle, Colchester Zoo (easy driving distance)

The Starr Restaurant with Rooms •••• ◉❀

Elegant, well-equipped bedrooms tucked away behind an award-winning restaurant

☎ 01371 874321 📠 01371 876337
✉ starrrestaurant@btinternet.com
www.zynet.co.uk/menu/starr

Map ref 4 - TL62

Market Place, GREAT DUNMOW, CM6 1AX
M11J8, E on A120 towards Colchester, in
Dunmow centre turn L into Market Place off
High St
8 Rooms, S £70-£90 D £110-£130, No
smoking in bedrooms or dining room ,
Closed 2-8 Jan

 RECOMMENDED IN THE AREA

Mountfitchet Castle and Norman village; Audley End House and Gardens; Saffron Walden

*A*n old stable block at the rear of the main building has been lovingly converted to provide quality individually-styled accommodation. All of the comfortable, spacious rooms have en suite bath and shower, and two rooms in particular are ideal for honeymooners, or a special romantic evening. All of the delightful bedrooms appeal particularly to diners in the award-winning (2 AA Rosettes) restaurant, where an excellent meal can be relished in the pleasant knowledge that bed is only a short walk away. The beamed restaurant extends into a sunny, bright conservatory, where an essentially English menu offers a good variety of dishes cooked to order from local produce. This establishment is renowned for its friendly but professional service, and a relaxed atmosphere is part of its charm. There are two private meeting/dining rooms catering for groups of up to 30 people. With Stansted Airport only 7 miles away, this is an excellent location for business meetings or family reunions.

Gloucestershire

A selection of places to eat from the AA Restaurant & AA Pub Guides

Restaurants

Lower Brook House
Lower Street, Blockley GL56 9DS
Tel 01386 700286 Fax 01386 700286

Dial House Hotel (Traditional, Country-house)
The Chestnuts, High St, Bourton-on-the-Water GL54 2AN
Tel 01451 822244 Fax 01451 810126

Le Petit Blanc (Modern, Chic)
The Promenade, Cheltenham GL50 1NN
Tel 01242 266800 Fax 01242 266801

Cotswold House (Modern, Chic)
The Square, Chipping Campden GL55 6AN
Tel 01386 840330 Fax 01386 840310

Restaurant on the Green (Informal)
The Green, Frampton on Severn GL2 7DY
Tel 01452 740077

947AD at The Royalist (Country-house, Chic)
Digbeth Street, Stow-on-the-Wold GL54 1BN
Tel 01451 830670 Fax 01451 870048

Pubs

The Village Pub
Barnsley GL7 5EF
Tel 01285 740421 Fax 01285 740142

Kings Head Inn & Restaurant
The Green, Bledington OX7 6XQ
Tel 01608 658365 Fax 01608 658902

The Churchill Arms
Paxford, Chipping Campden GL55 6XH
Tel 01386 59400 Fax 01386 594005

The Fox Inn
Lower Oddington GL56 0UR
Tel 01451 870555 Fax 01451 870669

Egypt Mill
Nailsworth GL6 0AE
Tel 01453 833449 Fax 01453 836098

Halfway Inn
Box, Stroud GL6 9AE
Tel 01453 832631 Fax 01453 835275

Gumstool Inn
Calcot Manor, Tetbury GL8 8YJ
Tel 01666 890391 Fax 01666 890394

The Old Bakery ◆◆◆◆◆

Warm hospitality and exceptional food in a delightful village setting

☎ 01386 700408
🖷 01386 700408

Map ref 3 - SP13

High Street, BLOCKLEY,
Moreton-in-Marsh, GL56 9EU
turn off A44 at Bourton-on-the-Hill
onto B4479. Proceed to Blockley
centre. Beyond Church Square, Old
Bakery on corner of High St/School
Lane
3 Rooms, S £85-£105 D £130-£200
(prices include dinner), No smoking,
Closed Dec-Jan & 2 wks Jun

The Old Bakery is a conversion of four cottages in a North Cotswolds' village, a perfect base for country walks and trips to Stratford-upon-Avon, Cheltenham or Oxford. The friendly proprietor, Linda Helme, creates a welcoming atmosphere for her guests and feeds them superbly well. She was overall national winner of the AA Best Breakfast Award 2001-2002, and her four-course dinners with fine wines are quite special. The meal is set, but personal preferences and special diets are taken into account. The bedrooms are luxuriously appointed and thoughtfully equipped. Guests have exclusive use of the sitting room, study and dining room, all beautifully furnished with antiques. No pets or children under 14.

RECOMMENDED IN THE AREA

Hidcote Manor Gardens (10 minutes' drive); Warwick Castle (30 minutes' drive); beautiful walks in the Cotswolds

Coombe House ♦♦♦

Peacefully located stone-built house convenient for the village centre

☎ 01451 821966
📠 01451 810477
✉ coombe.house@virgin.net
www.smoothhound.co.uk/
hotels/coombeho.html

Map ref 3 - SP12

Rissington Road, BOURTON-ON-
THE-WATER, GL54 2DT
exit A429, through village. House past
model village on L; or exit A424 at
Burford or Stow, continue into
Bourton-on-the-Water, 0.5m on R
6 Rooms, S £35-£50 D £45-£60, No
smoking, Closed Jan-Feb

An attractive property of mellow Cotswold stone, Coombe House is set in immaculate gardens, from where a short riverside walk leads to the historic centre of Bourton-on-the-Water. Bedrooms are both practical and comfortable with modern en suite bathrooms and plenty of welcoming extras, such as mini fridges, tea and coffee-making facilities, television and clock radios. A choice of continental or full English breakfast is served at individual tables in the pretty dining room. Guests enjoy a high level of personal service, which might include a drink in the lounge or outside on the garden terrace. Children under 12 are not accepted.

RECOMMENDED IN THE AREA

National Trust properties – Hidcote Manor Garden and Snowshill Manor; Blenheim Palace, Stratford upon Avon and Warwick Castle (within 60 minutes' drive); beautiful walks in the area

Cleeve Hill Hotel ♦♦♦♦♦

An elegant residence in the heart of the Cotswolds

☎ 01242 672052 📠 679969
✉ gbtoncleevehill@aol.com
www.smoothhound.co.uk/
hotels/cleeve.html

Map ref 2 - SO92

Cleeve Hill, CHELTENHAM, GL52 3PR
on B4632 2.5m from Cheltenham
between Prestbury and Winchcombe
9 Rooms, S £45-£55 D £75-£85,
No smoking

Cleeve Hill Hotel is in a superb location, overlooking the Malvern Hills in an area of outstanding natural beauty. There are spectacular views from all the bedrooms, either across the valley to the hills or to Cleeve Common. The rooms (including one with four-poster bed) are beautifully decorated and very well equipped, with en suite facilities, direct dial telephones with modem points, television, tea and coffee, radio alarms, toiletries and hairdryers. A trouser press is available on request. Spacious public rooms include a conservatory dining room where guests are served an excellent breakfast, and an elegant lounge where guests can relax and enjoy a drink from the licensed bar. Hosts Bob and Georgie Tracey provide friendly and attentive service.

The hotel makes a good base for visiting the tourist attractions of the Cotswolds, and there is a good range of places to eat in the locality

RECOMMENDED IN THE AREA

The Cotswolds Walk (direct access to rear); Sudeley Castle (3 miles); National Trust – Hidcote Manor (10 miles)

131

$\mathcal{M}$oorend Park Hotel ♦♦♦♦

Elegant Victorian property to the south of Cheltenham

☎ 01242 224441 ☏ 01242 572413
✉ moorendpark@freeuk.com
www.moorendpark.freeuk.com

Map ref 2 - SO92

Moorend Park Road, CHELTENHAM,
GL53 0LA
M5 J11A, A417 (Cirencester), A46
(Cheltenham). After 3m L at lights to enter
hotel car park.
9 Rooms, S £46-£50 D £56-£67, Smoking in
bar only

$\mathcal{M}$oorend Park dates from 1895 and retains many period features, including beautiful moulded cornices and original tiling. It is conveniently situated in a mainly residential area within walking distance of the town centre, and makes an ideal base for touring the Cotswold villages, Oxford and Bath. The Austrian/Australian owners offer the warmest of welcomes, and in addition to the cosy bar, where guests can relax with a pre-dinner drink by the fire, there is also a separate reading lounge. All the bedrooms have en suite facilities, colour televisions, direct dial telephones, hairdryers, radio alarms, hospitality trays and in-room control central heating. The area has a good choice of restaurants to choose from.

RECOMMENDED IN THE AREA

Bourton-on-the-Water (20 minute drive); Worcester Cathedral and porcelain factory (45 minute drive); Winchcombe (8 miles)

$\mathcal{H}$olly House ♦♦♦♦

Quietly situated house in the centre of a pretty Cotswold village

☎ 01386 593213
☏ 01386 593181
✉ hutsby@talk21.com
www.stratford-upon-avon.
co.uk/hollyhouse.htm

Map ref 3 - SP14

Ebrington, CHIPPING CAMPDEN,
GL55 6NL
from Chipping Campden take B4035
towards Shipston on Stour. After 0.5m
turn left to Ebrington & follow signs
3 Rooms, S £35-£42 D £44-£48,
No smoking, Closed 21-31 Dec

$\mathcal{A}$ picturesque Cotswold village is the appealing setting for this late Victorian guest house. Surrounded by quaint thatched cottages and close to the Norman village church, Holly House is ideally placed for visiting Stratford, Hidcote Manor Gardens, and Chipping Campden. The thoughtfully-equipped en suite ground floor bedrooms which are set around a courtyard have been cleverly converted from outbuildings, and each has its own private entrance. Guests can make use of the plethora of tourist information in the attractive Garden Room, and delicious Cotswold breakfasts are served in the cosy dining room. Parking spaces are plentiful, and the village pub serving traditional food is just a few minutes walk away.

RECOMMENDED IN THE AREA

Hidcote Manor Gardens (2 miles); Stratford upon Avon (10 miles); National Trust houses – Snowshill Manor, Charlecote Park, Upton House

The Old School House ♦♦♦♦♦

An old house of character offering spacious guest rooms

☎ 01452 740457
📠 01452 741721
📧 the oldies@
f-o-s.freeserve.co.uk

Map ref 2 - SO70

Whittles Lane, FRAMPTON ON SEVERN, GL2 7EB
from A38 take right turn onto B4071, at village green turn left
2 Rooms, S £26.50 D £53,
No smoking in bedrooms,
Closed 21-31 Dec

A picturesque canal-side village is the setting for this 18th-century property. No longer a school but retaining many original features of its former life, the house now offers homely accommodation in stylish surroundings. Bedrooms are roomy and comfortable, with modern en suite bathrooms and lots of useful extras. There is a drawing room for guests' exclusive use, furnished with fine period pieces and an open fire, and a separate dining room with a large polished table for breakfast. Frampton-on-Severn boasts the longest village green in England, and within reasonable touring distance are Slimbridge Wildlife and Wetlands Trust, Westonbirt Aboretum and Garden Show, Bath, Bristol and Cheltenham.

RECOMMENDED IN THE AREA

The Wildlife and Wetlands Trust at Slimbridge; Gloucester Docks; Berkeley Castle

Guiting Guest House ♦♦♦♦♦

16th-century former farmhouse in a village setting

☎ 01451 850470 📠 01451 850034
📧 guiting.guest_house@virgin.net
freespace.virgin.net/
guiting.guest_house/

Map ref 3 - SP02

GUITING POWER, Cheltenham, GL54 5TZ
A40, Andoversford lights R to Stow-on-the-Wold, 4m L to Lower Swell B4068, 1m L to Guiting Power. L into village, house in centre
4 Rooms, S £35 D £60, No smoking in bedrooms or dining room

A lovely old building of mellow Cotswold stone, this house retains many original features including exposed beams, inglenook fireplaces and polished wooden floors. Public areas have a warm, comfortable and cosy atmosphere, enhanced by open fires, decorative pottery and family memorabilia. Fresh flowers, fruit and a teddy to cuddle are among the thoughtful extras in the welcoming bedrooms. Four-poster beds are a feature along with generously filled hospitality trays, quality toiletries and bathrobes. Two rooms are en suite and the third has private facilities. Food is imaginative, cooked on the family Aga and well worth experiencing. Yvonne and Bernie Sylvester are warm and attentive hosts who greet arriving guests with a cup of tea and a slice of home-made cake.

RECOMMENDED IN THE AREA

Walking in local countryside; Snowshill Manor, Sudley Castle; Winchcombe (6 miles)

Northfield Bed & Breakfast ◆◆◆◆

Detached family house set in large gardens in open countryside

☎ 01451 860427
📠 01451 860427
✉ nrthfield0@aol.com

Map ref 3 - SP11

Cirencester Road, NORTHLEACH,
GL54 3JL
just off A429 Northleach to
Cirencester road, 1m from Northleach
traffic lights. Well signed from main
road
3 Rooms, S £30-£40 D £48-£54,
No smoking, Closed 23-27 Dec

*B*eautifully located in the Cotswolds and handy for visiting Cirencester, Gloucester and Stow-on-the-Wold, this delightful property is built of the honeyed local stone. Set in immaculate gardens with a pond, it offers tastefully-furnished bedrooms with good home comforts, and plenty of extras in the spacious bathrooms. Two rooms have direct access to the garden. Breakfast is taken overlooking the open countryside, with the owners' own hens providing the eggs, while delicious and imaginative evening meals using plenty of fresh local ingredients are served in the elegant dining room. Short breaks are available at a special inclusive price for two nights.

RECOMMENDED IN THE AREA

Chedworth Roman Villa; Keith Harding's World of Mechanical Music; Cotswold Heritage Centre

The Sodbury House Hotel ◆◆◆◆

Friendly small hotel offering smart bedrooms and delicious breakfasts

☎ 01454 312847
📠 01454 273105
✉ sodhousehotel@tesco.net

Map ref 2 - ST78

Badminton Road, OLD SODBURY,
BS37 6LU
from M4 J18 take A46 North, after 2m
turn L onto A432 (Chipping Sodbury)
hotel on L in 1m
17 Rooms, S £50-£54 D £78-£90,
Closed 21 Dec - 1 Jan

*F*ormerly a farmhouse, this 19th-century property stands in extensive grounds on the edge of the Cotswolds. The house has been sympathetically converted and extended to provide seventeen en suite bedrooms. These are spread between the main house and nearby buildings. All are well equipped and comfortably furnished with a range of thoughtful extras. Breakfast is a highlight of a stay here, with freshly squeezed orange juice and a good selection of cold dishes, including local gammon and eggs, or smoked salmon with scrambled eggs. Self-contained conference facilities in a period building are popular.

RECOMMENDED IN THE AREA

The historic city of Bath; beautiful towns and villages of the Cotswolds; Bristol

Rectory Farmhouse ♦♦♦♦♦

Superb bedrooms and public areas with stunning views across the countryside

☎ 01451 832351
✉ rectory.farmhouse@
cw-warwick.co.uk

Map ref 3 - SP12

Lower Swell, STOW-ON-THE-WOLD,
Cheltenham, GL54 1LH
From the A429 at Stow-on-the-Wold.
B4608 signed Lower Swell, L just
before Golden Ball Inn into a private
Road. Farmhouse on R at the far end
of the gravel drive.
3 Rooms, S £45-£50 D £70-£80,
No smoking

A listed 17th-century former farmhouse has been delightfully refurbished to provide luxury accommodation for the discerning guest. Built of traditional Cotswold stone and set in the pretty hamlet of Lower Swell, it enjoys stunning views over the open countryside towards Stow-on-the-Wold. Bedrooms are filled with thoughtful extras, and each has a superb en suite bathroom with immaculate fittings. A spacious lounge with wood-burning stove has an intrinsic charm, while in the homely kitchen/dining room guests enjoy tasty country breakfasts at a communal table. This property sits in attractive mature gardens, and is close to plenty of excellent restaurants and inns.

RECOMMENDED IN THE AREA

Gardens such as Hidcote and Barnsley House; walks in stunning countryside; theatre at Stratford upon Avon (easy driving distance)

Hodgecombe Farm ♦♦♦♦

Spectacular views from a peaceful farmhouse on the Cotswold Way

☎ 01453 860365
📠 01453 860365

Map ref 2 - ST79

ULEY, GL11 5AN
In Uley on B4066 follow signs for
Coaley via Fop Street, after approx.
1m take farm track on sharp L ben)
3 Rooms, D £40-£46, No smoking,
Closed mid-Oct – mid-March

Views towards the Malverns, River Severn and the Forest of Dean are afforded from this impressive Victorian house, situated beneath the Uley Bury Roman Fort. Guests are welcome to enjoy the large garden, where breakfast can be taken on sunny mornings, and there are woodland walks available close by.

The house retains many original features and provides spacious double bedrooms including one with an en suite shower, one with a washbasin, and one twin. The large shared bathroom has a shower over the bath. Full English breakfast, with home-made jams and bread, is served until 9am and dinner (by prior arrangement – book 24 hours in advance) at 7pm. Accommodation cannot be provided for dogs or children under five.

RECOMMENDED IN THE AREA

Slimbridge Wildfowl Trust; Westonbirt Aboretum; Berkeley Castle

135

Wesley House ••••

An elegant restaurant combined with homely bedrooms where guests come to be pampered

☎ 01242 602366
📠 01242 602405
www.wesleyhouse.co.uk

Map ref 3 - SP02

High Street, WINCHCOMBE, GL54 5LJ
5 Rooms, S £48-£55 D £70-£80, No smoking in bedrooms or dining room , Closed 14 Jan-10 Feb

RECOMMENDED IN THE AREA

Sudeley Castle; Cotswolds; Cheltenham

An immaculately preserved half-timbered house dating from around 1435 is the charming setting for this award-winning restaurant with rooms. Many original features have been carefully retained and restored, including the large open fireplaces and exposed beams inside and out which are an integral part of the medieval structure. Despite is great age, the building offers every modern convenience, including five comfortable bedrooms filled with a generous range of thoughtful extras. All rooms have en suite and highly efficient bathrooms, and are individually decorated to enhance the period style. Named after the Methodist John Wesley who is reputed to have stayed here in 1779, this house is centred around its restaurant which is the holder of two AA rosettes. This elegant room with its tasteful flower arrangements is the setting for imaginative dinners and memorable breakfasts. Log fires and plump sofas make the cosy lounge/bar a difficult place to resist, and staff ensure that guests are well pampered.

Sudeley Hill Farm ◆◆◆◆

Lovely old farmhouse with homely comforts and majestic views

☎ 01242 602344
🖷 01242 602344
✉ scudamore4@aol.com

Map ref 3 - SP02

WINCHCOMBE, GL54 5JB
turn off B4632 in Winchcombe into Castle St, White Hart Inn on corner. Farm 0.75m on L
3 Rooms, S £30-£36 D £48-£50, No smoking in bedrooms or dining room , Closed Xmas

*T*he beautiful Cotswold countryside makes a splendid backdrop for this 15th-century mellow stone farmhouse. Outside there are immaculately kept gardens which guests are encouraged to enjoy, while inside the log fires and exposed beams create a memorable atmosphere. The comfortable en suite bedrooms are filled with thoughtful extras, while delicious country breakfasts are taken around a large table in the smart dining room. A guests' sitting room with huge inglenook fireplace and deep armchairs is a cosy place to retreat to in all weathers. This impressive house with its friendly atmosphere is set above Sudeley Castle with panoramic views of the valley.

RECOMMENDED IN THE AREA

Sudeley Castle (0.25 mile); excellent walking from the farm; Cotswold villages (10 mile radius)

Hampshire

A selection of places to eat from the AA Restaurant & AA Pub Guides

Restaurants

◎ Banks Bistro (Modern, Bistro-style)
Bank Street, Bishop's Waltham SO23 1AE
Tel 01489 896352 Fax 01489 896288

◎◎ Simply Poussin (Modern)
The Courtyard, Brookley Rd, Brockenhurst SO42 7RB
Tel 01590 623063 Fax 01590 623144

◎◎ Master Builder's House (Modern)
Bucklers Hard SO42 7XB
Tel 01590 616253 Fax 01590 616297

◎ Fat Olives (Brasserie-style)
30 South Street, Emsworth PO10 7EH
Tel 01243 377914

◎ Hour Glass (Modern, Traditional)
Burgate, Fordingbridge SP6 1LX
Tel 01425 652060 Fax 01425 656022

◎◎ JSW (Chic)
1 Heath Road, Petersfield GU31 4JE
Tel 01730 262030

◎◎ Hotel du Vin & Bistro (Bistro-style)
14 Southgate Street, Winchester SO21 2LT
Tel 01962 863588 Fax 01962 842458

Pubs

🍴 Globe on the Lake
The Soke, Broad Street, Alresford SO24 9DB
Tel 01962 732294 Fax 01962 736211

🍴 The Sun Inn
Sun Hill, Bentworth GU34 5JT
Tel 01420 562338

🍴 The Bell Inn
Brook SO43 7HE
Tel 023 8081 2214 Fax 023 8081 3958

🍴 The Flower Pots Inn
Cheriton SO24 0QQ
Tel 01962 771318 Fax 01962 771318

🍴 The Chestnut Horse
Easton SO21 1EG
Tel 01962 779257 Fax 01962 779014

🍴 The Plough Inn
Main Road, Sparsholt SO21 2NW
Tel 01962 776353 Fax 01962 776400

🍴 Wykeham Arms
75 Kingsgate, Winchester SO23 9PE
Tel 01962 853834 Fax 01962 854411

137

$\mathcal{T}$ilehurst ◆◆◆◆

Charming hosts and well-maintained house in a rural setting

☎ 01264 771437
📠 01264 773651
📧 tilehurst@compuserve.com

Map ref 3 - SU24

Furzedown Lane, Amport, ANDOVER, SP11 8BW
(turn off A303 W of Andover in direction of Amport. At next T-junct turn R, R again at next T-junct. 4th house on L past St Mary's church
3 Rooms, S £30 D £60, No smoking

$\mathcal{A}$ delightful modern house in secluded gardens, backing onto the grounds of Amport House. This charming country property is close to Thruxton race circuit in a picturesque village, and offers comfortable accommodation that appeals to both the business and leisure guest. There are plenty of useful extras in the smart bedrooms, one of which has en suite facilities; hospitality trays and colour televisions are standard fittings.

A choice of breakfasts is offered in the dining room. In the summer, guests are welcome to sit in the gardens and swim in the outdoor pool.

RECOMMENDED IN THE AREA

The Hawk Conservancy (1.5 miles); Museum of Army Flying, Middle Wallop; golf, horseriding and fishing nearby

---

$\mathcal{T}$he Hatchings ◆◆◆◆

Ideal for the holiday or business guest, with particularly well-equipped rooms

☎ 01256 465279

Map ref 3 - SU64

Woods Lane, Cliddesden, BASINGSTOKE, RG25 2JF
(M3 J6, take Alton road A339 & pass under road bridge. Immediate R signed Cliddesden B3046, after 0.75m pass garage, take next R
3 Rooms, S £27.50-£29.50 D £50-£60, No smoking

$\mathcal{T}$he pretty village of Cliddesden is home to a welcoming guest house, ideal for the holiday or business guest. Bedrooms overlook the garden and are spacious and relaxing, each with its own dining table, comfortable chair or sofa and television. Rooms also have microwave ovens, toasters and fridges. Guests are very welcome to bring in evening meals to enjoy in their own room. Cereals, bread, jam, fruit and biscuits are freely available and a delicious cooked breakfast is served in the room at any time in the morning. The Hatchings is well located for places of interest in the South of England, plus fast trains to London, and there is a car park at the rear for secure parking.

RECOMMENDED IN THE AREA

Watercress Steam Railway at Old Alresford; Milestones Museum in Basingstoke; The Vyne (National Trust house and garden)

*T*he Cottage Hotel ◆◆◆◆

350 year old forester's cottage in the New Forest

☎ 01590 622296
📠 01590 623014
✉ terry_eisner@
compuserve.com
www.cottagehotel.org

Map ref 3 - SU20

Sway Road, BROCKENHURST,
SO42 7SH
from Lyndhurst on A337, turn R at
Careys Manor into Grigg Lane.
0.5m to x-roads, straight over,
cottage next to war memorial
7 Rooms, S £55-£85 D £70-£95, No
smoking in bedrooms or dining room ,
Closed Dec-Jan

*T*his small hotel, with its own charming garden and patio, and residents' car park, is just 200 yards from open forest and the centre of Brockenhurst. This is one of the few New Forest villages where ponies and cattle still have right of way as they roam and graze the land. The owners have a dog, so check with them if you want to bring yours. There are no facilities for children under ten. Low ceilings, oak beams, and the open fire in the snug lounge with bar, give the place all the character of a traditional cottage. The en suite bedrooms are fresh and cosy. The owners are happy to lend you binoculars, books, and boules for the garden. A hearty English breakfast is served, as well as afternoon tea (on the patio in summer).

RECOMMENDED IN THE AREA

National Motor Museum at Beaulieu (5 miles); Exbury Gardens (4 miles); walking, cycling and horseriding locally

*S*tar Inn ◆◆◆◆ ◉◉

Peaceful country inn with overnight accommodation and award-winning food

☎ 01794 340225
📠 01264 810954
✉ info@starinn-uk.com
www.starinn-uk.com

Map ref 3 - SU22

EAST TYTHERLEY, Nr Romsey,
SO51 0LW
N from Romsey on A3057, L on
B3084 at Dukes head, L in Dunbridge
at railway crossing R at end of road,
follow rd for 1.5 mile
3 Rooms, S £45 D £60, No smoking in
bedrooms or dining room , Closed 25-
26 Dec

A hand-carved children's playground is a recent popular addition.

*T*he local cricket ground adjoins the pleasant gardens of this quintessentially English country pub set in a quiet Hampshire village. The old coaching inn serves excellent, value for money food throughout the public areas - the beamed restaurant is the recipient of two AA Rosettes - offering very good value for money. Three en suite bedrooms are housed in a separate purpose-built annexe, with comfortable beds and plenty of peace to attract guests. Breakfast is another highlight of a stay here, with fresh food and a variety of hot and cold choices available.

RECOMMENDED IN THE AREA

Mottisfont Abbey (National Trust) (1 mile); fishing on the Test and Dun (1 mile); Romsey, Broadlands and New Forest (5 miles)

$\mathcal{A}$lderholt Mill ◆◆◆◆

Working water mill convenient for the New Forest

☎ 01425 653130
🖷 01425 652868
📧 alderholt-mill@zetnet.co.uk
www.alderholtmill.co.uk

Map ref 3 - SU11

Sandleheath Road,
FORDINGBRIDGE, SP6 1PU
M27 J1, B3078 through town, R hand
fork (Damerham/Sandleheath). L at
x-roads in Sandleheath, 0.5m over
bridge on R
4 Rooms, D £42-£50, No smoking

*O*ne of the many pleasures of staying at Alderholt Mill is the home-baked bread, made from wholemeal flour stone ground in the water mill that forms part of this delightful property. All the machinery is still intact and guests can watch milling demonstrations. Bedrooms are individually decorated and furnished and all have en suite facilities. A comfortable lounge is also provided. The dining room is decorated in lovely bold colours, and a super breakfast is served around one large table. Dinner is available by prior arrangement. This is the ideal spot from which to discover the New Forest with its wonderful walks and cycle paths. The Wiltshire Downs and Dorset coast are also within easy reach.

RECOMMENDED IN THE AREA

Salisbury Cathedral; Beaulieu National Motor Museum; Kingston Lacey

---

$\mathcal{T}$he Three Lions ◆◆◆◆◆ ◉◉◉

Restaurant with rooms set in extensive gardens

☎ 01425 652489
🖷 01425 656144
📧 the3lions@btinternet.com

Map ref 3 - SU11

Stuckton, FORDINGBRIDGE,
SP6 2HF
0.5m E of Fordingbridge from A338 or
B3078. At Q8 garage follow Three
Lions tourist signs
3 Rooms, S £59-£75 D £65-£85,
No smoking in bedrooms or dining
room , Closed 18 Jan-12 Feb

*T*he Three Lions began life as a farmhouse in 1863, it later became a pub and in the 1980s a restaurant of some repute. These days it is widely known and celebrated for the excellent cuisine of chef Michael Womersley. The establishment, owned and run by Michael and his wife Jayne, is quietly located in the hamlet of Stuckton, near Fordingbridge, on the edge of the New Forest. A cosy bar area leads into the restaurant, where a log fire is lit in cooler weather. Michael creates outstanding dishes using the freshest ingredients. His menu reflects international influences and is supported by a selection of fine wines from his cellar of some 150 bins. Accommodation in the Lions' Den comprises light and airy double rooms with modern furniture and bold fabrics. The house is surrounded by two and a half acres of gardens, including a hot tub, ideal for an hour's relaxation.

RECOMMENDED IN THE AREA

Breamore House and Museum; Hinton Ampner; Wilton House

$\mathcal{A}$uplands ♦♦♦♦

Town centre establishment close to the New Forest and coast

☎ 01590 675944
🖷 01590 675944
✉ s.broomfield@btinternet.com
www.btinternet.com/~auplands

Map ref 3 - SZ39

22 Southampton Road, LYMINGTON, SO41 9GG
on A337 just before town centre, almost opposite supermarket
3 Rooms, S £25-£40 D £38-£50,
No smoking

Sue and Graham Broomfield welcome guests to their comfortable guest house, conveniently located just a short walk from Lymington High Street. Private parking to the front and rear is a particular bonus in this popular New Forest location, as is the small outdoor swimming pool. Guests have access to bedrooms at all times, and a choice of double, twin and family rooms is available, all offering en suite facilities, remote control colour television and tea and coffee making equipment. A hearty breakfast is served in the attractive dining room, and for other meals there's a good range of pubs and restaurants nearby.

RECOMMENDED IN THE AREA

South coast beaches including Bournemouth (20 minute drive); Lymington harbour for sailing; explore the New Forest

$\mathcal{R}$ufus House Hotel ♦♦♦♦

Family-run Victorian hotel ideally located in the New Forest

☎ 023 8028 2930
🖷 023 8028 2930
✉ rufushousehotel@ dcintna.fsnet.co.uk

Map ref 3 - SU30

Southampton Road, LYNDHURST, SO43 7BQ
From centre of Lyndhurst turn towards Totton, on L opp open forest
11 Rooms, S £30-£40 D £55-£75,
No smoking in bedrooms or dining room

Comfy beds and super breakfasts are highlights of this friendly and immaculately maintained establishment - according to some very satisfied customers. The hotel overlooks the New Forest from its location on the edge of Lyndhurst, so is convenient for all local attractions, including lovely walks and forest trails. The guests' lounge and many of the bedrooms offer forest views, and all rooms have en suite facilities, tea and coffee-making equipment, colour television, video recorders and radios. The turret bedrooms also have their own lounge areas, while the guests' lounge or garden terrace provide a relaxing spot following a good day's sight-seeing.

RECOMMENDED IN THE AREA

The New Forest (opposite the house); Beaulieu Motor Museum (10 minute drive); Southampton – historical city and shopping centre (15 minutes)

*A*lma Mater ◆◆◆◆

Chalet-style bungalow within walking distance of the beach

☎ 01590 642811
🖶 01590 642811
✉ bandbalmamater@aol.com
www.newforest.demon.co.uk/
almamate.htm

Map ref 3 - SZ29

4 Knowland Drive, MILFORD ON SEA,
Lymington, SO41 0RH
from Lymington on A337, L onto
B3058 to Milford on Sea. Pass South
Lawn Hotel, turn R into Manor Road,
1st L into Knowland Drive. Alma Mater
is 3rd bungalow on R.
3 Rooms, S £35 D £45-£50, No
smoking

*E*ileen and John Haywood enjoy welcoming guests to their beautifully kept home, a large detached bungalow overlooking landscaped gardens in a quiet residential area. It is a good base for exploring the New Forest and coast, and the yachting centre of Lymington is close by. Ample secure parking is provided and the attractive village and the beach are just a walk away. A full four-course or continental breakfast is served in the dining room, and evening meals are available on request. The comfortable en suite bedrooms are all centrally heated and equipped with televisions, radios, and tea and coffee-making provisions.

RECOMMENDED IN THE AREA

Keyhaven with passenger ferry to Yarmouth and Hurst Castle (1 mile); Lymington – Saturday market and antique shops; Beaulieu village and Motor Museum (short drive)

*L*ittle Forest Lodge ◆◆◆◆◆

Delightful house in peaceful gardens, handy for Forest and coast. Dogs very welcome

☎ 01425 478848 🖶 01425 473564

Map ref 3 - SU10

Poulner Hill, RINGWOOD, BH24 3HS
1.5m E on A31
6 Rooms, S £30-£40 D £50-£70, No smoking in
bedrooms or dining room

*T*wo and a half acres of lovely gardens and woodland surround this spacious Edwardian house. Set in an ideal location for exploring the New Forest and the coast, it offers the opportunity to relax and be pampered.

High standards of hospitality and comfort are provided by the friendly owners, and the en suite bedrooms are well-equipped and inviting; a ground floor garden room provides spacious accommodation for families and pet owners.

A beautiful sitting room and bar with a log fire is the ideal place in which to relax after a busy day, with its views out over the garden. Enjoyable home-cooked food is served in the evening and at breakfast time.

RECOMMENDED IN THE AREA

Bournemouth; Beaulieu Motor Museum; Exbury Gardens

*T*he Old Cottage ♦♦♦♦

Lovely thatched cottage in a peaceful rural location

☎ 01425 477956
📠 01425 477956
✉ forestgatewines@
btinternet.com

Map ref 3 - SU10

Cowpitts Lane, North Poulner,
RINGWOOD, BH24 3JX
from A31 E/bound, 0.75m E of
Ringwood. L to Hangersley. 1st R,
0.5m to x-rds. Straight over, after
100yds cottage on R
3 Rooms, D £44-£56, No smoking,
Closed Dec

*T*his 300-year-old thatched cottage in a beautiful garden setting has a peaceful rural location in the New Forest. The market town of Ringwood is just a mile and a half away, and here visitors will find a good choice of pubs and restaurants for their evening meal. The cottage's original features, including beams and an inglenook fireplace, are full of old-world character, while modern plumbing ensures contemporary standards of comfort. Mr and Mrs Theobald are hospitable hosts, greeting their guests with offers of refreshment. The bedrooms are well equipped; one has a four-poster bed and all have en suite facilities. A freshly cooked breakfast is served in the elegant lounge/dining room.

RECOMMENDED IN THE AREA

New Forest; south coast; Salisbury

*O*ld Stacks ♦♦♦♦

Warm hospitality and well sprung beds in a pretty bungalow

☎ 01425 473840
📠 01425 473840
✉ oldstacksbandb@aol.com

Map ref 3 - SU10

154 Hightown Road, RINGWOOD,
BH24 1NP
A31 W towards Bournemouth. 1m
before Ringwood take slip road to
'Hightown' & Owl sanctuary. L into
Eastfield Ln. 0.5m R into Hightown
Rd. Old Stacks 2nd on L.
2 Rooms, S £30 D £40-£46, No
smoking, Closed Xmas & New Year

*J*oan and Brian Peck warmly welcome you to Old Stacks, their delightful spacious bungalow where home from home hospitality awaits in a truly relaxing atmosphere. Set in lovely gardens which are directly accessed from one of the bedrooms, Old Stacks is ideally placed for exploring the New Forest and the picturesque Dorset coast. A good night's sleep is guaranteed in well sprung beds. Both the twin en suite and the double bedroom with private bathroom have hospitality trays and television. Warming log fires are lit in the comfortable lounge in cold weather, and hearty breakfasts are served at a communal table in a sunny dining room. There is a country inn nearby.

RECOMMENDED IN THE AREA

New Forest Owl Sanctuary (0.5 mile); Beaulieu National Motor Museum and Palace House (30 minute drive); Kingston Lacey and Mompesson House (National Trust) (easy driving distance)

143

The Nurse's Cottage •••••

Former district nurse's cottage with luxury accommodation and a restaurant serving memorable freshly-cooked food

☎ 01590 683402
📠 01590 683402
✉ nurses.cottage@lineone.net
www.hants.gov.uk/tourist/hotels

Map ref 3 - SZ29

Station Road, SWAY, Lymington, SO41 6BA
off B3055 in village next to post office
3 Rooms, S £60 D £100, No smoking,
Closed 2wks Mar, 3wks Nov

RECOMMENDED IN THE AREA

The New Forest – walking, cycling etc.; ArtSway Gallery; Lymington – shops and yachting marina

*E*ach of the bedrooms is named after one of the district nurses who occupied this cottage from 1927 to 1983, although were those ladies to return they would scarcely recognise their old quarters. The property has been converted into luxury accommodation, with sumptuously comfortable bedrooms providing a host of extras, and de-luxe bathrooms kitted out with fluffy towels and lovely toiletries. There is a choice of twin room (Southerden, 1927-37), a single (Lipscombe (1937-67) and a double (Gibson (1967-83), all offering telephone with modem connections, television/video, fridge with fresh milk, fruit and chocolates. The Garden Room Restaurant, open to non-residents, serves a range of carefully-prepared dishes complemented by an extensive wine list, and award-winning breakfasts (AA Best Breakfast 2000/1) also served in this pretty room leave a delicious taste in the mouth. Hospitality from chef/owner Tony Barnfield is very warm and welcoming, and his high standards are maintained by his well-trained staff.

$\mathcal{L}$andguard Lodge ♦♦♦♦

Cosy, clean and comfortable accommodation in a quiet residential location, handy for amenities

☎ 023 8063 6904
🖷 023 8063 2258
✉ landguard.lodge@141.com
www.landguardlodge.co.uk

Map ref 3 - SU41

21 Landguard Road,
SOUTHAMPTON, SO15 5DL
north of railway station between Hill
Lane & Shirley Road
10 Rooms, S £29 D £49, No smoking
in bedrooms or dining room

A warm welcome awaits you at this professionally run establishment, which is conveniently located for the city centre, ferry terminals and docks. Bedrooms are neatly laid out and freshly decorated. All bedrooms have en suite shower rooms and are equipped with colour televisions and tea and coffee making facilities. A pretty lounge is also provided for guests' use. The dining room faces east and attracts all the morning sunshine, a tasty breakfast is served here including a good choice of hot items. Children under five years cannot be accommodated, neither can dogs (with the exception of guide dogs). Some car parking is provided.

RECOMMENDED IN THE AREA

Southampton Maritime Museum, medieval wall walks & West Quay shopping mall; Beaulieu (14 miles); Marwell Zoological Park (10 miles)

$\mathcal{M}$ay Cottage ♦♦♦♦

Period house in a picturesque village location

☎ 01264 771241
🖷 01264 771770

Map ref 3 - SU24

THRUXTON, Andover, SP11 8LZ
from A303 take sign Thruxton (village only), situated almost opposite George Inn
3 Rooms, S £35-£40 D £55-£70,
No smoking, Closed Xmas

May Cottage, dating from 1740, is set in a secluded garden next to a pretty thatch and cob barn. Originally the barn housed carriages and horses from the nearby George Inn, but during the 1700s and 1800s it was used as the village mortuary. These days it provides the attractive setting for Tom and Fiona Biddolph's splendid breakfasts. The cottage is comfortably furnished and the all-en suite bedrooms are equipped with televisions, radios, hairdryers and tea trays. The location is ideal for visiting Stonehenge, Salisbury and Winchester. Other attractions include the Hawk Conservancy and several stately homes and gardens. Ample private parking is provided.

RECOMMENDED IN THE AREA

Stonehenge (10 miles); Hawk Conservancy (1 mile); Salisbury (15 miles)

145

Herefordshire

A selection of places to eat from the AA Restaurant & AA Pub Guides

Restaurants

⊛⊛⊛⊛⊛ La Rive (Modern, Chic)
Bridge Street, Hereford HR4 9RG
Tel 01432 349008 Fax 01432 349012

⊛⊛ The Stagg Inn and Restaurant (Traditional)
Titley, Kington HR5 3RL
Tel 01544 230221

⊛ Feathers Hotel (Traditional)
High Street, Ledbury HR8 1DS
Tel 01531 635266 Fax 01531 638955

⊛ Chase Hotel (Traditional)
Gloucester Road, Ross-on-Wye HR9 5LH
Tel 01989 763161 Fax 01989 768330

⊛ Glewstone Court (Traditional, Country-house)
Glewstone, Ross-on Wye HR9 6AW
Tel 01989 770367 Fax 01989 770282

⊛⊛ Pengethley Manor (Country-house)
Pengethley Park, Ross-on-Wye HR9 6LL
Tel 01989 730211 Fax 01989 739238

⊛ The Salutation Inn (Traditional)
Market Pitch, Weobley HR4 8SJ
Tel 01544 318443

Pubs

⊛ Riverside Inn & Restaurant
Aymestrey HR6 9ST
Tel 01568 708440 Fax 01568 709058

⊛ The Roebuck Inn
Brimfield SY8 4NE
Tel 01584 711230 Fax 01584 711654

⊛ The Ancient Camp Inn
Ruckhall, Hereford HR2 9QX
Tel 01981 250449 Fax 01981 251581

⊛ Stockton Cross Inn
Kimbolton HR6 0HD
Tel 01568 612509

⊛ The Lough Pool Inn
Sellack HR9 6LX
Tel 01989 730236 Fax 01989 730462

⊛ Three Crowns Inn
Ullingswick HR1 3JQ
Tel 01432 820279 Fax 01432 820279

⊛ The Sun Inn
Winforton HR3 6EA
Tel 01544 327677 Fax 01544 327677

The Bowens Country House ♦♦♦♦

Country house by the church in a small Herefordshire village

☎ 01432 860430
🖷 01432 860430
✉ thebowenshotel@aol.com
www.thebowenshotel.co.uk

Map ref 2 - SO53

FOWNHOPE, HR1 4PS
6m SE of Hereford on B4224. In
Fownhope, premises opp church
10 Rooms, S £38 D £50-£65,
No smoking in dining room

*T*his 300-year-old stone house has been altered and extended, but it is still small enough to provide a cheerful, friendly atmosphere.

The owners have preserved the original character, rediscovering a magnificent inglenook fireplace in the oak-beamed lounge, and reclaiming the old lawn tennis court, which had been lost to a field for forty years. It is convenient for the Wye Valley, the Brecons and Malverns, and there is ample car parking space. The gardens are beautiful, with mature trees and shrubs. Besides the tennis court, there is a putting green.

Bedrooms, overlooking the gardens and countryside, all have modern en suite facilities, TV and telephone, four are ground floor Courtyard rooms. Delicious home-made meals are served in the oak-beamed dining room. The vegetable garden and greenhouse provide much of the produce.

RECOMMENDED IN THE AREA

Visit the 'black and white' villages of Herefordshire; Hereford Cathedral and the world famous Mappa Mundi; Eastnor Castle.

Felton House ◆◆◆◆

A former rectory of great charm where breakfast is always memorable

☎ 01432 820366
📠 01432 820366
✉ bandb@ereal.net
www.bandbherefordshire.co.uk

Map ref 2 - SO54

Felton, HEREFORD, HR1 3PH
signposted off A417 between A49 and
A465 beside Felton church
4 Rooms, S £25 D £50, No smoking,
Closed 24-28 Dec

A country house of immense character set in four acres of tranquil gardens looking out onto the Welsh mountains. The house is authentically furnished in 19th-century style, including comfortable four-poster and antique beds. Bedrooms are equipped with complimentary refreshments which may be enjoyed in the library, the garden room or the lovely gardens themselves, and en suites have quality towels and toiletries. Breakfast offers a real 'Flavour of Herefordshire', with a large choice of dishes using the finest local produce. Unsurprisingly this meal has won awards for its quality and innovation. This family home provides the highest levels of comfort, hospitality and service.

RECOMMENDED IN THE AREA

Hereford Cathedral chained library and Mappa Mundi; Eastnor Castle; Hay-on-Wye

Bodenham Farm ◆◆◆◆

Delightful 18th-century farmhouse set in a conservation area

☎ 01531 660222
✉ bodenhamfarm@lineone.net

Map ref 2 - SO63

Much Marcle, LEDBURY, HR8 2NJ
M50 J4 follow A449 towards Ledbury, property
4m on left
4 Rooms, S £22.50-£25 D £45-£50, No smoking

Set on the lower slopes of Marcle Ridge, just outside the village of Much Marcle, this Grade II listed farmhouse nestles in wooded grounds and offers spacious rooms, full of charm and character. Over two hundred years old, the house has been carefully restored and retains many original features, such as oak beams and polished elm floors.

There are two double bedrooms with four-poster bed, one en suite and one with private bathroom, plus another double en suite room. (Or a twin if preferred). All have colour television and tea and coffee making facilities. Guests have exclusive use of the large drawing room, and ample parking is available

RECOMMENDED IN THE AREA

Malvern Hills; Hellens House, Much Marcle; fine half-timbered buildings in Ledbury

Hills Farm ♦♦♦♦♦

Modern comforts and 16th-century features with glorious views

☎ 01568 750205
🖷 01568 750306
✉ conolly@bigwig.net

Map ref 2 - SO56

Leysters, LEOMINSTER, HR6 0HP
exit A4112 Leominster to Tenbury
Wells rd. On edge of Leysters
5 Rooms, S £43-£48 D £58-£62,
No smoking, Closed Nov-Feb

Guests are treated to a genuinely warm welcome at this attractive and peaceful farmhouse. With its glorious views across the surrounding countryside, the elevated property is ideal for those wanting to relax and absorb the rural ambience. The accommodation is a mixture of exposed 16th-century beams and modern comforts.

Two bedrooms in the main house and three in converted barns offer a high degree of luxury, with their en suite or private facilities, quality towels and toiletries, and spaciousness. Food is another important aspect of a stay

here, and the cosy dining room is the setting for delicious breakfasts and imaginative dinners. Jane Conolly was AA Landlady of the Year 1999-2000.

RECOMMENDED IN THE AREA

Ludlow (10 miles); Berrington Hall (National Trust) (4 miles); Hampton Court Gardens (6 miles)

Cwm Craig Farm ♦♦♦♦

Georgian farmhouse set amid lovely countryside

☎ 01432 840250
🖷 01432 840250

Map ref 2 - SO53

LITTLE DEWCHURCH, HR2 6PS
A49 from Ross rdbt, 2nd R from rdbt,
cont to Little Dewchurch, R in village.
Cwm Craig 1st farm on L
3 Rooms, D £38-£40, No smoking in
bedrooms and dining room

Cwm Craig Farm is situated midway between Hereford and Ross-on-Wye and stands on the edge of the village surrounded by superb countryside. It is a Georgian property retaining many original features and offering spacious accommodation furnished with fine period pieces.

The bedrooms are all en suite and include two doubles and a family room. Guests

have access to their rooms all day, and colour televisions and hospitality trays are provided. Home-cooked breakfasts are served in the dining room and morning room around large tables, and guests can relax in the sitting room or the games room with its three-quarter-size snooker/pool table and dartboard. Pets cannot be accommodated.

RECOMMENDED IN THE AREA

Hereford Cathedral and city; Forest of Dean; Wye Valley

Lumleys ♦♦♦♦

Victorian building with modern comforts in a lovely setting

☎ 01600 890040
📠 0870 7062378
✉ helen@lumleys.force9.co.uk
www.lumleys.force9.co.uk/

Map ref 2 - SO52

Kern Bridge, Bishopswood, ROSS-ON-WYE, HR9 5QT
A40 turn off at Goodrich onto B4229 over Kern Bridge. Right at Inn On The Wye approx 400yds past inn opp picnic ground
3 Rooms, D £46-£55, No smoking

An early Victorian roadside hostelry, Lumleys has been transformed into a quality modern guest house while retaining much of its original character. The house is situated south of the historic town, on the banks of the River Wye, in a designated area of outstanding natural beauty. From Lumleys you can see Goodrich Castle, with Symonds Yat and the Royal Forest of Dean not far away.

The comfortable en suite bedrooms offer plenty of thoughtful extras. There are some fine period pieces and ornaments in the public areas, all very much in keeping with the style of the property. Helen Mattis and Judith Hayworth are caring hosts, welcoming guests to their home with justifiable pride. They were 1999 AA Landlady of the Year finalists.

RECOMMENDED IN THE AREA

Symonds Yat; Forest of Dean; Goodrich Castle

Norton House ♦♦♦♦

Listed building set in an area of outstanding natural beauty

☎ 01600 890046
📠 01600 890045
✉ norton@
    osconwhi.source.co.uk
www.norton-house.com

Map ref 2 - SO51

Whitchurch, Symonds Yat, SYMONDS YAT [WEST], HR9 6DJ
A40 sliproad for Whitchurch, R over A40, 1st L to T-junct, turn L, located 300yd on R past Memorial Hall
3 Rooms, S £28-£32 D £44-£48, No smoking, Closed 25 Dec

Originally a farmhouse, dating back 300 years, the house has a wealth of character retained in the locally quarried stone walls, flagstone floors and oak beams. Friendly hospitality is a notable feature, and traditional English, vegetarian and continental along with a choice of speciality breakfasts are offered. Guests are seated at a mahogany table in a dining room full of curios, with a fine old dresser and inglenook fireplace. Evening meals are available, served by candlelight and oil lamp. Bedrooms, including one four-poster room, are all fully en suite, with remote control television, hot drinks and mineral water, patchwork quilts, crisp cotton sheets, fluffy white towels and fresh flowers. Dogs welcome by arrangement; no children under 12.

RECOMMENDED IN THE AREA

Symonds Yat and Royal Forest of Dean; Hereford city and Hay on Wye; border castles (within easy reach)

149

Kent

A selection of places to eat from the AA Restaurant & AA Pub Guides

Restaurants

Souffle Restaurant (Classic, French)
31 The Green, Bearsted ME14 4DN
Tel 01622 737065 Fax 01622 737065

West House Restaurant (Traditional)
28 High Street, Biddenham TN27 8AH
Tel 01580 291341 Fax 01580 291341

Augustine's Restaurant (Modern)
1 & 2 Longport, Canterbury CT1 1PE
Tel 01227 453063

The Dove (Rustic)
Plumpudding Lane, Dargate, Canterbury
ME13 9HB
Tel 01227 751360

Soho South (Rustic, Bistro-style)
23 Stone Street,Cranbrook TN17 3HF
Tel 01580 714666 Fax 01580 715653

Dunkerleys Hotel (Modern, English)
19 Beach Street, Deal CT14 7AH
Tel 01304 375016 Fax 01304 380187

Haxted Mill & Riverside Brasserie (Rustic)
Haxted Road, Edenbridge TN8 6PU
Tel 01732 862914 Fax 01732 865705

Sandgate Hotel Restaurant La Terrace
(Classic, French)
The Esplanade, Sandgate, Folkestone CT20 3DY
Tel 01303 220444 Fax 01303 220496

The Lime Tree (Classic, French)
8-10 The Limes, The Square, Lenham ME17 2PL
Tel 01622 859509 Fax 01622 850096

Fishermans Wharf (Rustic, Formal)
The Quay, Sandwich CT13 9RU
Tel 01304 613636 Fax 01304 620707

Rankins (French, Rustic)
The Street, Sissinghurst TN17 2JH
Tel 01580 713964

Right on the Green
15 Church Road, Southborough, Royal
Tunbridge Wells TN4 0RX
Tel 01892 513161 Fax 01892 513161

The Tagore (Modern Indian)
4 Neville Street, Royal Tunbridge Wells TN2 5SA
Tel 01892 615100 Fax 01892 549877

Wife of Bath Restaurant (Country-house,
Traditional)
4 Upper Bridge Street, Wye TN25 5AF
Tel 01233 812540 Fax 01233 813630

Pubs

The Three Chimneys
Biddenham Road TN27 8LW
Tel 01580 291472 Fax 01580 820042

The Castle Inn
Chiddingstone TN8 7AH
Tel 01892 870247 Fax 01892 870808

The Albion Tavern
Front Brents, Faversham Creek ME13 7DH
Tel 01795 591411 Fax 01795 591411

Green Cross Inn
Goudhurst TN17 1HA
Tel 01580 211200 Fax 01580 212905

Red Lion
The Green, Hernhill ME13 9JR
Tel 01227 752990 Fax 01227 752990

The Harrow Inn
Common Road, Ightham TN15 9EB
Tel 01732 885912

The Plough
High Cross Road, Ivy Hatch TN15 0NL
Tel 01732 810268 Fax 01732 810451

King William IV
4 High Street, Littlebourne CT3 1UN
Tel 01227 721244 Fax 01227 721244

The George Inn
44 The Street, Newnham ME9 0LL
Tel 01795 890237 Fax 01795 890587

The Dering Arms
Station Road, Pluckley TN27 0RR
Tel 01233 840371 Fax 01233 840498

The Chequers Inn
The Street, Smarden TN27 8QA
01233 770217 Fax 01233 770623

The Bottle House Inn
Coldharbour Road, Smarts Hill TN11 8ET
Tel 01892 870306 Fax 01892 871094

Royal Wells Inn
Mount Ephraim, Royal Tunbridge Wells
TN4 8BE
Tel 01892 511188 Fax 01892 511908

The Sportsman
Faversham Road, Whitstable CT5 4BP
01227 273370

*B*ishopsdale Oast ♦♦♦♦

Peaceful restored oast house with stunning views from all bedrooms

☎ 01580 291027
✆ 01580 292321
✉ drysdale@
**   bishopsdaleoast.co.uk**
www.bishopsdaleoast.co.uk

Map ref 4 - TQ83

BIDDENDEN, TN27 8DR
A28, Tenterden-Rolvenden road, first right after Tenterden into Cranbrook Rd, 2.5m to sign for B&B on L, turn L and follow signs
4 Rooms, S £45 D £50-£60, No smoking in bedrooms

Converted and restored from a ruin in 1984, this beautiful 18th-century oast house now offers stylish accommodation. Peacefully located in mature gardens with outstanding views, it offers a delightful terrace where meals can be taken in warm weather, and areas of wild flowers and grasses as well as lawns with croquet. Two of the comfortable bedrooms have direct access to the garden, and all rooms have luxury en suite bathrooms. Imaginative dinners cooked by prior arrangement feature vegetables and herbs from the organic garden, and there's a spacious sitting room with a roaring fire.

RECOMMENDED IN THE AREA

Hever, Bodiam and Leeds Castles; Chartwell, Knole and Ightham Mote; Sissinghurst Gardens

*M*agnolia House ♦♦♦♦♦

Late Georgian home near Canterbury centre, with luxury four-poster suite

☎ / ✆ 01227 765121
✉ magnolia_house_
**   canterbury@yahoo.com**
http://freespace.virgin.net/
magnolia.canterbury

Map ref 4 - TR15

36 St Dunstan's Terrace,
CANTERBURY, CT2 8AX
Leave A2 for Canterbury. L at 1st rdbt approaching city (signed University). 3rd R
7 Rooms, S £48-£65 D £78-£125, No smoking

Ann and John Davies welcome guests to their Late Georgian home (circa 1830), set in a quiet residential street just a five minute stroll from the city's West Gate Towers. There is a cosy lounge stocked with local and national information. The en suite bedrooms, (one with a four-poster bed) are tastefully decorated and equipped to the highest standard. Wallpapers with smart vertical stripes and fresh flowers give a bright touch of charm and elegance throughout. Breakfast is a generous meal, catering for all diets and includes home-made preserves. It is taken in the dining room overlooking the attractive walled garden with its fish pond and terraces – a quiet haven for guests in summer.

RECOMMENDED IN THE AREA

Canterbury Cathedral (20 minute walk); Museum of the City (15 minute walk); Canterbury Tales Museum (15 minute walk)

Beesfield Farm.....

A delightful farmhouse nestling in Garden of England countryside, yet convenient for major road networks and Brands Hatch

☎ 01322 863900
📠 01322 863900
✉ kim.vingoe@
    btinternet.com

Map ref 4 - TQ56

Beesfield Lane, FARNINGHAM,
DA4 0LA
Turn off A20 to A225 left to
Beesfield Lane, farm 0.5m on left.
3 Rooms, D £80, No smoking,
Closed Dec-Jan

RECOMMENDED IN THE AREA

Bluewater Shopping Centre (10 minute drive); beautiful walks (from the farm); Eagle Heights Bird of Prey Centre

*H*ospitable owners Kim and Douglas Vingoe welcome guests to Beesfield Farm, where close attention to detail is the key to customer satisfaction. The house lies in 300 acres of rural farmland in a designated Area of Outstanding Natural Beauty, an ideal location for exploring the Weald of Kent and visiting the nearby grand prix circuit at Brands Hatch. The bedrooms are individually appointed to a high standard and all of them have well designed en suite facilities. Options include the golden cupid room or the invigorating Roman shower room, though all the rooms have a luxurious feel with many welcoming touches, such as biscuits, chocolates, fresh flowers, milk and mineral water. A full English breakfast is served in the elegant dining room or outside on the garden patio in summer, and local organic produce is used wherever possible. A comfortable lounge is provided for guests and ample car parking in the grounds.

*H*arbourside B&B Hotel ♦♦♦♦♦

Exceptional accommodation with sea-views in this cliff-top location

☎ 01303 246824 📠 01303 241299
✉ joy@harboursidehotel.com
www.harboursidehotel.com

Map ref 4 - TR23

14 Wear Bay Road, FOLKESTONE, CT19 6AT
M20 J13, follow signs to country park. Turn off A259, then A260 into Wear Bay Rd, hotel 1m
6 Rooms, S £30-£40 D £80-£90, No smoking

On his retirement from the Royal Engineers, Colonel Ray Pye and his wife, Joy, opened their home on the harbour to guests. No detail is overlooked and personal attention is paid to guests' every requirement. All en suite bedrooms are individually designed, charmingly decorated and exceptionally well-equipped, with for instance television, radio alarm, trouser press, hair dryer. Additional, individual facilities come with different bedrooms and quality is in evidence throughout. This extends to breakfast, the lovely garden, and the three tastefully appointed lounges. Guests feel comfortable and at home here. Folkestone's attractions are within a short walking distance of the hotel.

RECOMMENDED IN THE AREA

Eurotunnel & Cross Channel ports; Canterbury Cathedral & Leeds Castle; Kentish Gardens & Coast

*S*outhgate-Little Fowlers ♦♦♦♦♦

Listed property with views over the Kent and Sussex borders

☎ 01580 752526
📠 01580 752526
✉ Susan.Woodard@
    southgate.uk.net
www.southgate.uk.net

Map ref 4 - TQ73

Rye Road, HAWKHURST, Cranbrook, TN18 5DA
On A268, approx 0.25m from traffic lights in village eastwards on Rye Rd
2 Rooms, Double/twin £55-£60, No smoking, Closed Nov-Feb

Dating back 300 years, the former dower house to Fowlers Park provides charming accommodation set in mature gardens; the perfect base for enjoying the coastline of Kent and Sussex and an area rich in castles, gardens and stately homes. Spacious bedrooms, in the 17th-century part of the house, are tastefully decorated and thoughtfully equipped with en suite facilities, televisions, radio alarms, fridges and complimentary tea and coffee. One room has an attractive four-poster bed. There is an oak-beamed sitting room, and breakfast is served in the Victorian conservatory, complete with Muscat vine and flowering plants, or in the elegant dining room. A choice of pubs and restaurants is but a stroll away.

RECOMMENDED IN THE AREA

Sissinghurst Gardens; Rye; Bodiam Castle

The Wren's Nest ♦♦♦♦♦

Friendly family-run guest house in a beautiful setting

☎ 01580 754919
🖷 01580 754919

Map ref 4 - TQ72

Hastings Road, HAWKHURST,
TN18 4RT
turn off A229 and bear L onto B2244,
0.75m on L before Hawkhurst Fish
Farm
3 Rooms, S £45-£49, D £55-£59

RECOMMENDED IN THE AREA

*Bodiam Castle; Sissinghurst Gardens;
Merriments Gardens*

Guests are assured of a warm welcome at this immaculately kept guest house, which is surrounded by lakes and open countryside rich in wildlife. It has its own lovely gardens providing ample secure parking.

Bedrooms are located in a barn conversion, traditional in style with oak-beamed vaulted ceilings. The rooms are luxuriously spacious, with a sitting area and coffee table, full en suite facilities, remote control televisions, radio alarms and hairdryers. The attractive dining room is part of the main house and breakfast is served at individual pine tables. Ideal base for Sissinghurst, Great Dixter, Merriments, Batemans and Bodiam Castle.

Conway House ♦♦♦♦

Quality accommodation with a homely atmosphere in a convenient location

☎ 01622 688287
🖷 01622 662589
🄴 conwayhouse@
    ukgateway.net
www.conwayhouse.
ukgateway.net

Map ref 4 - TQ75

12 Conway Road, MAIDSTONE,
ME16 0HD
exit M20 J5, L onto A20, at traffic
lights/crossroads (with BP petrol
station) R into Conway Rd
3 Rooms, S £30-£40 D £40-£45, No
smoking in dining room or lounge

Situated in a peaceful area with easy access to both the motorway and the town centre, Conway House is an ideal base for touring Kent, Sussex and Surrey and is just an hour from London or Dover. The private car parking is also an asset. Welcoming proprietors Sue and Tony Backhouse provide attractively presented, modern accommodation with co-ordinated décor and soft furnishings. Rooms are supplied with thoughtful extras, and one has en suite facilities. After a good night's sleep in one of the extremely comfortable beds, guests are served breakfast at one large table in the pleasantly appointed dining room. This room also offers lounge seating.

RECOMMENDED IN THE AREA

Leeds Castle (10 minute drive); Sissinghurst Gardens (30 minute drive); Hever Castle or Dover Castle and channel port (65 minute drive)

Langley Oast ♦♦♦♦

Huge circular bedrooms and welcoming, amenable hosts

☎ 01622 863523
📠 01622 863523
✉ margaret@
langleyoast.freeserve.co.uk

Map ref 4 - TQ75

Langley Park, Langley, MAIDSTONE,
ME17 3NQ
From junct 6 follow signs to
Maidstone town centre then Hastings.
At rdbt take the A274 to Tenterden.
Past Parkwood Business Estate turn
right into lane signposted Maidstone
Golf Centre
3 Rooms, S £28-£50 D £45-£70, No
smoking, Closed Xmas

A beautiful Kentish oast house once owned by the local brewery, and now providing superb guest accommodation for the discerning visitor. The converted and tastefully modernised accommodation includes two 24foot circular bedrooms housed in the roundel towers, one with a jacuzzi in its en suite bathroom. Two twin rooms also have half-tester canopies. Breakfast is taken in the airy roundel dining room with its views of the garden and countryside, and the nearby swan lake is a pleasant stroll away.

This quiet location makes an ideal base for touring around the many attractions of this part of Kent.

RECOMMENDED IN THE AREA

Leeds Castle, Hever Castle, Dover Castle; Sissinghurst Gardens; Canterbury and Rochester

Ringlestone Inn & Farmhouse Hotel ♦♦♦♦♦

An unspoilt Kentish inn with a wonderful atmosphere and exclusive accommodation

☎ 01622 859900
📠 01622 859966
✉ bookings@ringlestone.com
www.ringlestone.com

Map ref 4 - TQ85

Ringlestone Hamlet, Harrietsham,
MAIDSTONE, ME17 1NX
M20 J8 onto A20. At rdbt opp Great
Danes Hotel take L to Hollingbourne.
Through village, R at x-roads at top of
hill
4 Rooms, S £79-£96 D £89-£96, No
smoking in bedrooms, Closed 25 Dec

A 16th-century former monks' hospice has been converted to provide luxury exclusive accommodation in a picturesque Kentish village. Despite its many modern comforts and amenities, the farmhouse and adjacent inn have changed little since medieval times, and many original features remain intact. Bedrooms are beautifully decorated and furnished to a very high standard, and with their smart en suite bathrooms and many homely extras they offer a warm and comfortable place to stay. In the summer the garden is an idyllic spot in which to enjoy a meal or a drink, and a wide variety of food is served in the bar and restaurant. The hotel specialises in English fruit wines and liqueurs.

RECOMMENDED IN THE AREA

Chatham Historic Dockyard; Hever Castle; Sissinghurst

Merzie Meadows ♦♦♦♦♦

A delightful house set in extensive grounds with a swimming pool

☎ 01622 820500
🖷 01622 820500
www.smoothhound.co.uk/
hotels/merzie./html
Map ref 4 - TQ74
Hunton Road, MARDEN, Tonbridge,
TN12 9SL
from A229 Maidstone/Hastings rd,
take B2079 towards Marden, 1st right
into Underlyn Lane for app 2.5m.
Large Chainhurst sign, R into drive
2 Rooms, S £40 D £50-£60, No
smoking, Closed 15 Dec- 31st Jan

Merzie Meadows is a unique, beautifully situated country home, set in lovely rural surroundings in the heart of Kent, convenient for London, Maidstone and Ashford. A warm welcome is assured, and there are two luxurious double en suite bedrooms, one a suite, which provide guests with space, privacy and comfort. The tastefully decorated bedrooms have TV, tea and coffee making facilities, and overlook the extensive landscaped grounds, which include an outdoor swimming pool (unheated).

Parking is available for guests. Children under 14 cannot be accommodated.

RECOMMENDED IN THE AREA

Leeds Castle (20 minute drive); Sissinghurst Castle and gardens (20 minute drive); Scotney Castle Garden (20 minute drive)

Danehurst House ♦♦♦♦♦

Charming gabled house with pretty gardens in a Kent village

☎ 01892 527739
🖷 01892 514804
📧 danehurst@zoom.co.uk

Map ref 4 - TQ53

41 Lower Green Road, Rusthall,
ROYAL TUNBRIDGE WELLS,
TN4 8TW
from Tunbridge Wells take A264 W,
1.5m turn R past Spa Hotel, R at x-
rds, Lower Green Rd 200yds on L
4 Rooms, S £45-£60 D £50-£80, No
smoking, Closed Xmas, last week Aug

Just west of the historic spa town at Tunbridge Wells stands Angela and Michael Godbold's spacious Victorian home. The lovely garden has a waterfall and koi carp swim happily in the pond, while indoors style and flair in both décor and furnishings enhance the house's intrinsic charm.

There is a baby grand piano in the drawing room and the Victorian style conservatory is a delightful setting for breakfast, be it full English, fish, cold meats or continental. The four cosy bedrooms have en suite facilities, and are equipped with a wealth of thoughtful extras and notably comfortable beds. Private parking available. No children under eight. No pets.

RECOMMENDED IN THE AREA

Tunbridge Wells Museum and Art Gallery; Penshurst Place and Gardens; Scotney Castle Garden

Lancashire

A selection of places to eat from the AA Restaurant & AA Pub Guides

Restaurants

◎ Dunkenhalgh Hotel
Blackburn Road, Clayton-le-Moors, Accrington
BB5 5JP
Tel 01254 398021 Fax 01254 872230

◎ Kwizeen (Bistro-style)
47-49 Kings Street, Blackpool FY1 3EJ
Tel 01253 290045

◎ Shaw Hill Hotel (Traditional, Country-house)
Preston Road, Whittle-le-Woods, Chorley
PR6 7PP
Tel 01257 269221 Fax 01257 261223

◎◎◎ Paul Heathcote's Restaurant (Modern)
104-106 Higher Road, Longridge PR3 3SY
Tel 01722 784969 Fax 01772 785713

◎◎ Greens Bistro (Modern, Bistro-style)
3/9 St Andrews Road, St Annes on Sea, Lytham
FY8 1SX
Tel 01253 789990 Fax 01253 789908

◎ High Moor Inn (Rustic, Traditional)
Highmoor Lane, Wrightington WN6 9QA
Tel 01257 252364 01257 255120

Pubs

◧ Millstone Hotel
Church Lane, Mellor, Blackburn BB2 7JR
Tel 01254 813333 Fax 01254 812628

◧ Assheton Arms
Downham, Clitheroe BB7 4BJ
Tel 01200 441227

◧ The Bay Horse Inn
Forton LA2 0HR
Tel 01254 791204 Fax 01524 791204

◧ The Eagle & Child
Maltkiln Lane, Parbold L40 3SG
Tel 01257 462297 Fax 01257 462297

◧ The Spread Eagle
Sawley BB7 4NH
Tel 01200 441202 Fax 01200 441973

◧ The Inn at Whitewell
Forest of Bowland, Whitewell BB7 3AT
Tel 01200 448222 Fax 01200 448298

◧ The Mulberry Tree
Wrightington WN6 9SE
Tel 01257 451400 Fax 01257 451400

The Old Coach House ♦♦♦♦♦

Historic building close to the beach and pier

☎ 01253 349195
🖷 01253 344330
✉ blackpool@
theoldcoachhouse.freeserve.
co.uk
www.theoldcoachhouse.
freeserve.co.uk

Map ref 5 - SD33

50 Dean Street, BLACKPOOL,
FY4 1BP
at end of M55 follow signs for main car park, at 2nd mini rdbt turn R, at lights turn L, next lights L, Dean St 2nd on R
11 Rooms, S £45-£60 D £60-£70, No smoking in bedrooms or dining room

Claire and Mark Smith are charming hosts, offering a warm and friendly welcome to their lovely home. The Old Coach House is just a few minutes walk from Blackpool's famous Pleasure Beach and South Pier. The bedrooms are attractively decorated and furnished, including 3 rooms with four-poster beds, and a special Roman room. All the rooms have en suite facilities and offer many thoughtful extras, such as colour televisions, hairdryers, trouser presses, and tea and coffee making equipment. Guests enjoy their meals in the period-style dining room, while the delightful conservatory is a comfortable place to sit at the end of the day. For those seeking total relaxation, a huge open air jacuzzi is located in the pretty water garden and is popular with guests throughout the year.

RECOMMENDED IN THE AREA

Blackpool Tower; Pleasure Beach; Lytham St Annes

$\mathcal{M}$iddle Flass Lodge ◆◆◆◆

Attractive stone-built converted barn offering good food and smart accommodation

☎ 01200 447259
🖷 01200 447300
✉ joan@
   middleflasslodge.fsnet.co.uk
www.mflodge.freeservers.com

Map ref 5 - SD75

Settle Rd, BOLTON-BY-BOWLAND, BB7 4NY
A59 Skipton to Clitheroe rd, take turn for Sawley. Follow sign for Bolton-by-Bowland at Copynook, 2nd L signed Middle Flass Lodge 2m on R
5 Rooms, S £28-£35 D £44-£58, No smoking

*I*dyllically situated in beautiful countryside within the Forest of Bowland, this guest house offers professional standards in a highly personal manner. Converted from a cow byre and barn, it offers stylish accommodation with exposed timbers adding character throughout. The smart modern bedrooms, including some family rooms, are all en suite and benefit from countryside views of the Ribble Valley. There is a residents' lounge with walking books and maps to browse through. A restaurant open to non-residents is a welcome feature, and the accomplished chef/owner produces good quality dinners made where possible from fresh local produce, and enhanced by a selection of wines and spirits.

RECOMMENDED IN THE AREA

Beautiful walks around Gisburn Forest (10 minute drive); National Trust House Gawthorpe Hall; shopping at Discounts

$\mathcal{E}$aves Barn Farm ◆◆◆◆

Exclusive farmhouse accommodation a short distance from Burnley

☎ 01282 771591
🖷 01282 771591
✉ mavis@eavesbarnfarm.co.uk
www.eavesbarnfarm.co.uk

Map ref 5 - SD73

Hapton, BURNLEY, BB12 7LP
M65 J9, turn R onto A679, at Hapton Inn turn R & after approx 1m L into lane between shop and houses
3 Rooms, S £25-£35 D £50-£70, No smoking in bedrooms or dining room , Closed Xmas/New Year

*E*aves Barn is a delightful farmhouse peacefully situated at the centre of a 30-acre mixed farm but within easy reach of major centres such as Burnley, Blackburn, Preston and Manchester, through the extensive motorway network. For tourists, the Yorkshire Dales, the Lake District and the Fylde Coast are all accessible. Individually designed bedrooms are equipped with en suite facilities and colour television, and thoughtfully provided with tea and coffee-making equipment and a tin of home-made biscuits. Traditional English breakfast is served in the conservatory, overlooking the attractive garden, and an elegant lounge with antique furnishings and a welcoming log fire is also available for guests' use

RECOMMENDED IN THE AREA

Gawthorpe Hall (National Trust) (5 minutes); "Pendle Hill", home of the Lancashire Witches; Ribble Valley, and famous Mill Shops

New Capernwray Farm ◆◆◆◆◆

Old farmhouse in beautiful countryside conveniently close to the M6

☎ 01524 734284
📠 01524 734284
📧 newcapfarm@aol.com
www.newcapfarm.co.uk

Map ref 5 - SD57

Capernwray, CARNFORTH, LA6 1AD
M6 J35, follow signs for Over Kellet. L
at village green in Over Kellett, house
on L after 1.7m
3 Rooms, S £45-£51 D £66-£78, No
smoking, Closed Nov-Feb

*T*his is no longer a working farm, but the farmhouse stands in two acres of grounds in a delightful rural location, five minutes from the M6, between the Lake District and the Yorkshire Dales. Guests are given the warmest of welcomes, greeted on arrival and offered tea or coffee. Built in 1697, the lounge has exposed stone wall and oak beams. One bedroom has a private bathroom, the other two have facilities en suite; they are fresh and airy with lovely views over the countryside. The full English breakfast, served in the intimate green dining room, includes home baked bread, local free range eggs, traditionally cured bacon and sausages. Dinner is served in informal house-party style, with the table lit by candles, set with silver, porcelain, and crystal. Guests are invited to bring their own wine.

RECOMMENDED IN THE AREA

Lake District National Park (20 minutes' drive); Yorkshire Dales National Park (30 minutes' drive); Lune Valley

Parr Hall Farm ◆◆◆◆

A pleasant beamed farmhouse in an interesting rural location

☎ 01257 451917
📠 01257 453749
📧 parrhall@talk21.com

Map ref 5 - SD51

Parr Lane, ECCLESTON, Chorley,
PR7 5SL
from M6 J27 take A5209 for Parbold,
then immediately R B5250 for
Eccleston. After 5m Parr Lane on R,
1st property on L
4 Rooms, S £25-£35 D £40-£50, No
smoking

A property of immense character, peacefully located in the countryside yet only a few miles from the M6. Parr Hall was built in 1721 for a gentleman farmer, and much of its original atmosphere has been retained. Further additions over a century later have also been converted and renovated to provide comfortable guest rooms, all with spacious en suite facilities, colour television and hospitality tray. The house was once surrounded by fruit orchards, but these are now mature gardens which guests are invited to enjoy. There are many well-known attractions nearby, and this is a good stopover from Scotland or the Lake District.

RECOMMENDED IN THE AREA

Lancashire coast – Blackpool, Southport, Morecambe Bay; good local walking and West Pennine Moors (10 miles); Rufford Old Hall, Gawthorpe Hall and Formby Point (National Trust)

159

Tulketh Hotel ♦♦♦♦

Elegant Edwardian hotel run by friendly proprietors

☎ 01772 726250
📠 01772 723743

Map ref 5 - SD53

209 Tulketh Road, Ashton-on-Ribble,
PRESTON, PR2 1ES
M6 J31, L onto A59 Preston then R
onto A5085 towards Blackpool. L at
St Andrews Church after 3m onto
Tulketh Rd
13 Rooms, S £37.50 D £49.50-£60,
No smoking in dining room,
Closed 20 Dec-4 Jan

Situated in a leafy area of Preston, less than two miles from the town centre, The Tulketh Hotel is conveniently situated for the Fylde Coast and the Lake District. The lovely Edwardian building retains many original features, including an impressive period reception area. It is beautifully decorated throughout and the en suite bedrooms are thoughtfully equipped with television, telephone, clock radio alarm, hair dryer and facilities for making drinks. One room offers a four-poster bed.

There is a comfortable lounge bar with a plentiful supply of books and magazines, and evening meals and breakfasts are served in the spacious dining room. There is parking for 14 cars.

RECOMMENDED IN THE AREA

Blackpool (16 miles); Lake District (40 miles); Trough of Bowland (10 miles)

Leicestershire

A selection of places to eat from the AA Restaurant & AA Pub Guides

Restaurants

🍽 The Priest House on the River
Kings Mills, Castle Donnington DE74 2RR
Tel 01332 810649

🍽 Sketchley Grange (Modern)
Sketchley Lane, Burbage, Hinckley LE10 3HU
Tel 01455 251133 Fax 01455 631384

🍽 The Tiffin (Classic, Chic)
1 De Montfort Street, Leicester LE1 7GE
Tel 0116 247 0420 Fax 0116 255 3737

🍽 Watsons Restaurant & Bar (Modern, Chic)
5-9 Upper Brown Street, Leicester LE1 5TE
Tel 0116 222 7770 Fax 0116 222 7771

🍽 The Three Swans Hotel (Traditional, International)
21 High Street, Market Harborough LE16 7NJ
Tel 01858 466644 Fax 01858 433101

🍽 Stapleford Park (Classic, Country-house)
Stapleford, Melton Mowbray LE14 2EF
Tel 01572 787522 Fax 01572 787651

Pubs

🍺 The Nag's Head
Hilltop, Castle Donnington DE74 2PR
Tel 01332 850652

🍺 The Bell Inn
Main Road, East Langton LE16 7TW
Tel 01858 545278 Fax 01858 545748

🍺 The Old Barn & Restaurant
Andrew's Lane, Glooston LE16 7ST
Tel 01858 545215 Fax 01858 545215

🍺 The Berwicke Arms
1 Eastgate, Hallaton LE16 8UB
Tel 01858 555217 Fax 01858 555598

🍺 The Crown Inn
Debdale Hill, Old Dalby LE14 3LF
Tel 01664 823134 Fax 01664 822638

🍺 The Cock Inn
Twycross Road, Sibson CV13 6LB
Tel 01827 880357 Fax 01827 880976

🍺 The Bakers Arms
Main Street, Thorpe Langton LE16 7TS
Tel 01856 545201

*K*naptoft House Farm & The Greenway ••••

Set near the peaceful rural borders of Leicestershire, Northamptonshire and Warwickshire, a picturesque farmhouse and bungalow

☎ 0116 247 8388
📠 0116 247 8388
✉ info@knaptoft.com
www.knaptoft.com

Map ref 3 - SP68

Bruntingthorpe Road, Nr Shearsby,
BRUNTINGTHORPE, Lutterworth,
LE17 6PR
Bruntingthorpe/Saddington x-roads turn off A5199 (former A50) for Bruntingthorpe, premises on L after 1m
6 Rooms, S £28 D £44, No smoking,
Closed Xmas/New Year

*T*aking its name from the nearby deserted medieval village of Knaptoft, this working farm and adjacent bungalow are set peacefully in 135 acres of beautiful Leicestershire countryside. Comfortable beds are a top priority, and the pretty bedrooms in both the farmhouse and The Greenway have been carefully furnished and decorated to complement their rural setting. Generous hospitality trays bring a touch of home, and there are fridges in both houses with fresh milk and cold drinks. All rooms, apart from one with adjacent facilities, have well-fitted en suite bathrooms. Each building also has a cosy sitting room with wood-burning stove and a west-facing conservatory where the afternoon sun can be enjoyed. Freshly-cooked breakfasts, or something lighter, are served in the comfortable farmhouse dining room with its views out over the gardens. Guests are welcome to fish by arrangement in the restored medieval fishponds which are a short walk across fields. Secluded parking is a bonus in this quiet place.

RECOMMENDED IN THE AREA

Foxton Locks/Grand Union Canal; Stanford Hall; National Space Centre – Leicester

ℬadgers Mount ◆◆◆◆

A quietly-located guest house with well-kept gardens

☎ 01455 848161
🖷 01455 848161
🄴 info@badgersmount.com
www.badgersmount.com

Map ref 3 - SK49

6 Station Road, Elmesthorpe,
HINCKLEY, LE9 7SG
on B581
12 Rooms, S £35-£42 D £45-£60, No
smoking in bedrooms or dining room

𝒜 large detached house set in spacious gardens, with a pleasant sunny patio and an outdoor swimming pool, heated in summer. Bedrooms are decorated and furnished to a high specification, and en suite bathrooms and lots of thoughtful touches are standard to all. One large room is ideal for a whole family, sleeping up to six people.

A chicken run in the garden ensures a constant supply of fresh eggs for breakfast, and light meals or roast dinners are available with appropriate notice, served in the airy dining room. There is also a loyalty bar where guests may gather in the evenings.

RECOMMENDED IN THE AREA

Space Centre at Leicester; Warwick Castle (35 minutes); Mallory Park Race Circuit (3.5 miles)

ℒincolnshire

A selection of places to eat from the AA Restaurant & AA Pub Guides

Restaurants

🏵 Branston Hall (Formal, Country-house)
Branston Park, Branston LN4 1PD
Tel 01522 793305 Fax 01522 790549

🏵 Kingsway Hotel (Traditional)
Kingsway, Cleethorpes DN35 0AE
Tel 01472 601122 Fax 01472 601381

🏵🏵🏵 Harry's Place (Country-house)
17 High Street, Great Gonerby, Grantham
NG31 8JS
Tel 01476 561780

🏵🏵 Harvey's Restaurant (Modern, Classic)
2 Louth Road, Scartho, Grimsby DN33 2EN
Tel 01472 750560

🏵🏵 Magpies Restaurant (Traditional)
71-75 East Street, Horncastle LN9 6AA
Tel 01507 527004 Fax 01507 524064

🏵 Jew's House (Classic, Traditional)
15 The Strait, Lincoln LN2 1JD
Tel 01522 524851 Fax 01522 520084

🏵 Cley Hall (Country-house)
22 High Street, Spalding PE11 1TX
Tel 01775 725157 Fax 01775 710785

Pubs

🍺 The Black Horse Inn
Grimsthorpe, Bourne PE10 0LY
Tel 01778 591247 Fax 01778 591373

🍺 Hare & Hounds Country Inn
The Green, Fulbeck NG32 3JJ
Tel 01400 272090 Fax 01400 273663

🍺 Pyewipe Inn
Fossebank, Saxiby Road, Lincoln LN1 2BG
Tel 01522 528708 Fax 01522 525009

🍺 The Wig & Mitre
30/32 Steep Hill, Lincoln LN2 1TL
Tel 01522 535190 Fax 01522 532402

🍺 Masons Arms
Cornmarket, Louth LN11 9PY
Tel 01507 609525

🍺 Red Lion Inn
Raithby PE23 4DS
Tel 01790 753727

🍺 The George at Stamford
71 St Martins, Stamford PE9 2LB
Tel 01780 750750 Fax 01780 750701

Abbottsford House ◆◆◆◆

A friendly welcome to this charming house with a well-tended garden

☎ 01522 826696
🖷 01522 826696

Map ref 8 - SK97

5 Yarborough Terrace, LINCOLN,
LN1 1HN
L off A1102. A15 North, premises 1m
from A46 bypass & A57 into city
3 Rooms, S £30-£35 D £44, No
smoking, Closed Xmas and New Year

There are lovely gardens at the rear of this end-of-terrace property, and superb views from the front overlooking the Trent Valley. The charming bedrooms are decorated and furnished in Victorian style, and equipped with plenty of useful little extras. A hospitality tray, television, trouser press, hairdryer and radio are standard in each room, and all share the splendid views.

The smart lounge/dining room offers comfortable seating, and there are separate tables for breakfast, which always features freshly-laid eggs.

Off street parking is a bonus in this quiet cul-de-sac, and the city is just a short walk away. Expect a warm welcome from pleasant owners.

RECOMMENDED IN THE AREA

Lincoln Cathedral (10 minute walk); Lincoln Castle (10 minute walk); Usher Gallery (15 minute walk with lovely views)

Carholme Guest House ◆◆◆◆

Close to the marina and university, a friendly and immaculately kept guest house

☎ 01522 531059
🖷 01522 511590
✉ farrelly@talk21.com
www.smoothhound.co.uk/
hotels/carholme.html

Map ref 8 - SK97

175 Carholme Road, LINCOLN,
LN1 1RU
turn off A46 bypass, house situated
on A57 past Lincoln Racecourse
5 Rooms, S £25-£30 D £40-£42, No
smoking

A beautiful walled garden is a delightful feature of this restored Edwardian house located close to the city and the university. Most of the original features have been carefully retained while the house has been updated with modern comforts. In the smart dining room an old range is a constant topic of conversation for the guests who gather around a communal table for breakfast.

Bedrooms are attractively decorated and well equipped, with either en suite or private bathrooms, plus television and courtesy tray; one room is on the ground floor. A great advantage is the locked, undercover parking which all guests are invited to use.

RECOMMENDED IN THE AREA

Lincoln Castle; Lincoln Cathedral; Museum of Lincolnshire Life

163

Carline Guesthouse ◆◆◆◆

*Double-fronted Edwardian house
in the heart of historic Lincoln*

☎ 01522 530422
📠 01522 530422

Map ref 8 - SK97

1-3 Carline Road, LINCOLN, LN1 1HL
L off A1102, A15 N. Premises 1m from
A46 bypass & A57 into city
8 Rooms, S £30-£35 D £42-£44, No
smoking, Closed Xmas & New Year

*J*ust a short stroll from the Bailgate shopping and restaurant area, with great views of the city and county, this guesthouse is convenient for the centre and all the major sites of interest, including the cathedral, castle and museums.

The house is comfortably appointed in traditional style, with tourist literature on hand to help you plan your stay. The spacious bedrooms are particularly appealing, all with individual decor, en suite facilities, hairdryers and tea and coffee-making equipment.

Full English breakfast is served at individual tables in the smart dining room/sitting room. Private off-street parking and garaging are a particular benefit in this city location.

RECOMMENDED IN THE AREA

Lincoln Castle; Hemswell Antiques Centre; Whisby Nature Park

St Clements Lodge ◆◆◆◆

Delightful guest house close to the cathedral

☎ 01522 521532
📠 01522 521532

Map ref 8 - SK97

21 Langworth Gate, LINCOLN,
LN2 4AD
approx 350yds to E of Lincoln
Cathedral, down Eastgate into
Langworthgate, 1st house on L 50yds
past Bull & Chain pub
3 Rooms, S £35 D -£52, No smoking

*S*t Clements Lodge is renowned for its hospitality, presided over by the friendly owners Janet and Bill Turner. The house is conveniently located for the cathedral, the castle, the shops and a good range of restaurants to suit all tastes. Guests can relax and leave the car behind, as private off-street parking is provided.

The bedrooms are luxuriously appointed and individually decorated. Double and twin rooms are available, two with en suite facilities and one with a private bathroom. All the rooms are equipped with television, hospitality trays and hairdryers. Breakfasts are cooked to order and served at individual tables in the dining room.

RECOMMENDED IN THE AREA

Daily guided tours of Lincoln Cathedral; daily guided tours of Lincoln Castle; boat trips on river from Brayford Pool Marina

Black Swan
Guest House ◄◄◄◄

Very friendly hosts offering an excellent service to match the comfortable modern bedrooms

☎ 01427 718878
🖷 01427 718878
📧 reservations@
    blackswan-marton.co.uk
www.blackswan-
marton.co.uk

Map ref 8 - SK88

21 High Street, MARTON,
Gainsborough, DN21 5AH
on A156, at junct with A1500, 12m
from Lincoln, 5m from
Gainsborough
8 Rooms, S £30-£50 D £50-£65,
No smoking

*G*uests are invited to absorb the historic atmosphere at this delightfully restored 18th-century coaching inn. With a 17th-century cellar reputed to have sheltered Oliver Cromwell during the Battle of Gainsborough in 1643, the guest house is short of neither historical anecdote nor original features. Bedrooms in the house or converted stable block are homely and comfortable, and thoughtfully equipped, all with modern facilities including en suites. One of the bedrooms has a four-poster bed for special occasions. Visitors can also opt to stay on a self-catering basis in two of the bedrooms. Tasty breakfasts are served in the comfortable dining room, and there is also a very spacious and relaxing lounge where a wide selection of drinks is available from the bar servery. The hospitable owners offer an excellent standard of personal care to all their guests, and they are even willing to ferry people to and from the railway station, or the local pubs and restaurants.

RECOMMENDED IN THE AREA

Lincoln – Cathedral, Castle, Museums (15 minute drive); antiques at Hemswell, Swinderby and Newark (15-25 minutes); aviation heritage and memorials (10-30 minutes)

$\mathcal{B}$laven ✦✦✦✦

Hospitable establishment in a peaceful rural location

☎ 01673 838352
✉ blaven@amserve.net

Map ref 8 - TF19

Walesby Hill, Walesby, MARKET RASEN, LN8 3UW
from Market Rasen take A46 towards Grimsby, turn R at junct with A1103 then L at T-junct, Blaven 100yds on R
2 Rooms, No smoking

$\mathcal{G}$uests can expect a warm, friendly welcome and attentive service from Jacqy Braithwaite, the charming owner of this delightful house. It is situated in the village of Walesby at the foot of the Lincolnshire Wolds, and is surrounded by extensive, beautifully tended gardens.

The bedrooms are nicely furnished and equipped with a range of useful extras. Public rooms include a cosy dining room and a comfortably appointed conservatory, which overlooks the garden.

Blaven is conveniently located for visits to the coast and the historic city of Lincoln. It is also on the Viking Way and the Hull-Harwich cycle route.

A small parking area is provided at the front of the house.

RECOMMENDED IN THE AREA

Market Rasen Races (5 minutes); Cadwell Park (20 minutes); National Fishing Heritage Centre (30 minutes)

$\mathcal{L}$ondon

A selection of places to eat from the AA Restaurant & AA Pub Guides

Restaurants

◉ Restaurant Twentyfour (Modern, Minimalist)
Tower 42, Old Bond Street EC2N 1HQ
Tel 020 7877 2424 Fax 020 7877 7742

◉ Blue Print Café (Modern, Minimalist)
The Design Museum, 28 Shad Thames SE1 2YD
Tel 020 7378 7031 Fax 020 7357 8810

◉◉ Le Caprice Restaurant (Classic)
Arlington House, Arlington Street SW1A 1RT
Tel 020 7629 2239 Fax 020 7493 9040

◉◉ Bibendum (Classic)
Michelin House, 81 Fulham Road SW3 6RD
Tel 020 7581 5817 Fax 020 7823 7925

◉ Bistro 190 (Bistro-style)
190 Queen's Gate SW7 5EU
Tel 020 7581 5666 Fax 020 7581 8172

◉◉ Hilaire (Modern, Classic)
86 Old Brompton Road SW7 3LQ
Tel 020 7584 8993 Fax 020 7581 2949

◉◉ Archipelago (Eclectic)
110 Whitfield Street W1T 5ED
Tel 020 7383 3346 Fax 020 7383 7181

Pubs

◖ The Crown
223 Grove Road E3 5SW
Tel 020 8981 9998 Fax 020 8980 2336

◖ The Bleeding Heart Tavern
19 Greville Street EC1N 8SQ
Tel 020 7404 0333 Fax 020 7404 0333

◖ The Eagle
159 Farringdon Road EC1R 3AL
Tel 020 7837 1353 Fax 020 7689 5882

◖ The Salt House
63 Abbey Road NW8 0AE
Tel 020 7328 6626 Fax 020 7625 9168

◖ The Fire Station
150 Waterloo Road SE1 8SB
Tel 020 7620 2226 Fax 020 7633 9161

◖ Swag and Tails
10/11 Fairholt Street SW7 1EG
Tel 020 7584 6926 Fax 020 7581 9935

◖ The Cow Saloon Bar & Dining Room
89 Westbourne Park Road W2 5QH
Tel 020 7221 5400 Fax 020 7727 8687

The Gallery ••••

Opulent town house hotel with an artistic theme in a prime South Kensington location

☎ 020 7915 0000 📠 020 7915 4400 ✉ gallery@eeh.co.uk 🌐 www.eeh.co.uk

Map ref 3 - TQ27

8-10 Queensberry Place, South Kensington, LONDON SW7 2EA
turn off Cromwell Rd opposite Natural History Museum into Queensberry Place in South Kensington
36 Rooms, S £141-£171 D £152-£287, No smoking in dining room

RECOMMENDED IN THE AREA

Victoria and Albert Museum (5 minute walk); Harrods (10 minute walk); Kensington Palace (10 minute walk)

The concept behind The Gallery is 'the Victorian artist at home', and the hotel features original Victorian paintings and antiques throughout. The décor of the two master suites, 'Rosetti' and 'Leighton' is stunning. They each have a private roof terrace, Jacuzzi, fax and CD and DVD players. All the bedrooms are well appointed and have full en suite bathrooms with marble tiling, brass fittings and soft white bath towels. Sumptuous public rooms include the mahogany-panelled reception, lobby and lounge, and the Arts & Crafts-style Morris Room complete with an original Manxman piano and antique bar billiards table. The highest level of personal service is available 24-hours a day, and business guests benefit from two direct dial telephones in each room, ADSL links available round the clock in public areas, and a boardroom-style meeting room. For the culturally minded the Science, Natural History and Victoria & Albert Museums are virtually on the doorstep.

22 ◆◆◆◆

Quality and value in an outstanding London location between Baker Street and Oxford Street

☎ 020 7224 2990 📠 020 7224 1990 ✉ mc@22yorkstreet.prestel.co.uk
www.myrtle-cottage.co.uk/callis

Map ref 3 - TQ28

22 York Street, LONDON W1, W1U 6PX
From Marylebone Road go South into Baker Street towards Oxford Street, York Street is the second turning on the R.
12 Rooms, S £82.25 D £100, No smoking

RECOMMENDED IN THE AREA

Madame Tussauds, Regent's Park, London Zoo, Planetarium, Wallace Collection, Camden Lock

*I*deally located for the sights and the shops, this elegant town house is situated within walking distance of Oxford Street and very close to Baker Street tube station. A splendid staircase leads up to the bedrooms and comfortable first floor lounge, where guests can read, relax and make tea or coffee whenever it suits them. Breakfast is a convivial affair, with guests seated around the unusual antique dining table discussing their forays to the theatre, museums, restaurants and galleries. This is a continental-style meal, with hot croissants, toast, preserves, cheese, cereals and bananas, along with orange juice, tea, coffee or chocolate. The bedrooms all have en suite facilities, including a bath and shower. The rooms are also equipped with televisions and telephones. Other attractive features are the wooden floors, French antique pieces, and charming quilts and rugs. The house is strictly no-smoking throughout, though guests can go outside to smoke if they wish.

Norfolk

A selection of places to eat from the AA Restaurant & AA Pub Guides

Restaurants

Hoste Arms Hotel (Rustic)
The Green, Burnham Market PE31 8HD
Tel 01328 738777 Fax 01328 730103

Kings Head (Rustic)
26 Wroxham Road, Coltishall NR12 7EA
Tel 01603 737426 Fax 01603 737521

Ark Restaurant (Rustic)
The Street, Erpingham NR11 7QB
Tel 01263 761535 Fax 01263 761535

Rococo (Modern, British)
11 Saturday Market Place, King's Lynn
PE30 5DQ
Tel 01533 771483 Fax 01533 771483

Femi's (Modern)
42 King Street, Norwich NR1 1PD
Tel 01603 766010 Fax 01603 766010

Marco's Restaurant (Classic, Italian)
17 Pottergate, Norwich NR2 1DS
Tel 01603 624044

Lifeboat Inn (Traditional, Rustic)
Ship Lane, Thornham PE36 6LT
Tel 01485 512236 Fax 01485 512323

Pubs

The White Horse
Main Road, Brancaster Staithe PE31 8BY
Tel 01485 210262 Fax 01485 210930

Ratcatchers Inn
Easton Way, Eastgate NR10 4HA
Tel 01603 871430 Fax 01603 873343

Saracen's Head
Wolterton, Erpingham NR11 7LZ
Tel 01263 768909 Fax 01263 768993

The Rose & Crown
Old Church Road, Snettisham PE31 7LX
Tel 01485 541382 Fax 01485 543172

The Wildebeest Arms
82-86 Norwich Road, Stoke Holy Cross
NR14 8QJ
Tel 01508 492497 Fax 01508 494353

The Hare Arms
Stow Bardolph PE34 3HT
Tel 01366 382229 Fax 01366 385522

Three Horseshoes
Warham All Saints NR23 1NL
Tel 01328 710547

Shrublands Farm ♦♦♦♦

Eighteenth-century farmhouse in an area of outstanding natural beauty

☎ 01263 579297
📠 01263 579297
✉ youngman@farming.co.uk
www.broadland.com/shrublands

Map ref 4 - TG23

Church Street, Northrepps, CROMER,
NR27 0AA
turn off A149 to Northrepps, 2m from
Cromer. Through village, past Foundry
Arms on R for 50yds, house on L
behind trees
3 Rooms, S £27-£29 D £44-£48, No
smoking, Closed 23 Dec-1 Jan

Shrublands is a working family farm set in mature gardens amid 300 acres of arable farmland, ideal for exploring the coastline and countryside of rural North Norfolk. Old-fashioned hospitality is a distinguishing feature, with good farmhouse cooking from the Aga, based on home-grown and fresh local produce. Breakfast is taken at one large table in the dining room, and dinner is available October to March (bring your own wine). There is also a cosy lounge, with a log fire, books and television. All the bedrooms have colour television, radio alarms and tea and coffee-making facilities. One room is en suite and two have private bathrooms. No pets or children under 12.

RECOMMENDED IN THE AREA

National Trust houses – Blickling Hall and Felbrigg Hall (within 6 miles); safe sandy beaches at Cromer and Overstrand (2 miles); Blakeney Point – boat trips to see seals and bird sanctuary (15 miles)

*T*he Dial House ◆◆◆◆

An ideal guest house for a peaceful stay in West Norfolk

☎ 01366 388358
**✉ bookings@
   thedialhouse.co.uk**
www.thedialhouse.co.uk

Map ref 4 - TF60

12 Railway Road, DOWNHAM
MARKET, PE38 9EB
A10 follow signs for Downham
Market, at lights turn L & 1st R, follow
signs for Rail Station, at T-junct turn L,
house 100yds on R
3 Rooms, S £25-£33 D £35-£45, No
smoking

*G*uests to this delightful Georgian guest house are left in no doubt that Ann and David really care about their stay. A warm, friendly welcome is followed up by a high standard of hospitality, and this peaceful, comfortable house offers a chance to completely relax. The pretty en suite bedrooms are cosy and warm, especially in the winter, and well equipped with television and hospitality trays, with each decorated in co-ordinating colours. A bright and well-proportioned lounge makes a pleasant retreat. Breakfast and evening meals to suit all tastes are served at a large communal table in the dining room, and home-made bread and preserves are a house speciality.

RECOMMENDED IN THE AREA

Oxburgh Hall; Denver Windmill; the Wildfowl and Wetlands Trust at Welney

---

*H*eath Farmhouse ◆◆◆◆

A pretty pink-hued farmhouse serving good food

☎ 01986 788417

Map ref 4 - TM28

Homersfield, HARLESTON, IP20 0EX
turn off A143 onto B1062 towards
Flixton, over bridge past 'Suffolk' sign
& take 2nd farm entrance on left at AA
sign
2 Rooms, S £25 D £38, No smoking in
bedrooms or dining room

*H*eath Farmhouse dates from the 16th century, retaining many original features and a wealth of oak beams. Log fires are an appealing feature of winter stays. The bedrooms are spacious and comfortably furnished, with central heating in all rooms. The home-cooked dinners (available by prior arrangement) are produced in the farmhouse kitchen by the proprietor, Julia, and make use of local meat, fish and home-grown vegetables where possible. Special diets are catered for, and sandwich lunches can be prepared. The house is located near the river in the beautiful Waveney Valley, children are welcome.

RECOMMENDED IN THE AREA

Bungay Otter Trust; on the route of the Angles Way; Suffolk Coast and Southwold (30 minutes)

Claremont Guest House ♦♦♦♦

Versatile accommodation in a warm Victorian house

☎ 01485 533171

Map ref 4 - TF64

35 Greevegate, HUNSTANTON, PE36 6AF
off A149, turn L at Greevegate, opp
recreation ground. House is 300mtrs on R
before St Edmunds church
7 Rooms, S £23 D £38-£46, No smoking

A comfortable and welcoming guest house,
where visitors can expect warm hospitality
from the friendly owners. Bedrooms are individually
decorated and tastefully furnished, with plenty of
thoughtful extras to create a home-from-home
atmosphere. A ground floor room with access for
the disabled is a useful feature, and there are two
special bedrooms, one with a four-poster and the
other with a canopied bed. High standards of
cleanliness and maintenance make this attractive
property an inviting place for both the leisure and the
business guest. A weekly discount is available, as
are winter breaks (November–March).

RECOMMENDED IN THE AREA

*Sandringham, Holkham and Houghton Estates (within
12 miles radius); Snettisham and Titchwell Bird
Sanctuaries (within 4 miles); beautiful beaches and
resort attractions including the Princess Theatre (3
minute walk)*

The Gables ♦♦♦♦

*Stone-built property 100 yards
from the glorious sandy beach*

☎ 01485 532514

Map ref 4 - TF64

28 Austin Street, HUNSTANTON,
PE36 6AW
from A149 into Austin St, cross
Church St, Gables at bottom of road
on right at junct of Northgate/Austin
St
5 Rooms, S £25 D £36-£50, No
smoking

T he Gables, an Edwardian property built from traditional
Norfolk carrstone, makes an ideal base for exploring the
Norfolk coastline and countryside. Full English or continental
breakfast is served in the panelled dining room, and an
evening meal is offered, prepared from fresh local produce.
All the bedrooms have en suite facilities and most have
views of the sea and the new Boston Square Sensory Park.
Each room has central heating, double-glazing, colour
television, satellite channel, radio alarm, beverage-making
equipment and a razor point. Luxurious extras include bath
robes, hairdryers and toiletries. Guests have
access to rooms throughout the day.
Families are made very welcome, but pets
are not accommodated.

RECOMMENDED IN THE AREA

*Sandringham (5 miles); Heacham Lavender (2
miles); Titchwell RSPB Reserve (5 miles)*

Wallington Hall.....

Superior Grade I listed property in the West Norfolk countryside, offering smart, well-appointed accommodation

☎ 01553 811567
🖷 01553 810661
📧 luddington@ wallingtonhall.co.uk
www.wallingtonhall.co.uk

Map ref 4 - TF61

KING'S LYNN, PE33 0EP
Off A10 left heading North
3.5 miles from Downham Market
3 Rooms, S £50 D £80, No smoking in bedrooms or dining room

RECOMMENDED IN THE AREA

Sandringham House and Estate; Oxburgh Hall, Gardens and Estate; the Norfolk coast

Charming hosts welcome visitors to this impressive early Tudor house, and help to make even the shortest stay as memorable as possible. The Grade I listed property is set in landscaped gardens in a peaceful rural location, surrounded by 600 acres of a working family estate. Many interesting architectural features distinguish the rambling house, and despite its age, high levels of maintenance and care ensure that it continues to offer superior accommodation. Guests can enjoy lakeside walks, games of tennis and fishing within the grounds, and there are two sitting rooms in which to relax and savour the grand ambience. Breakfast is served at a large communal table in the paneled dining room, and all public facilities are exceptionally generous. The beautifully-appointed en suite bedrooms are individually decorated with attractive co-ordinated soft furnishings, and equipped with an abundance of useful extras. A newly-refurbished four poster master bedroom is superb.

Carr House ♦♦♦♦

Peacefully-located house, ideal for bird watchers and country lovers

☎ 01603 713041
✉ margotdunham@supanet.com

Map ref 4 - TG30

Low Road, Strumpshaw, NORWICH, NR13 4HT
from Norwich on A47 towards Gt Yarmouth turn R to Brundall, follow signs for RSPB to Low Rd. R & follow by-way sign 100yds to house
3 Rooms, S £25-£35 D £40-£50, No smoking in bedrooms or dining room

Just 15 minutes from the centre of Norwich and the Norfolk Broads, this attractive house overlooks Strumpshaw Fen RSPB reserve and its own large fishing lake. From this peaceful position in well-tended gardens it offers cheerfully-decorated bedrooms, thoughtfully equipped with many extras. Two rooms have en suite shower facilities, and the third has a private bathroom. Hospitality tray and television are standard. Guests have a choice of comfortable places in which to relax and unwind, and breakfast is served in the smart dining room looking out over the lake and bird breeding grounds; marsh harriers, swallowtail butterflies and Cetti's Warbler are the local speciality. There is plenty of parking space.

RECOMMENDED IN THE AREA

Blickling Hall, Felbrigg House and many more National Trust properties; How Hill conservation/Nature Reserve (10 miles); Audley End (20 miles), Castle Acre Priory (15 miles)

Northamptonshire

A selection of places to eat from the AA Restaurant & AA Pub Guides

Restaurants

⊛⊛ Fawsley Hall Hotel (Country-house)
Fawsley, Daventry NN11 3BA
Tel 01327 892000 Fax 01327 892001

⊛⊛ The Falcon Inn (Modern)
Fotheringhay PE8 5HZ
Tel 01832 226254 Fax 01832 226046

⊛ Kettering Park Hotel
Kettering Parkway, Kettering NN15 6XT
Tel 01536 416666 Fax 01536 416171

⊛ The Sun Inn (Classic, Country-house)
Main Street, Marston Trussel LE16 9TY
Tel 01858 465531 Fax 01858 433155

⊛ Roade House Restaurant (Modern)
16 High Street, Roade NN7 2NW
Tel 01604 863372 Fax 01604 862421

⊛ Bruernes Lock Restaurant
The Canalside, Stoke Bruerne NN12 7SB
Tel 01604 863654 Fax 01604 863330

⊛⊛ Vine House Restaurant (Modern)
100 High Street, Paulerspury, Towcester NN12 7NA
Tel 01327 811267 Fax 01327 811309

Pubs

🍺 The Queen's Head
High Street, Bulwick NN17 3DY
Tel 01780 450272

🍺 George and Dragon
Silver Street, Chacombe OX17 2JR
Tel 01295 711500

🍺 The Exeter Arms
Stamford Road, Easton-on-the-Hill PE9 3NS
Tel 01780 757503 Fax 01780 757503

🍺 The George Inn
Great Oxendon LE16 8NA
Tel 01858 465205 Fax 01858 465205

🍺 The White Swan
Seaton Road, Harringworth NN17 3AF
Tel 01572 747543 Fax 01572 747323

🍺 The Star Inn
Manor Road, Sulgrave OX17 2SA
Tel 01295 760389 Fax 01295 760991

🍺 The King's Head
Church Street, Wadenhoe PE8 5ST
Tel 01832 720024 Fax 01832 720024

$\mathcal{T}$hatches on the Green ◆◆◆◆

*Sixteenth-century former inn
located on the village green*

☎ 01536 266681
🖷 01536 266659
✉ tom@
   thatches-on-the-
   green.fsnet.co.uk
www.thatches-on-the-
green.fsnet.co.uk

Map ref 3 - SP98

9 School Lane, Weldon, CORBY,
NN17 3JN
on old A43 opposite The Woolpack on
village green
6 Rooms, S from £35 D from £60, No
smoking in bedrooms or dining room

$\mathcal{S}$ympathetic renovation of this thatched stone inn and adjoining cottages has provided a guest house of considerable charm set in superb landscaped gardens. Nothing is too much trouble for hosts Tom and Ann Nunnerley, who extend a very warm welcome to guests and are always on hand to help. Single, twin, double and family rooms are available, some in the main house and others in the courtyard. All are equipped with en suite facilities, television and tea/coffee provisions. A private thatched cottage sleeping three is also available. Breakfast and imaginative dinners are served in the attractive dining room, which also has a small bar.

RECOMMENDED IN THE AREA

Rockingham Speedway; Rockingham Castle; Deene Park

$\mathcal{N}$orthumberland

A selection of places to eat from the AA Restaurant & AA Pub Guides

Restaurants

◎ Victoria Hotel (Modern, Bistro)
Front Street, Bamburgh NE69 7BP
Tel 01668 214431 Fax 01668 214404

◎ Blue Bell Hotel (Classic)
Market Place, Belford NE70 7NE
Tel 01668 213543 Fax 01668 213787

◎ Riverdale Hall Hotel (Traditional, French)
Bellingham NE48 2JT
Tel 01434 220254 Fax 01434 220457

◎ Swallow George Hotel
Chollerford NE46 4EW
Tel 01434 681611 Fax 01434 681727

◎ Tillmouth Park Hotel (Classic, Country-house)
Cornhill-on Tweed TD12 4UU
Tel 01890 882255 Fax 01890 882540

◎ De Vere Slaley Hall (Modern)
Slaley, Hexham NE47 0BY
Tel 01434 673350 Fax 01434 673050

Pubs

◨ The Allenheads Inn
Allenheads NE47 9HJ
Tel 01434 685200 Fax 01434 685200

◨ The Manor House Inn
Carterway Heads DH8 9LX
Tel 01207 255628

◨ Queens Head Inn & Restaurant
Great Whittington NE19 2HP
Tel 01434 672267

◨ The Feathers Inn
Hedley on the Hill NE43 7SW
Tel 01661 843607 Fax 01661 843607

◨ Dipton Mill Inn
Dipton Mill Road, Hexham NE46 1YA
Tel 01434 606577

◨ Cook and Barker Inn
Newton the Moor NE65 9 JY
Tel 01665 575234 Fax 01665 575234

◨ Warenford Lodge
Warenford NE70 7HY
Tel 01668 213453 Fax 01668 213453

Low Dover ♦♦♦♦

Beach side property virtually surrounded by sea

☎ 01665 720291
🖷 01665 720291
✉ kathandbob@lowdover.co.uk
www.lowdover.co.uk

Map ref 10 - NU22

Harbour Road, BEADNELL, NE67 5BJ
from S leave A1 at Alnwick, onto
B1340 to Beadnell, from N leave A1 at
Belford onto B1342 thro' Seahouses
and on towards Beadnell. Follow
signpost to Beadnell Harbour, Low
Dover is last house on R, adj to beach
2 Rooms, D £54-£60, No smoking

Low Dover is located at the end of a peninsula at the village of Beadnell on the beautiful Heritage Coast. There is a sandy bay here and an 18th-century harbour incorporating National Trust lime kilns. Accommodation is provided in ground floor suites with bed linen for up to four people and independent access from the patio. The rooms are equipped with full en suite facilities and complimentary tea, coffee and biscuits. Both the patio and lounge overlook the gardens while the dining room affords panoramic sea views. The Farne Islands, Holy Island and several historic castles are within easy reach. Low Dover cannot accommodate divers, children under 12 or pets.

RECOMMENDED IN THE AREA

Farne Islands Nature Reserve (3 miles); Lindesfarne (Holy Island) (10 miles); Bamburgh Castle (5 miles)

Market Cross Guest House ♦♦♦♦

A fine period house where guests are cossetted and very well fed

☎ 01668 213013
✉ details@marketcross.net
www.marketcross.net

Map ref 10 - NU13

1 Church Street, BELFORD,
NE70 7LS
off A1 signposted Belford,
establishment 0.5m on R next to post
office
3 Rooms, S £25-£40 D £45-£55, No
smoking

Jill and John Hodge offer the sort of charming hospitality and friendship that encourages guests to return again and again to their attractive guest house. Added to the warmth of their presence is the comfort and quality of the accommodation: bedrooms are large and stylish, with sofas and armchairs, smart en suite facilities and hordes of pleasing extras like chocolates, flowers, and milk and fruit in the fridge.

Breakfast is a delightful feature, with an excellent choice of dishes which might include kedgeree, pancakes and griddle scones. A new lounge offers a really inviting place to relax after a busy day sightseeing or playing golf.

RECOMMENDED IN THE AREA

Lindesfarne (Holy Island) (15 minute drive); Bamburgh Castle (4 miles), Alnwick Castle ('Hogwarts' location in recent Harry Potter film) (13 miles); Farne Islands bird watching trips (10 miles)

*I*vy Cottage ♦♦♦♦♦

Care and comfort in a sleepy village setting

☎ 01890 820667
🖷 01890 820667

Map ref 10 - NT93

1 Croft Gardens, Crookham,
CORNHILL-ON-TWEED, TD12 4SY
A697, 10m N of Wooler, R into
Crookham village, 0.5m on R past
village hall.
2 Rooms, S £27.50-£29.50 D £55-
£59, No smoking

*T*op quality accommodation is offered at this stone-built property in the village of Crookham, surrounded by fabulous walking country and much of historic interest. There is a choice of twin or double bedrooms with private bathrooms, generous towels, bathrobes and Crabtree & Evelyn toiletries. Embroidered bed linen and fresh flowers provide a welcoming touch in the rooms, which are equipped with colour televisions, hairdryers and tea-making provisions. Breakfast is prepared from fresh local produce, home-made bread and preserves, and is served in the farmhouse-style kitchen or more formal dining room. Restaurant and bar meals are available at a pub in the village. Dogs can be accommodated by arrangement.

RECOMMENDED IN THE AREA

Holy Island, coastal castles and various historic houses (easy reach); walking in the Cheviot Hills, St Cuthbert's Way close by; horse riding, fishing, gliding and golfing nearby

*N*ottinghamshire

A selection of places to eat from the AA Restaurant & AA Pub Guides

Restaurants

Langar Hall (Country-house)
Langar NG13 9HG
Tel 01949 860559 Fax 01949 861045

Hart's Restaurant (Modern)
1 Standard Court, Nottingham NG1 6GN
Tel 0115 911 0666 Fax 0115 911 0611

Hotel des Clos (Classic)
Old Lenton Lane, Nottingham NG7 2SA
Tel 0115 986 6566 Fax 0115 986 0343

Merchants Restaurant (Modern, Chic)
29/31 High Pavement, Nottingham NG1 1HE
Tel 0115 958 9898 Fax 0115 852 3223

Rutland Square Hotel by the Castle (Modern, Chic)
St James Street, Nottingham NG1 6FJ
Tel 0115 941 1114 Fax 0115 941 0014

Sonny's (Modern, Minimalist)
3 Carlton Street, Hockley, Nottingham NG1 1NL
Tel 0115 947 3041 Fax 0115 950 7776

Pubs

Victoria Hotel
Dovecote Lane, Beeston NG9 1JG
Tel 0115 925 4049 Fax 0115 922 3537

Caunton Beck
Caunton NG23 6AB
Tel 01636 636973 Fax 01636 636828

The Martins Arms Inn
School Lane, Colston Bassett NG12 3FD
Tel 01949 81361 Fax 01949 81039

Robin Hood Inn
High Street, Elkesley DN22 8AJ
Tel 01777 838259

Ye Olde Trip to Jerusalem
1 Brewhouse Yard, Castle Road, Nottingham NG1 6AD
Tel 0115 947 3171 Fax 0115 950 1185

The Mussel & Crab
Tuxford NG22 0PJ
Tel 01777 870941 Fax 01777 871096

The Three Horse Shoes
High Street, Walkeringham DN10 4HR
Tel 01427 890959 Fax 01427 890437

Jerico Farm ♦♦♦♦

Peaceful rural setting for this quality farmhouse accommodation

☎ 01949 81733 ❺ 01949 81733
✉ info@jericofarm.co.uk
www.jericofarm.co.uk

Map ref 8 - SK63

Fosse Way, COTGRAVE, Nottingham, NG12 3HG
9m SE of Nottingham city centre. Jerico Farm on lane off A46 - 1m N of A46/A606 junction
3 Rooms, S £30 D £45, No smoking, Closed Xmas week

*I*deally located for both business and leisure guests, this family farm in 150 acres enjoys wonderful views over the Nottinghamshire wolds. Enjoy comprehensive farmhouse breakfasts, using fresh local produce, in the bright and attractive dining room. From here, you can look out on to the well-tended garden or, in cooler weather, relax by the wood-burning stove in the sitting room. Guest rooms are spacious and well furnished and equipped with practical and homely extras. Your hosts pride themselves on their high quality beds and bedding, making for a sound night's sleep. All rooms have private facilities, two are en suite.

RECOMMENDED IN THE AREA

Nottingham; Nottingham Universities; Trent Bridge Cricket; Holme Pierrepont Watersports Centre; Sherwood Forest

Browns ♦♦♦♦♦

Comfortable garden lodges, white doves, and exquisite cottage gardens

☎ 01909 720659
❺ 01909 720659
✉ browns@holbeck.fsnet.co.uk
www.brownsholbeck.co.uk

Map ref 8 - SK57

The Old Orchard Cottage, Holbeck, HOLBECK, S80 3NF
6m from M1 J30, 0.5m off A616 Sheffield/Newark road turn for Holbeck at x-rds
3 Rooms, S £38-£40 D £46-£56, No smoking in dining room or lounge, Closed Xmas week

*B*eautiful cottage gardens surround this delightful Queen Anne property, which nestles in a peaceful hamlet. Winding country lanes lead to this idyllic stone-built cottage, and guest rooms are housed in three separate lodges close to the main house, each offering high levels of comfort and guest en suite facilities. One room has a king-size four-poster and a fine spacious bathroom, and all the rooms have a television and courtesy tray. Breakfast is taken from a lengthy menu in the elegant dining room, and in the evening transport is provided to a nearby restaurant if required.

RECOMMENDED IN THE AREA

Sherwood Forest; Clumber Park; Bolsover Castle and other stately homes

177

Oxfordshire

A selection of places to eat from the AA Restaurant & AA Pub Guides

Restaurants

Blewbury Inn (Rustic, Country-house)
London Road, Blewbury OX11 9PD
Tel 01235 850496 Fax 01235 850496

The Goose (Modern)
Britwell Salome, OX9 5LG
Tel 01491 612304 Fax 01491 614822

Dexters Restaurant (Informal, Modern)
Market Place, Deddington OX15 0SE
Tel 01869 338813

White Hart Hotel (Country-house)
High Street, Dorchester-on-Thames OX10 7HN
Tel 01865 340073 Fax 01865 341082

Le Manoir Aux Quat' Saisons
(Modern French)
Great Milton OX44 7PD
Tel 01844 278881 Fax 01844 278847

The Crazy Bear Hotel (Chic)
Bear Lane, Stadhampton OX44 7UR
Tel 01865 890714 Fax 01865 400841

Spread Eagle Hotel (Traditional, French)
Cornmarket, Thame OX9 2BW
Tel 01844 213661 Fax 01844 261380

Pubs

The Boars Head
Church Street, Ardington OX12 8QA
Tel 01235 833254 Fax 01235 833254

The Inn for All Seasons
The Barringtons, Burford OX18 4TN
Tel 01451 844324 Fax 01451 844375

The Bull Inn
Sheep, Charlbury OX7 3RR
Tel 01608 810689

The Plough Hotel
Abingdon Road, Clifton Hampden OX14 3EG
Tel 01865 407811 Fax 01865 407136

The Five Horseshoes
Maidensgrove, Henley-on Thames RG9 6ET
Tel 01491 641282 Fax 01491 641086

The Jersey Arms
Middleton Stoney OX6 8SE
Tel 01869 343234 Fax 01869 343565

Crooked Billet
Stoke Row RG9 5PU
Tel 01491 681048 Fax 01491 682231

Dinckley Court ◆◆◆◆

Former farmhouse in mature gardens fronting the River Thames

☎ 01865 407763
🖷 01865 407010
✉ annette@dinckleycourt.co.uk

www.dinckleycourt.co.uk

Map ref 3 - SU59

Burcot, ABINGDON, OX14 3DP
from M40 J7 take A329, R onto A4074
Oxford rd, then A415 to Abingdon
4 Rooms, S £49 D £60, No smoking

Dinckley Court is a Victorian property set in 12 acres of grounds including a river frontage. The house has been carefully restored to provide comfortable accommodation for the modern business or leisure traveller. It is ideally situated for Oxford, Abingdon, Henley and routes to London. Fishing and boating facilities are available to guests. The cosy bedrooms have en suite bath and shower rooms, remote control televisions, and tea and coffee making equipment. Imaginative snacks and hot dishes are offered by room service, or dinner can be taken, by arrangement, in the homely kitchen at the large family table.

Annette Godfrey is a friendly and caring hostess, justifiably proud to welcome guests to her lovely home. Ample car parking is provided.

RECOMMENDED IN THE AREA

Historic village of Dorchester-upon-Thames (walking distance); Oxford's museums and colleges; Blenheim Palace

Rafters ....

Large modern half-timbered house in a pretty village setting close to Oxford and Abingdon

☎ 01865 391298 📠 391173
✉ b&b@graw.fsnet.co.uk

Map ref 3 - SU49

Abingdon Road, ABINGDON, OX13 6NU
from A34 take A415 towards Witney.
Rafters on A415 in Marcham by 1st
street light on R
3 Rooms, S £26-£45 D £38-£58,
No smoking

RECOMMENDED IN THE AREA

Visit Abingdon - one of England's oldest towns; walk the Ridgeway (10 minute drive); Blenheim Palace (15 minute drive away.)

Situated a mile from the A34 with its links to Oxford and the south coast, this imposing detatched house offers spacious bedrooms furnished in a mixture of British and Scandanavian styles. The superior double, with private balcony, has a big en suite bathroom while the other two rooms have private facilities. Many thoughtful extras all over the house invite guests to feel at home. You'll find bathrobes, fresh flowers and complimentary mineral water in your room, and be warmly welcomed with tea or coffee and a piece of homemade cake on arrival. Fresh orange juice, fruits, yoghurt and delicious homemade bread and preserves feature in the excellent breakfasts, as well as free-range eggs and local and organic produce. Ample off street parking is available.

The Knoll ♦♦♦♦

Peaceful home in landscaped gardens offering comfort and quality

☎ 0118 940 2705
🖷 0118 940 2705
✉ theknollhenley@aol.com
www.theknollhenley.com

Map ref 3 - SU77

Crowsley Road, Shiplake,
HENLEY-ON-THAMES, RG9 3JT
from Henley take A4155 towards
Reading, after 2m L at war memorial,
then 1st R into Crowsley Rd, 3rd
house on R
2 Rooms, S £45 D £54-£56, No
smoking in bedrooms or dining room

*D*iscover this lovingly restored home in the riverside village of Shiplake, close to Henley-on-Thames. Both ground floor bedrooms have en suite facilities, one featuring an adjoining children's room. Your host, a Landlady of the Year finalist, provides a tray laid with fine bone china and freshly made cookies, enticing you to make that morning cuppa or bedtime chocolate. Excellent breakfasts - full English or continental - feature home-made preserves, fresh fruit, juices and muffins. Breakfast is served in the family dining room, which is decorated in Regency style, with a Chinese influence. Details of local car tours and walks, with maps, and notes are provided by your hosts. Free Internet access is available.

RECOMMENDED IN THE AREA

Beautiful walks and drives in the Chilterns; Stonor Park and Basildon Park (easy driving distance); Beale Park (wildlife), River and Rowing Museum

Bould Farm ♦♦♦♦

Cotswold farmhouse with fabulous country views

☎ 01608 658850
🖷 01608 658850
✉ meyrick@
   bould-farm.fsnet.co.uk

Map ref 3 - SP22

IDBURY, OX7 6RT
leave A424 Burford/Stow-on-the-
Wold rd signed Idbury, through village,
farm on R. Or B4450 from Chipping
Norton, L after rail bridge signed
Idbury
3 Rooms, S £30D £45, No smoking,
Closed Dec-Jan

*L*ocated between Stow-on-the-Wold and Burford is the Meyrick family farm of 400 acres, part arable with a flock of pedigree Suffolk and Charollais sheep. The 17th-century farmhouse is set in attractive formal gardens and retains much of its original character, enhanced by the quality of the décor and furnishings. A cast iron stove and flagstone floor are features of the cosy breakfast room, and there is a comfortable sitting room where guests can relax. Two rooms, including the large family room, have en suite facilities, while the other double has a private bathroom. All are equipped with colour televisions, radios, hairdryers, and complimentary tea and coffee. Children under 12 stay half price.

RECOMMENDED IN THE AREA

Blenheim Palace; Stratford-upon-Avon; Snowshill Manor

Gables Guest House ♦♦♦♦

Very pleasant and attentive hosts and a comfortable, relaxing house

☎ 01865 862153
📠 01865 864054
✉ stay@gables-oxford.co.uk
www.oxfordcity.co.uk/
accom/gables

Map ref 3 - SP40

6 Cumnor Hill, OXFORD, OX2 9HA
M40 J9 take A34 towards Newbury, at junct with A420 exit A34 to rdbt, take Oxford/Botley turn off, turn R at T-junct, then 500yds on R
6 Rooms, S £28-£30 D £46-£55,
No smoking, Closed 24 Dec-1 Jan

As might be expected at the home of a former AA Landlady of the Year, standards of welcome, hospitality, and service exceed all expectations. Guests are made to feel at home at this comfortable house, quietly located on the edge of the city. The bedrooms are immaculately presented and well furnished, each with en suite facilities and satellite television, video and direct dial telephone.

The conservatory lounge overlooking an extensive garden is a natural place to sit and relax. Tasty breakfasts, whether the full English choice or some innovative alternatives, is a real treat, and one of the reasons for the high level of returning visitors.

RECOMMENDED IN THE AREA

Oxford University; Blenheim Palace; Cotswold towns and villages

The Star Inn ♦♦♦♦

Character inn a mile and a half from the Ridgeway

☎ 01235 751539
📠 01235 751539
✉ star.inn@amserve.net

Map ref 3 - SU38

Watery Lane, Sparsholt, WANTAGE, OX12 9PL
from B5507, 4m W of Wantage turn R to Sparsholt. The Star Inn is signed
8 Rooms, D £55, No smoking in bedrooms or dining room

Very much a focal point of the local community, this 17th-century village inn achieves a good balance between character and comfort. Original features include exposed beams and a polished flagstone floor in the attractive dining room, and a good selection of ales and home-cooked dishes are served. The modern bedrooms, all with en suite facilities, are located in a sympathetic conversion of a former barn and stable block. The rooms are tastefully furnished and equipped with televisions, radio alarms and hospitality trays. The Ridgeway runs right past the village, and White Horse Hill, with the huge figure of a horse cut into the chalk, is just a five-minute drive away.

RECOMMENDED IN THE AREA

The Ridgeway National Trail (1.5 miles); White Horse Hill (2 miles); Tom Brown's School Museum – Uffington (4 miles)

The White Horse ◆◆◆◆

Family-run inn with an old world village setting

☎ 01367 820726 🖷 01367 820566
✉ WHorseUffington@aol.com

Map ref 3 - SU28

WOOLSTONE, Faringdon, SN7 7QL
6 Rooms

The White Horse is a 16th-century inn set in the lovely village of Woolstone in the heart of the Oxfordshire countryside, beneath White Horse Hill. The inn is full of character with old oak beams and a welcoming atmosphere enhanced by crackling log fires and a fine collection of malt whiskies. Though in summer guests might prefer to sit out in the pretty gardens. The smart bedrooms are located in a purpose built annexe, and all have full en suite facilities, Sky television, hospitality trays and direct dial telephones. A comprehensive range of food, to suit all tastes and pockets, is served in the bar or a la carte restaurant.

RECOMMENDED IN THE AREA

Uffington White Horse (chalk hill figure); Tom Brown's Museum; Didcot Railway Museum

Shropshire

A selection of places to eat from the AA Restaurant & AA Pub Guides

Restaurants

⊛ The Studio (Informal)
59 High Street, Church Stretton SY6 6BY
Tel 01694 722672 Fax 01694 722672

⊛⊛ Country Friends Restaurant (Modern)
Dorrington SY5 7JD
Tel 01743 718707 Fax 01743 718707

⊛⊛ The Waterdine
Llanfair Waterdine LD7 1TU
Tel 01547 528214

⊛ The Courtyard (Bistro)
Quality Square, Ludlow SY8 1AR
Tel 01584 878080

⊛⊛ Goldstone Hall (Traditional, Country-house)
Goldstone, Market Drayton TF9 2NA
Tel 01630 661202 Fax 01630 661585

⊛ Sebastian's Hotel & Restaurant (French)
45 Willow Street, Oswestry SY11 1AQ
Tel 01691 655444 Fax 01691 653452

Pubs

◨ The Cholmondeley Riverside Inn
Cressage SY5 6AF
Tel 01952 510900 Fax 01952 510980

◨ The Malthouse
The Wharfage, Ironbridge TF8 7NH
Tel 01952 433712 Fax 01952 433298

◨ Unicorn Inn
Corve Street, Ludlow SY8 1DU
Tel 01584 873555

◨ Hundred House Hotel
Bridgnorth Road, Norton TF11 9EE
Tel 01952 730353 Fax 01952 730355

◨ The Bradford Arms
Llanymynech, Oswestry SY22 6EJ
Tel 01691 830582 Fax 01691 830728

◨ The Armoury
Welsh Bridge, Victoria Quay, Shrewsbury SY1 1HH
Tel 01743 340525 Fax 01743 340526

◨ The Countess's Arms
Weston Heath TF11 8RY
Tel 01952 691123 Fax 01952 691660

The Old Bake House ◆◆◆◆

Good cooking and a relaxed atmosphere in this lovely old house

☎ 01299 270193
✉ old-bake-house@amserve.com

Map ref 2 - SO67

46-47 High Street, CLEOBURY MORTIMER, Kidderminster, DY14 8DQ
on A4117 from Kidderminster. 100yds past church on R
2 Rooms, S £25 D £50, No smoking in bedrooms or dining room

*T*wo 18th-century cottages were knocked into one to produce this delightful house, complete with oak beams and large dormer windows. The charm of the house is matched by the hospitality of the owners, who offer a generous welcome and a relaxing environment. Guests can look forward to the pot of tea served on arrival. Each comfortable bedroom has a private bath or shower room, equipped to a very good standard. Public rooms are cosy, and filled with interesting collectables. A highlight of a stay here is the home cooking both at dinner and breakfast, when local produce is used with excellent results. Special dietary needs are happily catered for.

RECOMMENDED IN THE AREA

West Midlands Safari Park; Ludlow (castle and food); Severn Valley Railway

---

Strefford Hall Farm ◆◆◆◆

Well-proportioned Victorian farmhouse with stylish decorations and furnishings

☎ 01588 672383
📠 0870 132 3818
✉ streffordhallfarm@ farmersweekly.net

Map ref 2 - SO48

Strefford, CRAVEN ARMS, SY7 8DE
0.25m off A49. 1st house on right
3 Rooms, S £22-28 D £44-50, No smoking, Closed Xmas & New Year

A network of footpaths radiates out from this Victorian farmhouse, making it an ideal holiday spot for the walking enthusiast. Good views across the fields to the Wenlock Edge are enjoyed from most rooms, and the 300-acre farm is a constant source of interest, with its suckler cows and sheep, and piglets throughout the year. Spacious en suite bedrooms provide many appealing extras as well as quality beds and attractive decors. Public rooms are well proportioned and cosy, including the smart sitting room with open fire, and a sunny dining room where delicious farm breakfasts are served. Hospitality is warm, and the house is immaculately kept.

RECOMMENDED IN THE AREA

Shropshire Hills Discovery Centre (2 miles); Stokesay Castle (2.5 miles); Acton Scott Farm Museum (3 miles)

Ashton Lees ♦♦♦♦

Attractive family home in secluded gardens south of Shrewsbury

☎ 01743 718378

Map ref 2 - SJ40

Ashton Lees, DORRINGTON, Shrewsbury, SY5 7JW
from Shrewsbury, 6m S on A49, premises on R on entering Dorrington
3 Rooms, S £21-£24 D £42-£48, No smoking, Closed Dec-Jan

Ashton Lees is a well proportioned mid 20th-century house on the edge of the village. It is set in large tree-shaded gardens, providing a peaceful retreat just six miles from Shrewsbury. Bedrooms, with views across the garden towards the Stretton Hills, are thoughtfully equipped with televisions, radios, hospitality trays and baskets of fruit. Wine can also be supplied. Breakfast may be taken in your room, on the terrace or in the dining room. In summer teas are served in the garden, while in winter guests can warm themselves by the blazing log fires in the dining room or separate sitting room. Bicycles available for hire.

RECOMMENDED IN THE AREA

Ironbridge Gorge and Museums (10 miles); walking and exploring the Church Stretton Hills (5 miles); medieval town of Shrewsbury (6 miles); Roman lead workings near Snail Beach (8 miles); Stokesay Castle (8 miles); RAF Museum, Cosford (30 minutes)

Top Farm House ♦♦♦♦

Spacious black and white period guest house with a delightful atmosphere

☎ 01691 682582
📠 01691 682070
📧 p.a.m@
   knockin.freeserve.co.uk
www.topfarmknockin.co.uk

Map ref 5 - SJ32

KNOCKIN, SY10 8HN
in Knockin, past Bradford Arms & shop, past turning for Kinnerley, large black & white house on L
3 Rooms, S £27.50-£32, No smoking in dining room

Old-fashioned hospitality blends with modern comforts at this impressive old property, producing a very pleasing and comfortable guest house. Dating from the 16th century, the Grade I former farmhouse is splendidly decorative with its patterned black timbers against a white fascia. There is plenty of character inside too, with exposed beams and timbers creating a cosy atmosphere in the spacious drawing room, where a log fire burns on cool days. Bedrooms are large and well equipped, including one family room, and all are en suite. Breakfast is an enjoyable occasion, with dishes selected from an extensive menu in the period dining room.

RECOMMENDED IN THE AREA

Offa's Dyke (6 miles); Powys and Chirk Castles, (easy driving distance); medieval town of Shrewsbury (12 miles), Chester (25 miles)

$\mathcal{L}$ine Farm ♦♦♦♦♦

High levels of warmth and hospitality in gloriously peaceful surroundings

☎ 01568 780400

Map ref 2 - SO46

Tunnel Lane, Orleton, LUDLOW, SY8 4HY
signed from A49 in Ashton. Follow B&B signs in Tunnel Lane to Line Farm)
3 Rooms, S £40 D £50-£60,
No smoking, Closed Nov-Feb

$\mathcal{E}$njoy wonderful views out over the countryside, and relish the peace and tranquility of this unspoilt part of Shropshire. Line Farm offers all of this and more. Spacious en suite bedrooms, tastefully furnished and decorated in pretty colours provide high levels of comfort for the discerning visitor. All rooms are equipped with television, courtesy tray and plenty of homely extras. Fabulous breakfasts including free range eggs and home-made jams and marmalades are guaranteed to provide fuel for a day's sightseeing, and both the dining room where they are served and the sitting room are warm and comfortable. A very welcoming house where guest comfort is the priority.

RECOMMENDED IN THE AREA

Bernington Hall and Croft Castle (National Trust); Ludlow (5 miles); beautiful walks on Bircher Common (15 minute drive)

$\mathcal{N}$umber Twenty Eight ♦♦♦♦♦

A cluster of period houses run by welcoming owners

☎ 01584 876996
🖷 01584 876860
🖂 ross@no28.co.uk
www.no28.co.uk

Map ref 2 - SO57

28 Lower Broad Street, LUDLOW, SY8 1PQ
just off B4361
9 Rooms, S £60-£90 D £75-£95,
No smoking

$\mathcal{G}$uests come first at this period house, and the owners go to great lengths to prove it. The welcome is truly warm, and although accommodation is spread over several properties in the same street, most people gather for breakfast under the same roof. An early Georgian house, several Tudor cottages and a Victorian terraced house make up the broad period mix. All are decorated with taste and comfortably furnished for the discerning visitor. Bedrooms are not particularly large, but are mainly equipped with quality en suite shower and bath. Breakfast is an enjoyable meal made from local produce. Many excellent restaurants are just a walk away

RECOMMENDED IN THE AREA

Ludlow Castle; Stokesay Castle; Ironbridge

$\mathcal{M}$ickley House ◆◆◆◆

Attractive farmhouse accommodation amid a gardener's paradise

☎ 01630 638505
📠 01630 638505
📧 mickleyhouse@hotmail.com

Map ref 6 - SJ63

Faulsgreen, Tern Hill, MARKET DRAYTON, TF9 3QW
A41 to Tern Hill rdbt, then A53 towards Shrewsbury, 1st R for Faulsgreen, 4th house on R
3 Rooms, S £25-£30 D £44-£70, No smoking, Closed Xmas

$\mathcal{R}$ecommended for its warmth and hospitality, Mickley House is set in an acre of beautiful landscaped gardens with many species of plants and shrubs, a rose-covered pergola, ornamental trees and water features. Inside, original beams and oak doors reflect the character of the property. Relax in the spacious drawing room after a busy day's sightseeing. The all-en suite bedrooms are individually designed - a double and a twin upstairs, the latter with a balcony overlooking the garden; and a double and a twin on the ground floor, the double being particularly large and having an impressive Louis XV-style bed. Children and pets cannot be accommodated.

RECOMMENDED IN THE AREA

Wollerton Old Hall Garden (3 miles); Ironbridge and Shrewsbury (24 miles & 15 miles); Bridgemere, Dorothy Clive (10 miles)

$\mathcal{F}$ieldside Guest House ◆◆◆◆

Charming Victorian house standing in large, attractive gardens

☎ 01743 353143
📠 01743 354687
📧 robrookes@btinternet.com
www.fieldsideguesthouse.co.uk

Map ref 2 - SJ51

38 London Road, SHREWSBURY, SY2 6NX
from A5 take A5064, premises 1m on left
4 Rooms, S £35-£40 D £50-£54, No smoking

$\mathcal{F}$ieldside, which dates back to 1835, is conveniently located just a mile from the centre of Shewsbury and just five minutes' walk from Shrewsbury Abbey. With its own private car park, there is ample space for your car. This delightful house is tastefully furnished and decorated and offers both single and double/twin rooms, all of which are en suite. All bedrooms feature period-style furniture and are equipped with colour televisions and tea and coffee making facilities. Breakfast is served at individual tables in the spacious and relaxing dining room overlooking the garden. Traditional English or vegetarian or lighter alternatives are available.

RECOMMENDED IN THE AREA

Shrewsbury with Castle and Abbey (1 mile); National Trust house Attingham Park (1.5 miles); Ironbridge Gorge and Museums

$\mathcal{A}$venue Farm Bed & Breakfast ♦♦♦♦

*Set in a quiet, unspoilt village
with magnificent views*

☎ 01952 740253
📠 01952 740401
✉ jones@
   avenuefarm.fsnet.co.uk

Map ref 2 - SJ50

Uppington, TELFORD, TF6 5HW
from M54 J7 take B5061 for Atcham,
2nd L signed Uppington pass sawmill,
turn R farm 400yds on R
3 Rooms, S £25-£30 D £45-£50, No
smoking in bedrooms or dining room,
Closed Xmas

Superbly located in immaculate gardens, this 18th-century farmhouse offers magnificent views of the Wrekin and the surrounding countryside. The same outlook is shared by the spacious en suite bedrooms, which are filled with lots of thoughtful extras. A cosy sitting room is another plus. Many original Georgian features have been retained in the impressive old house, and the fine period furniture is perfectly in keeping with the style of the building. The effect is further enhanced by quality furnishing and décor schemes throughout. The owners creates a homely, friendly atmosphere in which guests are invited to relax completely.

RECOMMENDED IN THE AREA

Ironbridge Gorge and Museums; Weston Park, Attingham Hall, Boscobel House; RAF Museum Cosford, Severn Valley Railway

$\mathcal{D}$earnford Hall ♦♦♦♦♦

*The Bebbington family home
combining 18th-century elegance
with 21st-century comfort*

☎ 01948 662319
📠 01948 666670
✉ dearnford_hall@yahoo.com
www.dearnfordhall.com

Map ref 6 - SJ53

Tilstock Road, WHITCHURCH,
SY13 3JJ
at Tilstock rdbt on S Whitchurch by-
pass take B5476 to Tilstock. Premises
0.5m on L
2 Rooms, S £40-£50 D £70-£85,
No smoking, Closed Xmas

Guests may choose to play the Steinway in the hall, enjoy a game of boules on the lawn or fly-fishing on the 15-acre lake. Molly the flat-coat retriever will show you the way. This William and Mary house is surrounded by its own farmland, with a wildflower meadow close by. Antique furniture, family treasures and log fires feature in the drawing and dining rooms. King-size en suite bedrooms are bright and sunny, with rich fabrics, deep mattresses, fat duvets and fine linen. Recommendations can be made for local restaurants and country pubs. The genuine hospitality of the Bebbingtons makes a stay here truly memorable. Dogs by prior arrangement.

RECOMMENDED IN THE AREA

Ironbridge Gorge, Shrewsbury (30 minutes); Hodnet, Wollerton Old Hall Gardens (20 minutes); Chirk Castle & Erddig (National Trust) (30 minutes)

187

Soulton Hall ....

Elizabethan manor house with a lovely walled garden and fifty acres of oak woodland

☎ 01939 232786
📠 01939 234097
✉ j.a.ashton@farmline.com
www.soultonhall.fsbusiness.co.uk

Map ref 6 - SJ53

Soulton, WEM, SY4 5RS
turn off A49 onto B5065 towards Wem,
2m on L after small bridge
6 Rooms, S £37.50-£42.50 D £60-£75,
No smoking

RECOMMENDED IN THE AREA

Chester, Ironbridge, Shrewsbury and the castles of North Wales are within easy reach

The Ashton family can trace their tenure of this impressive hall back to the 16th century. Much evidence of the building's antiquity remains, notably the sloping floors! The comfortable entrance lounge leads into the bar on one side and a restaurant on the other, offering a good range of freshly prepared dishes. The house has central heating as well as log fires to ensure a warm environment. The bedrooms reflect the character of the house with mullioned windows and exposed timbers, one room also has wood panelling. Five bedrooms have en suite facilities, two of these are located in a converted coach house across the garden. Open farmland surrounds the house and guests are welcome to explore the grounds. These include one and half miles of river and brook where guests can go fishing. Farm and woodland walks to explore.

Somerset

A selection of places to eat from the AA Restaurant & AA Pub Guides

Restaurants

◎◎ Restaurant le Clos (Classic, French)
1 Seven Dials, Saw Close, Bath BA1 1EN
Tel 01225 444450 Fax 01225 404044

◎◎ The Moody Goose (Classic, Formal)
7a Kingsmead Square, Bath BA1 2AB
Tel 01225 466688 Fax 01225 466688

◎◎ No 5 Bistro (Bistro)
5 Argyle Street, Bath BA2 4BA
Tel 01225 444499 Fax 01225 318668

◎ Truffles (Modern)
95 High Street, Bruton BA10 0AR
Tel 01749 812255 Fax 01749 812255

◎ Ashwick House Hotel (Country-house)
Dulverton TA22 9QD
Tel 01398 323868 Fax 01398 323868

◎ The Ring O'Roses Country Inn
Stratton Road, Holcombe BA3 5EB
Tel 01761 232478

◎◎ Hunstrete House (Country-house)
Hunstrete BS39 4NS
Tel 01761 490490 Fax 01761 490732

◎ Periton Park Hotel (Country-house)
Middlecombe, Minehead TA24 8SW
Tel 01643 706885 Fax 01643 706885

◎◎◎ Andrews on the Weir (French, Country-house)
Porlock Weir, Porlock TA24 8PB
Tel 01643 863300 Fax 01643 863311

◎ Bowlish House (Classic)
Bowlish, Shepton Mallet BA4 5JD
Tel 01749 342022 Fax 01749 342022

◎◎ Ston Easton Park (Traditional, European)
Ston Easton BA3 4DF
Tel 01761 241631 Fax 01761 241377

◎ Brazz (Modern, Chic)
Castle Bow, Taunton TA1 1NF
Tel 01823 252000 Fax 01823 336066

◎◎ Bindon House (Traditional Country-house)
Langford Budville, Wellington TA21 0RU
Tel 01823 400070 Fax 01823 400071

◎ Market Place Hotel (Modern, Scandinavian)
One Market Place, Wells BA5 2RW
Tel 01749 836300 Fax 01749 836301

◎ Karslake House (Country-house)
Halse Lane, Winsford TA24 7JE
Tel 01643 851242 Fax 01643 851242

◎◎ Langley House Hotel (Country-house)
Langley Marsh, Wiveliscombe TA4 2UF
Tel 01984 623318 Fax 01984 624573

Pubs

🍺 The Globe Inn
Appley TA21 0HJ
Tel 01823 672327

🍺 Woolpack Inn
Beckington BA3 6SP
Tel 01373 831244 Fax 01373 831223

🍺 Crown Inn
The Batch, Skinners Lane, Churchill BS25 5PP
Tel 01934 852995

🍺 The Wheatsheaf
Combe Hay BA2 7EG
Tel 01225 833504 Fax 01225 833504

🍺 The Crown Inn
Exford TA24 7PP
Tel 01643 831554 Fax 01643 831665

🍺 The Haselbury Inn
North Street, Haselbury Plucknett TA18 7RJ
Tel 01460 72488 Fax 01460 72488

🍺 Kingsdon Inn
Kingsdon TA11 7LG
Tel 01935 840543

🍺 Royal Oak Inn
Luxborough TA23 0SH
Tel 01984 640319 Fax 01984 641561

🍺 The Notley Arms
Monksilver TA4 4JB
Tel 01984 656217

🍺 George Inn
High Street, Norton St Philip BA3 6LH
Tel 01373 834224 Fax 01373 834861

🍺 The Three Horseshoes
Batcombe, Shepton Mallet BA4 6HE
Tel 01749 850359 Fax 01749 850615

🍺 The Montague Inn
Shepton Montague BA9 8JW
Tel 01749 813213

🍺 The Carpenters Arms
Stanton Wick BS39 4BX
Tel 01761 490202 Fax 01761 490763

🍺 The Blue Ball
Triscombe, nr Crowcombe, Taunton TA4 3HE
Tel 01984 618242

🍺 The Fountain Inn
1 St Thomas Street, Wells BA5 2UU
Tel 01749 672317 Fax 01749 670825

🍺 The Royal Oak Inn
Winsford TA24 7JE
Tel 01643 851455 Fax 01643 851009

🍺 Royal Oak Inn
Withypool TA24 7QP
Tel 01643 831506 Fax 01643 831659

The Ayrlington •••••

Individually-themed bedrooms in a gracious listed hotel with high levels of comfort

☎ 01225 425495
🖷 01225 469029
✉ mail@ayrlington.com
www.ayrlington.com

Map ref 2 - ST76

24/25 Pulteney Road, BATH, BA2 4EZ
M4 junct 18, A46 then A4 to Bath. Follow signs for A367 Wells/Exeter, hotel on R 100mtrs beyond St Mary's church
12 Rooms, D £75-£145, No smoking, Closed 2 weeks at Xmas

*A*n impressive listed Victorian house filled with splendour and charm, set right in the heart of Bath. In a beautiful fusion of West and East, this elegant hotel uses oriental themes to stunning effect throughout. Asian antiques, artwork and fine fabrics sit comfortably alongside classical English fireplaces, drapes and seating. All of the spacious bedrooms are furnished and decorated to individual themes, including a Chinese room, an Empire room, and a Pulteney room with four-poster bed.

Bathrooms are equipped with quality fixtures and fittings, and luxurious towels and toiletries, and some have a spa bath. Guests can enjoy the superb views out over the walled garden to the Abbey and the rest of the city while eating a freshly-cooked breakfast in elegant surroundings. There is also a guests' bar, and a welcoming lounge. This hotel offers an atmosphere of peace and tranquility, and has ample parking for guests.

RECOMMENDED IN THE AREA

Roman Baths; Bath Abbey; Theatre Royal

$\mathcal{A}$psley House Hotel ◆◆◆◆◆

Attractive Georgian property on the outskirts of the city

☎ 01225 336966
📠 01225 425462
📧 info@apsley-house.co.uk
www.apsley-house.co.uk

Map ref 2 - ST76

Newbridge Hill, BATH, BA1 3PT
on A431 1m west of city
9 Rooms, S £55-£75 D £75-£120, No
smoking (except in bar), Closed 1 wk
Xmas

This elegant house, located about a mile from the city centre, was built for the Duke of Wellington. Hospitality is warm, friendly and enthusiastic from proprietors and staff alike. The spacious public areas are delightfully decorated and furnished and the lounge is full of period charm.

The bedrooms are individually styled, well maintained, and equipped with en suite bathrooms, colour televisions, direct dial telephones, and tea and coffee making facilities. A delicious variety of breakfast items is offered. Children under five and dogs cannot be accommodated (except for guide dogs). Smoking in bar only.

RECOMMENDED IN THE AREA

Roman Baths (5 minute drive); Stonehenge (60 minute drive); Wells Cathedral/Salisbury Cathedral (60 minute drive)

$\mathcal{B}$rocks Guest House ◆◆◆◆

Delightful Georgian property close to the Royal Crescent

☎ 01225 338374
📠 01225 334245
📧 marion@
    brocksguesthouse.co.uk
www.brocksguesthouse.co.uk

Map ref 2 - ST76

32 Brock Street, BATH, BA1 2LN
leave M4 J18 onto A46, Brocks is just
off A4 between Circus & Royal
Crescent
6 Rooms, S £49-£60 D £63-£75, No
smoking, Closed Xmas

Built by John Wood the younger in 1765, this handsome house is ideally located between the Circus and the Royal Crescent, where guests can experience the finest of Bath's architecture. The town centre, the Roman Baths and the Pump Room are just a few minutes' walk away. Bath is one of only three designated World Heritage Cities by the United Nations and has much to recommend it to the visitor. The interior of the house reflects all the elegance of the period with beautifully furnished en suite bedrooms. A traditional breakfast is served in the large dining room, which has its own lounge area where guests can relax in easy chairs.

RECOMMENDED IN THE AREA

Visit the Assembly Rooms and Museum of Costume; walk in Victoria Park; Roman Baths and Pump Room are just a few minutes' walk

Cheriton House ♦♦♦♦♦

*Attractive Victorian residence with
lovely views over the city*

☎ 01225 429862
📠 01225 428403
✉ cheriton@which.net
www.cheritonhouse.co.uk

Map ref 2 - ST76

9 Upper Oldfield Park, BATH, BA2 3JX
south of Bath, 0.5m on A367. Take 1st
R into Upper Oldfield Park. Cheriton
House is 300yds along on L
9 Rooms, S £48-£60 D £66-£90,
No smoking

Set just off a busy road in a quiet residential location, Cheriton House is a gracious property with wonderful views across the city. Careful restoration and redecoration have led to superb public rooms filled with antiques. Bedrooms are also of a high standard, with individual décor adding a delightful personal touch. This well-maintained Victorian property offers a warm welcome to guests, and there is plenty of tourist information to help get the most from a stay. A very attractive new breakfast room with bow window overlooking the garden is the setting for superb breakfasts, and Bath is just a short stroll away.

RECOMMENDED IN THE AREA

The Roman Baths; The Royal Crescent; Bath Museum of Costume

Holly Lodge ♦♦♦♦♦

*Gracious mansion with excellent
views, set in lovely gardens*

☎ 01225 424042
📠 01225 481138
✉ stay@hollylodge.co.uk
www.hollylodge.co.uk

Map ref 2 - ST76

8 Upper Oldfield Park, BATH, BA2 3JZ
0.5m SW of city centre off A367
7 Rooms, S £48-£55 D £79-£97,
No smoking

Set high above Bath and with expansive views across the city, this fine mansion is still within easy walking distance of the major tourist attractions. Renovated several years ago from near dereliction by dedicated owners, it now offers gracious accommodation decorated and furnished in rich colours and sumptuous fabrics. Many of the bedrooms enjoy the same superb views, and all are fitted with smart en suite facilities and plenty of personal touches. Breakfast is a delicious feast including exotic fresh fruits, smoked salmon and home-made croissants, served in a beautiful bright dining room at individual tables. Personal touring inventories are happily supplied on request.

RECOMMENDED IN THE AREA

Bath city – World Heritage Site; National Trust village of Lacock; Wells Cathedral

The County Hotel .....

Award-winning family-run hotel with outstanding accommodation and friendly hospitality

☎ 01225 425003
🖷 01225 466493
✉ reservations@ county-hotel.co.uk
www.county-hotel.co.uk

Map ref 2 - ST76

18-19 Pulteney Road, BATH, BA2 4EZ
22 Rooms, S £60-£80
D £100-£160, No smoking, Closed 22 Dec-15 Jan

*W*inner of the AA's 2000 English Guest Accommodation of the Year award, this elegant house is perfectly placed to enjoy Bath. Looking out over the cricket and rugby grounds towards nearby Bath Abbey, the hotel is just around the corner from the famous Pulteney Bridge. The accommodation is truly outstanding, with beautifully decorated and furnished rooms providing an appealing base from which to explore the city. The stylish Reading Room is the ideal place for afternoon tea or just relaxing in, while the Cricket Bar is a quiet place for a bar lunch or an evening drink. Bedrooms range from one with a four-poster and others of superior quality to more standard rooms, but all are comfortable furnished, and many have delightful views. Each room has an en suite bathroom, satellite television, and a plug for a computer. Breakfast is an impressive selection of fresh dishes, taken in the fine dining room. This exceptionally caring and friendly hotel is also able to offer secure parking.

RECOMMENDED IN THE AREA

Bradford upon Avon (20 minutes); Lacock (30 minutes) (location for Pride and Prejudice, Sense and Sensibility, and Harry Potter); horse riding (20 minutes), golf (15 minutes)

Cranleigh ....

Quietly-placed Victorian house where 'quality' is a watch-word and the hospitality is impeccable

☎ 01225 310197 📠 01225 423143
📧 cranleigh@btinternet.com
www.cranleighguesthouse.com

Map ref 2 - ST76

159 Newbridge Hill, BATH, BA1 3PX
on A431, west side of city
8 Rooms, S £45-£55 D £65-£80, No smoking

RECOMMENDED IN THE AREA

Bath's famous attractions and independent shops; Wells, Glastonbury and Cheddar (20 miles); walk the Cotswold Way (0.25 mile)

A warm, comfortable house decorated in tasteful colours, with many homely touches to create an appealing ambience. Located in a peaceful residential area of Bath, Cranleigh offers private parking and easy access to the centre of Bath via the nearby 'Park & Ride' scheme, or walking through Royal Victoria Park, past Royal Crescent. The bright and spacious bedrooms all have en suite shower rooms (two also have a bath), and most enjoy fantastic views across the city and the Avon Valley. One bedroom offers a stylish four-poster, another has a canopied bed, and three large rooms are ideal for families. All come with colour television, hospitality tray, radio alarm clock and hairdryer. As members of the 'Real Bath Breakfast', the owners provide freshly-prepared food made from locally-sourced ingredients with plenty of choice. Breakfast is served in the elegant lounge/dining room, and there is also a sunny south-facing garden. Guests are offered free golf, including club and trolley hire. This is a non-smoking house.

Devonshire House....

Exceptionally welcoming owners and a restful atmosphere

☎ 01225 312495
📠 01225 335534
✉ info@
devonshire-house-
bath.co.uk
www.devonshire-
house-bath.co.uk

Map ref 2 - ST76

143 Wellsway, BATH,
BA2 4RZ
1m from city centre on
A367 out of Bath
3 Rooms, S £38-£55
D £55-£75, No smoking

*T*his lovely Victorian house which dates from 1880 is within a comfortable strolling distance of the Georgian delights of Bath. Guests are made to feel at home by the friendly hosts, Eileen and Albie, who provide an attentive service and plenty of useful information on the special attractions of the city. Their charming home offers pretty bedrooms with en suite bath or shower and plenty of extras. Breakfast is taken in the dining room which was once a Victorian grocer's shop. Fresh fruit, smoked fish and the traditional cooked meal are all on offer, and special diets are also catered for. Guests wanting to recover after a day's touring will find the sitting room very relaxing, and the highly-polished brasswork shows how lovingly the building is cared for. In a city where parking is at a premium, the private car space available in the walled courtyard is an added bonus.

RECOMMENDED IN THE AREA

The Roman Baths; Jane Austen Museum; Pulteney Bridge

*H*aute Combe Hotel ....

Smart, upmarket hotel with committed owners and a high degree of personal attention

☎ 01225 420061
🄵 01225 446077
🄴 enquiries@
    hautecombe.com
www.hautecombe.com

Map ref 2 - ST76

174/176 Newbridge Road, BATH, BA1 3LE
Leave Queens Square in city centre along Upper Bristol Road (A4) towards Bristol, fork L onto Newbridge Rd at 2nd set of traffic lights, after Victoria Park, Hotel is on R
13 Rooms, S £45-£59 D £59-£89, No smoking in bedrooms or dining room

*A*n attractive Edwardian house within easy reach of the city centre. Hospitality is taken very seriously by the friendly owners, and guests are made to feel exceptionally welcome. Lifts to and from the railway station are offered, and there is also easy car parking on site. The bedrooms are of a good size and particularly well equipped with many modern facilities. While most rooms have en suite shower and wc, one room is available with bath.

Internet/e-mail access is also available for guests' use. There are two cosy lounges, one with a small, well-stocked bar. A tempting selection of home-cooked meals is offered at dinner, and various options are available at breakfast. All meals are served in the light and airy dining room. The hotel is kept in immaculate condition, and standards of cleanliness are very high.

RECOMMENDED IN THE AREA

The Roman Baths, and beautiful Georgian city of Bath; Cheddar Gorge and Caves (30 minute drive); Wells and Glastonbury (30 minute drive)

*H*ighways House ....

Handy for the centre of Bath, a well-decorated and furnished house high standards of hospitality

☎ 01225 421238
📠 01225 481169
✉ stay@
   highwayshouse.co.uk
www.highwayshouse.co.uk

Map ref 2 - ST76

143 Wells Road, BATH,
BA2 3AL
on A367 to Radstock
7 Rooms, S £35-£45 D £52-£69, No smoking

Cars may be left safely in the grounds of this elegant Victorian house, while their owners take the short stroll into the centre of the city. Such convenience is part of the attraction of this friendly guest house, where buses stop near the house every 10 minutes, and the railway station is not far away. Guests are assured of a warm welcome from the friendly owners. The comfortable lounge is a good place to plan sightseeing trips, with plenty of information available on what to see and where to eat. Bedrooms are homely and relaxing, with well-sprung beds, en suite facilities and plenty of extras. One twin room approached up a windy staircase is popular with teenagers. A generous choice of breakfast is on offer in the bright and cheerful dining room, where fresh fruit and home-made jams are always available. This peaceful house built from mellow Bath stone is strictly non-smoking.

RECOMMENDED IN THE AREA

The Roman Baths; the only hot springs public baths in England; Georgian Bath city centre

Kennard Hotel ♦♦♦♦♦

Elegant Georgian town house just over Pulteney Bridge

☎ 01225 310472
📠 01225 460054
✉ reception@kennard.co.uk
www.kennard.co.uk

Map ref 2 - ST76

11 Henrietta Street, BATH, BA2 6LL
from A4 London Road L onto A36
over river, R past fire station. Kennard
is top R on Henrietta Street
13 Rooms, S £48-£54 D £88-£108, No
smoking, Closed Xmas & New Year

The Kennard was built as a lodging house in 1794 during an era of great prosperity for the city as the fashionable place to 'take the waters'. It is located just a few minutes from the Roman Baths and proudly preserves its gracious heritage.

With views over the city, the bedrooms are beautifully decorated, their modern facilities include satellite televisions, direct dial telephones with modem points, hairdryers and hospitality trays. The en suite bathrooms are stylishly fitted and make good use of space.

A choice of full English or continental breakfast is offered, prepared with quality fresh produce and the finest teas and coffees. The meal is served in the original Georgian kitchen. Proprietors Malcolm Wright and Richard Ambler assure guests of a warm welcome with attention to detail.

RECOMMENDED IN THE AREA

Roman Baths & Museums; Kennet & Avon canal walks (10 minutes); the Cotswolds

Leighton House ♦♦♦♦♦

Victorian residence, close to city centre, with splendid bedrooms

☎ 01225 314769
📠 01225 443079
✉ welcome@
   leighton-house.co.uk
www.leighton-house.co.uk

Map ref 2 - ST76

139 Wells Road, BATH, BA2 3AL
leave A36 at Churchill Bridge in town
centre, take A367, 600mtrs, house on
L, at junct with Hayesfield Park
8 Rooms, S £45-£99 D £55-£99, No
smoking

By staying here, leaving your car in the private car park and taking a 10 minute walk into the centre of Bath, you discover the ideal way to explore this city.

The house, brought to life by a colourful assortment of flowers in the well-tended garden, overlooks the city and the surrounding hills. The bedrooms are king, queen and twin with period furniture and have both bath and shower en suite, direct dial telephone, colour TV, coffee and tea making facilities, radio alarm and hairdryers.

A gourmet breakfast is available in the breakfast room overlooking the garden. Fresh fruit salad is served every day with a choice of other fruits and cereals, followed by a full English breakfast or smoked salmon with scrambled eggs, kippers or smoked haddock.

RECOMMENDED IN THE AREA

Roman Baths, Bath Abbey, Stonehenge (40 minutes' drive)

Marlborough House ....

Elegant accommodation and very welcoming hosts specialising in irresistible vegetarian cooking

☎ 01225 318175
🖷 01225 466127
✉ mars@
   manque.dircon.co.uk
www.marlborough-
house.net

Map ref 2 - ST76

1 Marlborough Lane, BATH,
BA1 2NQ
on corner of A4 &
Marlborough Lane. W of
Queen Square in city centre
7 Rooms, S £45-£70 D £65-
£85, No smoking

*A*n enchanting Victorian town house, situated opposite Royal Victoria Park, which has been brought to life by friendly and enthusiastic hospitality. The bedrooms are sumptuously furnished and equipped with a range of thoughtful touches such as fresh flowers and decanters of sherry. Most rooms have en suite bath or shower, and some are fitted with four posters. Television, direct-dial telephone, radio, alarm and hairdryer are standard, and there is also internet access. Elegant antiques grace the house, but the atmosphere remains informal and relaxed. Vegetarian cooking is a speciality, using organic ingredients prepared with flair and imagination. The American-style French toast with real maple syrup, and omelettes at breakfast are a must! Room service is available during the day from a vegetarian menu, and delicious home-cooked dinners featuring exotic dishes are served in the evening by candlelight. Cars can be parked throughout a stay, and most of the city's places of interest are within easy walking distance.

RECOMMENDED IN THE AREA

Roman Baths and Pump Room; Jane Austen Centre; Museum of Costume and Assembly Rooms

Tasburgh House Hotel ····

Close to Bath city centre, yet enjoying all the peace and comfort of a country house

☎ 01225 425096
📠 01225 463842
✉ hotel@
bathtasburgh.co.uk
www.bathtasburgh.
co.uk

Map ref 2 - ST76

Warminster Road, BATH, BA2 6SH
on N side of A36 - adjacent to Bathampton Ln junct - approx 0.5m from Bathwick St rdbt & Sydney Gdns
12 Rooms, S £57-£67
D £82-£112, No smoking

*E*xtensive well-tended gardens and a meadow park running down to the Kennet and Avon canal are some of the delightful features of this hotel. From its unique position the charming Victorian property enjoys the best of both the city and the countryside. Bath is just a short walk away, yet spectacular views across the Avon valley make this setting a particularly peaceful and attractive one. Inside the hotel offers high levels of comfort and elegance, including smart public rooms. The tastefully decorated lounge leads into a sunny conservatory and a striking dining room, where enjoyable dinners cooked from fresh local produce are served by prior arrangement. Breakfast is also served in this room. Bedrooms range in size and shape, but all are individually furnished and decorated, with en suite facilities, direct dial telephone and modem connection point. Another strength of Tasburgh House is the relaxed, friendly atmosphere which is generated by very committed staff.

RECOMMENDED IN THE AREA

City of Bath – Royal Crescent, Circus etc; Roman Baths; Stonehenge

$\mathcal{M}$onkshill Guest House ♦♦♦♦♦

Edwardian property peacefully set in extensive gardens

☎ 01225 833028
📠 01225 833028
✉ monks.hill@virgin.net
www.monkshill.com

Map ref 2 - ST76

Shaft Road, Monkton Combe, BATH, BA2 7HL
A36 (Pulteney rd) towards Bristol. Turn L into A3062 (Prior Park Rd) towards Combe Down. Top of hill turn L (North Rd). 2nd R into Shaft Rd. Pass fields, down hill, Monkshill 100m on R
3 Rooms, S £50-£65 D £65-£80, No smoking, Closed 2 wks Xmas & New Year

This delightful house is set in attractive gardens, including a croquet lawn, and offers superb views across the Limpley Stoke Valley. The bedrooms are spacious, comfortably furnished and fully in keeping with the character of the building. Two of the rooms have en suite facilities and the third has a private bathroom. Plenty of thoughtful extras are provided, and each room has a colour television and tea and coffee making equipment. The attractive sitting room with its many personal touches has a real homely feel and is the perfect place in which to relax. A choice of dishes is offered at breakfast, which is served in the elegant dining room. and taken, family style, at one large table.

RECOMMENDED IN THE AREA

National Trust Gardens at Prior Park (15 minute walk); Wells & Wookey Hole Caves (25 minutes drive); Kennet & Avon Canal walks (15 minutes walk)

$\mathcal{T}$he Claire De Lune ♦♦♦♦

Good food and warm hospitality at this restaurant with rooms

☎ 01749 813395
📠 01749 813395
✉ drew.beard@virgin.net
www.clairedelune.co.uk

Map ref 2 - ST63

2-4 High Street, BRUTON, BA10 0AA
situated in centre of Bruton at eastern end of High Street
3 Rooms, S £35-£40 D £47.50-£55, No smoking in bedrooms or dining room, Closed Jan

The Claire De Lune is the perfect place to be pampered, well fed and cared for by enthusiastic proprietors Tanya and Andrew Beard. Quality is obvious throughout the establishment from the fine beds and bedding to the range of complimentary toiletries. The two double rooms are en suite, while the single has a private bathroom. A breakfast room and relaxing residents' lounge are provided, including a range of books and magazines for guests to read. Food, of course, is a highlight. Mediterranean dishes are a speciality, with fish as a feature and local Somerset produce predominating. In fine weather, dinner is served on the flower-decked garden terrace overlooking the church.

RECOMMENDED IN THE AREA

National Trust houses – Stourhead and Montacute House (easy driving distance); Fleet Air Arm and Haynes Motor Museums (easy driving distance); Glastonbury Abbey (20 minutes), Bath (45 minutes)

For BATH see also NORTON ST PHILIP page 206

Saltmoor House ◆◆◆◆◆

Listed Georgian property just five miles from the M5

☎ 01823 698092
✉ saltmoorhouse@amserve.net

Map ref 2 - ST33

Saltmoor, BURROWBRIDGE, TA7 0RL
from M5 J24 through Huntworth
Moorland towards Burrowbridge
3 Rooms, S £45 D £90, No smoking

Saltmoor is an elegant country home in an Environmentally Sensitive Area known for its withy-growing for the local basket-making industry. Nearby places of interest include historic houses and gardens, Glastonbury, Wells and Exmoor National Park. The house overlooks the River Parrett, with a large walled garden to the rear, old farm buildings beyond, and 12 acres of pasture with views across the moors to the Blackdown and Quantock Hills. Black and white bathrooms, flagstone floors, log fires and classical wall paintings characterise the stylish interior. One bedroom is en suite and the others have their own private bathrooms. A wide choice is offered at breakfast including home produced free-range eggs. A superb dinner, beautifully presented, is always available – prior notice is helpful.

RECOMMENDED IN THE AREA

Hestercombe Gardens (8 miles); Village Basket Makers (1-3 miles); Montacute House and Gardens (40 minutes)

Bellplot House Hotel ◆◆◆◆◆

Handsome Georgian property in the centre of town

☎ 01460 62600 🖷 01460 62600
✉ info@bellplothouse.co.uk
www.bellplothouse.co.uk

Map ref 2 - ST30

High Street, CHARD, TA20 1QB
located in the centre of Chard,
500yrds from Guildhall
7 Rooms, S £47-£57 D £57-£67, No smoking in dining room

This mid-Georgian house is set in classic surroundings in the centre of town, with ample parking provided. It is a family-run establishment based on personalised service, and the owner is an experienced chef. Facilities include a bar and restaurant where an innovative dinner menu is offered. The en suite bedrooms feature walk in power showers, and each room is equipped with a telephone, satellite television, video and computer workstation, hairdryer, trouser press, and tea and coffee-making equipment. E-mail and fax are available at reception. Guests have full use of a nearby golf and squash club and a members-only leisure club, with pool, sauna, Jacuzzi, fitness room and beauty treatments.

RECOMMENDED IN THE AREA

Forde Abbey and Gardens; Cricket St Thomas Wildlife Park; Perry's Cider Mills (5 miles)

Tor Farm ◆◆◆◆

A very rural farmhouse in a glorious setting

☏ 01934 743710
🖷 01934 743710
✉ bcjbkj@aol.com

Map ref 2 - ST45

Nyland, CHEDDAR, BS27 3UD
take A371 from Cheddar towards
Wells, after 2m turn R towards
Nyland. Tor Farm 1.5m on R
7 Rooms, S £35 D £45-£55, No
smoking in bedrooms or dining room

Truly fantastic views and a peaceful rural setting are two of the best reasons for choosing to stay at this comfortable farmhouse. Located on the Somerset Levels just three miles from Cheddar Gorge, this working farm is superbly set in an area of outstanding natural beauty. Smartly-furnished bedrooms, four of them on the ground floor, are all en suite and equipped with courtesy trays; some rooms have private patios, and one is fitted with a four-poster bed. A heated outdoor pool is popular in the warmer months, and guests can enjoy barbecues in the garden. On colder evenings the cosy sitting room is appreciated.

RECOMMENDED IN THE AREA

Spectacular Cheddar Gorge; Roman Bath; Wells – the smallest city in England

Manor Farm ◆◆◆◆

Off the beaten track Victorian farmhouse with extensive views

☏ 01460 78865 🖷 01460 78865
www.manorfarm.com

Map ref 2 - ST40

Wayford, CREWKERNE, TA18 8QL
from Crewkerne take B3165 to Lyme
Regis, after 3m in Clapton turn R into
Dunsham Lane, 0.5m up hill, farm
on R
4 Rooms, S £25-£35 D £50, No
smoking

Built of local hamstone and brick, this imposing farmhouse is set on a working farm of 20 acres, including three stocked ponds where guests can fish. The views are wonderful, across open country to the Axe Valley, and guests can bring their own horses. The farm is situated on the Liberty Trail, an ancient footpath, and close to several National Trust properties. Lyme Regis on the south coast is just 12 miles away. Bedrooms are comfortably furnished and equipped with en suite showers, remote control televisions, hospitality trays and ironing facilities. A self-catering apartment is also available. Breakfast is served in the cosy dining room, and a spacious lounge is provided.

RECOMMENDED IN THE AREA

Forde Abbey and Gardens (3 miles); Cricket St Thomas Wildlife Park (3 miles); Lyme Regis coast (12 miles)

Oakland House ♦♦♦♦

Friendly family home with spectacular country views

☎ 01934 744195

Map ref 2 - ST45

Wells Road, DRAYCOTT, Cheddar, BS27 3SU
M5 J22, follow signs into Cheddar on A371. Draycott 2.5m & house last on R before market gdn
3 Rooms, S £27-£35 D £42-£50 (family room £55-£70), No smoking in bedrooms or dining room, Closed late Dec-mid Jan

A short distance from Cheddar, in the Mendip Hills, Oakland House offers spacious accommodation surrounded by mature gardens, including plenty of car-parking space. Views of the Somerset Moors and Glastonbury Tor can be enjoyed from the sun lounge and attractively appointed bedrooms. Double or twin rooms are available, and one double room can be adapted for family use. All have television, tea and coffee-making equipment and en suite facilities. The dining room is furnished with individual tables, and in cooler weather a log fire is lit. A good dinner is available featuring fresh fruit and vegetables from the garden. Opportunities for walking, golf, horse riding and swimming are available nearby.

RECOMMENDED IN THE AREA

Wells Cathedral (5 miles); Glastonbury Tor (8 miles); Stourhead (20 minute drive), Longleat (20 minute drive)

Town Mills ♦♦♦♦

Georgian mill house peacefully located in the centre of Dulverton

☎ 01398 323124

Map ref 2 - SS92

High Street, DULVERTON, Somerset, TA22 9HB
Dulverton is on B3222, Town Mills 200 yds on left after crossing River Barle next to the Mill Leat
5 Rooms, S £30-£45 D £45-£55, Closed Xmas

All the advantages of a town centre property are available at this lovely mill house, with nearby shops, pubs and restaurants, yet the situation is quiet and secluded, with private car parking provided. It is an ideal base for exploring Exmoor, with many outdoor pursuits available locally. A good choice of rooms is offered - doubles and twins - including four with en suite facilities (one on the ground floor), and one with a large private bathroom. Two rooms have log fires in colder weather. Guests have unrestricted access to their rooms, which are furnished with easy chairs and a dining table. Full English or continental breakfast is served to the room each morning.

RECOMMENDED IN THE AREA

Exmoor (5 minute drive); Knightshayes Court (National Trust) (15 minute drive); Dunster Castle (National Trust) (20 minute drive)

Garden House ◆◆◆

Highly personalised guest house providing countless extra touches in a lovely garden setting

☎ 01373 301951
www.garden-househotel.co.uk

Map ref 2 - ST74

30 Fromefield, FROME,
BA11 2HE
2 Rooms, D £55-£65, No
smoking

RECOMMENDED IN THE AREA

Longleat (3 miles); Bath (13 miles); Glastonbury (17 miles)

This peaceful Georgian house is full of charm and elegance. It is named after one of its best features, a beautiful garden set within high walls, where fishponds, sweeping lawns and a shaded patio with lovely views make a delightful place to walk or sit. The two comfortable themed guest rooms are named after Beau Nash and Mozart, and they offer a host of extra items such as CD players, sherry, chocolates, fresh fruit and bath robes. Coffee/tea making facilities, trouser press, hairdryers and large cooling fans are standard in both rooms. Dinners, by prior arrangement, are served in the smart dining room, and feature fresh local produce. Well-cooked and carefully-prepared candle-lit breakfasts are also presented in style in this room. Because of the small number of guests accepted, the owners offer a very personalised service. This guest house is particularly well placed for many local attractions including Longleat, Stourhead, Glastonbury and Bath.

The Old Rectory ◆◆◆◆◆

Thatched rectory in a rural location

☎ 01460 54364
📠 01460 57374
📧 theoldrectory@
malherbie.freeserve.co.uk
malherbie.freeserve.co.uk

Map ref 2 - ST31
Cricket Malherbie, ILMINSTER,
TA19 0PW
from rdbt junct A358/A303 take A358
S towards Chard. After Donyatt turn L
towards Ilminster, R to Cricket
Malherbie, Old Rectory on L
5 Rooms, S £48 D £75-£85,
No smoking

This Grade II listed house has been beautifully restored and makes a delightful place to stay, with its thatched roof, sandstone walls and grand windows overlooking green lawns. Your charming hosts Michael and Patricia Fry-Foley take particular trouble to offer fine local produce at breakfast and dinner, cooked with flair and imagination. The comfortable bedrooms are well equipped, all are en suite and have tea and coffee making facilities and colour television. The house is licensed and children over 16 can be accommodated, no dogs are allowed except for guide dogs.

There is plenty of guest parking space and most credit cards are accepted. Yeovil, Taunton and the South coast are within easy reach by car.

RECOMMENDED IN THE AREA

Dorset Coast (35 minutes); Cricket St Thomas Wildlife Park (2 miles); many beautiful houses & gardens within 30 minutes

Monmouth Lodge ◆◆◆◆◆

RECOMMENDED IN THE AREA

Longleat Safari Park; Castle Combe (National Trust Village), Farley Hungerford; Stourhead

Historic village setting close to Bath

☎ 01373 834367

Map ref 2 - ST75
NORTON ST PHILIP, Bath, BA2 7LH
leave Bath on A36, after 7m right onto A366
to Norton St Philip
3 Rooms, D £65-£70, No smoking,
Closed 20 Dec-2 Jan

A delightful house, set in an acre of attractive garden with an orchard and views of the Somerset Hills which surround this charming village. The three attractively decorated en suite ground floor rooms are spacious and comfortable, with king-size beds, television, tea and coffee making facilities and patio doors opening onto the terrace. The same attention to detail is apparent in the sitting room and stylish dining room, where a good choice of excellent breakfast is served. Bath is just a ten minute drive away, and Monmouth Lodge is ideally situated for exploring Wells, Cheddar and Stonehenge. The famous 13th-century George Inn is nearby.

Andrews on the Weir... ✦✦✦ ❀❀❀

Restaurant with rooms in a delightful location with panoramic views over Porlock Bay

☎ 01643 863300
📠 01643 863311
✉ reservations@
   andrewsontheweir.co.uk
www.andrewsontheweir.co.uk

Map ref 2 - SS84

Porlock Weir, PORLOCK, TA24 8PB
A39 from Minehead to Porlock,
through village, 1st R signposted
Harbour (Porlock Weir) for 1.5m
5 Rooms, S £45-£80 D £65-£100,
No smoking in bedrooms or dining
room, Closed 2nd/3rd wk Jan &
2nd/3rd wk Nov & Mon

An elegant Georgian building on Porlock Weir provides the setting for a rather special establishment combining an AA three Rosette restaurant with beautifully presented en suite bedrooms in the country house style. Each room has its own character, including one with a romantic four-poster bed, and all have wonderful sea views. The highlight of a visit here must be the cooking, especially at dinner, for the innovation of the dishes and the delivery of all the promised flavours. Your evening might begin with an aperitif by the log fire in the attractive lounge, with olives or home-roasted almonds to nibble. Moving into the restaurant, local produce is a feature of the menu, including freshly caught fish from the weir, locally reared meats and West Country cheeses. All diets are catered for with the same imaginative approach. Breakfasts are also memorable, prepared from the best quality produce and with variety enough to suit all tastes and preferences.

RECOMMENDED IN THE AREA

Colborne Church (walking distance); Dunster Castle and Coneygar Tower (20 minutes) beautiful Exmoor walks (5 minute drive)

$\mathcal{B}$arkham ....

Peace and privacy in a traditional 18th-century farmhouse in Exmoor National Park

☎ 01643 831370
📠 01643 831370
✉ adie.exmoor@
   btinternet.com
www.exmoor-vacations.co.uk

Map ref 2 - SS73

Sandyway, SIMONSBATH, EX36 3LU
exit A361 to North Molton, through village & onto moor signed Sandyway, L at X-rds signed Simonsbath, 400mtrs turn R
3 Rooms, S £35 D £60-£70, No smoking

*T*his was one of the first farmhouses built in the Old Royal Park on Exmoor, the extensive grounds include a valley of steep woodland, pasture with a stream running through it, and a large treehouse. Walks, riding, trout and salmon fishing in season, are all close at hand.

The drawing room has an inglenook fireplace and French windows opening onto the croquet lawn. Bedrooms are attractive and satisfyingly simple, one has an en suite bathroom and king-sized double bed. An excellent dinner is available by arrangement, served by candlelight around a long central table in the oak-panelled dining room. The premises are licensed. One of the barns has been converted into an art gallery where concerts take place. A number of courses are run at Barkham and it is a lovely setting for weddings and functions.

RECOMMENDED IN THE AREA

National Trust Arlington Court (10 miles); Dunkery Beacon (10 miles); Quince Honey Farm (8 miles)

Greyhound Inn ◆◆◆◆

Friendly family-run guest accommodation in an atmospheric old building

☎ 01823 480227
📠 01823 481117

Map ref 2 - ST21

STAPLE FITZPAINE, Taunton,
TA3 5SP
M5 J25 take A358 Yeovil road, follow
signs to Staple Fitzpaine
4 Rooms, S £45 D £60-£69.90, No
smoking in bedrooms or restaurant

Originally built as a coaching inn, the Greyhound is a series of rambling rooms with flagstone floors, old timbers and natural stone walls. Four appealing bedrooms are furnished and equipped to a very high standard, with en suite bathrooms and plenty of toiletries. The candle-lit pub with its roaring fires and separate locals' bar is full of character, and a wide choice of imaginative food cooked from fresh local produce is served here. Real ale drinkers will enjoy the choice of beers on offer. Hospitality and service are of a high order, and the family owners create a warm welcome and relaxing atmosphere.

RECOMMENDED IN THE AREA

Walking in the Blackdown Hills or on Exmoor. Hestercombe Gardens; South Devon or North Somerset coasts (short drive)

Northam Mill ◆◆◆◆

Former mill house in an area of Outstanding Natural Beauty

☎ 01984 656916
📠 01984 656144
✉ bmsspicer@aol.com
www.northam-mill.co.uk

Map ref 2 - ST13

Water Lane, STOGUMBER, Taunton,
TA4 3TT
A358 approx 11m NW of Taunton. L at
1st sign Stogumber, down lane, pass
1st lane L in dip, uphill, downhill, next
L, 100yds on R into Water Ln
6 Rooms, S £30-£37.50 D £55-£75,
No smoking in bedrooms or dining
room

Hidden for 300 years, and full of character and timeless charm, this 16th-century mill house is located in beautiful countryside within a mile of Exmoor National Park; its pretty garden of four acres borders a trout stream. The all-en suite bedrooms include two in the main house, plus a garden suite and a self-catering apartment in the Old Mill Barn. Dinner varies from a barbecue to a formal dinner, with a daily menu based on fresh local ingredients, including home-produced bread, preserves, eggs and vegetables. Breakfast is a feast, and picnic lunches can be ordered. An honesty bar is also provided. Stabling is available for horses and purpose built kennels for guests' dogs. Children cannot be accommodated.

RECOMMENDED IN THE AREA

Exmoor – beautiful walking (30 minute drive); Quantocks walking and home of Wordsworth and Coleridge at Nether Stowey; Hestercombe Gardens (designed by Lutyens & Jekyll) (30 minute drive)

209

Creechbarn Bed & Breakfast ◆◆◆◆

Converted Somerset longbarn in a beautiful rural location

☎ 01823 443955
📠 01823 443509
✉ mick@somersite.co.uk
www.somersite.co.uk

Map ref 2 - ST22

Vicarage Lane, Creech-St-Michael, TAUNTON, TA3 5PP
M5 J25; A358. Turn to Creech St Michael via Ruishton. Follow canal boat signs to end of Vicarage Lane
3 Rooms, S £27-£29 D £40-£44, No smoking in bedrooms or dining room, Closed 20 Dec-6 Jan

*V*isitors are assured of a warm welcome from Hope & Mick Humphreys at this charming country home, a lovingly converted stone-built Somerset longbarn. It is peacefully situated at the end of a private drive, and surrounded by nearly an acre of well tended gardens with access to the Taunton/Bridgwater Canal. The bedrooms are comfortably furnished, one double room has an en suite shower and the other is a twin with a separate private bathroom. A further double room is available. There is a studio sitting room where a host of books, table tennis equipment and a television are provided for guests. Good home cooked dinners (by prior arrangement) and hearty breakfasts are served at one large table in the dining room. Guests should be sure to ask about the unique revolving log fire.

RECOMMENDED IN THE AREA

Temple of Harmony, Haswell Park; Hestercombe Gardens (3 miles); Wells

---

Lower Farm ◆◆◆◆

Thatched farmhouse in a lovely country setting

☎/📠 01823 443549
✉ lowerfarm@talk21.com
www.somersite.co.uk
Map ref 2 - ST22
Thornfalcon, TAUNTON, TA3 5NR
2m SE of M5 J25, on A358
Ilminster/Yeovil rd, turn L opp Nags Head PH. Lower Farm is 1m on L, signed on driveway
3 Rooms, S £25-£35 D £50, No smoking

*D*oreen and John Titman invite guests to relax in the peace of their late 15th-century Somerset longhouse, with its beamed ceilings and inglenook open fires. The house, which is Grade II listed, is set in large gardens, with parking provided, surrounded by open countryside. The accommodation comprises an en suite family room, an en suite double room (with additional bed), and a twin with separate facilities, all with colour televisions. There is a comfortable guests' lounge, and a dining room that is part of the old farmhouse kitchen, complete with traditional Aga. Full English or continental breakfast is served, and home-cooked evening meals by arrangement, featuring home-produced meat, and local produce, and seasonal vegetables from the garden. 2002 provides new holiday accommodation in a converted granary.

RECOMMENDED IN THE AREA

Hestercombe Gardens (designed by Lutyens and Jekyll) (15 minute drive); explore west Somerset by Steam Train through the Quantock Hills; Exmoor National Park and the Quantock and Blackdown Hills (easy driving distance)

Meryan House Hotel ◆◆◆◆

Historical house and fine restaurant set in beautiful grounds

☎ 01823 337445
📠 01823 322355
✉ info@meryanhouse.co.uk
www.meryanhouse.co.uk

Map ref 2 - ST

Bishop's Hull, TAUNTON, TA1 5EG
from Taunton take A38 towards
Wellington. After crematorium on left
take 1st right & house approx 600yds
12 Rooms, S £40-£55 D £50-£65,
No smoking in dining room

*D*ating back some 400 years, Meryan House is full of architectural interest, with old beams, inglenook fireplaces and a 30-foot deep well. It is located a mile from Taunton in delightful gardens that recently won a Taunton in Bloom award. The bedrooms are individually designed and furnished with antiques, including a half tester bed in the sumptuous honeymoon room. All rooms have en suite facilities, hospitality trays, radio/baby alarms, direct dial telephones and remote control colour televisions with video and satellite channels. Extra touches are the luxury toiletries, sweets and tissues. The house has its own restaurant with a menu based on seasonal local produce and vegetables from the garden.

RECOMMENDED IN THE AREA

West Somerset Railway; Willows and Wetlands Visitor Centre; Somerset County Museum

---

Beaconsfield Farm ◆◆◆◆◆

Period farmhouse in an area of outstanding natural beauty

☎ 01749 870308
📠 01749 870308
✉ carol@
  beaconsfieldfarm.co.uk
www.beaconsfieldfarm.co.uk

Map ref 2 - ST54

Easton, WELLS, BA5 1DU
2.5m from Wells on A371, on right just
before village of Easton
3 Rooms, S £35-£40 D £42-£46,
No smoking in bedrooms or dining
room, Closed 22 Dec-24 Jan

A peaceful retreat is provided by this lovely non-working farmhouse, set in its own four acres with views of the Mendip Hills to the north and the Somerset Levels to the south. The little city of Wells is just three miles away, and Glastonbury, Wookey Hole, Cheddar, Longleat, Weston-Super-Mare and Bath are within easy reach. Two rooms have en suite facilities and another a private bathroom. All are luxuriously appointed, with remote control television, mini fridges, hospitality trays, alarm clocks, bathrobes, hairdryers and direct dial telephones. Recommendations are offered for local pubs and restaurants including one within walking distance. No children under eight; credit cards not accepted.

RECOMMENDED IN THE AREA

National Trust Woodland Trail at Ebbor Gorge; Wookey Hole Caves and Mill; Clarks Village Designer and Factory Outlet

The Old Farmhouse ◆◆◆◆◆

A fine 17th-century farmhouse in the heart of Wells

☎ / 🖷 01749 675058
📧 theoldfarmhouse@
talk21.com
www.plus44.com/oldfarmhouse
Map ref 2 - ST54
62 Chamberlain Street, WELLS,
BA5 2PT
On A39 follow signs for city centre, R
at lights into Chamberlain St. House
on R opposite Almshouses
2 Rooms, S £40-£45 D £45-£50,
No smoking

Only in Wells, England's smallest cathedral city, would you expect to find an old farmhouse within a pretty walled garden, so well preserved and right in the centre. It only takes a short stroll to reach the Gothic cathedral, the 13th-century marketplace or the oldest medieval street in Europe. With Bath, Glastonbury and the unique Somerset Levels within easy driving distance, and secure private parking, this is the perfect base for exploring the city on foot, or the surrounding area by car. It is well worth coming back for dinner, available by prior arrangement. Felicity is a Cordon Bleu chef, and the food is truly delicious. Freshly cooked breakfasts are multi-choice, with homemade bread and preserves. Colours throughout the home are subtle and warm. Both bedrooms have en suite bathrooms, as well as colour TV, radio and tea and coffee. There is a payphone available to guests. The beds are extremely comfortable.

RECOMMENDED IN THE AREA

Bishop's Palace, Wells; The City Arms, Wells (pub); Cheddar Gorge

---

Riverside Grange ◆◆◆◆◆

Converted tannery in a quiet position on the river edge

☎ 01749 890761
Map ref 2 - ST54
Tanyard Lane, North Wootton,
WELLS, BA4 4AE
take A39 towards Glastonbury. On
leaving Wells take 1st L signed North
Wootton, through village to T-junct,
turn L & 2nd L
2 Rooms, S £27.50-£29.50 D £44-
£45, No smoking

Riverside Grange is an old tannery built in 1853 to supply leather to Clarks the Shoemakers. Its foundations are actually laid in the bed of the River Redlake which flows gently past. The bedrooms overlook a cider orchard, and the peaceful surroundings have been designated an area of outstanding natural beauty. It is a convenient location for visiting Wells, Glastonbury, Bath and Street (with its factory shopping outlet). Both bedrooms have been tastefully decorated with comfortable furnishings, tea and coffee and TV in the rooms. One room has an en suite shower room, the other has a private bathroom. Breakfast is served around one large table. Mrs English, an AA Landlady of the Year finalist, and her family greet their guests with a warm welcome.

RECOMMENDED IN THE AREA

Wookey Hole Caves; Cheddar Gorge; Clarks Village (Factory shopping outlet)

Tynings House ◆◆◆◆

Charming owners offer a relaxing stay at their beautifully-located guest house

☎ 01749 675368
🖷 01749 675368
✉ b+b@tynings.co.uk
www.tynings.co.uk

Map ref 2 - ST54

Harters Hill Lane, Coxley, WELLS, BA5 1RF
A39 to Coxley from Wells or Glastonbury. Turn off at Coxley Church School, take 4th L onto private road over cattle grid to house
3 Rooms, S £35-£40 D £50-£60, No smoking, Closed Nov-Mar

Well placed between Wells and Glastonbury, this peaceful 17th-century house makes the most of its rural outlook. The attractive, spacious bedrooms enjoy views out over the large garden and the unspoilt Somerset countryside beyond, as well as offering plenty of home comforts. Two of the en suite rooms are equipped with king-sized beds, and the third has two large twin beds. Bathrooms are neatly fitted, and include quality towels and toiletries. Delicious home-cooked dinners are served in the dining room, and there is also a very pleasant guests' lounge which opens out onto the garden. The friendly hosts are attentive and welcoming.

RECOMMENDED IN THE AREA

City of Wells; Glastonbury (2 miles); Bath (easy driving distance); walking on Mendip Hills

Bashfords Farmhouse ◆◆◆◆◆

Period farmhouse on the southern slopes of the Quantocks

☎ 01823 432015
🖷 0870 167 1587
✉ charlieritchie@ netscapeonline.co.uk
www.bashfordsfarmhouse.co.uk

Map ref 2 - ST13

WEST BAGBOROUGH, TA4 3EF
follow main road through village for approx 1.5m. Bashfords 3rd on left after pub
3 Rooms, S £27.50-£30 D £45-£50, No smoking

Bashfords is a beautifully restored farmhouse located in an area of outstanding natural beauty, rich in wildlife, with wonderful walks straight from the door. Most of the house dates from the 18th century, though some parts are over 400 years old. It has been carefully appointed to provide a superb level of comfort, with open fireplaces, wood burning stoves and a huge pine table in the dining room. Imaginative dinners prepared from local produce and homegrown vegetables are available, and the local pub is within walking distance. There is a double room with en suite shower facilities, and another double and a twin with private shower and bath respectively.

RECOMMENDED IN THE AREA

Beautiful walks on the Quantocks (from front door); West Somerset Steam Railway (10 minute drive); Hestercombe Gardens (15 minute drive)

*R*est and be Thankful Inn ♦♦♦♦

Former coaching inn surrounded by lovely countryside

☎ 01643 841222
📠 01643 841813
📧 enquiries@
    restandbethankful.co.uk
www.restandbethankful.co.uk

Map ref 2 - SS93

Wheddon Cross, WHEDDON CROSS, TA24 7DR
on crossroads of A396 & B3224, 5m S of Dunster
5 Rooms, S £26-£30 D £52-£60, No smoking in bedrooms or dining room, Closed 24-26 Dec

*T*he inn is beautifully located in a moorland village overlooking Dunkery Beacon, the highest point in Exmoor. A warm welcome is extended by the resident proprietors, who go out of their way to make guests feel at home.

The comfortable bedrooms all have en suite facilities. Colour televisions, direct dial telephones, and tea and coffee making equipment are provided for guests' comfort.

The restaurant, popular with residents and non-residents alike, offers a good selection of dishes, ranging from bar snacks to more substantial house specialities. There is a comfortable guest lounge. Additional amenities include darts, pool and a skittle alley. No pets or children under the age of 11 can be accommodated. Parking is available.

RECOMMENDED IN THE AREA

Exmoor National Park, walking, riding, cycling etc; medieval village of Dunster; Lorna Doone country

*K*arslake House ♦♦♦♦ ◉

Good food and comfortable accommodation in a 15th-century malthouse

☎ 01643 851242
📠 01643 851242
📧 karslakehouse@aol.com
www.karslakehouse.co.uk

Map ref 2 - SS93

Halse Lane, WINSFORD, Exmoor National Park, TA24 7JE
leave A396 (Winsford). In village turn L beyond village stores signed Karslake Hse. Around corner and just beyond Royal Oak
6 Rooms, S £45-£67.50 D £60-£95, No smoking in bedrooms, Closed Feb and Mar

*K*arslake House is a small country hotel surrounded by some of the most beautiful countryside in Exmoor and an ideal base for a peaceful and relaxing break. Original beams and fireplaces are a feature of the public rooms and quality is evident in the furnishings throughout the house. The newly decorated rooms are very attractive and the accommodation is thoughtfully equipped with colour televisions, hairdryers, complimentary toiletries, tea, coffee and mineral water. Four bedrooms have full en suite facilities, including one with a four-poster bed. Food is a highlight here, and interesting menus, including home-baked bread, and homemade preserves, are offered in the spacious restaurant, which has an AA Rosette award. Riding, fishing and shooting can all be arranged for guests.

RECOMMENDED IN THE AREA

Tarr Steps (medieval clapper bridge); Selworthy (National Trust village); Barle Valley Safaris – see the countryside by Landrover

Staffordshire

A selection of places to eat from the AA Restaurant & AA Pub Guides

Restaurants

◉ Three Horseshoes Inn (Traditional)
Buxton Road, Blackshaw Moor, Leek ST13 8TW
Tel 01538 300296 Fax 01538 300320

◉◉ Moat House (Classic)
Lower Penkridge Road, Acton Trussel, Stafford
ST17 0RJ
Tel 01785 712217 Fax 01785 715344

◉ Haydon House Hotel (Traditional)
Haydon Street, Bashford, Stoke-on-Trent
ST4 6JD
Tel 01782 711311 Fax 01782 717470

Pubs

🍺 The Old Boat
Alrewas DE13 7DB
Tel 01283 791468 Fax 01283 791468

🍺 The Black Lion Inn
Butterton ST13 7SP
Tel 01538 304232

🍺 The George
Castle Street, Eccleshall ST21 6DF
Tel 01785 850300

🍺 Ye Olde Royal Oak
Wetton, Leek DE6 2AF
Tel 01335 310287 Fax 01335 310336

🍺 The Hollybush Inn
Salt, Stafford ST18 0BX
Tel 01889 508234 Fax 01889 508058

🍺 Yew Tree Inn
Cauldon, Waterhouses, Stoke-on-Trent ST10 3EJ
Tel 01538 308348

🍺 Ye Olde Dog & Partridge Inn
High Street, Tutbury DE13 9LS
Tel 01283 813030 Fax 01283 813178

*B*ank House ✦✦✦✦✦

*Delightful former farmhouse in a
scenic location*

☎ / 🖷 01538 702810
📧 john.orme@dial.pipex.com
www.dialspace.dial.pipex.com
/town/parade/fi88

Map ref 7 - SK04
Farley Lane, OAKAMOOR, ST10 3BD
In Oakamoor pass church, then pub
(both on L), 80yds turn R. Bank House
0.3m on R
3 Rooms, S £45-£54 D £60-£78,
No smoking, Closed Xmas week

*O*riginally a farmhouse, this delightful
property has been lovingly restored by
John and Muriel Orme over many years.
Bedrooms are spacious and well equipped,
and one has a four-poster bed. Every
conceivable luxury is provided and the
comfort and well-being of guests is the
prime objective. An elegant drawing room is
available, where a cheerful log fire burns in
cooler weather. There is an abundance of
reading material throughout the house and
leaflets on local walks are created to order
by Muriel.

Hospitality is a major strength and there is a relaxing and
peaceful atmosphere. Excellent meals are provided and the
gardens are a joy to behold. Muriel is a recent winner of the
AA's prestigious Landlady of the Year award.

RECOMMENDED IN THE AREA

*The Potteries; Alton Towers Theme Park; The Peak National
Park*

*B*etley Court Farm ••••

A friendly guest house on a working farm, offering country pursuits, cosy bedrooms and good breakfasts

☎ 01270 820229

Map ref 5 - SJ74

BETLEY, CW3 9BH
leave M6 J16 onto A500 towards Crewe & to 2nd rdbt, then A531, farm in 2.5m on R
3 Rooms, S £28-£32 D £45-£48, No smoking

Recommended in the area

Stoke on Trent and the Potteries (8 miles); Bridgemere Garden World (6 miles); Chester and Alton Towers (both 40 minutes' drive); Keele University (5 miles)

*A*n impressive farmhouse surrounded by 250 acres of mixed farming in the picturesque village of Betley. This comfortable property offers attractively-decorated and well-equipped bedrooms themed around colours such as blue and pink, with spacious en suite facilities. Breakfast is a notable feature of a stay here, with home-produced sausages and bacon, farm fresh milk, and home-made jams and preserves adding to the enjoyment of the meal. Visitors are welcome to explore the farm, and in particular the beautiful 26-acre Betley Mere where bird watching and coarse fishing can be enjoyed along with other traditional country pursuits; specialist carp fishing can also be tried in a smaller pool. Betley Court Farm plays an integral part in village life, hosting the annual village show in August, and the Betley Bonfire on November 5th. The farm is easy to locate, and a wide selection of pubs and hotels serving meals can be found nearby.

Oak Tree Farm .....

*Comfortable
accommodation in a
lovely country house
with a river frontage*

☎ 01827 56807
📠 01827 56807

Map ref 3 - SK10

Hints Road, Hopwas,
TAMWORTH, B78 3AA
take A51 Lichfield to
Tamworth rd & turn into
Hints Rd at Tame Otter
pub. Last house on L
where road divides
7 Rooms, S -£54 D -
£70, No smoking in
bedrooms or dining
room

RECOMMENDED IN THE AREA

*Snow Dome (indoor wet snow ski slope) at Tamworth (2 miles); Lichfield
and Cathedral, (5 miles); Birmingham NEC (16 miles away).*

This beautifully renovated farmhouse is situated on the edge of the village of Hopwas, north west of Tamworth. It is surrounded by spacious gardens and overlooks the River Thame. There is an attractively appointed breakfast room, where separate tables are provided. Other facilities include an indoor swimming pool and steam room. Mrs Purkis creates a friendly and relaxing atmosphere and really enjoys welcoming guests into her home. Two rooms are located in the main house and the others are on the first and ground floors of a cleverly converted former grain store and farm building. All of them have en suite facilities. There is an attractively appointed breakfast room, where separate tables are provided. Other facilities include an indoor swimming pool and steam room. Mrs Purkis creates a friendly and relaxing atmosphere and really enjoys welcoming guests into her home. Despite the peace and tranquillity assured by its rural location, the house is a convenient base for visitors to Tamworth, Lichfield, Birmingham and the National Exhibition Centre.

Suffolk

A selection of places to eat from the AA Restaurant & AA Pub Guides

Restaurants

Lighthouse (Modern, British)
77 High Street, Aldeburgh IP15 5AU
Tel 01738 453377 Fax 01728 453377

Leaping Hare Restaurant (Chic, Country-house)
Stanton, Bury St Edmunds IP31 2DW
Tel 01359 250287 Fax 01359 252372

Scott's Brasserie (Modern)
4a Orwell Place, Ipswich IP4 1BB
Tel 01473 230254 Fax 01473 218851

Angel Hotel (Classic, Traditional)
Market Place, Lavenham CO10 9QZ
Tel 01787 247388 Fax 01787 248344

Ivy House Farm (Rustic, Traditional)
Beccles Road, Oulton Broad, Lowestoft
NR33 8HY
Tel 01502 501353 Fax 01502 501539

The Crown & Castle (Bistro)
Orford IP12 2LJ
Tel 01394 450205 Fax 01394 450176

Pubs

The Swan Inn
Swan Lane NR34 7QF
Tel 01520 476646

The Trowel & Hammer Inn
Mill Road, Cotton IP14 4QL
01449 781234 Fax 01449 781765

The Red Lion
The Street, Icklingham IP28 6PS
Tel 01638 717802 Fax 01638 515702

Angel Hotel
Market Place, Lavenham CO10 9QZ
Tel 01787 247388 Fax 01787 248344

The Cock Inn
The Green, Polstead CO6 5AL
Tel 01206 263150 Fax 01206 263150

Crown Hotel
The High Street, Southwold IP18 6DP
Tel 01502 722275 Fax 01502 727263

The Angel Inn
Stoke-by-Nayland CO6 4SA
Tel 01206 263245 Fax 01206 263375

The Six Bells Country Inn ♦♦♦♦

Set in peaceful countryside, a charming inn with lovely views

☎ 01359 250820
🖷 01359 250820
✉ sixbellsbardwell@aol.com
www.sixbellsbardwell.co.uk

Map ref 4 - TL97

The Green, Bardwell, BURY ST
EDMUNDS, IP31 1AW
A143, take turn marked Bardwell
Windmill/Six Bells. Inn 1m on L before
village green
10 Rooms, S £45-£55 D £50-£85,
No smoking in dining room,
Closed 25 & 26 Dec

Its origins are in the 16th century, and this tranquil country inn has been extended and modernised over the years without losing any of its intrinsic charm. The cottage-style bedrooms are located in a conversion of a barn and stables, with comfortable en suite facilities and great views over unspoilt countryside. The inn is a delightful building with many original features still in place. Delicious well-cooked food is prepared from fresh local ingredients and served either in the pretty conservatory or the beamed dining room. A very friendly team of staff offers a personal service to inn and guest house patrons, and there are good-value bed, breakfast and dinner breaks.

Recommended in the area

*Ickworth House (National Trust),
Sandringham, Kentwell Hall; Bury St
Edmunds with Abbey and Cathedral;
Cambridge. (All less than an hour's drive)*

Earsham Park Farm ••••

*Substantial Victorian
farmhouse with sweeping
views over the Waveney Valley
on the Norfolk/Suffolk border*

☎ 01986 892180
🖷 01986 894796
✉ watchorn_s@freenet.co.uk

Map ref 4 - TM38

Harleston Road, Earsham,
BUNGAY, NR35 2AQ
3m SW of Bungay on A143, on
RHS of road in SW direction
3 Rooms, S £34-£40 D £48-£60,
No smoking

RECOMMENDED IN THE AREA

*Earsham Otter Trust (0.5 mile);
Southwold (15 miles); Bressingham
Gardens (10 miles)*

Once part of the Duke of Norfolk's Deer Park, this elegant Victorian farmhouse is set amid lovely gardens on a 600-acre working farm, close to the Earsham Otter Sanctuary. The house has been carefully renovated to retain original features while emphasising its qualities of light and spaciousness. Hand stencilling is a feature of the bedrooms, along with antique furnishings, en suite facilities, remote control television, radio, hairdryer, in-room refreshments (tea, coffee, hot chocolate and biscuits), embroidered linen and fluffy towels. The rooms have playfully bucolic titles, including the Pig Sty with its king size bed and adjoining dressing room (which can be used to create a family suite), the Duck Pond with its four-poster, and the cosy twin-bedded Cow Shed with its luxurious bathroom. Breakfasts deserve a healthy appetite to do full justice to the farm's own sausages and bacon, home-made bread and preserves, and local free-range eggs. Lighter options include fresh fruit salad, dried fruit compote, Greek yoghurt and croissants. Vegetarian and special diets are happily catered for.

The Hatch ◆◆◆◆◆

15th-century thatched, timber frame house in a delightful rural setting

☎ / 🖷 01284 830226

Map ref 4 - TL85

Pilgrims Lane, Cross Green,
HARTEST, IP29 4ED
A143 towards Haverhill, B1066 to
Glemsford. 1st road on L on entering
village
2 Rooms, S £35-£45 D £60-£70,
No smoking

A lovely medieval house situated in a no through road, formerly the Pilgrims Way to the shrine of St Edmund at Bury St Edmunds. It is just outside the village of Hartest, surrounded by rolling countryside. Bridget and Robin Oaten are the charming hosts, greeting their guests with a cup of tea and home-made cakes on arrival. There is an acre of grounds including a wildflower meadow and a wonderful array of both old and new roses. Inside, antique pieces and fine fabrics complement the period architecture and attractive original features. The accommodation comprises a large double or twin ground floor room, with separate access, nearby parking and a sunny private terrace; and a family suite with a cosy single and double bedroom. Both the drawing room and dining room have splendid inglenook fireplaces where log fires burn on cooler evenings. The breakfast buffet is followed by English or continental choices.

RECOMMENDED IN THE AREA

The National Stud & National Horseracing Museum; National Trust Houses - Ickworth, Lavenham Guildhall & Melford Hall; antiques in Long Melford

Mockbeggars Hall ◆◆◆◆

A peaceful, relaxing environment for an away-from-it-all break

☎ 01473 830239
🖷 01473 832989
✉ pru@mockbeggars.co.uk
www.mockbeggars.co.uk

Map ref 4 - TM14

Claydon, IPSWICH, IP6 0AH
off A14 signed Gt Blakenham B1113.
Follow signs for Travel Inn along
Paper Mill Ln. Pass entrance, take
farm track on L 300 mtrs
5 Rooms, S £32-£40 D £45-£52, No
smoking in bedrooms

*E*xpect a warm welcome at this impressive Grade II listed Jacobean house. Set in an elevated spot in 12 acres of gardens and paddocks, it is surrounded by the rolling farmland. As befits a grand house with an interesting history, the elegant rooms are tall and spacious, and filled with antique and period furniture. The en suite bedrooms are filled with thoughtful extras, and there is also a self-contained flat in a converted old barn. Breakfast is eaten at the long family table in the dining room, and an evening meal by appointment or various snacks on request are also available. Yacht sailing weekend breaks are offered.

RECOMMENDED IN THE AREA

Christchurch Mansion, Ipswich, Constable country and Flatford Mill (15 minute drive); 'Invitation to view' scheme – tours of private historic houses

Lavenham Priory.....

Magnificent timber framed Priory, Grade I listed, in a celebrated Suffolk village

☎ 01787 247404
📠 01787 248472
✉ mail@
lavenhampriory.co.uk
www.lavenhampriory.co.uk

Map ref 4 - TL94

Water Street, LAVENHAM, Sudbury, CO10 9RW
A1141 to Lavenham, turn by side of Swan into Water St & right after 50yds into private drive
6 Rooms, S £59-£69 D £78-£116, No smoking, Closed 21 Dec-2 Jan

Gilli and Tim Pitt have created a sumptuous haven in the midst of historic Lavenham, one of England's prettiest medieval villages. The Priory dates back to the 13th century and retains many fine historical features, including an oak Jacobean staircase, leading to beautiful bedrooms with crown posts, Elizabethan wall paintings and oak floors. Each room has a spectacular bed, a four-poster, lit bateau or polonaise; and all have en suite facilities, television and tea and coffee making equipment. Lavenham Priory received the AA Guest Accommodation of the Year Award for 1999-2000.

The house is set in three acres of private grounds, all attractively landscaped and stocked with period herbs, plants and shrubs. Breakfast is taken in the merchants room at an imposing polished table. The great hall with its Tudor inglenook fireplace and an adjoining lounge are comfortable places to relax and are very well stocked with books.

RECOMMENDED IN THE AREA

Kentwell Hall (10 minutes); Ickworth House (20 minutes); Guildhall Lavenham

$\mathcal{F}$ield End Guest House ◆◆◆◆

Tastefully-decorated and pristine clean guest house that welcomes children

☎ 01728 833527
📠 01728 833527
✉ pwright@
   fieldend-guesthouse.co.uk
www.fieldend-guesthouse.co.uk

Map ref 4 - TM46

1 Kings Road, LEISTON, IP16 4DA
A12/A1094, turn L after 3m onto
B1069. After Leiston town sign turn R
at Aldeburgh/Leisure Centre sign, last
house on R
5 Rooms, S £28-£35 D £48-£55,
No smoking

*I*deally placed for touring the Suffolk coast, this large detached Edwardian house is close to several RSPB reserves including Minsmere and North Warren. Refurbished to a very high standard, it offers comfortable family accommodation with children and babies welcomed. Simple diets catered for. There's a range of puzzles and games in the dining room, where a large sofa encourages visitors to relax, and where breakfast is served. Bedrooms are tastefully decorated and fitted with wash basins (private bathrooms are available for each room) and one family room has the benefit of an en suite shower. Field End is close to Aldeburgh and Snape, and therefore attractive to visitors to the music festival and proms.

RECOMMENDED IN THE AREA

The Suffolk coast (1.5 miles); the Suffolk Cycle Route (1 mile); Long Shop Steam Museum

---

$\mathcal{A}$bbè House Hotel

Victorian townhouse a short walk from the beach

☎ 01502 581083
📠 01502 514327
✉ abbehouseh@cwcom.net

Map ref 4 - TM59

322 London Road South,
LOWESTOFT, NR33 0BG
on A12 (London rd) northbound -
Hotel on right. Approx 1.5m from town
outskirts
3 Rooms, S £35-£40 D £46-£70,
No smoking

*F*riendly hospitality and a high standard of accommodation are offered at this small, family-run hotel, with home-made cake and tea served on arrival. Two rooms are en suite and the third has private facilities. All have colour televisions, radio alarms, hairdryers, bathrobes, toiletries and hospitality trays. Public areas comprise a lounge with a corner bar and a dining room where a fantastic choice is offered at breakfast, including locally dry-cured bacon and award-winning sausages from a local master butcher, and Lowestoft kippers, smoked haddock and smoked salmon from the local smokehouse (the oldest in Britain). The garden has won the Lowestoft in Bloom Gold Award for the last several years.

RECOMMENDED IN THE AREA

Lowestoft Ness – Britain's most easterly point (few minutes' drive); The Broads National Park (5 minute drive); the Otter Trust and Suffolk Wildlife Trust (easy driving distance)

*T*he Albany Hotel ◆◆◆◆

Delightful privately-owned hotel close to the town and beach

☎ 01502 574394 📠 01502 581198
📧 geoffrey.ward@btclick.com
www.albanyhotel-lowesoft.co.uk

Map ref 4 - TM59

400 London Road South, LOWESTOFT,
NR33 0BQ
on A12 to Lowestoft from S. Hotel on right
just after entering one-way system from
Pakefield
8 Rooms, S £20-£28 D £42-£52,
No smoking in bedrooms or dining room

*K*nown as 'the small hotel with the big welcome', it is not surprising to find that hospitality is high on the agenda here. Much of the original style and elegance of the Edwardian age was preserved when the terraced townhouse was converted into a hotel. It now offers stylish, comfortable bedrooms, each one individually decorated and furnished with well-chosen pieces; six of the rooms are en suite. A licensed bar is a useful feature of the pleasant lounge, and in the elegant dining room delicious breakfasts offering plenty of choice are served. Home-cooked evening meals are also provided here.

RECOMMENDED IN THE AREA

Somerleyton Hall & Gardens (4-5 miles); Fritton Lake Countryworld (5-6 miles); Lowestoft Maritime Museum (1 mile)

*S*urrey

A selection of places to eat from the AA Restaurant & AA Pub Guides

Restaurants

◎ Le Petit Pierrot Restaurant (Chic, French)
4 The Parade, Claygate KT10 0NU
Tel 01372 465105 Fax 01372 467642

◎ Chalk Lane Farm (Country-house)
Chalk Lane, Woodcote End, Epsom KT18 7BB
Tel 01372 721179 Fax 01372 727878

◎◎ Lythe Hill Hotel (Modern-French)
Petworth Road, Haslemere GU27 3BQ
Tel 01428 651251 Fax 01428 644131

◎◎ Langshott Manor (Country-house)
Langshott Lane, Horley RH6 9LN
Tel 01293 786680 Fax 01293 783905

◎◎ The Dining Room (Modern)
59a High Street, Reigate RH2 9AE
Tel 01737 226650 Fax 01737 226650

◎◎ Kinghams
Gomshall Lane, Shere GU5 9HE
Tel 01483 202168

◎ Gemini (Modern)
28 Station Approach, Tadworth KT20 5AH
Tel 01737 812179 Fax 01737 812179

Pubs

🍺 The Crown Inn
The Green, Chiddingfold GU8 4TX
Tel 01428 682255 Fax 01428 685736

🍺 The Stephan Langton
Friday St, Abinger Common, Dorking RH5 6JR
Tel 01306 730775

🍺 The Woolpack
The Green, Elstead GU8 6HD
Tel 01252 703106 Fax 01252 703106

🍺 King William IV
Byttom Hill, Mickleham
Tel 01372 372590

🍺 Bryce's at The Old School House
Ockley RH5 5TH
Tel 01306 627430 Fax 01306 628274

🍺 The Inn @ West End
42 Guildford Road, West End GU24 9PW
Tel 01276 858652 Fax 01276 485842

🍺 Brickmakers Arms
Chertsey Road, Windlesham GU20 6HT
Tel 01276 472267 Fax 01276 451014

$\mathcal{T}$rumbles ◆◆◆◆

Victorian house peacefully located close to Gatwick Airport

☎ 01293 863418/862925
🖷 01293 862925
✉ trumbles.gatwick@tesco.net
www.trumbles.co.uk

Map ref 3 - TQ24

Stan Hill, CHARLWOOD, RH6 0EP
J8 M25. A217 to Gatwick, turn R at
rdbt to Charlwood Village, through
village bear R to Leigh, 1st L into Stan
Hill, Trumbles 300yds on R
4 Rooms, S £40-£45 D £50-£55,
No smoking

*I*n a pleasant village location, on the outskirts of a charming Surrey village, this family-run guest house is just minutes away from Gatwick Airport, and rail and road links to London and the south coast. The house was built in 1872 and was once a cottage hospital, a country club and a small hotel/restaurant. Recently refurbished, it has comfortable, spacious and well equipped bedrooms, all with en suite facilities, hairdryers, colour televisions, clock radios and hospitality trays. Larger deluxe rooms also have ironing facilities. A payphone is available at reception. There is a sunny conservatory/breakfast room and an inviting garden patio. A continental breakfast is served, including hot croissants and fresh fruit salad. Complimentary transport can be provided to Gatwick at any time. Parking available.

RECOMMENDED IN THE AREA

Limes Bistro & local inns; Charlwood village and zoo

$\mathcal{T}$he Lawn Guest House ◆◆◆◆

Well-equipped guest house for the international traveller

☎ 01293 775751
🖷 01293 821803
✉ info@lawnguesthouse.co.uk
www.lawnguesthouse.co.uk

Map ref 3 - TQ24

30 Massetts Road, HORLEY,
RH6 7DE
M23 J9, follow signs to A23 (Redhill),
at rdbt by Esso garage take 3rd exit,
Massetts Rd 200yds on R
12 Rooms, S £40-£45 D £50-£55,
No smoking

*H*andily-placed for Gatwick airport, this imposing Victorian house set in pretty gardens is particularly popular with air travellers. Late arrival is no problem, and there are free airport transfers between 9am and 10pm. Guests may leave their cars for a fee while they are away. Bedrooms and bathrooms are nicely decorated and bright, and equipped with many extras including hairdryers, tea/coffee/chocolate facilities, direct dial phones, pumped showers and computer modem sockets, all of which are attractive to the many North American visitors. An ice machine and an on-line computer are available for guests' sole use. A choice of well-prepared hot and cold breakfast dishes is served in the attractive dining room. Service is very efficient.

RECOMMENDED IN THE AREA

Hever Castle (10 miles); Chessington World of Adventure (30 minute drive); Leonardslee Gardens (5 miles)

Sussex

A selection of places to eat from the AA Restaurant & AA Pub Guides

Restaurants

Black Chapati (Modern, Minimalist)
12 Circus Parade, Brighton, East Sussex
BN1 4GW
Tel 01273 699011

One Paston Place (Chic)
1 Paston Place, Brighton, East Sussex BN2 1HA
Tel 01273 606933 Fax 01273 675686

Sundial Restaurant (Chic, French)
Herstmonceux, East Sussex BN27 4LA
Tel 01323 832217 Fax 01323 832909

Hungry Monk Restaurant (Country-house)
Jevington, East Sussex BN26 5QF
Tel/Fax 01323 482178

Landgate Bistro (Bistro, Modern)
5-6, Landgate, Rye, East Sussex TN31 7LH
Tel 01797 227907

The Wild Mushroom Restaurant (Modern)
Woodgate House, Westfield Lane, Westfield, East
Sussex TN35 4SB
Tel 01424 751137

Millstream Hotel (Classic Country-house)
Bosham Lane, Bosham, West Sussex PO18 8HL
Tel 01243 573234 Fax 01243 573459

Cliffords Cottage Restaurant (Traditional)
Bracklesham Lane, Bracklesham, West Sussex
PO20 8JA
Tel 01243 670250

Comme Ça (Chic)
67 Broyle Road, Chichester West Sussex
PO19 4BD
Tel 01243 788724 Fax 01243 530052

Taylors Barn Restaurant (Rustic)
Brook Street, Cuckfield, West Sussex RH17 5JJ
Tel/Fax 01444 455826

Jeremy's at Borde Hill
Balcomb Hill, Haywards Heath, West Sussex
RH16 1XP
Tel 01444 441102 Fax 01444 441102

Lickfold Inn (Minimalist)
Lickfold, West Sussex GU28 9EY
Tel 01798 861285 Fax 01798 861342

Fleur de Sel (Country-house)
Manleys Hill, Storrington West Sussex
RH20 4BT
Tel 01903 742331 Fax 01903 740649

Alexander House
East Street, Turners Hill, West Sussex RH10 4QD
Tel 01342 714914 Fax 01342 717328

Pubs

Rose Cottage Inn
Alciston, East Sussex BN26 6UW
Tel 01323 870377 Fax 01323 871440

The Cricketers Arms
Berwick, East Sussex BN26 6SP
Tel 01323 870469 Fax 01323 87411

The Jolly Sportsman
Chapel Lane, East Chiltington, East Sussex
BN7 3BA
Tel 01273 890400 Fax 01273 890400

The Tiger Inn
East Dean, East Sussex BN20 0DA
Tel 01323 423209 Fax 01323 423209

Star Inn
Church St, Old Heathfield, East Sussex
TN21 9AH
Tel 01435 863570 Fax 01435 862020

The Ypres Castle Inn
Gun Garden, Rye, East Sussex TN31 7HH
Tel 01797 223248

The Dorset Arms
Withyham, East Sussex TN7 4BD
Tel 01892 770278 Fax 01892 770195

George & Dragon
Burpham, West Sussex BN18 9RR
Tel 01903 883131

The White Horse at Chilgrove
High St, Chilgrove West Sussex PO18 9HX
Tel 01243 535219 Fax 01243 535301

The King's Arms
Midhurst Road, Fernhurst, West Sussex
GU27 3HA
Tel 01428 652005 Fax 01428 658970

Black Horse Inn
Nuthurst, West Sussex RH13 6LH
Tel 01403 891272 Fax 01403 891148

The Halfway Bridge Inn
Halfway Bridge, Petworth, West Sussex
GU28 9BP
Tel 01798 861281 Fax 01798 861878

The Fox Goes Free
Charlton, Singleton, West Sussex PO18 0HU
Tel 01243 811641 Fax 01243 811461

The Horse Guards Inn
Tillington, West Sussex GU28 9AF
Tel 01798 342332 Fax 01798 344351

Bates Green ◆◆◆◆◆

18th-century gamekeeper's cottage on a quiet country village lane

☎ 01323 482039
📠 01323 482039

Map ref 4 - TQ50

ARLINGTON, East Sussex, BN26 6SH
2m W of A22 towards Arlington turn R
Old Oak Inn
3 Rooms, D £70, No smoking, Closed
22-27 Dec

Bates Green is an idyllic rural retreat. There is an oak-panelled sitting room, with an open log fire. The bedrooms are decorated in cottage style, brightened by fresh flowers, with en suite bathrooms and colour TV. Children and pets cannot be accommodated.

There is an impressive two-acre plantsman's garden: a rockery with pond; an enclosed garden with colourful borders; and a shaded, foliage garden. There is usually a selection of plants for sale, and garden chat is always welcome. Bates Green also has pasture with 300 sheep, as well as deciduous woodland, with spectacular vistas of bluebells towards the end of April and beginning of May.

On arrival guests are welcomed with tea and home made cakes. A substantial English breakfast is served that includes freshly squeezed orange juice, dried fruit compote, oak-smoked Sussex bacon and home made preserves.

RECOMMENDED IN THE AREA

Michelham Priory & Gardens (5 minute drive); Charleston (Bloomsbury Group country house, 10 minute drive); Lewes Castle & Anne of Cleves House (20 minutes drive)

Bonham's Country House ◆◆◆◆◆

Charming house with relaxing atmosphere, and luxury designer accommodation

☎ 01243 551301
📠 01243 551301
✉ bonhams@
compass_rose.org.uk

Map ref 3 - TQ90

Barnham Road, Yapton, ARUNDEL,
West Sussex, BN18 0DX
A27/A29 towards Bognor Regis, turn
L at first rdbt on B2233 through
Barnham. House after S-bend but
before Black Dog pub, on L
3 Rooms, S £42 D £50-£70, No
smoking in bedrooms or dining room

Pleasantly located between Chichester and Arundel, and handy for the coast, this charming mid 18th-century house continues to offer the elegant lifestyle for which it was designed. Luxurious bedrooms are attractively decorated and spacious, with en suite facilities and plenty of discerning extras to make guests feel at home. Good home-cooked breakfasts are taken in the oak-panelled dining room, and there's a comfortable, sunny lounge. An all-weather tennis court, indoor swimming pool, snooker and boules are ideal for the energetic visitor, and the landscaped walled garden with a pond is a charming amenity for everyone. Yacht charter is also available.

RECOMMENDED IN THE AREA

Arundel Castle, Cathedral and town (5 miles); Portsmouth Historic Ships and Submarine Museum; Fishbourne Roman Palace (10 miles); Petworth House

Farthings Farm ♦♦♦♦

Superb elevated position for this Edwardian House serving memorable breakfasts

☎ 01424 773107
✉ penny.rodgers@
   btopenworld.com
www.farthingsfarm.co.uk

Map ref 4 - TQ71

Catsfield, BATTLE, East Sussex,
TN33 9BA
from Battle on A271. Turn L onto
B2204 towards Catsfield for 1m. Farm
on L of sharp S-bend & farmhouse
0.5m down farm lane
1 Room, D £50-£55, No smoking in
bedrooms or dining room

Farthings is positioned down the farm lane in 70 acres of peaceful countryside, half a mile from the road. The south facing house and guest wing overlooks woodland, fields and lake; you might enjoy a 20 minute walk across the fields to reach the historic town of Battle, after tea and home-made cake served on arrival. Dinner is available at Farthings, and breakfast, with its varied menu, is served in the combined lounge/dining room or on the terrace. The well appointed versatile en suite room is attractively furnished and decorated.

RECOMMENDED IN THE AREA

Batemans – Rudyard Kipling's house (National Trust); Great Dixter house and gardens; Bodiam Castle

White Barn Guest House ♦♦♦♦

Architecturally unique house in a harbour village setting

☎ 01243 573113
📠 01243 573113
✉ whitebarn@compuserve.com

Map ref 3 - SU80

Crede Lane, BOSHAM, Chichester,
West Sussex, PO18 8NX
A259 Bosham rdbt, turn S signed
Bosham Quay, 0.5m to t-junct, L
signed White Barn, 0.25m turn L
signed White Barn, 50yds turn R
3 Rooms, S £35-£60 D £60-£75,
No smoking

The location of this single-storey house is very peaceful, in a private road in the beautiful Saxon harbour village of Bosham, close to the city of Chichester, glorious Goodwood, the West Sussex beaches and the South Downs. The all-en suite bedrooms are compact but well appointed and thoughtfully equipped, with colour televisions, electric blankets and tea and coffee making materials. Hairdryers and ironing facilities are available for guests' use. The glass walled dining room, overlooking the garden, is the setting for a choice of English or continental breakfast, and a four-course dinner prepared from fresh local ingredients (available October-March). White Barn is not suitable for pets or children under 10.

RECOMMENDED IN THE AREA

Chichester – cathedral, theatre, Fishbourne Roman Palace; Bosham/Itchenor – sailing, water tours and coastal walks; Portsmouth – historic ships and harbour tours

Kenwood •••••

*Large Victorian
house overlooking
Bosham Harbour*

☎ 01243 572727
📠 01243 572738

Map ref 3 - SU80

Off A259, BOSHAM,
Chichester, West
Sussex, PO18 8PH
400m W of Bosham
roundabout on A259
3 Rooms, No
smoking in
bedrooms or dining
room

Sheena Godden's friendly hospitality ensures an enjoyable stay at this fine property, which is set in several acres of well maintained gardens with extensive views over the harbour. The decor and furnishings reflect the period charm, creating a warm, homely atmosphere.

The comfortably appointed bedrooms are all en suite and have many thoughtful extras. A generous breakfast is served in the bright conservatory, which also contains a fridge and microwave oven for guests who wish to cater for themselves in the evening.

The lounge is the ideal setting in which to relax after a busy day, and other amenities include a pool table and solar heated swimming pool covered by a dome.

RECOMMENDED IN THE AREA

*Goodwood Festival of Speed & Races;
Fishbourne Roman Palace; Chichester Marina*

Trouville Hotel ◆◆◆◆

Conveniently situated seafront hotel with efficient owners and attractive rooms

☎ 01273 697384

Map ref 3 - TQ30

11 New Steine, Marine Parade, BRIGHTON,
East Sussex, BN2 1PB
A259 approx 300yds from Palace Pier
8 Rooms, S £29 D £59-£65, No smoking in
dining room, Closed Xmas & Jan

RECOMMENDED IN THE AREA

National Trust gardens at Sheffield Park and Nyman's Place (10 miles); stately homes – Firle and Glynde Place (8 miles); South Downs area of Outstanding Natural Beauty (5 miles)

A Regency seafront square is the smart setting for this Grade II listed building. The small period hotel has been well restored, and is tastefully decorated and furnished to provide comfortable, appealing accommodation. Most rooms have en suite facilities, and one large room boasts a four-poster bed and balcony with sea views. Trouville is run to a high standard under the personal supervision of the resident owners, and guests are assured of a pleasant stay. Well-cooked breakfasts are served in the bright open-plan lounge/dining room. All the attractions of Brighton are an easy walk away, such as the Pavilion, the Lanes, the Marina, and the conference centres.

Paskins Town House ◆◆◆◆◆

Environmentally friendly house within walking distance of the seafront

☎ 01273 601203 📠 01273 621973
📧 welcome@paskins.co.uk
www.paskins.co.uk

Map ref 3 - TQ30

18/19 Charlotte Street, BRIGHTON,
East Sussex, BN2 1AG
A23 to pier, turn left, Charlotte Street on L
19 Rooms, S £25-£47.50 D £55-£110

L ocal organic produce, fair trade tea and coffee, and cruelty-free toiletries are examples of the thoughtful approach to hospitality at this attractive town house. It provides stylish accommodation in a residential area convenient for the town centre and the seafront. Sixteen bedrooms are en suite, some have luxurious four-poster beds and all have colour televisions, direct dial telephones and hospitality trays. Breakfast is a treat with options like home-made spiced compote, traditionally cured bacon, speciality sausages and imaginative vegetarian and vegan dishes. The fully licensed lounge provides a relaxing setting for a lunchtime or early evening drink. Freshly made sandwiches can be ordered with your drink or in your room.

RECOMMENDED IN THE AREA

Brighton – excellent shopping, two piers, Regency Pavilion, great atmosphere

Cedar House ◆◆◆◆

Quietly located house to the west of the city

☎ 01243 787771
📠 01243 538316
✉ mel.judi@talk21.com

Map ref 3 - SU80

8 Westmead Road, CHICHESTER,
West Sussex, PO19 3JD
from 'Fishbourne' rdbt on A27 W of
city, proceed for city centre. Then 1st
L into Fishbourne Rd East, R into Clay
Lane, 1st R
4 Rooms, S £20-£30 D £45-£50,
No smoking

*J*udi and Mel Woodcock's lovely home is set in spacious gardens at the end of a cul-de-sac, just 12 minutes' walk from the city centre. It makes a convenient base for visiting the cathedral, Festival Theatre, Fishbourne Roman Palace, Goodwood House and Racecourse, Bosham village and the South Downs. Bedrooms are stylishly decorated and all have television, tea/coffee and en suite facilities (except one room with a private bathroom). Breakfast is served at a large table in the dining room. There are two village pubs within five minutes' walk, both offering food and real ale, and a good range of restaurants in Chichester.

RECOMMENDED IN THE AREA

Chichester town centre; Fishbourne Roman Palace; Bosham

Chichester Lodge ◆◆◆◆

Delightful gate cottage to a manor house, with comfortable, tasteful bedrooms

☎ 01243 786560
📠 01243 784525

Map ref 3 - SU80

Oakwood, CHICHESTER,
West Sussex, PO18 9AL
3 miles west of Chichester off the
B2178. Establishment 170 metres on L
after Salthill Road)
2 Rooms, D £60, No smoking

*C*harming Gothic lodge set peacefully amidst pretty, secluded gardens of one and a half acres, yet only a few miles from Chichester. Flagstoned floors, lots of polished wood, and beautiful Gothic windows lend character to the inside as well, and there's a welcoming wood-burning stove in the hallway. The spacious bedrooms are well furnished and decorated in tasteful designs, all with en suite bathrooms and televisions. There are plenty of places in which to relax, including a garden room and a conservatory filled with plants and shrubs. Breakfast is served in the elegant dining room.

RECOMMENDED IN THE AREA

Chichester Festival Theatre (1.5 miles); Fishbourne Roman Palace (5 minute drive); West Dean Gardens (National Trust)

Wilbury House Bed & Breakfast ◆◆◆◆

*Modern home near Roman palace
and Goodwood racing*

☎ 01243 572953
🖷 01243 572953
✉ jackie.penfold@talk21.com

Map ref 3 - SU80

Main Road, Fishbourne,
CHICHESTER, West Sussex,
PO18 8AT
from A27 Chichester by-pass, take
A259 W to Fishbourne and Bosham,
1m on L from Tesco rdbt
3 Rooms, S £30-£35 D £50-£60, No
smoking, Closed mid Dec-mid Jan

Jackie and Maurice Penfold welcome guests to their family home, a comfortable, modern house of warm brown brick, built in 1994 by Maurice himself. The design and décor of the house reflects the loving care that they have bestowed upon it. It is on the outskirts of Chichester, just a quarter of a mile from the Fishbourne Roman Palace, one of the biggest and best preserved Roman sites in the country.

The rooms look out over farmland towards Goodwood, ten minutes away, where there is horse racing, as well as events at the famous car-racing track. One room has en suite bathroom facilities. A generous breakfast is served.

Guests may use the patio and gardens in the summer, and there is ample off-road parking.

RECOMMENDED IN THE AREA

Chichester Cathedral; West Dean Gardens; Uppark (National Trust)

Forge Hotel ◆◆◆◆◆

*Delightful restored cottage with superior
views and excellent food*

☎ 01243 535333 🖷 01243 535363
✉ enquiries@forgehotel.com
www.forgehotel.com

Map ref 3 - SU81

CHILGROVE, Chichester, West Sussex,
PO18 9HX
off B2141, adjacent to White Horse Inn, 6m
NW of Chichester
5 Rooms, S £35-£45 D £79-£99, No smoking
in bedrooms, Closed last wk Oct & 1 wk Feb

This typical 17th-century Sussex brick and flint cottage is surrounded by beautiful downland countryside in an area of outstanding natural beauty. Completely restored by its owner, Chef Neil Rusbridge, it offers tasteful accommodation in keeping with the building's style, with superior fabrics and designs to enhance the rustic character. Bedrooms are thoughtfully laid out, with well-planned en suite bathrooms (one room has private facilities), and plenty of extras. The stairs to three rooms are steep, but two are on the ground floor. Breakfast and gourmet dinners are cooked in front of guests, who share a communal table. Expect a warm welcome and congenial hospitality.

RECOMMENDED IN THE AREA

Goodwood (5 miles); Chichester (6 miles); Portsmouth (25 miles)

$\mathcal{P}$innacle Point ♦♦♦♦♦

Celebrity retreat in a desirable location overlooking Eastbourne

☎ 01323 726666
🖷 01323 643946
www.pinnaclepoint.co.uk

Map ref 4 - TQ69

Foyle Way, Upper Duke's Drive,
EASTBOURNE, East Sussex,
BN20 7XL
Take A22 past station, follow signs to
seafront. Head W along promenade
towards South Downs. At foot of hill is
St Bedes school, immediately after
school turn L. Pinnacle Point is 80m
beyond metal gate
3 Rooms, S £50-£60 D £80-£100, No
smoking, Closed Xmas & New Year

*I*n a unique position on Pinnacle Point, with views over the town, this superb modern establishment has all the qualities that ensure an enjoyable stay. The proprietors, Mr and Mrs Pyemont, aim to pamper their guests, and as such the house is a favourite retreat for the stars of television, theatre and international sport. The spacious bedrooms are appointed to the highest level with an extensive range of facilities, and the en suite bathrooms are thoughtfully designed, with effective lighting and an excellent range of toiletries. There are plenty of relaxing areas, with an outside pool and verandas for summer use as well as the open-plan lounge and dining room.

RECOMMENDED IN THE AREA

Opera at Glyndebourne (30 minutes); walk the South Downs Way to Beachy Head (from the gate); gardens at Great Dixter (60 minutes); Leonardslee (45 minutes); Borde Hill (45 minutes)

Old Corner Cottage ♦♦♦♦♦

Extended period cottage in a village setting

☎ / 🖷 01435 863787
✉ hamishcjbrown@aol.com

Map ref 4 - TQ52

Little London Road, HEATHFIELD,
East Sussex, TN21 0LT
A267 to Heathfield 1st R past Cross
in Hand pub, signed Horam &
Eastbourne into Little London Rd
3 Rooms, S £30 D £45-£50,
No smoking

A warm welcome is assured at this pretty cottage from Cynthia Brown, who offers hospitality of the highest standard. Corner Cottage is close to the village centre, and makes a convenient base from which to visit Eastbourne, Beachy Head, Hastings and Brighton. There are also several notable houses and gardens within a short drive. Half a mile distant is the start of the Cuckoo Trail cycle track, on the old railway line, which runs from Heathfield to Polegate through pretty countryside. The bedrooms are spacious and comfortably appointed with many thoughtful extras. All of the rooms have modern en suite facilities. A generous breakfast is served in the charming dining room, including a variety of cereals, fruit and yoghurt as well the traditional English breakfast. Guests can relax in the conservatory lounge overlooking the attractive garden.

RECOMMENDED IN THE AREA

Batemans (home of Rudyard Kipling, 4 miles); Glyndebourne Opera House (short drive); cliff walks

Wartling Place .....

A Georgian country house, formerly a rectory, set in two acres of mature secluded gardens

☎ 01323 832590
📠 01323 831558
✉ accom@
wartlingplace.prestel.co.uk
www.countryhouseaccomoda
tion.co.uk

Map ref 4 - TQ60

Wartling Place, Wartling,
HERSTMONCEUX, Hailsham,
East Sussex, BN27 1RY
take A271 signed Herstmonceux
after Windmill Hill turn R continue
following signs, at Wartling village,
Wartling Place on R opp church
3 Rooms, S £55-£70 D £72-£95,
No smoking

ormerly the rectory for the Parish of Wartling, this listed period property has been carefully refurbished to provide accommodation of the highest quality. The standard of the furnishings and décor are matched by equally high levels of hospitality and service. Two of the bedrooms have four-poster beds and have a bath and shower en suite, tea and coffee making facilities, remote control colour televisions and hairdryers. Guests can relax in the stylish comfort of the drawing room and a fine breakfast is served in the elegant dining area. Wartling Place is set in extensive mature gardens, with some impressive trees, and private parking is provided within the grounds. The house is ideally situated for visiting many historic towns, castles, and National Trust houses and gardens in the South East. Golf, tennis, riding, walking, cycling and watersports can all be enjoyed in the immediate vicinity and the town of Eastbourne is just five miles away.

RECOMMENDED IN THE AREA

Herstmonceux Castle; Monk's House (home of Virginia Woolf); Sissinghurst Castle

Nightingales ♦♦♦♦♦

Fantastic gardens at the foot of the South Downs

☎ 01273 475673
📠 01273 475673
✉ Nightingales@totalise.co.uk
www.users.totalise.
co.uk/~nightingales/

Map ref 3 - TQ30

The Avenue, Kingston, LEWES,
East Sussex, BN7 3LL
A23 S/A27 E signposted Lewes. At
1st rdbt take 3rd exit, R at 30mph
sign, premises 2nd from end on R
2 Rooms, S £35 D £50-£55,
No smoking

Nightingales is situated in a quiet country road, surrounded by beautifully kept gardens. There is a wonderful pink bougainvillea growing in the conservatory. Guests are free to explore the well-kept grounds, perhaps in the company of Ben, the resident black labrador who gives everyone a warm welcome. The bedrooms are comfortably furnished, both with en suite facilities, and have colour television and tea and coffee making facilities for guests. The range of thoughtful extras in the rooms includes fresh fruit, flowers, chocolate and sherry. Breakfast is served by the Aga. Although dinner is not available here, Jean is happy to recommend local restaurants and a 15th-century real ale pub nearby.

RECOMMENDED IN THE AREA

Anne of Cleves House Museum & Lewes Castle

Pendragon Lodge ♦♦♦♦♦

Former village bakery, now beautifully maintained guest house

☎ 01424 814051
📠 01424 812499
✉ pendragon-
lodge@hotmail.com
www.pendragonlodge.co.uk

Map ref 4 - TQ81

Watermill Lane, PETT, Rye,
East Sussex, TN35 4HY
A259 from Hastings, turn R opposite
Beefeater inn, onto minor road signed
Pett Rd. Proceed 1m, pass shops on
R, 2nd turning L, house R
3 Rooms, S £30-£35 D £50-£64,
No smoking

This impressive Edwardian building, in a tranquil country lane, is very near to the quaint old town of Rye. Hastings, Battle and Bodiam are all equally accessible. The spotless accommodation boasts tastefully furnished en suite bedrooms, (including one with four-poster bed) with real attention to detail: pretty china plugs in wash basins, hand wrapped soap and so on. The dining area overlooks the immaculately tended gardens and imaginative cooked breakfasts, which also include home-made bread, muesli, and preserves, are traditionally prepared on the Aga and served at one family table. There is a relaxed, professional ambience at Pendragon Lodge where you will be warmly welcomed. Parking space available for guests.

RECOMMENDED IN THE AREA

Ancient town of Rye; National Trust properties at Sissinghurst Castle and Scotney Castle; Battle and Battle Abbey

Mizzards Farm ◆◆◆◆◆

16th-century stone house, with peaceful gardens and lake

☎ 01730 821656
🖷 01730 821655
✉ julian.francis@hemscott.net

Map ref 3 - SU82

ROGATE, West Sussex, GU31 5HS
from x-rds in Rogate S for 0.5m, cross river, 300yds then turn R, signed Mizzards Farm
3 Rooms, S £34-£45 D £58-£70, No smoking, Closed Xmas

The River Rother skirts around the landscaped gardens and the lake, filled with carp. Beyond, there are views of woods and rolling farmland with pedigree Charolais sheep and Bantam chickens. Guests can use the covered swimming pool or the croquet lawn in summer. The owners are very welcoming, and are happy to help with suggestions of activities to enjoy in the area.

Roses climb around the front door, leading into a vaulted hall, where breakfast is served, the traditional range of dishes includes kedgeree and kippers. There is an elegant split-level drawing room with a grand piano, and a log fire in winter. There is also a conservatory furnished with wicker.

The largest of the bedrooms has a four-poster bed on a dais, and a big marble bathroom. All have en suite bathroom, fresh flowers and fine bed linen.

RECOMMENDED IN THE AREA

Famous ships at Portsmouth; walks on the South Downs; houses & castles - Uppark, Petworth, Parham, Arundel

Kenmore Guest House ◆◆◆◆

A warm welcome for international travellers to an English home

☎ 01903 784634
🖷 01903 784634
✉ kenmoreguesthouse@ amserve.net

Map ref 3 - TQ00

Claigmar Road, RUSTINGTON, Littlehampton, West Sussex, BN16 2NL
A259 follow signs for Rustington, turn for Claigmar Rd between War Memorial & Alldays. Kenmore on R as Claigmar Rd bends
7 Rooms, S £23.50-£26 D £47-£52, No smoking

There is much to interest the visitor to this area, particularly the coastline, South Downs, Roman villas at Bignor and Fishbourne, Arundel Castle, and Chichester with its celebrated cathedral and theatre. The best nearby beaches are at Rustington itself and at Clymping with its stretch of sand dunes. Sylvia and Ray Dobbs' comfortable home affords spacious accommodation, including a lounge with ample reading material and a bright dining room with a good choice at breakfast. The all-en suite bedrooms are equipped with a fridge, television, radio alarm, hairdryer and tea and coffee making facilities. Reduced rates for under 12s, babies free, and a small charge for dogs. Parking provided.

RECOMMENDED IN THE AREA

Arundel Castle; Brighton; Leonardslee Gardens, West Dean Gardens

Jeake's House •••••

*17th-century former wool
store situated on one of
Rye's ancient cobbled streets*

☎ 01797 222828
📠 01797 222623
✉ jeakeshouse@
btinternet.com
www.jeakeshouse.com

Map ref 4 - TQ92

Mermaid Street, RYE,
East Sussex, TN31 7ET
within the cobbled medieval
town centre, approached
either from High St or from
The Strand Quay
12 Rooms, S £31.50-£65
D £61-£101, No smoking in
dining room

A fine old building in one of the most beautiful parts of Rye, Jeake's House dates from 1689 and during its colourful history it has been both a wool store and a Baptist school. In the early 20th century it was the home of American poet and author Conrad Potter Aiken and was the setting for many a literary get-together. The house is owned and run by Jenny Hadfield who offers guest accommodation of a high standard. The comfortable public rooms include an oak beamed lounge and a book lined bar where guests can relax over a drink. The original galleried chapel has been converted into a dining room where a traditional country breakfast is served. A vegetarian option is also available. The bedrooms are individually styled with sumptuous furnishings. Nine rooms have en suite facilities, and all offer telephones, televisions and hospitality trays. There is the added advantage of a private car park nearby.

RECOMMENDED IN THE AREA

*National Trust properties,
historical sites (Bodiam,
Canterbury, Battle, Hastings),
Rye museum, church,
potteries, art galleries and
antique shops*

King Charles II Guest House ♦♦♦♦♦

Quality and luxury in a medieval town-centre property

☎ 01797 224954

Map ref 4 - TQ92

4 High Street, RYE, East Sussex,
TN31 7JE
centrally in Rye High St
3 Rooms, S £55-£65 D £80-£95,
No smoking

King Charles was a frequent visitor to this half-timbered house, and in the 1930s it was the home of the novelist Radclyffe Hall. Its current owners have sensitively restored the early 15th-century building, bringing a touch of luxury to the medieval framework. Ancient brick fireplaces are adorned with beautiful flower arrangements, and antique furniture and fine quality fabrics and furnishings grace the rooms. The original character of the tastefully decorated bedrooms has been retained, and combined with modern comforts and plenty of welcome extras. A tiny walled garden with patio is filled with flowers and plants. Parking is available nearby.

RECOMMENDED IN THE AREA

Bodiam Castle; Great Dixter House and gardens; beautiful walks on the cliffs – Fairlight Country Park. All within easy driving distance

Little Orchard House ♦♦♦♦♦

Period property in the heart of the medieval town

☎ 01797 223831
📠 01797 223831
www.littleorchardhouse.com

Map ref 4 - TQ92

West Street, RYE, East Sussex,
TN31 7ES
follow one way system to town centre, through Landgate Arch into High St. West St is 3rd turning on L, house on LHS
2 Rooms, S £45-£65 D £64-£90, No smoking in bedrooms or dining room

Both the house and garden are full of character at this quietly located but central property. The house dates from around 1720 and has been lovingly renovated and meticulously maintained. Views over the cobbled street or walled garden are offered from beautifully appointed rooms with four-poster beds. All have en suite facilities, hospitality trays, fridges, hairdryers, radio alarms and hand-stitched quilts. The panelled book room provides books and games, and in the sitting room guests can relax by the fire and check out selected menus from local restaurants. Breakfast, served at a large communal table in the dining room, features local organic, free-range and home-made products. Off-street private parking available.

RECOMMENDED IN THE AREA

Sissinghurst and Great Dixter gardens (within 30 minutes' drive); Saxon Shore Way and many other walks from Rye; Lamb House (connections with Henry James and E.F. Benson) in Rye

Manor Farm Oast ◆◆◆◆

Rest and excellent food with orchards all around

☎ 01424 813787
📠 01424 813787
✉ manor.farm.oast@lineone.net

Map ref 4 - TQ81

Workhouse Lane, RYE, East Sussex, TN36 4AJ
A259 Rye to Hastings rd, from Rye in Icklesham pass church on L, turn L at x-rds into Workhouse Lane. After sharp L bend turn L into Orchards
3 Rooms, S £32-£40 D £55-£64, No smoking, Closed 28-31 Dec

*B*uilt in 1860, and still surrounded by a working orchard, on the edge of the village, Manor Farm Oast is ideally situated for rest and relaxation, quiet breaks and country walks. It has been carefully converted keeping the unusual original features both inside and out, the double bedroom inside one of the oast towers is completely round.

Owner Kate Mylrea provides a very friendly welcome. Guests can enjoy tea and home made cake in one of the two lounges. Kate is passionate about food and as well as a traditional English breakfast or a healthier alternative, she will prepare a top quality five-course dinner by arrangement, all exquisitely presented.

Two of the rooms are en suite; all have colour TV and lots of thoughtful extras, such as bathrobes, home made biscuits, bottled water and fresh flowers.

RECOMMENDED IN THE AREA

Battle Abbey (15 minute drive); historic town of Rye (10 minute drive); Ellen Terry's House (20 minute drive)

The Old Vicarage Guest House ◆◆◆◆

Outstanding breakfasts in a Georgian house on a cobbled square

☎ 01797 222119
📠 01797 227466
✉ oldvicaragerye@tesco.net
www.oldvicaragerye.co.uk

Map ref 4 - TQ92

66 Church Square, RYE, East Sussex, TN31 7HF
from A259 follow town centre signs, through Landgate Arch, 3rd L in High St into West St, by St Mary's Church footpath leads to Vicarage
4 Rooms, S £54-£65 D £61-£104, No smoking, Closed 24-26 Dec

*T*he Old Vicarage is an elegant detached property; it is right in the town centre, but free from traffic and noise. The rooms have wonderful views of the medieval houses and cobbled streets. Breakfast is a leisurely, gastronomic extravaganza, with home made jams and marmalade, scones and crusty caraway bread hot from the oven, along with wholesome local produce. This is served in the dining room, overlooking the pretty walled garden. In the bedrooms, Laura Ashley prints and fabrics set off the Georgian architecture. All the en suite bedrooms have colour TV, books and information packs, and a hot drinks tray with homemade fudge and biscuits. In the evening you can sip a glass of sherry in the guest lounge. There is a blazing log fire in winter.

RECOMMENDED IN THE AREA

Nature reserve & Camber Castle (0.5 mile); Great Dixter (5 miles); (N.T.) Lamb House (1 minute walk), Sissinghurst Castle Garden (12 miles)

$\mathcal{A}$vondale Hotel ♦♦♦♦

Friendly and attractively presented seaside hotel

☎ 01323 890008
✆ 01323 490598
www.avondalehotel.co.uk

Map ref 4 - TV49

Avondale Road, SEAFORD,
East Sussex, BN25 1RJ
from Seaford town centre take A259
towards Eastbourne. Avondale is on L
opposite town memorial
13 Rooms, S £20-£38 D £38-£55,
No smoking

$\mathcal{G}$uests frequently comment on how well they sleep in the tastefully decorated, centrally heated, spotlessly clean bedrooms at the Avondale Hotel. The beds are certainly comfortable, but the friendly service and relaxed atmosphere also play their part in creating the home-from-home experience. Bedrooms are accessible by lift, and 11 have en suite facilities. All are well equipped with colour televisions, hospitality trays, radios and alarms. An inviting lounge is provided, and enjoyable home-cooked food is served in the attractive dining room, using fresh local produce wherever possible. The hotel is conveniently placed for both the town centre and the seafront, and Seaford Leisure Centre is close by.

RECOMMENDED IN THE AREA

South Downs; Seven Sisters cliffs; Brighton and Eastbourne

$\mathcal{S}$t Andrews Lodge Hotel ♦♦♦♦

Friendly family-run hotel with a warm welcome

☎ 01243 606899
✆ 01243 607826
✉ info@standrewslodge.co.uk
www.standrewslodge.co.uk

Map ref 3 - SZ89

Chichester Road, SELSEY,
West Sussex, PO20 0LX
turn off A27 onto the B2145 for 7
miles. Hotel is on right past Police
Station just before the church
10 Rooms, S £30-£50 D £58-£85,
No smoking in bedrooms, dining room
or lounge, Closed 24 Dec-1 Jan

$\mathcal{S}$even miles south of Chichester, in the town of Selsey, St Andrews Lodge is located close to local beaches and countryside where golf, fishing, horse riding and seasport facilities can all be enjoyed. You will find a peaceful relaxed atmosphere in this comfortable accommodation, with ample private parking space. The en suite bedrooms are bright and spacious offering tea/coffee making facilities, colour television, hairdryer and a modem point. Individual thermostats allow you to control the temperature in your room and one room is specifically appointed to accommodate two guests with wheelchairs. Breakfast and, by prior arrangement, home-cooked evening meals are served in the front dining room.

RECOMMENDED IN THE AREA

Chichester (7 miles); South Downs; Uppark (National Trust)

$\mathcal{M}$oorings ◆◆◆◆

*Double fronted Victorian villa
close to the town centre*

☎ 01903 208882
🅕 01903 236878

Map ref 3 - TQ10

4 Selden Road, WORTHING,
BN11 2LL
on A259 towards Brighton, pass
indoor pool on R and hotel opp car
showroom
6 Rooms, S £25-£27 D £46-£50,
No smoking, Closed 19 Dec-4 Jan

*T*he Moorings is an elegant property set in a quiet residential street to the east of the town centre and just a short walk from the seafront. It is a family run establishment where a warm welcome is assured.

The bedrooms are smart and spacious offering a good range of extras, including en suite showers, direct dial telephones, double glazed windows, colour televisions, shaver points, hairdryers and tea and coffee making facilities.

There is a cosy residents' lounge and a full English breakfast is served in the comfortably furnished dining room. Guests have access to the hotel at all times. Some off-street parking is available and bicycles can be safely stored.

RECOMMENDED IN THE AREA

Brighton (10 miles); Cissbury Ring (3 miles); City of Chichester, and Arundel

$\mathcal{W}$arwickshire

A selection of places to eat from the AA Restaurant & AA Pub Guides

Restaurants

◉◉ Ettington Park Hotel (Classic, Country-house)
Alderminster CV37 8BU

◉ The Howard Arms
Lower Green, Ilmington CV36 4LT
Tel 01608 682226 Fax 01608 682226

◉◉ Restaurant Bosquet (Traditional)
97a Warwick Road, Kenilworth CV8 1HP
Tel 01926 852463

◉◉ Amor's (Modern French)
15 Dormer Place, Royal Leamington Spa
CV32 5AA
Tel 01926 778744 Fax 01926 778744

◉◉ Desports
13/14 Meer Street, Stratford-upon-Avon
CV37 6QB
Tel 01789 269304 Fax 01789 269304

◉◉ The Shakespeare (Traditional)
Chapel Street, Stratford-upon-Avon CV37 6ER
Tel 0870 400 8182 Fax 01789 415411

Pubs

🍺 The Bell
Alderminster CV37 8NY
Tel 01789 450414 Fax 01789 450998

🍺 The Golden Cross
Ardens Grafton B50 4LG
Tel 01789 772420 Fax 01789 773697

🍺 King's Head
21 Bearley Road, Aston Cantlow B95 6HY
Tel 01789 488242 Fax 01789 488137

🍺 The Chequers Inn & Restaurant
Ettington CV37 7SR
Tel 01789 740387 Fax 01789 748097

🍺 The Boot
Old Warwick Road, Lapworth B94 6JU
Tel 01564 782464 Fax 01564 784989

🍺 Golden Lion Inn
Easenhall, Rugby CV23 0JA
Tel 01788 832265 Fax 01788 832878

🍺 The Fox and Goose Inn
Armscote, Stratford-upon-Avon CV37 8DD
Tel 01608 682293 Fax 01608 682293

*G*lebe Farm House •••••

Ideally located in an excellent touring area, a welcoming house set in landscaped grounds

☎ 01789 842501
🖶 01789 841194
✉ scorpiolimited@msn.com
www.glebefarmhouse.com

Map ref 3 - SP25

Stratford Road, Loxley, STRATFORD-UPON-AVON, CV35 9JW
S from Stratford, cross river, immediately L onto B4086 Tiddington rd, then immediately R onto Loxley rd. Farm 2.5m on L
3 Rooms, S £69.50-£75 D £95-£105, No smoking

RECOMMENDED IN THE AREA

Stratford-upon-Avon; Warwick and Kenilworth Castles; Cotswolds

*R*elax in comfort at this delightful country house, and enjoy the attentions of the friendly and ever-willing hostess. Guests' enjoyment is the number one priority here, and everyone is encouraged to unwind and feel at home. This modernised 18th-century house is set in beautiful lawned gardens which extend into 30 acres of farmland. Indoors the walls are covered with the artist owner's own work, and rooms are decorated and furnished with impeccable taste. The en suite bedrooms are spacious and comfortable, particularly one room above the barn, and all enjoy lovely views out over the countryside. Rooms are fitted with antique pine furniture and plenty of homely extras, creating a really welcoming atmosphere. One of the highlights of a stay here is the home cooking, with delicious meals being served in the evening and at breakfast. Glebe Farm is only 2 miles from Stratford, ten minutes from Warwick, and 20 minutes from the Cotswolds.

$\mathcal{L}$oxley Farm ◆◆◆◆

Quintessentially English thatched cottage with tasteful accommodation

☎ 01789 840265
📠 01789 840645

Map ref 3 - SP25

Loxley, STRATFORD-UPON-AVON, CV35 9JN
Loxley is signposted off A422 Stratford-Banbury rd, 4m from Stratford on L. Through village to bottom of hill. Turn L, 3rd house on R
2 Rooms, D £60-£64, No smoking in dining room or lounge, Closed Xmas & New Year

$\mathcal{D}$elightful cottage gardens extending to about an acre surround this picture-postcard property in the heart of Shakespeare country. The thatched 16th-century, Grade II listed building once entertained Charles I, and is little changed today with its exposed beams and stone floors. A nearby large barn conversion has resulted in two spacious suites, one with a vaulted ceiling and the other having an unusual oval sitting room. Both suites are tastefully decorated and furnished, with double beds and en suite bathrooms, and fridges with fresh milk. Breakfast is taken around a family table in the period dining room. The village pub is just a few minutes walk away.

RECOMMENDED IN THE AREA

Warwick Castle (7 miles); Stratford-upon-Avon (3.5 miles); Cotswolds

$\mathcal{M}$onk's Barn Farm ◆◆◆◆

Riverside farm two miles from Stratford-on-Avon

☎ 01789 293714
📠 01789 205886
✉ rmeadows@hotmail.com

Map ref 3 - SP25

Shipston Road, STRATFORD-UPON-AVON, CV37 8NA
on A3400 approx 2m S
7 Rooms, S £18.50-£21 D £35-£39, No smoking, Closed 25-26 Dec

$\mathcal{M}$onks Barn Farm dates from the 16th-century and lies alongside the River Stour just south of Stratford-on-Avon, centrally situated for visiting Stratford, Warwick and the Cotswolds. The farmhouse has been modernised to provide comfortable accommodation while retaining much of its character. There are three rooms in the main house, and three ground floor rooms in the Garden Annexe, all with en suites, televisions and hospitality trays, and four at ground floor level (no steps). Full breakfast is served in the dining room, or continental breakfast to your room. There are lovely riverside walks to Clifford Chambers where good food is served at the village pub. Credit cards not accepted.

RECOMMENDED IN THE AREA

Stratford-upon-Avon – Shakespearean properties and Theatre (2 miles); Warwick Castle (8 miles); Cotswolds and various National Trust properties (easy driving distance)

Sequoia House Private Hotel ♦♦♦♦

Large Victorian house in a prime Stratford location

☎ 01789 268852 ☉ 01789 414559
✉ info@sequoiahotel.co.uk
www.stratford-upon-avon.co.uk/
sequoia.htm

Map ref 3 - SP25

51-53 Shipston Road, STRATFORD-UPON-AVON, CV37 7LN
on A3400 close to Clopton Bridge
23 Rooms, S £45-£59 D £69-£79, No smoking in bedrooms or dining room,
Closed 21-27 Dec

*T*he hotel is superbly situated across the River Avon from the Royal Shakespeare Theatre, and takes its name from the 175-year-old sequoia tree in the garden. Parking is provided in the grounds, from where you can stroll along the 'Old Tramway' to explore the delights of Stratford. There is a choice of standard size double/twin cottage bedrooms, spacious main house rooms with king size or twin beds, and superior rooms with king, queen or Victorian brass beds. All of them have en suite facilities, telephones, televisions, hairdryers, toiletries and hospitality trays. There is a guest lounge furnished with antiques, and breakfast is taken in the air-conditioned dining room overlooking the garden.

RECOMMENDED IN THE AREA

Royal Shakespeare Theatre (5 minute walk); the Cotswolds (20 minute drive); Warwick Castle (8 miles)

Victoria Spa Lodge ♦♦♦♦

Former hotel and pump rooms beautifully restored to offer charming accommodation

☎ 01789 267985
☉ 01789 204728
✉ ptozer@
  victoriaspalodge.demon.co.uk
www.stratford-upon-avon.co.uk/victoriaspa.htm

Map ref 3 - SP15

Bishopton Lane, Bishopton, STRATFORD-UPON-AVON, CV37 9QY
1.5m N on A3400/A46 junct. 1st exit left Bishopton Lane, 1st house on R
7 Rooms, S £50 D £65, No smoking

*O*pened in 1837 by Princess Victoria, whose coat-of-arms is built into the gables, this attractive house is peacefully located in a country setting on the edge of town. The Grade II listed building was once the home of cartoonist Bruce Bairnsfather, and many original period features still grace the property. Seven beautifully-appointed bedrooms offer spacious comfort with quality furniture, stylish fabrics and several thoughtful touches. Guests can also relax in the dramatic drawing room with its stripped hardboard floor and inviting furniture. Expect a warm welcome and high standards of service and maintenance. Stratford is a gentle 20 minute walk away.

RECOMMENDED IN THE AREA

Warwick Castle; Chipping Camden and the Cotswolds; Blenheim Palace

*H*igh House ♦♦♦♦

A peaceful niche in a country setting with delightful accommodation

☎ 01926 843270 ✆ 01926 843689

Map ref 3 - SP26

Old Warwick Road, Rowington, WARWICK,
CV35 7AA
N from Warwick on A4177, turn L after
Waterman Inn onto B4439. After 3rd x-rds
0.5m on L, down long farm drive
3 Rooms, S £40 D £60, No smoking in
bedrooms or dining room, Closed Xmas &
New year

Seclusion and tranquility surround this charming Queen Anne farmhouse, and high levels of comfort ensure an enjoyable stay. The listed property provides tasteful bedrooms that are full of character, and furnished with antiques and period pieces. Plenty of thoughtful, homely extras are provided, and standards of housekeeping are immaculate. Two of the rooms have en suite bath and shower, and one room has a shower room. Public areas are spacious yet cosy, including a sitting room with French windows opening onto a colourful garden. A warm welcome is extended to all visitors, and this peaceful house is ideal for either the leisure or business guest.

RECOMMENDED IN THE AREA

Baddesley Clinton, Packwood House (National Trust); Warwick Castle; Heritage Motor Centre

*W*est Midlands

A selection of places to eat from the AA Restaurant & AA Pub Guides

Restaurants

◎◎ Bank (Modern)
4 Brindley Place, Birmingham B1 2JB
Tel 0121 633 7001 Fax 0121 633 4465

◎ Chung Ying Garden (Oriental)
17 Thorp Street, Birmingham B5 4AT
Tel 0121 666 6622 Fax 0121 622 5860

◎ Shimla Pinks (Chic, Modern)
214 Broad Street, Birmingham B15 1AY
Tel 0121 633 0366 Fax 0121 643 3325

◎ Brooklands Grange (Modern)
Holyhead Road, Coventry CV5 8HX
Tel 024 6770 1601 Fax 024 7660 1277

◎◎ Manor Hotel
Main Road, Meriden CV7 7NH
Tel 01676 522735 Fax 01676 522186

◎◎ New Hall (Country-house)
Walmley Road, Sutton Coldfield B76 1QX
Tel 0121 378 2442 Fax 0121 378 4637

◎◎ The Fairlawns at Aldridge (Modern, Chic)
178 Little Aston Road, Walsall WS9 0NU
Tel 01922 455122 Fax 01922 743210

Pubs

◀ The Malt Shovel
Barston Lane, Barston B92 0JP
Tel 01675 443223 Fax 01675 443223

◀ The Rose and Castle
Ansty CV7 9HZ
Tel 024 7661 2822

◀ Little Dry Dock
Windmill End, Netherton DY2 9HU
Tel 01384 235369

◀ Waggon & Horses
17a Church Street, Oldbury B69 3AD
Tel 0121 552 5467

◀ Beacon Hotel
129 Bilston Road, Sedgley DY3 1JE
Tel 01902 883380

◀ The Vine
Roebuck Street, West Bromwich B70 6RD
Tel 0121 553 2866 Fax 0121 525 5450

*B*ridge House Hotel ◆◆◆◆

Well-located hotel offering smartly-maintained rooms in a friendly atmosphere

☎ 0121 706 5900 🖷 0121 624 5900
✉ emailenquiries@
   bridgehousehotel.co.uk
www.bridgehousehotel.co.uk

Map ref 3 - SP18

49 Sherbourne Road, Acocks Green,
BIRMINGHAM, B27 6DX
46 Rooms, S £45-£50 D £60-£65,
Closed Xmas

A friendly family-run hotel set in the village of Acocks Green, and handy for both Birmingham Airport and the National Exhibition Centre. Most of the 51 bedrooms offer en suite facilities, and all are comfortably furnished and well equipped. Guests can relax in the spacious reception area, the television lounge or the residents' bar, and there is also an à la carte restaurant. A large split-level function room offers conference facilities for around 80 people, and can be used for social or other functions for up to 120 people. This hotel has the added advantage of plenty of parking.

RECOMMENDED IN THE AREA

Birmingham NEC; Birmingham Botanical Gardens; the Jewellery Quarter Discovery Centre

*W*iltshire

A selection of places to eat from the AA Restaurant & AA Pub Guides

Restaurants

◉◉ Raffles Restaurant (Traditional)
The Green, Aldbourne SN8 2BW
Tel 01672 540700 Fax 01672 540038

◉◉ Georgian Lodge (Modern)
25 Bridge Street, Bradford-upon-Avon BA15 1BY
Tel 01225 862268 Fax 01225 862218

◉◉ The Grosvenor Arms (Bistro-style, Informal)
High Street, Hindon SP3 6DJ
Tel 01747 820696 Fax 01747 820869

◉◉ The Harrow Inn (Country-house)
Little Bedwyn SN8 3JP
Tel 01672 870871 Fax 01672 870871

◉◉ Old Bell Hotel (Classic)
Abbey Row, Malmesbury SN16 0AG
Tel 01666 822344 Fax 01666 825145

◉◉ The Pear Tree at Purton (Country-house)
Church End, Purton SN5 4ED
Tel 01793 772100 Fax 01793 772369

◉ Langley Wood Restaurant (Traditional, Country-house)
Redlynch, Downton SP5 2PB
Tel 01794 390348

Pubs

🍺 The Kings Arms & Chancel Restaurant
Monkton Farleigh, Bradford-on-Avon
BA15 2QQ
Tel 01225 858705

🍺 The Dove Inn
Corton BA12 0SZ
Tel 01985 850109 Fax 01985 851041

🍺 The Horseshoe
Handley St, Ebbesbourne Wake SP5 5JF
Tel 01722 780474

🍺 Compasses Inn
Lower Chicksgrove SP3 6NB
Tel 01722 714318 Fax 01722 714318

🍺 The Seven Stars
Bottlesford, Pewsey SN9 6LU
Tel 01672 851325 Fax 01672 851583

🍺 The George and Dragon
High Street, Rowde SN10 2PN
Tel 01380 723053 Fax 01380 724738

🍺 The Boot Inn
High Street, Berwick St James, Stapleford
SP3 4TN
Tel 01722 790243

245

WILTSHIRE

*H*ome Farm ♦♦♦♦

Handsome farmhouse accommodation convenient for many tourist attractions

☎ 01225 764492
🖷 01225 764492
✉ info@homefarm-guesthouse.co.uk
www.homefarm-guesthouse.co.uk

Map ref 2 - ST85

Farleigh Road, Wingfield,
BRADFORD-ON-AVON, BA14 9LG
exit A36 onto A366 to Fairleigh
Hungerford, pass castle into
Wingfield, gate to premises after three
cottages
3 Rooms, S £25 D £50, No smoking

*H*ome Farm is an imaginative conversion of what was originally cattle stalls, feeding rooms and a hay loft belonging to Wingfield House. It fronts onto the original farmyard, which provides ample private parking. Guests have the run of the two-acre garden with views over neighbouring farmland, and can relax in the large, comfortably furnished lounge. The Aga-cooked breakfasts offer a wide selection including fish dishes, and home-made bread is a feature. Spacious bedrooms comprise a family room, a double, and a ground-floor twin suitable for wheelchair users. All rooms have en suite facilities, dual aspect windows, a colour television, radio, hairdryer, trouser press and hospitality tray. Ironing facilities are also available.

RECOMMENDED IN THE AREA

Barton Farm Country Park and 14th century Tithe Barn; National Trust village of Lacock and Lacock Abbey; Bath; Saxon Church, Bradford-on-Avon

*T*he Old Rectory ♦♦♦♦

Spacious Georgian accommodation in an area ideal for touring

☎ 01747 820226
🖷 01747 820783
✉ vbronson@old-rectory.co.uk
www.old-rectory.co.uk

Map ref 2 - ST93

CHICKLADE, Salisbury, SP3 5SU
Situated on the A303 immediately
behind the lay-by
3 Rooms, S £30 D £55, No smoking,
Closed 18 Dec-Jan

*F*ull of Georgian charm, and with the well-proportioned rooms typical of the period, this former rectory provides pleasing accommodation. Dating from the 17th century, it has been tastefully decorated and furnished in keeping with its style. Bedrooms are large and comfortable, and guests are provided with bathrobes as the rooms are not en suite; tea and coffee are available on request. A comfortable lounge/dining room is ideal for relaxing in, and for taking breakfast. The Old Rectory also enjoys a good local reputation for its restaurant, where quality home-cooked food is served by prior arrangement. Nearby attractions include Bath, Stonehenge and Longleat.

RECOMMENDED IN THE AREA

Bath (60 minute drive); Salisbury (40 minute drive); Stonehenge (30 minute drive)

*H*ome Farm ◆◆◆◆

A working farm in a lovely village setting

☎ 01249 714475
📠 01249 701488
📧 audrey.smith@
   homefarmbandb.co.uk
www.homefarmbandb.co.uk

Map ref 2 - ST87

Home Farm, Harts Lane, Biddestone,
CHIPPENHAM, SN14 7DQ
A4 between Bath & Chippenham, at
Corsham turn off to Biddestone at
lights. In village take 1st R off village
green, farm signed
4 Rooms, S £27-£32 D £45-£50, No
smoking, Closed Xmas & New Year

A traditional 17th-century Cotswold stone farmhouse which oozes character from its flagstone floors, log fires and oak beams. The Smith family offer a warm welcome to their working farm set in the picturesque village of Biddestone. Guests will appreciate the bright, fresh bedrooms, most with en suite facilities, and the many thoughtful extras like razors, shoeshine, and toiletries. Breakfast is served at one large table in the homely dining room, and is cooked to order using the freshest ingredients. Home Farm is handily placed for the M4, M5 and access to Bath, and two good pubs are just a stroll away.

RECOMMENDED IN THE AREA

Bath – Roman Baths; Georgian architecture (8 miles); Lacock Abbey and Fox Talbot Museum (4 miles); Stonehenge and Wiltshire's white horses

*A*t the Sign of the Angel ◆◆◆◆◆

16th-century wool merchant's house with excellent restaurant

☎ 01249 730230
📠 01249 730527
📧 angel@lacock.co.uk
www.lacock.co.uk

Map ref 2 - ST96

6 Church Street, LACOCK,
Chippenham, SN15 2LB
M4 J17, follow Chippenham signs, 3m
S of Chippenham on A350 Lacock
signed L, follow 'local traffic' sign
10 Rooms, S £68-£85 D £99-£137.50,
No smoking in bedrooms, Closed 23
Dec-30 Dec

T he log fires and oak panelling, low beams and squeaky floors create all the atmosphere of an old English Inn; the house is situated in the National Trust village of Lacock, a history lesson in itself, and a perfect base for seeing the sights and the countryside of Wiltshire, Somerset and Gloucestershire. All of the bedrooms are en suite; four are in the cottage over the footbridge, across the stream. They are all furnished with antique wooden furniture - one has an enormous bed that was owned by the Victorian engineer, Isambard Kingdom Brunel. The restaurant is internationally renowned for its traditional English cooking, with herbs and vegetables (asparagus is a speciality) fresh from the garden. The Angel's own hens provide eggs for breakfast; lunch is available every day except Monday; and there is a daily changing menu and a full carte, by candlelight, in the evening.

RECOMMENDED IN THE AREA

Bowood House; Lacock Abbey; Longleat House

*L*ovett Farm ◆◆◆◆

Delightful farmhouse with lovely views over the Dauntsey Vale

☎ 01666 823268
🖷 01666 823268
✉ lovettfarm@btinternet.com

Map ref 2 - ST98

Little Somerford, MALMESBURY,
SN15 5BP
3m from Malmesbury on B4042
(Wootton Bassett/Swindon road) on L
opp 2nd signpost to the Somerfords
2 Rooms, S £25-£30 D £47-£50,
No smoking

*G*uests are warmly welcomed at this modern, working farmhouse situated within easy access of the M4 and M5 and an ideal base from which to visit The Cotswolds, Bath, Stonehenge and Avebury. Both bedrooms have en suite showers and are well equipped with extras: colour television, radio alarm, tea and coffee-making facilities. Attractively decorated, roomy and comfortable, guests will feel at ease here. Traditional home-cooked breakfast is served at one large table in the sunny dining room/lounge. Though dinner is not available, the proprietors recommend several pubs nearby - one within walking distance - serving a wide choice of good food.

RECOMMENDED IN THE AREA

Abbey and Abbey House Gardens in Malmesbury (3 miles); Lacock village (National Trust) and Abbey Gardens; Westonbirt Arboretum

---

*C*hetcombe House ◆◆◆◆

Elegant 1930's property with wonderful country views

☎ 01747 860219 🖷 860111
✉ mary.butchers@lineone.net

Map ref 2 - ST83

Chetcombe Road, MERE, Warminster,
BA12 6AZ
located off A303 when heading
westbound
5 Rooms, S £30 D £55, No smoking

*C*hetcombe is a charming house set in an acre of carefully tended gardens looking towards Gillingham and the Blackmore Vale. Mr and Mrs Butchers create a warm and welcoming atmosphere for their guests, and overseas visitors may be interested to know that German is also spoken here. The accommodation is pleasantly spacious, with five well-equipped bedrooms all with impressive en suite facilities, teletext televisions and tea and coffee making equipment. Four of the rooms are south facing with splendid views over open countryside. A substantial breakfast is served in the attractive dining room, and for other meals there is a good range of pubs and restaurants in the village.

RECOMMENDED IN THE AREA

Stourton House Gardens; Stourhead; Longleat

Clovelly Hotel ♦♦♦♦

Friendly family hotel close to the city centre

☎ 01722 322055
🖷 01722 327677
🄴 clovelly.hotel@virgin.net
www.clovellyhotel.co.uk

Map ref 3 - SU13

17-19 Mill Road, SALISBURY, SP2 7RT
approx 5 mins from Market Square &
Cathedral, & 2 mins from station
14 Rooms, S £40-£50 D £55-£65,
No smoking

Professionally run by Rowena and Haydn Ingram, the Clovelly offers lovely accommodation suitable for business and leisure guests alike. A friendly atmosphere prevails and staff are always available to give advice on where to dine and what to see. Rowena is a Blue Badge Guide and also offers personalised tours around Wessex. The house is just five minutes' level walk from the city centre, close to the railway station. Bedrooms are smartly decorated with co-ordinating soft furnishings, comfortable beds and modern facilities. All the rooms have fresh, bright en suite bathrooms, television and tea and coffee making equipment. Some rooms are located on the ground floor, including accommodation for disabled guests. There is a cosy lounge and a super dining room where a good cooked breakfast is served. Car parking is provided for residents.

RECOMMENDED IN THE AREA

Salisbury Cathedral (10 minute walk); Stonehenge (8 miles); Wilton House (2 miles)

The Old House ♦♦♦♦

Seventeenth-century property conveniently located for the city centre

☎ 01722 333433
🖷 01722 335551

Map ref 3 - SU13

161 Wilton Road, SALISBURY,
SP2 7JQ
on A36 between Wilton & Salisbury,
close to police station
7 Rooms, S £30-£35 D £40-£50,
No smoking in bedrooms or dining
room

Charming accommodation, full of character, is offered at this historic house, located on the Wilton road within walking distance of the city centre. Ground floor areas are beautifully furnished to maintain the period style, and there is a cosy cellar bar, the only place in the house where smoking is permitted. The mature gardens are a lovely surprise, with three distinct areas providing privacy for a drink outside on summer evenings. Bedrooms have been tastefully decorated and equipped with modern facilities, including en suite bath or shower rooms. There are two rooms at ground floor level and one room with a splendid four-poster bed, all with hairdryers, televisions and hospitality trays.

RECOMMENDED IN THE AREA

Stourhead (5 miles); Heale Garden (15 minute drive); Wilton House (5 minute drive)

249

Stratford Lodge ◆◆◆◆

Attractive Victorian house enjoying a peaceful location within walking distance of the city centre

☎ 01722 325177
📠 01722 325177
✉ enquires@stratfordlodge.co.uk
www.stratfordlodge.co.uk

Map ref 3 - SU13

4 Park Lane, off Castle Road,
SALISBURY, SP1 3NP
take A345 Castle Rd past St Francis
Church on right & Victoria Park on left.
Park Lane is an unadopted road
between park & Alldays store
8 Rooms, S £47.50-£55 D £65-£70,
No smoking

Stratford Lodge, a detached Victorian property, is quietly situated in a lane overlooking Victoria Park, with all the attractions and amenities of Salisbury close by. The bedrooms have en suite facilities and are decorated in relaxing soft shades with pretty co-ordinated fabrics. There is an emphasis on quality food, and the meals are carefully prepared using local produce and fresh vegetables, fruit and herbs. As well s the traditional British breakfast, you might have kedgeree, musrooms on toast, or scrambled egg. Muesli, fresh fruit, compotes and local honey are also a feature, with a choice of beverages including tea, coffee, herbal infusions and hot chococlate. There is a daily dinner menu, with vegetarian dishes always available. Other diets can also be catered for. For relaxation, there is a sheltered and secluded garden. Log fires in winter.

RECOMMENDED IN THE AREA

Salisbury Cathedral; Stonehenge; Old Sarum

The Barn ◆◆◆◆

Converted milking parlour in a quiet country situation

☎ 01985 841138
📠 01985 841138

Map ref 2 - ST84

The Marsh, Longbridge Deverill,
WARMINSTER, BA12 7EA
A36 Salisbury/Bath, then A350 into
Longbridge Deverill, turn 300yds past
BP garage on L, house 1st R
2 Rooms, S £30-£35 D £50-£55, No
smoking in bedrooms or dining room

Originally built in the mid 19th century, The Barn has been sympathetically extended and converted into a family residence with on-site parking, guests are welcomed with warm hospitality. It is in an idyllic rural position with a stream running by.

All rooms have en suite facilities; colour TV, radio alarm, hairdryers, tea and coffee are provided. One room has French windows leading out onto the lawn in the back garden. There is a spacious lounge with oak beams and a gallery, and plenty of books and magazines to look at.

A generous breakfast, English or continental, with home baked bread and fresh pastries, is served around a large pine table in the kitchen, or even out in the garden on warm sunny days.

RECOMMENDED IN THE AREA

Longleat (stately home and safari park); Corsham Court; Wilton House

Newton Farmhouse ◆◆◆◆◆

*16th-century listed building
offering quality accommodation*

☎ 01794 884416
📠 01794 884416
📧 reservations@
  newtonfarmhouse.co.uk
www.newtonfarmhouse.co.uk

Map ref 3 - SU22

Southampton Road, WHITEPARISH,
Salisbury, SP5 2QL
Just S of Salisbury- 6 miles, on A36
1m S of junct with A27
8 Rooms, D £38-£60, No smoking

This delightful historic farmhouse, originally part of the Trafalgar Estate, has been thoughtfully restored, providing modern amenities whilst retaining many original features: beams, flagstones, inglenook fireplace and even, in the conservatory, a well. All bedrooms have en suite facilities and are tastefully furnished - five feature period four-poster beds. Extra touches, such as home-made biscuits and fresh flowers in the rooms, make for additional comfort. Sumptuous breakfasts start the day; enjoy free range eggs, seasonal fruits from the kitchen garden, and home-made bread and preserves. By arrangement, delicious dinners are a speciality. Conveniently located next to Salisbury and on the fringe of the New Forest.

RECOMMENDED IN THE AREA

*Stonehenge (18 miles); Salisbury (6 miles);
New Forest (2 miles)*

The Woodfalls Inn ◆◆◆◆

*Village inn convenient for
Salisbury and the New Forest*

☎ 01725 513222
📠 01725 513220
📧 woodfallsi@aol.com
www.woodfallsinn.co.uk

Map ref 3 - SU11

The Ridge, WOODFALLS, SP5 2LN
on B3080
10 Rooms, S £45-£52 D £59.90-£72,
No smoking in bedrooms or dining
room

Established in 1870, this attractive inn is located on an old road leading from the forest's coast to the city of Salisbury. With recent refurbishment and the addition of accommodation, it has reverted to its original name after a few decades as the Bat & Ball (a reference to the adjacent cricket ground). Bedrooms are comfortably furnished in traditional style, including two four-poster rooms, one family suite and facilities for disabled guests. All the rooms have en suite bathrooms, telephones and tea and coffee makers. There is a public bar, lounge bar and a cosy restaurant, but breakfast is served in the airy conservatory. Children and well-behaved pets are welcome.

RECOMMENDED IN THE AREA

Beaulieu Estate and Buckler's Hard; Salisbury Cathedral; Wilton House

251

Worcestershire

A selection of places to eat from the AA Restaurant & AA Pub Guides

Restaurants

⊛⊛ Lygon Arms (Traditional)
High Street, Broadway WR12 7DU
Tel 01386 852255 Fax 01386 858611

⊛⊛ Brockencote Hall (Classic, Country-house)
Chaddesley Corbett DY10 4PY
Tel 01562 777876 Fax 01562 777872

⊛⊛ Riverside Hotel (Modern)
The Parks, Offenham Road, Evesham WR11 5JP
Tel 01386 446200 Fax 01386 40021

⊛⊛ Cottage in the Wood (Country-house)
Holywell Road, Malvern Wells, WR14 4LG
Tel 01684 575859 Fax 01684 560662

⊛⊛ The Venture In Restaurant (Traditional, Rustic)
Main Road, Ombersley WR9 0EW
Tel 01905 620552 Fax 01905 620552

⊛ Brown's Restaurant
The Old Cornmill, South Quay, Worcester WR1 2JJ
Tel 01905 611120 Fax 01905 616616

Pubs

◼ Horse & Jockey
Far Forest, Bewdley DY14 9DX
Tel 01299 266239 Fax 01299 266227

◼ The Fleece Inn
The Cross, Bretforton WR11 5JE
Tel 01386 831173

◼ Walter de Cantelupe Inn
Main Road, Kempsey WR5 3NA
Tel 01905 820572 Fax 01905 820572

◼ The Talbot at Knightwick
Knightwick WR6 5PH
Tel 01886 821235 Fax 01886 821060

◼ Farmers Arms
Birts St, Birtsmorton, Malvern WR13 6AP
Tel 01684 833308

◼ Crown & Sandys Arms
Main Road, Ombersley WR9 0EW
Tel 01905 620252 Fax 01905 620769

◼ The Fountain Inn
Oldwood, St Michaels, Tenbury Wells WR15 8TR
Tel 01584 810701 Fax 01584 819030

Leasow House ♦♦♦♦

Early 17th-century Cotswold stone farmhouse

☎ 01386 584526
🖷 01386 584596
🖅 leasow@clara.net
www.leasow.co.uk

Map ref 3 - SP03

Laverton Meadows, BROADWAY, WR12 7NA
B4632 to Winchcombe for 2m, turn R to Wormington then 1st on R
7 Rooms, S £35-£55 D £55-£65, No smoking, Closed Xmas and New Year

Leasow House is situated south of the town in a peaceful rural setting. Parts of the building date from the early 1600s and renovation has been carried out sympathetically to ensure that much of the original charm and character is retained. Bedrooms are comfortable and well equipped with en suite facilities, central heating, colour television, direct dial telephones and hospitality trays. Some have low beams set off by pretty decorative schemes. Two bedrooms are located in a former barn and one has been adapted for disabled guests. Delicious breakfasts are taken in the attractive dining room, which overlooks the gardens. The library lounge is a comfortable and relaxing room where guests can enjoy a complimentary glass of sherry.

Barbara and Gordon Meekings are friendly and caring hosts who delight in welcoming guests to their lovely home.

RECOMMENDED IN THE AREA

Hidcote Manor Gardens (National Trust); Snowshill Manor (National Trust); Warwick Castle

Milestone House ◆◆◆◆

Grade II listed Cotswold Town House

☎ 01386 853432
📠 01386 853432
✉ milestone.house@talk21.com
www.milestone-broadway.co.uk

Map ref 3 - SP03

122 Upper High Street, BROADWAY, WR12 7AJ
from Broadway by-pass (A44) follow signs to Broadway. House on L at Upper High St
4 Rooms, S £45D £55-£65, No smoking

*D*ating from the early 17th century Milestone House is situated in the secluded Upper High Street of this lovely Cotswold village, but within easy walking distance of all the antique shops, galleries and restaurants. Stratford-upon-Avon, Oxford with Blenheim Palace nearby, Warwick Castle, Hidcote Gardens, Sudeley Castle and many beautiful villages are close for a full day's sightseeing. All the bedrooms are en suite, they also have colour TV, hot drinks tray and hairdryers plus many extras.

Two comfortable sitting rooms are available for guests with plenty of reading material. Breakfast is served in the conservatory overlooking the garden which guests can wander through to the private parking.

RECOMMENDED IN THE AREA

Snowshill Manor (2 miles); Warwick Castle (22 miles); many National Trust properties in the area

Southwold House ◆◆◆◆

Handy for touring the Cotswolds, with good quality facilities

☎ 01386 853681
📠 01386 854610
✉ sueandnick.southwold@ talk21.com

Map ref 3 - SP03

Station Road, BROADWAY, WR12 7DE
on B4632 opp turning signposted to Winchcombe
8 Rooms, S £27-£32 D £50-£60, No smoking

*O*ne of the loveliest villages in Britain houses this impressive Edwardian house in the Cotswolds. Just a few minutes walk from the village centre, it offers high quality in all areas from comfy beds to plenty of choice at breakfast. Bedrooms are individually decorated and mainly spacious, with en suite facilities and a selection of toiletries. Guests can relax in the pleasant sitting room with a video, and breakfast is taken at separate tables in the bright dining room. Broadway is on the Cotswold Way, and has a good choice of pubs and restaurants. Southwold House is also handy for touring Stratford, Warwick and Oxford.

RECOMMENDED IN THE AREA

Snowshill Manor; Sudeley Castle; Blenheim Palace

Mill Hay House •••••

*Elegant Queen Anne country house
located in extensive gardens*

☎ 01386 852498
🖷 01386 858038
✉ millhayhouse@aol.com
www.broadway-
cotswolds.co.uk/milhay.html

Map ref 3 - SP03

Snowshill Road, BROADWAY,
WR12 7JS
turn off A44 (at Broadway Main Green)
towards Snowshill. House 0.75m on R
3 Rooms, S £108-£144 D £120-£160, No
smoking in bedrooms or dining room

*M*ill Hay is a handsome country house set in three acres of landscaped gardens including a medieval pond and moat. Adjacent to the house is the site of a water mill dating from the 12th century. Built of red brick and mellow Cotswold stone, Mill Hay has been lovingly restored to provide quality accommodation in a peaceful rural location. The bedrooms are comfortably furnished and all have en suite facilities. Direct dial telephones, colour televisions, and tea and coffee making equipment are also provided. Original features including floors and panelling are enhanced by fine period pieces in the public areas. Children under 12 are not accommodated, neither are dogs (except guide dogs).

RECOMMENDED IN THE AREA

Broadway Tower (country retreat of William Morris); Warwick Castle; Stratford-upon-Avon

$\mathcal{B}$uttercup House ♦♦♦♦

Beautifully located Edwardian red brick house overlooking the Vale of Evesham

☎ 01386 830724
✉ mary@buttercup-house.com
www.buttercup-house.com

Map ref 3 - SP04

Long Hyde Road, South Littleton,
EVESHAM, WR11 5TH
B4035 from Evesham, L to Offenham
(B4510), cont for 3m; R at sign for
Bennetts Hill opp Oakfield Nursery
2 Rooms, D £39.75-£49.75, No
smoking

$\mathcal{P}$retty gardens, developed from scratch by Martin Heywood-Thomas, surround this stylishly decorated house. Unique decor, reflecting craft and art interests, contribute to the charm of 'The Buttercup Experience'. Afternoon tea, featuring mouth-watering home-made fare, may be served in the orchard or in front of the sitting room fire. The many things to do and see locally include Cotswold villages, Stratford, Cheltenham and Worcester, and the riverside towns of Evesham, Tewkesbury and Pershore. Both en suite bedrooms are filled with thoughtful extras – and there are always fresh flowers in the bathrooms. Top quality, local and organic food, together with home-made preserves and cakes. are prepared by trained Home Economist Mary Heywood-Thomas.

RECOMMENDED IN THE AREA

Warwick Castle (20 minute drive); Broadway Tower and Country Park; Avoncroft Museum of Historic Buildings (20 minute drive)

$\mathcal{S}$t Just ♦♦♦♦

Constantly-improving guest house with a tranquil, inviting atmosphere

☎ 01684 562023
✉ stjust@lineone.net

Map ref 2 - SO74

169 Worcester Road, MALVERN,
WR14 1ET
M5 J7 follow A449 for 5m through
Malvern Link Shopping Ctr. 350yds
on, turn R into Albert Pk Rd, R into
green gates)
3 Rooms, S £20-£25 D £40-£56, No
smoking, Closed Xmas

$\mathcal{T}$he elegance of the late Georgian age blends easily with the comforts expected by a modern guest at this delightful country property. Gothic pillars, high ceilings and a galleried landing all lend a gracious feel to the house. Spacious en suite bedrooms are in keeping with the overall design, and plenty of extras such as mineral water and armchairs make the place feel homely. Another bonus is a large sitting area with a plentiful supply of books. Overlooking the Malvern Links Common with views towards the Malvern Hills, the house is set in pretty, mature gardens.

Guests are assured of a warm welcome, and their individual needs are willingly catered for.

RECOMMENDED IN THE AREA

Morgan Motor Factory (less than a mile); Malvern Hills for walking (less than a mile); Royal Worcester Porcelain Factory (8 miles)

*T*he Peacock Inn ♦♦♦♦ ⊚

A welcoming old inn serving good quality food

☎ 01584 810506
🖷 01584 811236
📧 jvidler@fsbdial.co.uk

Map ref 2 - SO66

Worcester Road, Boraston, TENBURY WELLS, WR15 8LL
on A456 from Worcester follow A443 to Tenbury Wells. Inn 1.25m E of Tenbury Wells
3 Rooms, S £45-£55 D £55-£70, No smoking in bedrooms

*V*isitors feel like honoured guests at this 14th-century inn, such is the warmth of the welcome. Nestling in the River Teme valley, the inn retains many original features including exposed beams and open fires. Public areas, like the oak-panelled lounge, use soft lighting and plenty of memorabilia to create a homely atmosphere. Hand-crafted four poster beds grace the comfortable, spacious bedrooms which are filled with thoughtful extras. All rooms have en suite showers, and all are non-smoking. Memorable dinners are taken in the friendly and relaxed restaurant which boasts an AA Rosette. Fringes of hops dangle from the beams in this charming room, where another open fire burns.

RECOMMENDED IN THE AREA

West Midlands Safari Park; Severn Valley Railways; Ludlow (13 miles)

*Y*orkshire

A selection of places to eat from the AA Restaurant & AA Pub Guides

Restaurants

⊚⊚ Crab and Lobster Restaurant (Modern)
Dishforth Road, Asenby, North Yorkshire YO7 3QL
Tel 01845 577286 Fax 01845 577109

⊚ The Dining Room (Chic, Formal)
20 St James Square, Boroughbridge, North Yorkshire YO51 9AR
Tel 01423 326426

⊚⊚ Dusty Miller (Classic, Traditional)
Summerbridge, Harrogate, North Yorkshire HG3 4BU
Tel 01423 780837

⊚⊚ Angel Inn (Rustic)
Hetton, North Yorkshire BD23 6LT
Tel/Fax 01756 730263

⊚ White Swan (Classic)
Market Place, Pickering, North Yorkshire YO18 7AA
Tel 01751 472288 Fax 01751 475554

⊚⊚ Restaurant Martel (Modern, Country-house)
Gateforth, Selby, North Yorkshire YO8 9LJ
Tel 01757 228225 Fax 01757 228189

⊚ Coniston Hall Lodge (Bistro-style)
Coniston Cold, Skipton, North Yorkshire BD23 4EB
Tel 01756 748080 Fax 01756 749487

⊚⊚ Melton's (Modern, British)
7 Scarcroft Road, York, North Yorkshire YO23 1ND
Tel 01904 634341 Fax 01904 635115

⊚ Greenhead House (Country-house)
84 Burncross Road, Chapeltown, South Yorkshire S35 1SF
Tel/Fax 0114 246 9004

⊚⊚ Richard Smith at Thyme (Bistro)
34 Sandygate Road, Sheffield, South Yorkshire S10 5RY
Tel 0114 266 6096 Fax 0114 266 0279

The Spring Rock (Formal, Modern)
Upper Greetland, Halifax, West Yorkshire
HX4 8PT
Tel 01422 377722

The Harlequin Restaurant (Modern)
139 Keithley Road, Cowling, Keithley, West
Yorkshire BD22 0AH
Tel 01535 633277 Fax 01535 633927

Pool Court at 42 (Chic, Minimalist)
44 The Calls, Leeds, West Yorkshire LS2 7EW
Tel 0113 244 4242 Fax 0113 234 3332

The Old Hall (Modern, Country-house)
Todmorden, West Yorkshire OL14 7AD
Tel 01706 815998 Fax 01706 810669

Pubs

The Black Bull Inn
6 St James Square, Boroughbridge, North
Yorkshire YO51 9AR
Tel 01423 322413 Fax 01423 323915

The Abbey Inn
Byland Abbey, North Yorkshire YO61 4BD
Tel 01347 868204 Fax 01347 868678

The Fox & Hounds
Carthorpe, North Yorkshire DL8 2LG
Tel 01845 567433 Fax 01845 567155

The Blue Lion
East Witton, North Yorkshire DL8 4SN
Tel 01969 624273 Fax 01969 624189

The Plough Inn
Main Street, Fadmoor, North Yorkshire
YO62 7HY
Tel 01751 431515

Stone Trough Inn
Kirkham Abbey, Kirkham, North Yorkshire
YO60 7JS
Tel 01653 618713 Fax 01653 618819

Sandpiper Inn
Market Place, Leyburn, North Yorkshire
DL8 5AT
Tel 01969 622206 Fax 01969 625367

The Sportsmans Arms Hotel
Wath-in-Nidderdale, Pateley Bridge, North
Yorkshire HG3 5PP
Tel 01423 711306 Fax 01423 712524

West Riding Licensed Refreshment Rooms
Dewsbury Railway Station, Wellington Road,
Dewsbury, West Yorkshire WF13 1HF
Tel 01924 459193 Fax 01924 507444

The Three Acres Inn
Roydhouse, West Yorkshire HD8 8LR
Tel 01484 602606 Fax 01484 608411

The Millbank at Millbank
Sowerby Bridge, West Yorkshire HX6 3DY
Tel 01422 825588 Fax 01422 822080

Ring O'Bells
212 Hilltop Road, Thornton, West Yorkshire
BD13 3QL
Tel 01274 832296 Fax 01274 831707

$\mathcal{S}$hallowdale House ✦✦✦✦✦

*1960s property in the Hambleton
Hills affording spectacular views*

☏ 01439 788325
📠 01439 788885
✉ stay@shallowdalehouse.
demon.co.uk
www.shallowdalehouse.demon.
co.uk

Map ref 8 - SE57
West End, AMPLEFORTH,
North Yorkshire, YO62 4DY
B1363 from York, L at Brandsby
3 Rooms, S £44-£55 D £65-£80,
No smoking, Closed Xmas/New Year

Shallowdale House is a beautiful example of a modern architect-designed house, carefully sited in a stunning landscape. All the rooms boast wonderful views through huge picture windows, and the interior design is restful, uncluttered and comfortable. In addition to the spacious bedrooms (two en-suite, one with private bathroom), there is a downstairs drawing room with open fire in winter, and an upstairs sitting room, perfect for enjoying the view and studying a good collection of books and local information. The attractive garden covers more than two acres of sheltered south-facing hillside. Food is a highlight, with delicious home-baking, and a memorable four course dinner featuring the best of regional produce in simple freshly-cooked imaginative dishes. There is a small and well-chosen wine list. Anton van der Horst and Phillip Gill spare no effort in providing a warm welcome and attentive hospitality.

RECOMMENDED IN THE AREA

*Castle Howard; Rievaulx Abbey; Nunnington
Hall*

*W*hitfield ♦♦♦♦

A sunny, peaceful setting overlooking the dales and distant fells.

☎ 01969 650565
📠 01969 650565
✉ empsall@askrigg.yorks.net
www.askrigg-cottages.co.uk

Map ref 7 - SD99

Helm, ASKRIGG, Leyburn,
North Yorkshire, DL8 3JF
off A684 at Bainbridge by Rose &
Crown, signed Askrigg, over river to t-
junct, 150mtrs to No Through Road
sign, L up hill for 0.5m
2 Rooms, D £42-£46, No smoking,
Closed 23 - 27 Dec.

Spectacular views of Wensleydale can be enjoyed from this very welcoming property set in a tranquil fellside location. Whitfield has been converted from a Yorkshire limestone barn into a warm and comfortable home furnished in the traditional manner. Both bedrooms have the benefit of either en suite shower or bath and shower, and guest rooms are provided with books and magazines, toiletries,

tea/coffee facilities and televisions. A hearty breakfast is served around a communal table in the open-plan lounge/dining room. This antique-filled room also has a television and video recorder, plenty of books and an open log fire to encourage visitors to relax.

RECOMMENDED IN THE AREA

Dales Countryside Museum; Bolton Castle; Wensleydale Creamery

*S*tow House Hotel ♦♦♦♦

High levels of service and comfort combined with a gorgeous rural setting

☎ 01969 663635
✉ davidpeterburton@aol.com
www.wensleydale.org

Map ref 7 - SE08

AYSGARTH, Leyburn, North Yorkshire,
DL8 3SR
7m W of Leyburn on A684, 0.6m before
Aysgarth village
9 Rooms, S £32-£40 D £64-£70, No smoking
in bedrooms or dining room

Fantastic views across two dales can be enjoyed from this imposing Victorian house set in breathtakingly scenic countryside. The large house, formerly the home of the Rural Dean of Wensleydale, sits in secluded grounds away from the road. Accommodation is furnished and decorated along traditional lines, with each bedoom having en suite facilities, and two luxury rooms making the most of the views. Hearty well-cooked breakfasts using local produce are served in the smart dining room, and evening meals are also available using fresh Wensleydale ingredients. There is also a cosy bar and a large lounge in which guests can relax. The friendly hosts offer a great welcome.

RECOMMENDED IN THE AREA

The Wensleydale Creamery (10 miles); Bolton Castle (3 miles); outstanding walks (from the door)

The Castle Arms Inn ••••

Convivial inn dating back to the 1300s, with luxury bedrooms and traditional hospitality

☎ 01677 470270
📠 01677 470837
✉ castlearms@aol.com

Map ref 7 - SE28

Snape, BEDALE,
North Yorkshire, DL8 2TB
A1 to Leeming Bar, then A684
to Bedale and B6268 to
Masham. After 2m turn left
signed Thorp Perrow
Arboretum. 1m past
arboretum left into Snape
9 Rooms, S £45 D £59,
No smoking in bedrooms or
dining room

A 14th-century inn has been given a touch of modernity with the addition of several smart bedrooms. The conversion of a cluster of old barns has resulted in a stylish courtyard development, where every room comes with its own luxury bathroom. This quiet annexe has kept many of the original architectural features, and these blend in well with the pine doors and furniture of the bright bedrooms. An inglenook fireplace complete with roaring fire is the focal point of the bar, where guests are encouraged to relax with plenty of reading material on hand to keep them occupied. A good range of traditional ales is another attraction. Lunch and dinner are served in the cosy restaurant, with the best local produce going into the good home cooking, and all dishes created to order. Guests to this pretty village inn are treated to a warm welcome from the friendly owners

RECOMMENDED IN THE AREA

Walks on the North York Moors and Northern Yorkshire Dales; Thorp Perrow Arboretum; many golf courses and race courses

$\mathcal{E}$lmfield Country House ◆◆◆◆

*Extended gamekeeper's cottage
with uninterrupted country views*

☎ 01677 450558
🖷 01677 450557
✉ stay@elmfieldhouse.
    freeserve.co.uk
www.countryhouseyorkshire.
co.uk

Map ref 7 - SE29

Arrathorne, BEDALE, North Yorkshire,
DL8 1NE
from A1 follow A684 through Bedale
towards Leyburn. After Patrick
Brompton turn R towards Richmond.
Premises 1.5m on R
9 Rooms, S £35 D £50-£60, No
smoking in dining room

$\mathcal{A}$ friendly establishment in a quiet country location, Elmfield is ideal for business or leisure, and a good base for touring the Yorkshire Dales and Moors. York, Durham, Richmond, Bedale, Ripon and Northallerton are all within striking distance and, after a busy day, guests can enjoy a drink in the garden, where the waterfall plays, or relax in the lounge bar or conservatory/games room. Home-cooked evening meals are also available. The modern en suite bedrooms are superbly equipped with direct dial telephones, colour televisions, movie channel, radio alarms and teasmades. There is one four-poster bed, and two rooms for disabled guests. Private fishing lake, four-wheel drive and paintballing on site, and outdoor activities arranged.

RECOMMENDED IN THE AREA

Richmond Castle (5 miles); Lightwater Valley and Fountains Abbey (12 miles); Yorkshire Dales National Park (2 miles)

$\mathcal{A}$shley House Hotel ◆◆◆◆

*Friendly, relaxed hotel in a
peaceful part of town*

☎ 01423 507474
🖷 01423 560858
✉ ashleyhousehotel@
    btinternet.com
www.ashleyhousehotel.com

Map ref 7 - SE35

36-40 Franklin Road, HARROGATE,
North Yorkshire, HG1 5EE
on entering Harrogate follow signs for
conference centre. Opp centre turn
into Strawberry Dale Ave, L into
Franklin Rd, premises on R
18 Rooms, S £39.50-£70 D £59.50-
£90, No smoking in dining room or
lounge

$\mathcal{T}$hree gracious Victorian townhouses have been carefully converted into this immaculately maintained and decorated hotel. Set in a quiet tree-lined part of Harrogate close to all amenities, it offers superbly-equipped bedrooms with en suite bath or shower rooms. A comfortable lounge with leather furniture and rich colours offers a stylish retreat after a day's shopping or sightseeing, and there's also a cosy bar lounge with a warm tartan theme. An extensive collection of whiskies (over 100 at the last count) provides a challenge for malt drinkers. A friendly, informal atmosphere is one of the proud boasts of this quiet hotel.

RECOMMENDED IN THE AREA

Yorkshire Dales (20 minute drive); city of York (45 minutes by train); Fountains Abbey (20 minute drive)

_K_imberley Hotel ◆◆◆

An elegant hotel of character close to the conference centre and all the town's amenities

☎ 01423 505613
🖷 01423 530276
✉ info@
thekimberley.co.uk
www.thekimberley.co.uk

Map ref 7 - SE35
11-19 Kings Road,
HARROGATE, North Yorkshire,
HG1 5JY
follow signs for Harrogate
International Centre or Kings
Rd, premises on L approx
150yds past the centre
48 Rooms, S £50-£74.50 D
£70-£104.50, No smoking in
dining room

Conveniently located in the centre of this lovely spa town, the Kimberley is equally well placed for discovering Yorkshire and the Dales. This Victorian townhouse hotel is close to the conference centre, and caters for both the business and leisure guest. Five well-equipped meeting and syndicate rooms provide facilities for up to 50 delegates. A lift to each floor services the bedrooms which offer an impressive range of accessories; each room is individually furnished and decorated, with en suite facilities and hospitality trays, telephone and satellite television. Executive rooms also feature king-size beds, fax machines and modem points. Stylish public areas include the large but cosy lounge and a well-stocked bar. An extensive choice of breakfast dishes is provided, with guests invited to help themselves from the buffet table. There is a friendly and relaxed atmosphere which is supported by an efficient level of service. Ample car parking is also available.

RECOMMENDED IN THE AREA

Royal Turkish Baths and Pump Room Museum; designer shops, tea rooms and antiques; Yorkshire Dales National Park

$\mathcal{F}$ountains Hotel ◆◆◆◆

Elegant Victorian property in a convenient location

☎ 01423 530483
📠 01423 705312
✉ dave@
    fountains.fsworld.co.uk
www.webart.co.uk/clients/fount
ains/index.htm

Map ref 7 - SE35

27 Kings Road, HARROGATE,
North Yorkshire, HG1 5JY
A1(M) J47, then A661 to Harrogate.
A59 off Skipton/Knaresborough/Ripon
rdbt. Continue on A59 for approx
1.5m, L into Kings Rd, Fountains
approx 0.75m on R
10 Rooms, S £32-£38 D £52-£60,
No smoking

$\mathcal{F}$ountains is a delightful bed and breakfast hotel, overlooking a wooded coppice, less than two minutes' walk from the Conference and Exhibition Centre and five minutes' walk from the town centre and all its amenities, including some excellent restaurants. A good choice is offered at breakfast in the dining room - cooked or continental with vegetarian alternatives. The spacious en suite bedrooms are equipped with colour televisions and well-stocked hospitality trays. A hairdryer and ironing facilities are also available on request. Off-road parking is provided, or a guest permit for free street parking.

RECOMMENDED IN THE AREA

Beautiful walks in Yorkshire Dales (10 minute drive); Castle Howard (25 minute drive); Royal Baths and Pump Rooms (10 minute walk)

$\mathcal{W}$eaver's Bar Restaurant with Rooms ◆◆◆◆ ◉

Cosy accommodation at this family-run restaurant and bar

☎ 01535 643822 📠 01535 644832
✉ weavers@amserve.net
www.weaversmallhotel.co.uk

Map ref 7 - SE03

15 West Lane, HAWORTH, West Yorkshire,
BD22 8DU
A629/B6142 towards Haworth, Stanbury and
Colne. At top of village pass Bronte Weaving
Shed on R. Turn L after 100 yds to Parsonage
car park
3 Rooms, S £55 D £80, No smoking in dining
room

$\mathcal{A}$ fascinating conversion of three weavers' cottages, stuffed with bric-a-brac, this restaurant with rooms is located close to the Brontë Parsonage Museum in the centre of town. It is a cosy property and the bedrooms are furnished with great panache and plenty more curios. They have full en suite facilities (baths and showers) and are equipped with television, trouser presses, hairdryers and complimentary tea and coffee. Colin and Jane Rushworth and family are the friendly owners, and are also responsible for the cooking. Food, served in generous portions, is locally sourced and strong on tradition, including some good old-fashioned puddings. Meals are available in both the restaurant and bar.

RECOMMENDED IN THE AREA

Brontë Parsonage Museum; moorland walks; Salts Mill David Hockney exhibition

*L*askill Grange....

Stunning scenery for this working farm, offering impressive accommodation divided between main house and luxurious converted barns

☎ 01439 798498
📠 01439 798268
✉ suesmith@
  laskillfarm.fsnet.co.uk
www.laskillfarm.co.uk

Map ref 8 - SE59

Hawnby, HAWNBY,
North Yorkshire, YO62 5NB
6m N of Helmsley on B1257
6 Rooms, S £30-£35 D £60,
No smoking, Closed 25 Dec

RECOMMENDED IN THE AREA

Rievaulx Abbey; lots of National Trust properties; York (40 minutes)

Country lovers will adore this charming 19th-century property situated in one of England's finest National parks. This is James Herriot and Heartbeat country - a haven of peace and tranquillity, and the perfect base from which to explore North Yorkshire's spectacular and varied scenery. Alternatively, try a spot of fishing in the River Seph, which runs through the 600 acre grounds, while children can play in the activity centre. High standards prevail throughout, with neatly furnished rooms hosting a range of homely extras. All bedrooms are en suite, charmingly decorated and equipped with TV and tea/coffee-making facilities. In the comfortable guest lounge you can sit by the open fire on cooler days or if you get wet on your travels, perhaps exploring one of the nature walks signposted from the farm, drying facilities are available. Delicious breakfasts, and, by arrangement, evening meals, are served in the smart dining room. Wherever possible meals feature home grown local produce and Laskill's own natural spring water.

*T*he Weavers Shed
Restaurant with Rooms ♦♦♦♦

A nearly self-sufficient restaurant serving quality food, with luxurious accommodation in peaceful surroundings

☎ 01484 654284
📠 01484 650980
✉ info@weaversshed.co.uk
www.weaversshed.co.uk

Map ref 7 - SE11

Knowl Road, Golcar, HUDDERSFIELD,
West Yorkshire, HD7 4AN
from Huddersfield A62 Oldham Rd, right
into Milnsbridge. L into Scar Lane at
Kwiksave, then to top of hill,
establishment on right before church.
Follow Colne Valley Museum signs.
5 Rooms, S £40-£50 D £55-£65,
Closed Xmas/New Year

 RECOMMENDED IN THE AREA

Royal Armouries Museum; National Museum of Film and Television; National Coal Mining Museum

*C*onverted from a cloth-finishing mill in the 1970s, with many of the original features making an interesting talking point amongst guests, the Weavers Shed continues to impress. Chef/patron Stephen Jackson has achieved his ideal of providing a near self-sufficient restaurant where guests can retire after a superb meal for a luxurious night's sleep. His superior bedrooms are a blend of traditional and classic styles with modern comforts. All five rooms, named after local textile mills, offer individually decorated en suite facilities in light and airy surroundings. The restaurant, where delicious breakfasts including home-made preserves are served in the morning, specialises in modern British cooking with simply-prepared and presented dishes. The restaurant has its own kitchen garden supplying virtually all of its fruit, herb and vegetable requirements, and allowing the chef to offer excellent seasonal dishes on the menus. The wines of Southwest France dominate the wine list, selected from less well-known producers who concentrate on small quality growths.

*B*ank Villa Guest House ◆◆◆◆

Grade II listed house with a wealth of antique furniture

☎ 01765 689605
🖷 01765 689605
http://www.smoothHound.co.uk
/hotels/bankvill.html

Map ref 7 - SE28

MASHAM, Ripon, North Yorkshire, HG4 4DB
on A6108 from Ripon, premises 100yds after 30mph sign on right on entering Masham
6 Rooms, S £30-£35 D £40-£52, No smoking

*B*ank villa is a charming Georgian house featuring old beams and antique pine furniture in the bedrooms. Four of the rooms have en suite facilities, the remaining two have private facilities. Two comfortable and inviting lounges are provided, where guests can relax after a day out, perhaps exploring the Yorkshire Dale National Park and James Herriot country. Good home cooking is served in the delightful dining room, using fresh local produce where possible. Service, from the proprietors Bobby and Lucy Thomson is attentive and friendly. Children under five cannot be accommodated, neither can dogs (except guide dogs). Guest parking is available.

RECOMMENDED IN THE AREA

Rievaulx Abbey & Fountains Abbey (short drive); The World of James Herriot (12 miles); Yorkshire Dales

*T*he Old Manse ◆◆◆◆

Conveniently and quietly situated former manse

☎ 01751 476484
🖷 01751 477124

Map ref 8 - SE78

19 Middleton Road, PICKERING, North Yorkshire, YO18 8AL
from A169, L at rdbt, through lights, 1st R into Potter Hill follow rd to L. From A170 turn L at 'local traffic only'
10 Rooms, S £22.50-£28 D £44-£52, No smoking

*W*hat was once a Methodist minister's home is now a comfortable and very well furnished guest house. The Old Manse is peacefully located within easy walking distance of the town and the North Yorkshire Moors Steam Railway (which runs from Pickering to Grosmont), and makes an ideal base from which to explore the moors, the Yorkshire coast and the historical city of York.

The comfortable bedrooms all have en suite facilities. A cosy lounge is available for guests' use, and excellent hospitality is assured from the resident owners. There is a private car park and a large secluded garden where guests can wander and relax.

RECOMMENDED IN THE AREA

North Yorkshire Moors Railway (0.5 mile); Eden Camp living history museum (6 miles) Flamingoland Theme Park & Zoo (5 miles)

*B*ay Tree Farm ♦♦♦♦

A delightful working farm close to Fountains Abbey

☎ 01765 620394
📠 01765 620394

Map ref 7 - SE26

Aldfield, RIPON, North Yorkshire,
HG4 3BE
approx 4m W, take unclass road S off
B6265
6 Rooms, D £50-£55, No smoking

*B*ay Tree Farm covers 400 acres of land with beef and arable farming. Situated between the Yorkshire Dales and the North York Moors, there is ample opportunity to explore the countryside or to visit Fountains Abbey nearby. The farmhouse itself is in the quiet village of Aldfield, near Ripon, with spacious accommodation in a converted barn. Family and ground floor rooms are available, all are en suite with colour television and tea and coffee making facilities. Dinner is available and the wholesome farm fare uses fresh local produce.

A comfortable lounge is available for guests to relax in, a wood-burning stove is lit here in colder weather. Proprietors Valerie and Andrew Leeming are attentive hosts. Visa and Mastercard are accepted.

RECOMMENDED IN THE AREA

Studley Park; Brimham Rocks; Yorkshire Dales

---

*T*he Sawley Arms ♦♦♦♦♦

Delightful accommodation in an area of exceptional beauty

☎ 01765 620642
📠 01765 620642

Map ref 7 - SE26

Sawley, Fountains Abbey, RIPON,
North Yorkshire, HG4 3EQ
Leave A1 to Ripon on B6265,
continue to Risplith, turn left into
Sawley village, inn in centre
2 Rooms, S £75 D £80-£95,
No smoking

*H*ospitable proprietor Mrs June Hawes has created a haven of luxury in a modern stone-built cottage adjoining the Sawley Arms. It offers accommodation in two suites, each with its own comfortable lounge, twin-bedded room, kitchen and lavish en suite shower or Jacuzzi. Additional facilities in the rooms include remote control televisions, radios, books, games, pay phones and an iron and ironing board. Good meals are served in the restaurant of the Sawley Arms, and breakfast can be taken here or in your room. Guests can also relax in the award-winning gardens. Sawley is located in an area of Outstanding Natural Beauty, close to Brimham Rocks, surrounded by open country.

RECOMMENDED IN THE AREA

*Fountains Abbey at Studley Royal Park
(National Trust); Castle Howard; Ripley Castle*

Westbourne House
Hotel ••••

Former Victorian gentleman's residence in a conservation area close to the university and hospitals

☎ 0114 266 0109
📠 0114 266 7778
www.westbournehouse
hotel.com

Map ref 8 - SK38

25 Westbourne Road,
Broomhill, SHEFFIELD,
South Yorkshire, S10 2QQ
10 Rooms, S £45-£65 D £75-
£85

Sue Hoey and Nick Currie's family-run hotel occupies an elegant town house dating from 1860. It is set in attractive gardens in the pleasant suburb of Broomhill, just a few minutes from the city centre and all its amenities. Sue, Nick and their staff aim to ensure an enjoyable stay for every guest, providing a 'home-from-home' experience. Bedrooms are individually furnished and decorated to retain their period elegance while providing modern comforts. Nine are en suite, one has private facilities, and all are equipped with complimentary tea and coffee, colour Ceefax televisions, direct dial telephones and radio alarms. Additional items, such as shoe cleaning materials, sewing kits, trouser presses, irons and toiletries are also available. The restaurant is open for dinner and functions, as well as breakfast. Cooking is second nature to Sue, who is responsible for the home-made food. A comfortable lounge is also provided, overlooking the terrace and garden.

RECOMMENDED IN THE AREA

Peak District National Park (5 minute drive); Meadowhall Shopping Centre; Sheffield Art Galleries (including the new Millenium Gallery)

Low Skibeden Farmhouse ♦♦♦♦

Genuine warm hospitality coupled with home-from-home comforts

☎ 01756 793849
🖷 01756 793804
✉ skibhols.yorksdales@
   talk21.com
www.yorkshirenet.co.uk/
accgde/lowskibeden/index.html

Map ref 7 - SD05

Skibeden Road, SKIPTON,
North Yorkshire, BD23 6AB
at E end of Skipton bypass off A65/59
5 Rooms, S £28-£40 D £40-£48,
No smoking

A lovely stone farmhouse set in its own well-tended gardens on the outskirts of town. Heather Simpson is the perfect host who offers all guests afternoon tea, suppertime drinks, and generous breakfasts. The warm hospitality and home comforts extend to the bedrooms, where spacious accommodation, with some en suite facilities, includes family rooms. All of the rooms enjoy stunning views over the surrounding countryside and gardens, and there is safe parking. A very strong emphasis is placed on cleanliness, and the bedrooms, the cosy lounge and the dining room are immaculately tended. Harrogate and York are within easy driving distance, and there is plenty to do in the immediate vicinity.

RECOMMENDED IN THE AREA

Bolton Abbey and Parcival Hall Gardens (3-5 miles); Brontë Parsonage and East Riddlesden Hall (National Trust) (5 miles); Eden Camp; Settle to Carlisle Railway

---

Spital Hill ♦♦♦♦

Victorian country house set in extensive grounds

☎ 01845 522273
🖷 01845 524970
✉ spitalhill@amserve.net
www.wolsey-lodges.co.uk

Map ref 8 - SE47

York Road, THIRSK, North Yorkshire,
YO7 3AE
from A1(M) take A168, then A170, at rdbt take A19 to York for 1m. House set back 600yds from road on R, drive marked by 2 white posts
5 Rooms, S £44-£53 D £72-£90, No smoking

R obin and Ann Clough welcome guests warmly to their beautiful home, a fine country house set in its own gardens and parkland surrounded by open countryside. The atmosphere is very relaxing; there is a lovely lounge and meals are taken house-party style at one large table in the dining room. Ann produces a set dinner each evening, using good fresh produce, much of which comes from the garden. The well-prepared breakfast is also a highlight.

Bedrooms are furnished with quality and style, and thoughtfully equipped to include items such as bathrobes, fresh fruit, shortbread, mineral water, books, alarm clocks and hairdryers. There is no tea making equipment in the rooms as Ann prefers to offer tea as a service. The excellent dinner is an optional extra.

RECOMMENDED IN THE AREA

Yorkshire Dales and North York Moors; Castle Howard; Fountains Abbey

*A*llerston Manor House ♦♦♦♦

Queen Anne house well positioned for York and the moors

☎ 01723 850112
🖷 01723 850112
✉ aa@allerston-manor.com
www.allerston-manor.com

Map ref 8 - SE88

THORNTON LE DALE, North Yorkshire, YO18 7PF
from A64 (east of Malton) take B1258. On leaving Yedingham, turn L and then immediately R (signed to Allerston). In Allerston, the driveway is on R just after Church Lane.
3 Rooms, S £50-£55 D £70-£85,
No smoking

*T*he Manor was built in the 18th century around the remains of a 14th-century Knights Templar Hall, on the site of an old castle. It borders the North York Moors National Park so is ideal for walkers. Hens grazing on the surrounding fields provide free-range eggs for breakfast, and natural water is supplied via a beck running through the village from a spring on the moors. The house is beautifully furnished throughout, and the comfortable en suite bedrooms include two doubles and a twin, all with hospitality trays, clock radios and colour televisions. Dinner is often available, with guests bringing their own wine.

RECOMMENDED IN THE AREA

Nunnington Hall (National Trust); Rievaulx Abbey; Castle Howard; North York Moors; Steam Railway; Heritage Coast

Brimham Rocks

*T*he Hazelwood ....

Impressive Victorian property quietly located in the very heart of the ancient city

☎ 01904 626548
📠 01904 628032
www.thehazelwoodyork.com

Map ref 8 - SE65

24-25 Portland Street, Gillygate,
YORK, YO31 7EH
approaching York from north on
A19 turn L before City Gate and
take 1st turning L
14 Rooms, S £49-£95 D £75-
£100, No smoking

RECOMMENDED IN THE AREA

York Minster; National Railway Museum; Jorvik Centre

*O*nly 400 yards from York Minster, The Hazelwood is an elegant Victorian town house retaining many original features. It has its own car park - a great advantage in such a central location - and is an ideal base from which to explore the historic city and its shops and restaurants.

The bedrooms are individually styled and have been tastefully fitted to the highest standard using designer fabrics. All the rooms have en suite bathrooms, which are well equipped and imaginatively lit. The breakfast room is graced with stylish fabrics and smart linen and the walls are hung with an interesting collection of floral prints. Enjoy a traditional hearty Yorkshire breakfast or vegetarian alternative, or for those with lighter tastes, croissants and Danish pastries. The cosy lounge offers a variety of reading material, and tea, coffee and freshly baked home-made biscuits are always available.

Holmwood House Hotel ♦♦♦♦

Delightful pair of early Victorian townhouses backing onto a pretty private square

☎ 01904 626183
📠 01904 670899
✉ holmwood.house@
    dial.pipex.com
www.holmwoodhousehotel.co.uk

Map ref 8 - SE55

114 Holgate Road, YORK,
North Yorkshire, YO24 4BB
on A59 Harrogate road on R 300yds
past traffic lights at The Fox pub
14 Rooms, S £45-£85 D £65-£105,
No smoking

Two townhouses built in the middle of the 19th century have been beautifully restored and converted into this delightful hotel. It still has the feel of a private house, and once guests have registered and been shown to their rooms they are free to come and go as if it were their own home. Bedrooms come in a variety of sizes, but all are richly decorated and pleasantly furnished, mostly with antiques. Each room has its own bathroom or shower, while some luxurious rooms, including one with a four-poster bed, have spa baths. In addition to colour televisions, direct-dial telephones and hospitality trays there are many extras to make a stay more comfortable. A charming sitting room has an open fire. There is a display with books and plenty of local information to browse through. A substantial choice is offered for breakfast, served at separate tables in the dining room. Holmwood House is within easy walking distance of York and all its attractions. A free car park is available for guests' use.

RECOMMENDED IN THE AREA

Fountains Abbey; Castle Howard (12 miles); Yorkshire Dales and North Yorkshire Moors

Channel Islands

A selection of places to eat from the AA Restaurant Guide

Restaurants

Rozel Harbour, Jersey

Da Nello (Modern)
46 La Pollet, St Peter Port, Guernsey
Tel 01481 721552 Fax 01481 724235

Le Nautique (Traditional)
Quay Steps, St Peter Port Guernsey
Tel 01481 721214 Fax 01481 721786

Jersey Pottery Restaurant (Modern)
Gorey Village, Jersey JE3 9EP
Tel 01534 851119 Fax 01534 856403

Château La Chaire (Country-house)
Rozel Bay, Jersey JE3 6AJ
Tel 01534 863354 Fax 01534 865137

Somerville Hotel (Classic, Country-house)
Mont du Boulevard, St Aubin JE3 8AD
Tel 01534 741226 Fax 01534 746621

Green Island Restaurant (Bistro-style, Rustic)
Green Island, St Clement, Jersey JE2 6LS
Tel 01534 857787 Fax 01534 619309

La Sablonnerie (Chic, French)
Sark, GY9 0SD
Tel 01481 832061 Fax 01481 832408

*B*on Air Hotel ♦♦♦♦

A sunny, south-facing hotel overlooking the sea

☎ 01534 855324
🖷 01534 857801

Map ref 13

Coast Road, Pontac, ST CLEMENT,
Jersey, JE2 6SE
18 Rooms, D £52-£74, No smoking in
dining room, Closed Nov-Feb

A very large indoor heated swimming pool is an undoubted attraction at this pretty small hotel just 10 minutes from St Helier. Set opposite St Clement's beach, it exudes a warm and welcoming atmosphere which is matched by the sunny position. The comfortable bedrooms, which come in a variety of sizes, are identically furnished and decorated to good modern standards. All have en suite facilities, and some have the benefit of balconies overlooking the sea. Visitors are encouraged to relax in the lounge and cosy bar, and enjoy breakfast in the beamed dining room. Sunny patios also make the most of the south-facing position.

RECOMMENDED IN THE AREA

Visit St Aubin's harbour; Beauport, Corbiere Lighthouse; daytrips to Sark

The Panorama ••••

Peaceful, elevated hotel overlooking St Aubin's Bay and offering delightful views from its sea-facing rooms

☎ 01534 742429 📠 01534 745940
www.panoramajersey.com

Map ref 13

La Rue du Crocquet, ST AUBIN, Jersey, JE3 8BZ
overlooking St Aubin's Bay, and out to sea, situated in the village
17 Rooms, S £20-£47 D £40-£94, No smoking, Closed early Nov-mid Mar

Some of the finest views in the Channel Islands can be enjoyed from this well-named hotel nestling beside cottages in a pretty seafront street. Guests are encouraged to linger on the sunny terrace to savour the glorious outlook, and front-facing rooms are much sought after. The well-equipped bedrooms vary in size and standard, with the superior rooms in particular offering high levels of comfort and luxury. All rooms are en suite and fitted with quality beds, many of them extra long to accommodate tall visitors. Public rooms feature antique fireplaces, and the hotel is notable for its huge collection of teapots - over 500 at the last count. Cream teas are served several times a week, and excellent breakfasts featuring the likes of Welsh Rarebit along with more traditional dishes are recommended. The area around the Panorama is well served with restaurants, many within walking distance, and the owners are happy to make recommendations on request.

RECOMMENDED IN THE AREA

Explore picturesque village of St Aubin; follow the Railway Walk to Corbiere; visit Beauport and Les Creux Country Park; use the cycle track into St Helier

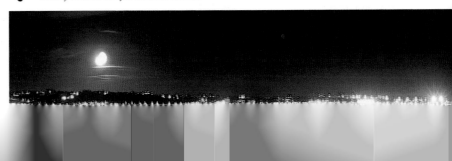

Millbrook House ****

Gracious Georgian mansion set in 10 acres of gardens and parklands overlooking the sea

☎ 01534 733036 ☎ 01534 724317

Map ref 13

Rue de Trachy, Millbrook, ST HELIER, Jersey, JE2 3JN
1.5m W of town on A1
27 Rooms, S £38-£44 D £76-£88, No smoking in dining room, Closed 6 Oct-3 May

RECOMMENDED IN THE AREA

Spectacular coastal walks; Elizabeth Castle; Jersey Museum

'The past improved but not forgotten' is a philosophy exemplified in the traditional service, values and appearance of Millbrook House, which is ideal for the independently-minded traveller seeking a hotel of character at reasonable cost. The house has been in the same family since 1848, but is now much extended to provide modern accommodation on three floors to the rear. The hotel is peacefully located in lovely gardens just 600 metres from the sea, and the grounds include ample car parking and a five-hole pitch and putt golf course. The comfortably appointed bedrooms all have private bathrooms and most have garden and sea views. A lift is provided, and guests will find a colour television, direct dial telephone, coffee/tea-maker and hairdryer in every room. Three fully equipped self-catering studio apartments are also available. The hotel has a residential license and lounge bar, and an imaginative menu supported by an extensive wine list is offered in the dining room.

Champ Colin •••••

Traditional old stone house with original features in peaceful surroundings

☎ 01534 851877
📠 01534 854902

Map ref 13

Rue du Champ Colin,
ST SAVIOUR,
Jersey, JE2 7UN
from airport, signs to St Helier, through tunnel.
1st L to lights/middle lane, up Mont Millais.
B28 to Hougue Bie, then Rue du Champ Colin
3 Rooms, S £18-£22 D £36-£44, No smoking, Closed 18 Dec-5 Jan

Champ Colin dates back to 1815. It sits in a quiet rural spot, only 10 minutes from the town centre by car, and 10 minutes from the nearest beach. It has a garden with a luscious long front lawn, and there is plenty of parking space. The bedrooms are lovely and snug, with heavy wooden antique furniture; two of them have half-tester beds. All three have en suite bathrooms, colour TV, tea and coffee making facilities. Beamed ceilings, some exposed stone walls and more antique furniture downstairs make the house feel cosy and rustic. You can take a moment to relax in the drawing room, and you can savour a delicious full English breakfast in front of the imposing granite fireplace in the breakfast room

RECOMMENDED IN THE AREA

Durrell Wildlife Conservation Trust; Mont Orgueil Castle; La Houge Bie (neolithic burial mound with medieval chapels)

*H*otel Petit Champ ◆◆◆◆

Wonderful coastal scenery and charming, friendly accommodation

☎ 01481 832046
℻ 01481 832469
✉ hpc@island-of-sark.co.uk
www.island-of-sark.co.uk

Map ref 13
SARK, GY9 0SF
from Methodist Chapel take lane,
signposted, towards sea & turn left
13 Rooms, S £51.50-£60 D £99-£116,
No smoking in dining room, Closed
Nov-Etr

*M*agnificent sea views and stunning sunsets set this small hotel way above the norm. Set on the small car-free island of Sark, its unique position overlooking the sea and neighbouring islands is matched by very high standards of hospitality and service. Nothing is too much trouble for the cheerful staff, and standards of cleanliness are high. The en suite bedrooms have no televisions or hospitality trays, but guests are brought a morning tea or coffee in bed, and there is a separate TV lounge. There is excellent use of fresh local produce in the breakfasts and five-course dinners, and a well-stocked wine cellar.

RECOMMENDED IN THE AREA

Beautiful cliff walks for coastal scenery, birds and wild flowers; horse and carriage tours, boat trips; La Seigneurie Gardens

*I*sle of Man

A selection of places to eat from the AA Restaurant Guide

Restaurants

⊛ The Chablis Cellar (Classic, French)
21 Bank Street, Castletown IM9 1AT
Tel 01624 823527 Fax 01624 824016

⊛ Bradda Glen Café (Chic, Classic)
Port Erin IM9 6PJ
Tel 01624 833166

Horse tram on Douglas Promenade

Rowany Cottier ♦♦♦♦♦

Impressive modern house overlooking Port Erin Bay

☎ 01624 832287 ☏ 01624 835685

Map ref 5 - SC27

Spaldrick, PORT ERIN, IM9 6PE
on entering Port Erin, proceed up promenade, passing hotels, rd levels off and dips down to Spaldrick. House on R opp path to Bradda Glen
5 Rooms, S £30-£40 D £52-£60, No smoking

Rowany Cottier is a newly-built guest house set in extensive grounds offering stunning coastal views. Friendly Manx proprietors, Heather and John Keggin, have a wealth of local knowledge to share with guests, and their house has a welcoming and relaxed atmosphere. There is a choice of double and twin bedrooms all with en suite facilities, colour televisions, radios, alarm clocks and complimentary tea and coffee. One ground floor room is suitable for wheelchair users and has a walk in shower. Public rooms include a comfortable lounge and an attractive breakfast room with individual tables. Continental and traditional breakfasts are served with Manx kippers as a feature.

RECOMMENDED IN THE AREA

Calf of Man Nature Reserve; Cregneash Village Folk Museum and coastal scenery; steam railway and museum

---

The River House ♦♦♦♦♦

Top breakfasts in a Georgian house overlooking the river

☎ 01624 816412
☏ 01624 816412

Map ref 5 - SC69

RAMSEY, IM8 3DA
3 Rooms, S £39-£49 D £71-£89

Built in about 1820, with Victorian additions, the house is five minutes' walk from the town centre. It is found in a private lane and has large mature gardens and a river passing nearby. All the spacious bedrooms have views across the river. The rooms are furnished with pretty chintzes, and have luxury bathrooms en suite, and colour TV. You can also see the river from the Garden Room, where breakfast is served from 7.30am to 9.30am, featuring an ample full breakfast, home made bread and preserves. All food is cooked on the traditional Aga, using fresh produce from the vegetable garden. Cordon Bleu dinners can be arranged from Sunday to Thursday, around the table in the elegant dining room, with its beautiful antique furniture and pictures. There is no licence but guests can bring their own wine.

RECOMMENDED IN THE AREA

The Grove Rural Life Museum; Ramsey harbour and beach; The Story of Mann

Scotland

A selection of places to eat from the AA Restaurant & AA Pub Guides

Restaurants

◉◉ Green Inn (Traditional)
9 Victoria Road, Ballater, Aberdeenshire
AB35 5QQ
Tel 01339 755701 Fax 01339 755701

◉◉ Waterfront Restaurant (French, Bistro-style)
Railway Pier, Oban, Argyll & Bute PA34 4LW
Tel 01631 563110 Fax 01631 563110

◉◉ Ivy House (Modern, Chic)
Alloway, South Ayrshire KN7 4NL
Tel 01292 442336 Fax 01292 445572

◉◉ Plumed Horse Restaurant (Classic, Chic)
Crossmichael, Castle Douglas, Dumfries &
Galloway DG7 3AU
Tel 01556 670333 Fax 01556 670333

◉◉ Iggs (Modern)
15 Jeffrey Street, City of Edinburgh, EH1 1DR
Tel 0131 557 8184 Fax 0131 441 7111

◉◉ Restaurant Martin Wishart (French,
Minimalist)
54 The Shore, Leith, City of Edinburgh EH6
6RA
Tel 0131 553 3557 Fax 0131 467 7091

◉◉ The Inn at Lathones (Country-house)
Largoward, St Andrews, Fife KY9 1JE
Tel 01334 840494 Fax 01334 840694

◉ Shish Mahal (Modern, Minimalist)
Park Road, City of Glasgow G4 9JF
Tel 0141 334 1057 Fax 0141 572 0800

◉◉ 2 Quail Restaurant (Victorian Town House)
Dornoch, Sutherland, Highland IV25 3SN
Tel 01862 811811

◉ Moorings Hotel (Country-house)
Banavie, Fort William, Highland PH33 7LY
Tel 01397 772797 Fax 01397 772441

◉ The Riverhouse (Classic)
1 Greig Street, Inverness, Highland IV3 5PT
Tel 01463 222033 Fax 01463 220890

◉◉ The Albannach (Country-house)
Baddidarroch, Lochinver, Highland IV27 4LP
Tel 01571 844407 Fax 01571 844285

◉◉ Champany Inn (Traditional, Formal)
Linlothgow, West Lothian EH49 7LU
Tel 01506 834532 Fax 01506 834302

◉◉ Old Monastery Restaurant (Modern)
Drybridge, Moray AB56 5JB
Tel 01542 832660 Fax 01542 839437

◉◉ Let's Eat (Traditional)
77/79 Kinnoull St, Perth, Perth & Kinross
PH1 5EZ
Tel 01738 643377 Fax 01738 621464

Pubs

🍺 Lairhillock Inn and Restaurant
Netherley, Aberdeenshire AB39 3QS
Tel 01569 730001 Fax 01569 731175

🍺 Loch Melfort Hotel
Arduaine, Argyll & Bute PA34 4XG
Tel 01852 200233 Fax 01852 200214

🍺 Tayvallich Inn
Tayvallich, Argyll & Bute PA31 8PL
Tel 01546 870282 Fax 01546 870333

🍺 The Bridge Inn
27 Baird Road, Ratho, City of Edinburgh
EH28 8RA
Tel 0131 333 1320 Fax 0131 333 3480

🍺 Ubiquitous Chip
12 Ashton Lane, City of Glasgow G12 8SJ
Tel 0141 334 5007 Fax 0141 337 1302

🍺 Creebridge House Hotel
Newton Stewart, Dumfries & Galloway
DG8 6NP
Tel 01671 401121 Fax 01671 403258

🍺 Drovers Inn
5 Bridge St, East Linton, East Lothian EH40 3AG
Tel 01620 860298

🍺 The Ship Inn
The Toft, Elie, Fife KY9 1DT
Tel 01333 330246 Fax 01333 330864

🍺 Applecross Inn
Shore St, Applecross, Highland IV54 8LR
Tel 01520 744262 Fax 01520 744400

🍺 Cawdor Tavern
The Lane, Cawdor, Highland IV12 5XP
Tel 01667 404777 Fax 01667 404777

🍺 Glenelg Inn
Glenelg, Highland IV40 8JR
Tel 01599 522273 Fax 01599 522283

🍺 The Ceilidh Place
14 West Argyle St, Ullapool, Highland IV26 2TY
Tel 01854 612103 Fax 01854 612886

🍺 The Bein Inn
Glenfarg, Perth & Kinross PH2 9PY
Tel 01577 830216 Fax 01577 830211

🍺 The Killiecrankie Hotel
Killiecrankie, Perth & Kinross PH16 5LG
Tel 01796 473220 Fax 01796 472451

🍺 Burts Hotel
Market Sq, Melrose, Scottish Borders TD6 9PN
Tel 01896 822285 Fax 01896 822870

🍺 Wheatsheaf Hotel
Main St, Swinton, Scottish Borders TD11 3JJ
Tel 01890 860257 Fax 01890 860688

Glen Lui Hotel ◂◂◂◂ ◉

Hotel of individuality and character with a beautiful and tranquil setting

☎ 013397 55402
📠 013397 55545
✉ infos@glen-lui-hotel.co.uk
www.glen-lui-hotel.co.uk

Map ref 10 - NO39

Invercauld Road,
BALLATER, Royal Deeside,
Aberdeenshire, AB35 5RP
Invercauld Road is off A93 in
Ballater
19 Rooms, £25-£45 per
person B&B, £35-£61 per
person including dinner, No
smoking in bedrooms or
dining room

Friendly staff at this small country hotel take pride in providing personal attention to every guest. The location, in the heart of Royal Deeside with views over Ballater Golf Course towards Lochnagar, is ideal for exploring an area with much to offer the visitor. For those with a spirit of adventure a wide range of outdoor activities can be arranged: abseiling, archery, canoeing, clay pigeon shooting, climbing, fly fishing, gliding, horse riding, mountain biking, off road driving, orienteering, skiing and white water rafting. Guests coming in from a day's sport, business or leisure will appreciate the provision of a coin-operated laundrette, drying facilities and cycle storage. All the bedrooms, in the main house or annexe, have en suite facilities and are equipped with colour televisions, direct dial telephones, trouser presses, hairdryers and tea and coffee making materials. Executive suites are also available. The French chef offers a taste of the Auld Alliance in the imaginative menus and supporting wine list.

RECOMMENDED IN THE AREA

The Cairngorm and Grampian Mountains; Crathes Castle; Kildrummy Castle Gardens; Balmoral Castle; fishing and shooting

Callater Lodge Hotel ◆◆◆◆

Peaceful, comfortable guest house in historic village of Braemar

☎ 013397 41275
📠 013397 41345
✉ mariaaa@
   hotel-braemar.co.uk
www.hotel-braemar.co.uk

Map ref 12 - NO19

9 Glenshee Road, BRAEMAR,
Aberdeenshire, AB35 5YQ
adjacent to A93, 300yds S of Braemar
centre
7 Rooms, S £24-£28 D £48-£96,
No smoking in dining room or lounge

Named after the beautiful loch five miles to the south, Callater Lodge lies in grounds of over an acre in the heart of the proposed Cairngorms National Park. The granite stone Victorian building, some eight miles from Balmoral, is well situated for walking, fishing, skiing and touring. The provision of packed lunches, a drying room and secure storage may be particularly welcome for outdoor enthusiasts. The thoughtfully equipped bedrooms, individually decorated by the owners, vary in size. Public areas are comfortable and inviting and include a lounge with an open fire. Breakfast, served in the well-proportioned attractive dining room, offers a good choice. Enjoyable, home-cooked dinners are available by arrangement.

RECOMMENDED IN THE AREA

Balmoral Castle (8 miles); Glenshee Ski Centre (8 miles); walking in the Cairngorms and Grampians

Kirkton House ◆◆◆◆◆

Quiet location 25 minutes from Glasgow Airport

☎ 01389 841951
📠 01389 841868
✉ AA@kirktonhouse.co.uk
www.kirktonhouse.co.uk

Map ref 9 - NS37

Darleith Road, CARDROSS, A&B,
G82 5EZ
Turn N off A814 into Darleith Rd at W
end of village. Kirkton House 0.5m on R
6 Rooms, S £38.50-£45 D £57-£70,
No smoking in dining room, Closed
Dec-Jan

Kirkton House is a converted 17th-18th century farmhouse in a peaceful country location, enjoying panoramic views of the River Clyde. Loch Lomond is only ten minutes' drive away. Licensed to sell alcohol, guests may wine and dine to good home cooking, from an extensive daily menu, at individual oil lamplit tables. The farmhouse retains a rustic style and cosy ambience (with open fire on chilly evenings), yet has modern amenities and comforts. All bedrooms have en suite bathrooms and all the facilities of a hotel, such as an ironing board, tea/coffee making facilities, direct dial phones, modem plugs, TV and hairdryer. Two downstairs rooms are suitable for those with mobility or respiratory problems (one has wheelchair access, with grab rails in the bathroom). Four rooms are suitable for family occupation. There are excellent local golf courses (open to visitors on weekdays).

RECOMMENDED IN THE AREA

Loch Lomond for hiking & boating (10 minute drive), Hill House, (Charles Rennie Mackintosh) (10 minute drive); Glasgow (30 minute drive)

$\mathcal{D}$unvalanree ◆◆◆◆

Hospitable hotel in a lovely location at the water's edge

☏ 01583 431226
🖷 01583 431339
🖂 bookin@dunvalanree.com
www.dunvalanree.com

Map ref 9 - NR83

Port Righ Bay, CARRADALE, Kintyre, A&B, PA28 6SE
In Carradale centre, L at sign for Portrigh Bay, follow rd to end
7 Rooms, S £22-£32 D £44-£56, No smoking

Stunning views across the Kilbrannan Sound to the hills of Arran are afforded from Alyson and Alan Milstead's welcoming hotel, situated beside a small bay and a sheltered beach. Public areas include an inviting lounge with a television and an attractive dining room with individual tables. Food is a particular highlight, with interesting menus utilising the best local produce. All the meals are home-made and vegetarian dishes are included. Five of the smart bedrooms have en suite facilities, all have tea and coffee provisions and colour TV, and one ground floor room is suitable for unassisted wheelchair users. The premises are licensed and parking is available for guests.

RECOMMENDED IN THE AREA

Forest and hill walks from the house; Campbeltown Heritage Centre; local nature reserves

$\mathcal{D}$unchraigaig House ◆◆◆◆

Comfortable accommodation in historic Kilmartin Glen

☏ 01546 605209
🖂 dunchraig@aol.com

Map ref 9 - NR89

KILMARTIN, Lochgilphead, A&B, PA31 8RG
from Lochgilphead take A816 Oban Rd, 7m on right opposite Ballymeanoch Standing Stones, 1m S of Kilmartin
5 Rooms, S £25-£28 D £44-£50, No smoking

The area around Dunchraigaig House is rich in ancient remains, and it stands opposite the Ballymeanoch Standing Stones, close to the Dunchraigaig Cairn. In the village churchyard there are examples of early Christian crosses and grave slabs from the 9th to the 13th century, and the award-winning museum in the village is well worth a visit. The house is set in a large garden and has an inviting lounge, well stocked with books, and a separate dining room where breakfast is served and a home-cooked evening meal by arrangement. Smart bedrooms include two doubles, two twins and one family room, all with en suite facilities, complimentary tea and coffee and televisions.

RECOMMENDED IN THE AREA

Kilmartin House Museum; Carassarie Castle; many standing stones and cairns in the area

Glenbervie House ♦♦♦♦

One of Oban's premier guest houses offering traditional Highland hospitality

☎ 01631 564770
🖷 01631 566723

Map ref 9 - NM83

Dalriach Road, OBAN, A&B, PA34 5NL
A82 to Oban, L at Kings Knoll Hotel.
Straight through x-roads. Tennis
courts & swimming pool on L.
Glenbervie on R
8 Rooms, S £22-£30 D £44-£60,
No smoking

*W*onderful views over to the islands of Mull, Lismore and Kerrera are commanded from this elevated Victorian house set above Oban Bay. The tastefully-decorated property includes several bedrooms of varying sizes, most with en suite showers, and the newly-refurbished first-floor lounge makes the most of the amazing views. Good Scottish home cooking is a feature here, and hearty breakfasts and delicious evening meals are served in the charming dining room.

Owners Joan and Iain offer an unusually warm welcome to their home, and guests are indulged in traditional highland fashion. The town of Oban with its harbour and promenade is only a few minutes walk away.

RECOMMENDED IN THE AREA

Rare Breeds Park (2 miles); Oban Sea Life Centre (12 miles); Oban Distillery (walking distance)

Glenburnie Private Hotel ♦♦♦♦

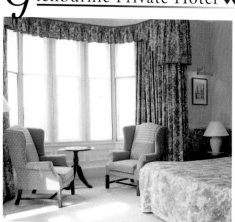

Elegant Victorian villa situated on the seafron

☎ 01631 562089
🖷 01631 562089
✉ graeme.strachan@
  btinternet.com
www.argyllinternet.co.uk/
glenburnie

Map ref 9 - NM83

The Esplanade, OBAN, A&B, PA34 5AQ
directly on Oban seafront, follow signs
for Ganavan
14 Rooms, S £25-£30 D £50-£70,
No smoking, Closed Dec-Mar

*F*rom its prime position on the esplanade, this handsome establishment offers dazzling views over the bay to the Isle of Mull. The house has been lovingly restored and refurbished by its dedicated owners, the Strachan family. The bedrooms, which include a superior four-poster room and mini suite, are beautifully decorated, comfortably furnished and equipped with modern facilities, including en suites in every room. There is a lovely sitting room with a fire for the cooler evenings. Guests are greeted with tea and shortbread on arrival, and delicious breakfasts, featuring the best of local produce and home made preserves, are served in the attractive dining room. For dinner, the Strachans are happy to advise guests on the many local restaurants located in the town centre, which is just a leisurely five-minute stroll away. Private car parking is provided.

RECOMMENDED IN THE AREA

Crarae and Arduaine Gardens; fishing and golf; boat hire and cruises

*L*erags House ••••

Enchanting rural retreat in super location, providing a relaxing environment with comfort and style

☎ 01631 563381
📠 01631 563381
✉ stay@leragshouse.com
www.leragshouse.com

Map ref 9 - NM82

Lerags by Oban, OBAN, A&B, PA34 4SE
from Oban follow signs for Campbeltown taking A816 S for 2m. Turn R at sign to Lerags. House on L 2.5m down single track
7 Rooms, S £35-£45 D £70-£90, No smoking

Set in mature grounds on the shores of a tidal inlet on the northern banks of Loch Foechan, this secluded Georgian country house is just a short drive from Oban. You can really feel at home here in the informal, yet professional, atmosphere created by Charlie and Bella Miller. There are five spacious bedrooms and three mini-suites, all tastefully designed with en suite facilities and some extra luxury touches, like the range of Arran toiletries you may either use or take home with you at the end of your stay. An attractive lounge with an open fire for cooler evenings provides a cosy place to relax.

Dinner, by prior arrangement and hearty breakfasts, featuring the best of local produce, are served in the elegant dining room. Bella is an accomplished cook and the Millers like nothing better than for you to feel as though you are enjoying a stay with good friends. To this end, no detail in ensuring your comfort is overlooked.

 ## RECOMMENDED IN THE AREA

Oban Distillery; Arduaine Gardens; Scottish Sea Life and Marine Sanctuary

Gruline Home Farm ◆◆◆◆◆

An immaculate, welcoming house with quality stamped all over

☎ 01680 300581 🖷 01680 300573
✉ aa@gruline.com
www.gruline.com

Map ref 9 - NM53

Gruline, SALEN, Isle of Mull, A&B, PA71 6HR
from Craignure ferry turn R and travel 10m to
Salen. In village turn L on B8035 and drive for
2m, keep L at fork, past church, farm L
2 Rooms, S £45-£60 D £60-£70, No smoking

𝒜 spectacular water feature and lovely gardens vie with the scenic foothills of Ben More for the most attractive outlook at this granite farmhouse. Set in two and a half acres of pastureland, this Georgian/Victorian guest house is a haven of de-luxe accommodation and wonderful hospitality. Both delightful bedrooms are elegantly furnished with period pieces, and luxurious en suite bathrooms. Downstairs, a tastefully-decorated lounge invites peaceful relaxation, while the splendid conservatory makes the most of the views. A highlight of a stay here is the evening meal, served at a communal table, featuring good local produce freshly prepared by the chef-owner.

RECOMMENDED IN THE AREA

Duart, Torosay and Moy Castles; boat trips to Treshnish Isles and Isle of Staffa; bird and sealife watching in and around Mull

Ben Doran Guest House ◆◆◆◆

Stylish Edinburgh architecture and genuinely warm hospitality

☎ 0131 667 8488
🖷 0131 667 0076
✉ info@ben-doran.co.uk
www.ben-doran.co.uk

Map ref 10 - NT27

11 Mayfield Gardens, EDINBURGH,
EH9 2AX
from east side of Princes Street, take
A701, Ben Doran on left, approx 1m)
10 Rooms, S £35-£85 D £50-£120,
No smoking

𝒯 his centrally-located guest house is the ideal choice for anyone wishing to leave the car safely behind and take the short bus ride into the city. Packed lunches are also available for those setting off on a day's sightseeing. The handsome Georgian listed property was built in the distinctly Edinburgh style, and provides smart accommodation which reflects a discerning approach to interior design. Bedrooms are mainly en suite, and charmingly decorated, with lovely hillside views to be enjoyed. A hearty Scottish breakfast is served at separate tables in the elegant dining room, and the obliging hosts offer a very pleasing standard of service.

RECOMMENDED IN THE AREA

Edinburgh Castle; golf clubs; theatres and museums

Ashcroft Farmhouse •••••

Immaculate and delightful, a friendly guest house with an obvious commitment to the well-being of guests

☎ 01506 881810
🖷 01506 884327
✉ scottashcroft7@
   aol.com
www.ashcroftfarmhouse.
com

Map ref 10 - NT06

East Calder, West Lothian,
NEAR EDINBURGH,
EH53 0ET
on B7015, off A71, 0.5m E of
East Calder, near to Almondell
Country Park
6 Rooms, D £56-£60,
No smoking

Surrounded by open countryside yet only 10 miles from the centre of Edinburgh, this sprawling modern bungalow is set in five acres of beautifully landscaped gardens. Elizabeth and Derek Scott have been welcoming guests to their home for 39 years, and their hospitality has been recognised: Elizabeth has twice been a top 20 finalist of the AA Landlady of the Year Award recently. In this caring environment, the well-proportioned bedrooms are immaculately kept and comfortably furnished. Each room is named after a Scottish championship golf course, and offers en suite facilities, colour television, hospitality tray with shortbread biscuits, fluffy towels and good toiletries.

A collection of golf memorabilia is a talking point in the dining room, and in here delicious breakfasts made from fresh Scottish produce are served at individual tables. Home-made sausages and whisky marmalade are part of the morning treat. Guests are invited to relax in the pleasant lounge and make use of the video library.

RECOMMENDED IN THE AREA

Almondell Country Park; Almond Valley Heritage Centre; McArthur Glen Designer Outlet

Ellesmere House ♦♦♦♦

Victorian town house hotel overlooking Bruntsfield Links

☎ 0131 229 4823
🖷 0131 229 5285
📧 celia@edinburghbandb.co.uk
www.edinburghbandb.co.uk

Map ref 10 - NT27

11 Glengyle Terrace, EDINBURGH, EH3 9LN
central Edinburgh off A702
overlooking Bruntsfield Links
6 Rooms, S £28-£38 D £56-£76,
No smoking in dining room

Ellesmere House is part of a handsome Victorian terrace overlooking Bruntsfield Links. The latter was once an 18-hole golf course - reputedly the oldest in the world. The location is convenient for the city centre and all the major tourist attractions, including the castle, Princes Street, the Royal Mile, the Edinburgh International Conference Centre, the universities and the museums. The en suite bedrooms are individually designed and vary in size, one featuring a four-poster bed. All are equipped with colour televisions and tea and coffee making facilities. Breakfast is prepared from the best of local produce and is served in the combined lounge and dining room.

RECOMMENDED IN THE AREA

Edinburgh Castle and Royal Mile (approximately 20 minute walk); Princes Street (0.75 mile); Holyrood Palace (3 miles – bus service available)

Elmview ♦♦♦♦♦

Fine Victorian terraced house in a central location

☎ 0131 228 1973
📧 marny@elmview.co.uk
www.elmview.co.uk

Map ref 10 - NT27

15 Glengyle Terrace, EDINBURGH, EH3 9LN
take A702 S up Lothian Rd, turn 1st left past Kings Theatre into Valley Field St, one-way system leading to Glengyle Terrace
3 Rooms, D £75-£95, No smoking

Occupying the garden level of a substantial Victorian property, Elmview offers superior bed and breakfast accommodation, with constantly upgraded decoration and facilities, which appeals to both tourist and business travellers. The tastefully furnished bedrooms have stylish en suite bathrooms and a good level of comfort, which compensates for the absence of a lounge. the rooms are exceptionaly well equipped, including thoughtful extras such as wine glasses and a fridge with fresh milk. Marny and Richard Hill are caring and attentive hosts who are always on hand when needed. The highlight of your stay will be the excellent breakfasts taken at one large, elegantly appointed table.

RECOMMENDED IN THE AREA

Edinburgh Castle (1 mile); Edinburgh Old Town (1 mile); Museum of Scotland (0.5 mile)

The International Guest House ◆◆◆◆

Luxurious modern facilities in a 19th-century setting

☎ 0131 667 2511 📠 0131 667 1112
✉ intergh@easynet.co.uk
www.s-h-systems.co.uk/hotels/internat.html

Map ref 10 - NT27

37 Mayfield Gardens, EDINBURGH, EH9 2BX
1.5m S of Princes St on A701 (4m from Straiton Junction on Edinburgh City by-pass)
9 Rooms, S £30-£50 D £50-£90, No smoking in dining room or lounge

RECOMMENDED IN THE AREA

Edinburgh Castle (1.5 miles); Holyrood Palace (1.5 miles); University of Edinburgh (0.5 mile)

This attractive stone-built terrace house lies on the south side of the city. There is ample private parking, and it is on a main bus route, giving easy access to the town centre. The high ceilings and large windows, wooden staircase, and décor, with ornate plasterwork on the ceilings, embody the splendour of the Victorian era. All the bedrooms, decorated and fitted in matching period floral prints, and brightened with fresh flowers, have modern en suite facilities and colour TV. Some rooms enjoy magnificent views across to the extinct volcano known as Arthur's Seat.

A hearty Scottish breakfast is served, on the finest bone china, at separate tables in the dining room; the marble fireplace with mirror above it is a lovely feature in this room. The International has received top accolades for quality and hospitality.

Kew House ◆◆◆◆

Part of a smart Victorian terrace, offering high levels of comfort and service

☎ 0131 313 0700
🖷 0131 313 0747
🖳 kewhouse@ednet.co.uk
www.kewhouse.com

Map ref 10 - NT27

1 Kew Terrace, Murrayfield,
EDINBURGH, EH12 5JE
on A8 Glasgow road, 1m W of city
centre, close to Murrayfield Rugby
Stadium
6 Rooms, S £50-£55 D £70-£100,
No smoking

Murrayfield Rugby Stadium is nearby, and all major tourist attractions are easily accessible from this mellow stone guest house. Boasting the facilities of a hotel, it offers extremely comfortable bedrooms, stylishly decorated and furnished to satisfy the needs of both the business and leisure traveller. A full Scottish breakfast is served at separate tables in the smart dining room, and guests can relax in the tranquil sitting room after a busy day's shopping or sightseeing. Princes Street and the city centre are a 10 minute walk away, and the attentive but unobtrusive hosts are always on hand to look after their guests.

RECOMMENDED IN THE AREA

City centre and castle (10-15 minute walk); Edinburgh Zoo (10-15 minute walk); International Conference Centre (10 minute walk)

The Lodge Hotel ◆◆◆◆◆

Charming Georgian house, centrally located in Edinburgh's fashionable west end

☎ 0131 337 3682
🖷 0131 313 1700
🖳 thelodgehotel@
btconnect.com
www.thelodgehotel.co.uk

Map ref 10 - NT27

6 Hampton Terrace, West Coates,
EDINBURGH, EH12 5JD
on A8, 1m W of city centre
10 Rooms, S £38-£60 D £50-£98,
No smoking, Closed 22-27 Dec

Conveniently situated within easy walking distance of the city, and also on a main bus route, The Lodge prides itself on extremely high standards of accommodation, hospitality and service. The stylish en suite bedrooms are beautifully decorated and immaculately presented. New guests are thoughtfully welcomed with fresh flowers and a small decanter of port, and can enjoy hearty breakfasts, featuring quality local produce, in the elegant dining room. A cosy, atmospheric bar and comfortable fire lit lounge are available for guests' use. You will feel very much at home in The Lodge, a tranquil retreat for the discerning guest.

RECOMMENDED IN THE AREA

City centre (1 mile); Edinburgh Castle; Edinburgh Zoo

Newington Cottage •••••

*Combining elegance and
friendliness, a superb house
offering beautifully maintained,
luxury accommodation*

☎ 0131 668 1935
🖷 0131 667 4644
✉ fmickel@
   newcot.demon.co.uk
www.newcot.demon.co.uk/m
ewcot1.htm

Map ref 10 - NT27

15 Blacket Place, EDINBURGH,
EH9 1RJ
from N, S, or airport, approach from
city bypass, exiting at Straiton junct
follow city centre signs to Minto
Hotel on R, next R
3 Rooms, S £70 D £80-£110,
No smoking

*B*uilt on classical Italian lines of mellow stonework with a colonnaded porch, this high-class guest house offers the sort of accommodation more usually associated with smart hotels. The house was rescued from serious disrepair ten years ago, and lovingly returned to its former glory. Keeping it in immaculate condition has become a labour of love for its owners. The three en suite bedrooms are luxurious, quiet and spacious, with large beds and comfortable chairs or sofas. Each is equipped with colour television, CD player, iron and ironing board, fridge and many thoughtful extras like decanters of sherry. The elegant dining room is a beautiful place in which to take breakfast, and like all the other rooms in the house it is tastefully decorated and delightfully maintained. Princes Street and the city centre are a mile away, and the Royal Mile, with the Castle and Holyrood Palace at either end, is even closer.

RECOMMENDED IN THE AREA

*Museum of Scotland; the Royal Mile, the Castle
and the Palace of Holyrood; Princes Street*

$\mathcal{S}$outhside Guest House ◆◆◆◆

Blonde sandstone town house of elegant design on the south side of Edinburgh

☎ 0131 668 4422
📠 0131 667 7771
📧 fionasouthside@
aol.com
www.southsideguesthou
se.co.uk

Map ref 10 - NT27

8 Newington Road,
EDINBURGH, EH9 1QS
8 Rooms, S £35-£50 D £60-
£150, No smoking

RECOMMENDED IN THE AREA

Dynamic Earth (15 minute walk through Queens Park); Holyrood Palace and Parliament (5 minute drive); Queen's Hall and Festival Theatres

$\mathcal{D}$esigned to be distinctly different, this exclusive guest house offers contemporary-style accommodation with dramatic décor making highly effective use of colour. The south side is a culturally rich area of the city, good for pubs, restaurants, theatre and cinema, and the house is located in the Meadows, at the heart of the university campus, close to Arthur's Seat and a 15 minute-walk from Princes Street. It offers a choice of individually styled bedrooms, all with en suite facilities. Rooms are well equipped with power showers, remote control televisions, radio alarms, central heating, hot water bottles, hairdryers, toiletries, irons and ironing boards. A laundry service is also available. For special occasions there is a particularly luxurious suite with a four-poster bed, a sofa and fluffy towels and bathrobes. Continental or hearty Scottish breakfasts are served in the bright Café South, which is open throughout the day for light meals and Italian coffee, and where in winter you can warm yourself by the welcoming log fire.

$\mathcal{P}$riory Lodge ♦♦♦♦

Purpose built guest house attractively situated close to Edinburgh

☎ / 🖷 0131 331 4345
✉ calmyn@aol.com
www.queensferry.com

Map ref 10 - NT17

The Loan, SOUTH QUEENSFERRY,
Edinburgh, EH30 9NS
just off High St, at the westerly end
5 Rooms, S £40-£54 D £54-£60,
No smoking

$\mathcal{F}$riendly owners Calmyn and Gordon Lamb enjoy welcoming people to their delightful guest house. It is located just off the quaint cobbled High Street in South Queensferry, which sits between the two famous bridges on the south side of the Firth of Forth. The town offers a good choice of pubs and restaurants and the City of Edinburgh is just 20 minutes away. The attractive bedrooms are maintained to a high standard and are comfortably furnished in antique pine. Each room has a remote control colour television, hospitality tray, iron/board and fridge. Bathrobes and fresh towels are provided in the en suite shower room daily. A small lounge is provided, and guests are welcome to use the kitchen facilities. Tartan has been used to good effect in the attractive dining room where hearty Scottish breakfasts are served at individual tables, with a vegetarian option. Pets are not accommodated.

RECOMMENDED IN THE AREA

Hopetoun House and Dalmeny House (15 minute walk); Deep Sea World (2 miles); ferry trip to the Abbey on Inchcolm Island

$\mathcal{L}$ongacre Manor ♦♦♦♦♦

Edwardian country house conveniently close to town

☎ 01556 503576
🖷 01556 503886
✉ ball.longacre@btinternet.com
www.aboutscotland.co.uk/
SOUTH/longacre.html

Map ref 5 - NX76

Ernespie Road, CASTLE DOUGLAS,
D&G, DG7 1LE
Leave A75 at rdbt signed Castle
Douglas A745, continue 0.75m,
Manor on L.
4 Rooms, S £35-£50 D £60-£90, No
smoking in bedrooms or dining room

$\mathcal{L}$ongacre is a private manor house hotel set in secluded wooded gardens, overlooking green fields, yet is still within walking distance of the town. Limed oak panelling, antiques and four-poster beds are features of the interior, including twin four-posters in one room. Bedrooms retain the period style, though all have en suite facilities, televisions, direct dial telephones, radios, trouser presses, hairdryers and complimentary tea and coffee. Among the choices at breakfast are smoked haddock and haggis, along with the usual kippers, bacon and sausage. A three-course Taste of Scotland dinner is also available, and there's a licensed bar for guests' use. Special diets can be catered for with advance notice.

RECOMMENDED IN THE AREA

Threave Castle (National Trust) and Threave Gardens; Kirkcudbright; beautiful walks and drives

Auchenskeoch Lodge ✦✦✦✦✦

Victorian shooting lodge in twenty acres of grounds surrounded by lovely countryside

☎ 01387 780277
🖷 01387 780277
✉ Brmsmth@aol.com
www.auchenskeochlodge.com

Map ref 5 - NX95
DALBEATTIE, D&G, DG5 4PG
5m SE off B793
3 Rooms, S £39 D £59-£62,
No smoking in dining room,
Closed Nov-Etr

Situated to the south east of the town, this fine house enjoys a peaceful setting with extensive grounds including woodland walks, a vegetable garden, croquet lawn, a maze and a small fishing loch. Christopher and Mary Broom-Smith have carefully retained the original character of the house, which is full of charm, graced with antiques, period furniture, books, painting and sculptures. Two of the well proportioned bedrooms have a lounge area and one of these can also be used as an additional single bedroom. The spacious ground floor room is ideally suited for disabled or elderly guests. A set four-course dinner is served house party style at 8pm and features Mary's home-cooked dishes, which include vegetables picked from the garden. There is a good wine list and guests are invited to help themselves to drinks in the billiard room, where they will also find a full size billiard table.

 ## RECOMMENDED IN THE AREA

Threave Castle and Gardens; coastal walks at Colvend and Southwick

Southpark Country House ◆◆◆◆

Gorgeous views and warm, comfortable accommodation in a friendly guest house

☎ 0800 9701588
🖷 01387 711155
📧 ewan@southparkhouse.co.uk
www.southparkhouse.co.uk

Map ref 5 - NX98

Quarry Road, Locharbriggs, DUMFRIES, D&G, DG1 1QG
A75/A701 (Edinburgh, Glasgow & Dumfries), past Curries European Transport, L into Quarry Rd, house last on L
4 Rooms, S £25 D £39,
No smoking

Guests are invariably impressed with the breathtaking views and genuine hospitality that go hand in hand with a stay here. The warm welcome and pleasant service are part of a genuine desire to offer a truly enjoyable experience, an aspiration helped by the natural beauty of the location. This substantial house is situated on the edge of town and therefore still handy for town centre amenities. Brightly-coloured fabrics and attractive furnishings lend an appealing look to the comfortable bedrooms, and bath robes, television and courtesy trays are standard to all rooms.

Hearty Scottish breakfasts are served in the open-plan dining room, and there's also a spacious lounge. Ewan Maxwell was an AA Landlady of the Year Top Twenty Finalist in 2000 and 2001.

RECOMMENDED IN THE AREA

Caerlaverock Castle (20 minute drive); Ae and Mabie Forest (20 minute drive); Burns heritage including Burns Mausoleum (5 minute drive)

Rosehill Guest House ◆◆◆◆

Detached Victorian house in a lovely garden setting

☎ 01576 202378
🖷 01576 202378

Map ref 5 - NY18

Carlisle Road, LOCKERBIE, D&G, DG11 2DR
south end of town
5 Rooms, S £20-£25 D £40,
No smoking

Rosehill is surrounded by its own large garden in a peaceful residential area on the way into town, just a few minutes from the M74. Proprietors, Mr and Mrs Callander, create a friendly atmosphere and maintain high standards throughout. The period feel has been retained in the public rooms, with original fireplaces, polished Victorian tiles in the hall and stripped pine in the lounge. Antique furniture, Laura Ashley

fabrics and impressive oil paintings take up the theme, and in the elegant dining room a hearty breakfast is served. Bedrooms are generally spacious, three have en suite facilities and all are equipped with televisions, radio alarms and complimentary tea and coffee.

RECOMMENDED IN THE AREA

Wildlife Sanctuary at Glencaple; countryside walks and hill walking; many golf courses and loch and river fishing

Hartfell House ♦♦♦♦

A large, striking house in a lofty position with superior rooms and food

☎ 01683 220153
📧 mary.whitsell@virgin.net
www.hartfellhouse.co.uk

Map ref 10 - NT00

Hartfell Crescent, MOFFAT, D&G,
DG10 9AL
exit A74(M) J15, A701, to town centre.
At clock tower turn R up Well St.
Straight on into Old Well Rd. 1st R is
Hartfell Crescent
8 Rooms, S £25 D £48, No smoking,
Closed Xmas & New year

From its peaceful rural setting high above the town, this fine Victorian house enjoys splendid views over the countryside around Moffat. Only five minutes from the M74, it is the ideal base for touring and walking; Edinburgh, Glasgow and the east and west coasts are about an hour's drive, and the surrounding hills are a delight to explore. This listed stone-built house offers bedrooms with plenty of character and comfort, with private facilities and television, radio alarm and hospitality tray. Delicious home-cooked meals are served in the smart dining room, and guests can relax in a charming first floor lounge.

RECOMMENDED IN THE AREA

Caerlaverock Castle; Shambellie House Museum of Costume; New Lanark (World Heritage Site)

Blinkbonnie Guest House ♦♦♦♦

Comfortable coastal villa with stunning views

☎ 01776 810282
📠 01776 810792

Map ref 5 - NX05

School Brae, PORTPATRICK,
Stranraer, D&G, DG9 8LG
Follow A77. On entering Portpatrick,
pass parish church on L. Take next
road on L into School Brae. 2nd
house on L
5 Rooms, S £25-£26 D £38-£40,
No smoking, Closed Dec

Ruby Robinson, a Top 20 Landlady of the Year finalist, is a superb host. Her modern villa stands in landscaped gardens complete with palm trees in an elevated position overlooking the town and harbour. The seafront, shops and restaurants are all within easy walking distance, and safe off street parking is provided. All the bedrooms, double and twin, are located on the ground floor and have en suite facilities, central heating, double glazing, colour television and tea-making equipment. The lounge has a huge picture window with views of the Irish Sea, as does the dining room, where a full Scottish breakfast is served at individual tables.

RECOMMENDED IN THE AREA

Logan Botanic Gardens (5 miles); Southern Upland Way (beautiful walks – starts nearby); Galloway Forest Park & Deer Range (25 miles)

Kippielaw Farmhouse ◆◆◆◆◆

Former farmhouse in a superb setting with magnificent views

☎ 01620 860368
🖷 01620 860368
✉ info@
  kippielawfarmhouse.co.uk
www.kippielawfarmhouse.co.uk

Map ref 10 - NT57

EAST LINTON, East Lothian,
EH41 4PY
leave A1 at E Linton, follow Traprain
sign 0.75m, take single track road on
R after farm. Premises 0.5m on L opp
CP
2 Rooms, S £35-£36 D £50-£52,
No smoking

Liz and Bill Campbell's cosy farmhouse is set in an elevated position, sheltered by lovely gardens, overlooking the Tyne valley. It is centrally situated for the sea, the city and the countryside, and is perfect for walking, cycling, bird watching or playing golf. The comfortable lounge with its open staircase and log fire is a focal point. Excellent meals are served in the elegantly appointed dining room with rosewood table, overlooking the attractive courtyard. Liz is an experienced cook and her candlelit dinners are quite a draw. Her interesting menus rely on locally sourced produce wherever possible and the dishes are freshly prepared. The country-style bedrooms are equipped with hairdryers and radios and have either en suite or private facilities.

RECOMMENDED IN THE AREA

Walking; golf (16 courses within 20 minutes); John Muir Country Park (10 minutes); Museum of Flight (10 minutes)

Faussetthill House ◆◆◆◆

Edwardian house in a peaceful coastal village

☎ 01620 842396
🖷 01620 842396
✉ faussetthill@talk21.com

Map ref 10 - NT48

20 Main Street, GULLANE, East
Lothian, EH31 2DR
on A198, from A1 follow A198 to
Gullane
3 Rooms, S £40-£45 D £54-£60,
No smoking, Closed Nov-Mar

George and Dorothy Nisbet welcome you to their delightful home, which stands in well tended gardens in the picturesque village of Gullane. Spotlessly clean and immaculately maintained, the house is both comfortable and inviting. Bedrooms are well proportioned and attractively decorated. Three rooms are en suite, and all have tea and coffee making equipment. There is a first-floor lounge with well filled bookshelves, and breakfast is served at one table in the elegant dining room. From Gullane, North Berwick is just 10 minutes away, and Edinburgh 30 minutes by car, there are many places of interest to visit in the area. Keen golfers will be pleased to note that there are 19 golf courses within easy reach, with five in the village itself, including Muirfield. Children under 10 are not accepted at Faussethill House, and dogs are not premitted in the rooms. This is a non smoking house.

RECOMMENDED IN THE AREA

*Beautiful walks around Gullane beach;
Scottish Seabird Centre (10 minute drive);
Dirleton Castle and Gardens (5 minute drive)*

Hillview House ♦♦♦♦

Italian and English are spoken at this delightful 1920s house. The location makes it an ideal base for visitors touring Scotland; with Edinburgh, Perth, St Andrews, Glasgow and Stirling all within an hour's drive. Your hosts can help you plan an itinerary and offer local information.

The attractively decorated en suite bedrooms all have video, colour television and tea and coffee making facilities.

Breakfast is taken at individual tables in the dining room, and a choice of traditional dishes or continental selection is available.

Close to Dunfermline town centre, M90 and Pitreavie Business Park

☎ 01383 726278
📠 01383 726278
✉ info@hillviewhouse
   dunfermline.co.uk
www.hillviewhousedunfermline.
co.uk

Map ref 10 - SE56

9 Aberdour Road, DUNFERMLINE,
Fife, KY11 4PB
from Edinburgh exit M90 J2 & follow
A823 for Dunfermline, after 3rd rbt
turn R at traffic lights into Aberdour
Road for Hillview House 200m on
the R
4 Rooms, S £25-£28 D £40-£44,
No smoking

RECOMMENDED IN THE AREA

*Andrew Carnegie Birthplace Museum;
Dunfermline Abbey; Pittencrieff House
Museum*

Pitreavie Guest House ♦♦♦♦

Easy atmosphere and professional care in a comfortable home

☎ 01383 724244 📠 01383 724244
✉ Info@pitreavie.com
www.pitreavie.com

Map ref 10 - NT18

3 Aberdour Road, DUNFERMLINE, Fife,
KY11 4PB
at west end of Aberdour Rd at junct with
A823. 0.5m S of Dunfermline town centre
5 Rooms, S £25-£35 D £45-£50, No smoking

Pitreavie Guest House is a family run establishment conveniently located on the bus route for Edinburgh and the Fife coast. The atmosphere is relaxed and friendly, you can enjoy a complimentary glass of sherry on arrival. Anne and John Walker are well practised and skilled at attending to their guests needs. Pitreavie has recently been refurbished to a high standard and can provide some of the best accommodation to be found in the locality. The bedrooms reflect this, and facilities include TVs, videos, direct dial phones with modem links, hospitality trays, hairdryers and clock radio alarms. Four of the rooms are en suite, the fifth has a shower/wc next door. Impressive breakfasts are served in the dining room, evening meals by arrangement.

RECOMMENDED IN THE AREA

*Dunfermline Heritage Trust; Dunfermline Abbey;
Dunfermline Museum and Small Gallery*

$\mathcal{F}$ossil House Bed & Breakfast ♦♦♦♦♦

Victorian house and cottage in a pretty village setting

☎ 01334 850639
📠 01334 850639
✉ the.fossil@virgin.net
www.fossil-guest-house.co.uk

Map ref 10 - NO41

12-14 Main Street, Strathkinness,
ST ANDREWS, Fife, KY16 9RU
A91 towards St Andrews,
Strathkinness signed. Fossil House at
top end of village close to pub
4 Rooms, D £44-£55, No smoking

$\mathcal{F}$ossil House is located in the village of Strathkinness two miles west of St Andrews. The en suite bedrooms are divided between the main house and a converted cottage to the rear. They are all at ground floor level with direct access to the courtyard, garden and car park, and guests have their own keys for easy access at any hour. Each room has been carefully designed to make the best use of available space, and is equipped with remote control colour television, trouser press, central heating, fridge, radio alarm, hairdryer, shaver point, and tea and coffee making facilities. One room is suitable for family occupation, and a cot and highchair are also available. There is a choice of comfortable lounges in the cottage, including a conservatory, and both have an ample supply of books, board games and videos. An imaginative breakfast menu offers something to suit everyone.

RECOMMENDED IN THE AREA

Close to The Old Course and The Royal and Ancient; historic St Andrews; and the picturesque East Neuk of Fife

$\mathcal{G}$lenderran ♦♦♦♦

Thoughtfully-appointed Victorian townhouse just a stone's throw from the town's amenities

☎ 01334 477951
📠 01334 477908
✉ glenderran@telinco.com
www.glenderran.com

Map ref 10 - NO51

9 Murray Park, ST ANDREWS, Fife,
KY16 9AW
enter St Andrews on A91 straight over
rdbt 2nd left into Murray Place R into
Murray Park Glenderran on L
5 Rooms, S £28-£56 D £56-£90,
No smoking

$\mathcal{W}$arm North American hospitality blends effortlessly with ancient Scottish golfing traditions at this smart guest house in St Andrews. Set just 250 yards from the first tee of the famous Old Course, the 19th-century townhouse is also perfectly located for the university and the miles of surrounding beaches. The five beautifully-appointed bedrooms are fitted with many extras, including CD/cassette/ AM-FM stereos, colour television and tasteful hospitality trays, while the en suite or private bathrooms are provided with quality toiletries. A cosy lounge is inviting on cold Scottish days, while breakfast is served at separate tables in the attractive dining room.

RECOMMENDED IN THE AREA

The Byre Theatre (5 minute walk); British Museum of Golf (2 minute walk); St Andrews Aquarium (2 minute walk)

297

*F*ern Villa ◆◆◆◆

A warm and cosy guest house with comfortable bedrooms and serving good food

☎ 01855 811393
🖷 01855 811727
✉ aa@fernvilla.com
www.fernvilla.com

Map ref 9 - NN05

Loanfern, BALLACHULISH, Highland, PH49 4JE
leave A82 & take L turn on entering village, house 150yds on L
5 Rooms, D £42-£46, No smoking

You are assured of a warm and friendly welcome to this elegant Victorian guest house, located just one mile from the Pass of Glencoe. Surrounded by mountains yet easily accessible, it is well placed for walking, climbing, skiing and cycling. The en suite bedrooms are comfortable and well equipped, and guests can unwind in the cosy lounge with a selection of board games. Delicious home cooking can be sampled in the attractive dining room, where dinner is a very sociable experience and service efficient. A utility room for drying wet outdoor clothes is a particularly useful amenity.

RECOMMENDED IN THE AREA

Superb walking around the Pass of Glencoe; steam train to Mallaig; Glen Orchy, Ben Nevis, Fort William, Rannoch Moor and Oban (all within easy driving distance)

*L*yn-Leven Guest House ◆◆◆◆

Welcoming Highland house beside the scenic Loch Leven

☎ 01855 811392
🖷 01855 811600
✉ lynleven@amserve.net
www.lynleven.co.uk

Map ref 9 - NN06

West Laroch, BALLACHULISH, Highland, PH49 4JP
off A82
12 Rooms, S £25-£30 D £40-£50, Closed Xmas

Friendly and beautifully situated, this guest house maintains consistently high standards in all areas. The Highland welcome and hospitality ensure that guests are put at their ease, and the spectacular views out towards Loch Leven guarantee plenty to talk about. Bedrooms of varying sizes are prettily decorated and comfy, with en suite showers and some thoughtful extras. The spacious lounge and smart dining room make the most of the scenic outlook, and delicious home-cooked evening meals and breakfasts are served at separate tables. Guests are encouraged to enjoy the lovely gardens which surround the property, and there is ample car parking.

RECOMMENDED IN THE AREA

Visit historic Glencoe (1 mile); Loch Ness Visitor Centre (60 minute drive); Inverary Castle and Jail (60 minute drive)

Beechwood ◆◆◆

A peaceful property in a glorious Highland setting, with warmly welcoming owners and smart bedrooms

☎ 01456 476377
📠 01456 476377
✉ cdou793101@
aol.com
www.olstravel.com/gues
t/beechwood

Map ref 12 - NH43

Marchfield, Balnain,
DRUMNADROCHIT,
Highland, IV63 6TJ
A82 to Drumnadrochit then
bear R on A831 signed
Cannich for 5.5 miles
2 Rooms, S £23 D £40,
No smoking

*B*reathtaking views over Loch Meikle and beyond can be enjoyed to the full from the first-floor lounge at this elevated family home. The beautiful scenery of Glen Urquhart is the backdrop to this immaculate house, where the smart, comfortable accommodation matches the striking landscape. The pretty twin and double bedrooms are stylishly furnished and colour co-ordinated, with good quality en suite facilities, colour television and hospitality trays, and many imaginative extras. On the ground floor the dining room offers a bright and airy place in which to enjoy a hearty traditional Scottish breakfast. Rural activities such as fishing,

horse riding and boat trips are available in the area, and can be arranged by the owner. Although Beechwood House offers an enviable degree of Highland peace and tranquility, it is still within easy reach of the village with all its facilities. Inverness is just 25 minutes away, and boasts plenty of shops and restaurants. There is a local bar/restaurant within walking distance.

 RECOMMENDED IN THE AREA

Loch Ness/Urquhart Castle; Culloden Battlefield; walks in Glen Affric

Inistore House ✦✦✦◉◉

Not only a B&B, but also a restaurant

☎ 01862 811263
✉ theAA@inistore.co.uk
www.inistore.co.uk

Map ref 12 - NH78

Castle Street, DORNOCH, Highland, IV25 3SN
on L hand side of main street, 200mtrs before cathedral
2 Rooms, D £50-£80, No smoking in bedrooms

*I*nistore House has a warm, comfortable atmosphere, created by its owners Kerensa and Michael Carr, who look after their guests with a great deal of care.

You can stay in one of two traditionally-decorated bedrooms which have en suite or private facilities. Guests also have a homely lounge where they can read books or just listen to music.

An added attraction is '2 Quail Restaurant', which has been awarded two AA Rosettes, it serves exceptionally good food in one of two intimate dining rooms. Space is limited, so booking is always advisable.

The World ranked Royal Dornoch Championship Golf Course and fine sandy beaches are only 5 minutes walk away from this Victorian Highland Townhouse.

RECOMMENDED IN THE AREA

Glenmorangie Distillery visitor centre (15 minute drive); Dunrobin Castle and Gardens (15 minute drive); Timespan Heritage Centre (30 minute drive)

Distillery House ✦✦✦✦

Substantial Highland property on the banks of the River Nevis

☎ 01397 700103
☎ 01397 702980
✉ disthouse@aol.com
www.fort-william.net/distillery-house

Map ref 12 - NN17

Nevis Bridge, North Road, FORT WILLIAM, Highland, PH33 6LR
from S A82 3rd rdbt on left. From N A82 just before Glen Nevis rdbt, on R
7 Rooms, S £25-£35 D £45-£70, No smoking

*D*istillery House is a conversion of three semi-detached houses in the extensive grounds of the former Glenlochy Distillery, originally used to house distillery staff. It is located on the banks of the River Nevis at the end of the West Highland Way (a long distance walk from Glasgow), but just a five-minute walk from the centre of Fort William. Well-equipped bedrooms offer en suite facilities, television, tea/coffee and hairdryers. Guests are greeted with a hot drink, home-made shortbread and tablet, and there's a reading lounge furnished with chesterfield sofas. Breakfast, including kippers, haggis, home baking, seasonal fresh fruits, jams and cereals, is served at individual tables in the airy dining room.

RECOMMENDED IN THE AREA

Ben Nevis – climbing (10 minute walk); gondola at Aonach Mor – skiing (5 minute walk); West Highland Way and lovely local walks

*A*shburn House.....

Victorian home in a stunning location, close to the centre of Fort William, overlooking Loch Linnhe

☎ 01397 706000
📠 01397 702024
✉ ashburn.house@
   tinyworld.co.uk
www.highland5star.co.uk

Map ref 12 - NN07

8 Achintore Road, FORT WILLIAM, Highland, PH33 6RQ
junct A82 and Ashburn Ln
500yds from large rbt at south end of High St or 400yds on R after entering 30mph zone from S
7 Rooms, S £30-£45 D £60-£90, No smoking, Closed Dec-Jan

The Hendersons have restored their elegant home with love and care to provide their guests with top standards of quality and comfort. The pretty flowers in the front garden, and the cheerful white and yellow painted exterior make for a happy welcome, and the big bay windows make the rooms light and airy. The bedrooms are charming and spacious, all with en suite bathrooms and a wide range of amenities including colour TV, and tea and coffee making facilities, and each with its own look - most have the added luxury of super king-size beds. Breakfast is highly commended. It is served at separate tables in the dining room. There is also a conservatory lounge for a peaceful moment of relaxation. Throughout their home the Hendersons instil a friendly atmosphere with their unique Highland charm.

 ### RECOMMENDED IN THE AREA

Ben Nevis; Jacobite Steam Train; Glenfinnan Bonnie Prince Charlie Monument

The Grange ♦♦♦♦♦

Victorian villa with lovely loch views

☎ 01397 705516 📠 701595
✉ jcampbell@
grangefortwilliam.com
www.thegrange-lochaber.co.uk

Map ref 12 - NN07

Grange Road, FORT WILLIAM,
Highland, PH33 6JF
leave Fort William on A82 S-300yds
from rdbt take L onto Ashburn Ln.
The Grange is at top on L
4 Rooms, D £78-£92, No smoking,
Closed Nov-Mar

Over the years, a lot of careful planning and hard work has gone into the restoration of this lovely property, to ensure that only the highest standards are offered to guests. Meticulous attention to detail is evident throughout the house, and warm Highland hospitality is assured.

Attractive decor and pretty fabrics have been used to stunning effect in the charming bedrooms, all of which enjoy beautiful views over Loch Linnhe. All the rooms have quality en suite facilities.

There is an abundance of books and fresh flowers in the comfortable lounge, and the dining room provides a lovely setting for the extensive breakfast, which gives guests a really good start to the day.

RECOMMENDED IN THE AREA

The West Highland Railway; Ben Nevis; Glen Nevis

Acorn House ♦♦♦♦

Comfortable Highland guest house offering traditionally warm hospitality

☎ 01463 717021
📠 01463 714236
✉ enquiries@
acorn-house.freeserve.co.uk
www.acorn-
house.freeserve.co.uk

Map ref 12 - NH64

2A Bruce Gardens, INVERNESS,
Highland, IV3 5EN
Acorn House is on W side of
Inverness. Bruce Gdns 1st on R
leaving Tomnahurich St onto
Glenurquhart Rd leading onto A82.
6 Rooms, S £30-£40 D £55-£65, No
smoking in bedrooms or dining room

A strong Scottish theme, with much memorabilia and bold use of tartan in the decoration and fabrics, distinguishes this Highland guest house. Acorn House is an attractive property set in a quiet residential area, just 5 minutes' walk from the city centre where guests are offered comfortable, well-equipped accommodation. All rooms are en suite, some with the extra luxury of four poster beds, and there is a sauna and a jacuzzi which are very popular after a busy day touring. Traditional Scottish food is served in the pretty dining room at breakfast and in the evening, and after-dinner coffee can be enjoyed in the comfortable lounge. Expect a warm, friendly welcome.

RECOMMENDED IN THE AREA

Eden Court Theatre (2 minute walk); Fort George (15 minute drive); Loch Ness (10 minute drive)

Culduthel Lodge ....

Elegant Georgian villa in an elevated position overlooking the River Ness

☎ 01463 240089
🖷 01463 240089
✉ AA@
   culduthel.com
www.culduthel.com

Map ref 12 - NH64

14 Culduthel Road,
INVERNESS, Highland,
IV2 4AG
follow B861 Castle St
from town centre
12 Rooms, S £45 D
£80-£105, No smoking
in bedrooms or dining
room

*D*avid and Marion Bonsor have carefully restored and sympathetically extended this Grade 11 listed residence to provide a high standard of accommodation in a pleasant residential area just a short walk from the town centre. The house is set in its own attractive grounds, which provide ample parking and wonderful views of the River Ness and the surrounding countryside. Guests are greeted with fresh fruit, flowers and a decanter of sherry in their rooms, and in the dining room freshly prepared dishes are offered from Marion's daily changing menu. The emphasis is on Scottish cooking from local produce, and a choice of wines is available to accompany your meal. In the morning, a continental or Scottish breakfast is served. Bedrooms are individually designed and thoughtfully equipped to include CD/cassette players, and all have en suite facilities. At the end of the day, guests can relax in the welcoming atmosphere of the drawing room.

RECOMMENDED IN THE AREA

Loch Ness (7 miles); Cawdor Castle (7 miles); riverside walks (5 minute walk)

Ballifeary House Hotel ◆◆◆◆◆

A lovely, imposing house with a beautiful, neat garden

☎ 01463 235572
🖷 01463 717583
✉ info@
ballifearyhousehotel.co.uk
www.ballifearyhousehotel.co.uk

Map ref 12 - NH64

10 Ballifeary Road, INVERNESS,
Highland, IV3 5PJ
off A82, 0.5m from town centre, turn L
into Bishops Rd & sharp R into
Ballifeary Rd
5 Rooms, D £72-£78, No smoking,
Closed mid Oct-Etr

Built in the early Victorian era, the house is situated in a quiet, residential area, an easy walk away from some excellent restaurants, and 10 minutes' walk from the town centre, along the banks of the River Ness. It is not suitable for young families, as the minimum age for guests is 15 years. There is ample parking. The house is immaculately kept. The pretty bedrooms are decorated in soft colours with simple floral prints on the fabrics. All have their own en suite bathroom, colour TV, hairdryer and radio alarm.

There is a charming sitting room with potted plants, and an elegant dining room with deep burgundy curtains and tablecloths, where excellent Scottish breakfasts are served at separate tables. Malt whiskies and wines are available from the list of refreshments.

RECOMMENDED IN THE AREA

Culloden Battlefield (3 miles); beautiful walks around Inverness; Golf Courses (from 0.5 mile)

Moyness House ◆◆◆◆◆

Gracious Victorian villa with a pretty walled garden

☎ 01463 233836
🖷 01463 233836
✉ stay@moyness.co.uk
www.moyness.co.uk

Map ref 12 - NH64

6 Bruce Gardens, INVERNESS,
Highland, IV3 5EN
off A82 Fort William road, almost
opposite Highland Regional Council
HQ
7 Rooms, S £33-£65 D £66-£74, No
smoking

Jenny and Richard Jones' elegant villa is located in a quiet residential area just minutes from the city centre. Car parking is provided, and the house makes an ideal base from which to explore the beautiful Highlands.

Inviting public rooms overlook the garden to the front, and guests are welcome to use the secluded and well-maintained back garden. The bedrooms are attractively decorated and are all fitted with en suite bath or shower rooms. Facilities in the bedrooms include colour televisions and tea and coffee making equipment.

RECOMMENDED IN THE AREA

Culloden Battlefield (5 miles); Caledonian Canal & Loch Ness (1-5 miles); Cawdor Castle (10 miles)

Taransay ♦♦♦♦

Comfortable modern bungalow adjacent to the family farm

☎ 01463 231880
📠 01463 231880
✉ aileen@
  munro2.freeserve.co.uk
www.scotland-info.co.uk/
taransay

Map ref 12 - NH74

Lower Muckovie Farm, INVERNESS,
Highland, IV2 5BB
A9, B9177, past Drumossie Hotel,
down hill, yellow B&B sign at end of
farm rd on R
2 Rooms, D £40-£45, No smoking

A warm Highland welcome awaits guests at Aileen Munro's spacious modern farmhouse, located on the family dairy farm just 10 minutes' from the city centre. Picture windows take full advantage of spectacular views over the Moray Firth, Black Isle and the hills beyond. A comfortably furnished guests' sitting room is provided, complete with colour television, and a full breakfast is served in the large dining room. Evening meals are available locally. Accommodation comprises a double room with en suite facilities and a large twin, suitable for family occupation, with a private bathroom. Both offer televisions, radios, tea/coffee and electric blankets. Price reduction for children under 12.

RECOMMENDED IN THE AREA

Culloden Battlefield; Cawdor Castle; many whisky distilleries

Trafford Bank ♦♦♦♦♦

A gracious 19th-century house with friendly hosts and good food

☎ 01463 241414
✉ traff@pop.cali.co.uk
www.ibmpcug.co.uk/~ecs/
guest/trafford/trafford html

Map ref 12 - NH64

96 Fairfield Road, INVERNESS,
Highland, IV3 5LL
Turn off A82, 2nd road on L is Fairfield
Rd, 600yds on L
5 Rooms, S £45-£60 D £60-£75, No
smoking

Expect a genuine Highland welcome to this impressive Victorian villa standing in well-tended gardens in a quiet area close to the canal. Guests are invited to join the owners for a convivial nightcap, and in the morning gourmet breakfasts featuring venison sausages, black pudding, smoked salmon and kippers are served at a communal table in the elegant dining room. Evening meals made from quality ingredients are also available by arrangement. Bedrooms are attractively furnished, and thoughtfully provided with fresh fruit and flowers, as well as televisions and hospitality trays. This guest house is within easy reach of Loch Ness, Culloden, whisky distilleries and championship golf courses.

RECOMMENDED IN THE AREA

Culloden; Cawdor Castle; Loch Ness; Eden Court Theatre (10 minute walk)

$\mathscr{A}$rdsheal House ◆◆◆◆◆

Beautiful gardens, elegant reception rooms and comfortable bedrooms in a wonderful setting

☎ 01631 740227
📠 01631 740342
✉ info@ardsheal.co.uk
www.ardsheal.co.uk

Map ref 9 - NM95

KENTALLEN, Highland, PA38 4BX
off A828, 4m S of Ballachulish Bridge.
Between Glencoe (on A82) & Appin
(on A828). 1m private road from A828
6 Rooms, S £45-£50 D £90-£100, No
smoking in dining room

$\mathscr{A}$ beautiful old country house occupying a magnificent position on the shores of Loch Linnhe. The lovely gardens are open to guests, as is the rest of the 800-acres estate which include one of the oldest natural woodlands in Scotland. The gracious style of a bygone age has been maintained by the owners, who extend an exceptional welcome and offer warm hospitality. The comfortable bedrooms are all en suite, including one four-poster, and guests are invited to relax in two sitting rooms and a billiard room, while breakfast and four-course dinners (by prior arrangement) are served in either of the two dining rooms.

RECOMMENDED IN THE AREA

Walks & sightseeing at Glencoe; National Trust for Scotland Visitor Centre; Gondola to viewing point on Ben Nevis; day trip to Isle of Mull

---

Corriechoille Lodge ◆◆◆◆

Fine country house in a spectacular location

☎ 01397 712002 📠 01397 712002
✉ enquiry@corriechoille.com
www.corriechoille.com

Map ref 12 - NN27

SPEAN BRIDGE, Highland, PH34 4EY
off A82, signed Corriechoille, for 2.25m,
keeping L at road fork at 10mph sign. At end
of tarmac road, turn R up hill & then L
5 Rooms, S £29-£33 D £44-£52, No smoking,
Closed Nov-Feb

$\mathcal{D}$ating in parts from the 18th century, Corriechoille (forest of the glen) has been in its time a farmhouse and a fishing lodge for the Inverlochy Estate. Today it provides stylish accommodation in a rural location with views towards the Nevis Range and surrounding mountains. Full advantage of these is taken in the first floor lounge and some of the bedrooms, including a choice of two doubles, a twin and two family suites. All are spacious and thoughtfully equipped with en suite facilities, colour television, and tea/coffee provisions. In addition to a hearty breakfast, home-cooked candlelit dinners are offered along with a varied wine list and a range of single malts.

RECOMMENDED IN THE AREA

Ben Nevis (25 minute drive); Loch Ness (within easy driving distance); Isle of Skye (easy driving distance)

$\mathcal{A}$ldie House ◆◆◆◆

Victorian house and gardens surrounded by magnificent Highland scenery

☎ 01862 893787
🖷 01862 893787
✉ info@aldiehouse.co.uk
www.aldiehouse.co.uk

Map ref 12 - NH78

TAIN, Highland, IV19 1LZ
from Inverness, 500yds before Tain on A9, turn left and follow private road
3 Rooms, S £32 D £48-£52, No smoking

$\mathcal{T}$his proud house has six acres of woods and beautiful gardens, full of rare and exotic plants. The surrounding area is rich in flora and fauna, with spectacular hills and lochs, and possibilities for a range of sporting activities. Guests are free to use the private car park.

The house has been beautifully decorated, and filled with elegant Victorian antiques, to preserve the feel of a Scottish country home, and the Belgian owners, Chris and Charles, make you feel very pleased you came - on arrival, guests are welcomed with tea in the drawing room. The bedrooms are grand and spacious, each with individual features and design; all have en suite bathrooms.

English or continental breakfast is served in the dining room, on delicately patterned china. It is lovely to sit in the sun lounge overlooking the gardens.

RECOMMENDED IN THE AREA

Tour the Highlands; 15 golf courses within a 15 minute drive; walks, castles, a beach and a distillery nearby. Watch the salmon leaping!

$\mathcal{G}$olf View House ◆◆◆◆

Panoramic views and traditional Highland hospitality in a peaceful house

☎ 01862 892856
🖷 01862 892172
✉ golfview@btinternet.com
www.golf-view.co.uk

Map ref 12 - NH78

13 Knockbreck Road, TAIN, Highland, IV19 1BN
1st R off A9 at Tain (B9174), follow for 0.5m, house signposted on R
5 Rooms, S £25-£35 D £46-£50, No smoking, Closed Dec-Jan

$\mathcal{A}$ delightful rural retreat offering an exemplary welcome and high standards of care. This former Victorian manse stands in immaculately-tended grounds of two acres, with stunning views from the front lawn across the golf course to Dornoch Firth. The warmest of Highland hospitality is guaranteed to guests, and the house is extremely comfortable as well as peacefully located in a picturesque setting. Bedrooms are well-proportioned and attractively decorated in a mixture of modern and traditional styles. Guests can relax in the inviting lounge, and in the dining room enjoy a traditional Highland breakfast including eggs from the family hens.

RECOMMENDED IN THE AREA

At least 10 18-hole golf courses in the area (including Royal Dornoch); Loch Ness (60 minute drive); Glenmorangie Distillery

Knockomie Lodge ♦♦♦♦

Traditional Scottish lodge providing superior en suite accommodation

☎ 01309 676785
🖷 01309 676785
✉ welcome@knockomie.com

Map ref 12 - NJ05

FORRES, Moray, IV36 2SG
A940, Forres to Grantown-on-Spey road, 1m from Forres on R
3 Rooms, S £30-£35 D £40-£45, No smoking

Situated one mile outside the beautiful garden town Forres, Knockomie Lodge is a 100 year old lodge in a semi-rural position. Each of the attractively decorated en suite bedrooms is equipped with television, radio and hospitality tray. The Lodge is ideally situated for touring Inverness and the Grampians, and there are plenty of opportunities for leisure activities, with ten golf courses within a 12-mile radius and both loch and sea-fishing close by. A warm welcome is assured, with tea and home made cakes offered to guests on arrival. There is a new lounge, and the bright dining room provides a comfortable setting for a hearty Scottish breakfast, with home made jams and pancakes as a welcome addition to the options available.

RECOMMENDED IN THE AREA

Dallas Dhu and Ben Romach Distilleries; Brodie Castle and the lovely coastal village of Findhorn within a 4 mile radius.

The Haughs Farm ♦♦♦♦

Traditional farmhouse offering cheerful well-equipped accommodation

☎ 01542 882238
🖷 01542 882238
✉ jiwjackson@aol.com

Map ref 10 - NJ45

KEITH, Moray, AB55 6QN
0.5m from Keith off A96, signed Inverness
3 Rooms, D £38-£40, No smoking in bedrooms or dining room, Closed Nov-Mar

Jean Jackson has been welcoming guests to The Haughs for some 40 years, so it not surprising that hospitality and guest care are major features. The farmhouse provides comfortable accommodation with plenty of thoughtful extras. The three spacious en suite bedrooms are bright, airy and well equipped. Public areas include a lounge where guests can relax and a separate dining room overlooking the garden. Traditional Scottish fare is offered and special diets can be catered for. The farmhouse is ideally located for touring the north east of Scotland and enjoying its many attractions, such as the whisky trail and the castle trail.

RECOMMENDED IN THE AREA

Strathisla Distillery tours; golf; falconry

$\mathcal{L}$ea-Mar ◆◆◆◆

Friendly, relaxed guest house with hospitable owners and comfy bedrooms

☎ 01475 672447
🖷 01475 672447
✉ leamar.guesthouse@
fsbdial.co.uk
www.smoothhound.co.uk/
hotels/leamar.html

Map ref 9 - NS26

20 Douglas Street, LARGS, North Ayrshire, KA30 8PS
take A78, on reaching town turn left at sign for Brisbane Glen/Inverclyde Sports Centre. Lea-Mar 100yds on R
4 Rooms, D £46-£50, No smoking, Closed Feb, Xmas & New Year

$\mathcal{A}$ small, well-run guest house close to the seafront at Largs, surrounded on three sides by green hills and with the Firth of Clyde nearly on its doorstep. Guests can expect a very warm welcome to this quiet property, where the owners strive constantly to offer the best possible service and a relaxed atmosphere. Twin or double beds are available in the smart en suite rooms, with their attractive pine furniture and colour televisions. The delicious Scottish breakfasts served in the pretty dining room are the subject of much praise, and there is a cosy sitting room where guests can unwind at the end of the day.

RECOMMENDED IN THE AREA

Vikingar!; Kelburn Castle and Country Centre; Big Idea (approximately 15 miles)

$\mathcal{S}$outh Whittlieburn Farm ◆◆◆◆

Panoramic views from farmhouse accommodation in Brisbane Glen

☎ 01475 675881
🖷 01475 675080
✉ largsbandb@
southwhittlieburnfarm.
freeserve.co.uk

Map ref 9 - NS26

Brisbane Glen, LARGS, North Ayrshire, KA30 8SN
2m NE of Largs town centre, off road signed Brisbane Glen, just past leisure complex
3 Rooms, S £20-£25.50 D £40-£51, No smoking in bedrooms or dining room

$\mathcal{A}$ warm welcome is assured from Mary Watson at this superb farmhouse, part of a working sheep farm in a peaceful glen (birthplace of Sir Thomas MacDougall Brisbane – founder of Brisbane, Australia). Just five minutes from the popular seaside town of Largs, and convenient for the ferries to Arran, Bute, Cumbrae and Dunoon, and 40 minutes from Glasgow/Prestwick airports. Activities available nearby include golf, horse riding, fishing, diving and hill walking, while Loch Lomond, Inverary, Culzean Castle or the Robert Burns Centre are ideal for day trips. The en suite bedrooms are bright and cheerful, and well equipped with television, radio alarms, tea and coffee facilities and hairdryers. The atmosphere is very friendly, and enormous delicious breakfasts are served.

RECOMMENDED IN THE AREA

Vikingar!; yacht marina and ferries to the Islands; Kelburn Castle and Country Centre

$\mathcal{D}$uncraggan ◆◆◆◆

Smart and unusual property standing in gorgeous gardens

☎ 01250 872082
🖷 01250 872098

Map ref 10 - NO14

Perth Road, BLAIRGOWRIE, P&K, PH10 6EJ
on A93 from Perth pass National service station on L, 2 bungalows, Duncraggon on corner of Essendy and Perth road
4 Rooms, S £20 D £40, No smoking, Closed mid Oct-Feb

$\mathcal{T}$he first impression of Duncraggan is the lovely, well-tended garden, in which this striking turreted house makes an appealing place to stay. Built at the turn of the century by the town architect for his own use, it provides comfortably-proportioned rooms - one with four poster - with attractive colour schemes. Guests are encouraged to use the cosy lounge, where ample reading material and board games are kept. In this friendly and relaxing atmosphere, breakfast, light suppers and evening meals (by prior arrangement) are served in the smart dining room.

There is a warm welcome from Christine McClement, and an added bonus is the 9-hole putting for guests' enjoyment.

RECOMMENDED IN THE AREA

Six golf courses nearby; Glamis Castle and Scone Palace on the doorstep; hill walking, and skiing in winter

$\mathcal{K}$innaird ◆◆◆◆

Traditional Scottish hospitality at a charming Georgian house overlooking a park

☎ 01738 628021
🖷 01738 444056
✉ tricia@
   kinnaird-gh.demon.co.uk
www.kinnaird-guesthouse.co.uk

Map ref 10 - NO12

5 Marshall Place, PERTH, P&K, PH2 8AH
From Edinburgh on M90 J10, follow signs for Perth City Centre. At 2nd set of traffic lights turn L, guesthouse on R.)
7 Rooms, S £25-£30 D £45-£50, No smoking, Closed 22 Dec-14 Jan

$\mathcal{B}$uilt in 1806, this elegant property is part of a Georgian terrace just minutes from the city centre. Guests are assured of a warm welcome and the personal attention of the owners throughout their stay. Breakfast is a highly enjoyable meal served at individual tables in the dining room, offering a wide choice of dishes including cold items from the attractive buffet. The comfortable bedrooms are attractively decorated, with en suite facilities to all seven, plus colour televisions, clock/radios and courtesy trays. The residents' lounge is just the place to relax after a day's sightseeing or walking.

RECOMMENDED IN THE AREA

Beautiful walks beside the River Tay; Scone Palace (10 minute drive); Bells Cherrybank Centre – National Heather Collection (10 minute drive)

Park Lane
Guest House ••••

Stylishly-decorated rooms in a fine Georgian terrace just a few minutes from the town centre

☎ 01738 637218 📠 01738 643519
✉ stay@parklane-uk.com
www.parklane-uk.com

Map ref 10 - NO12

17 Marshall Place, PERTH, P&K, PH2 8AG
Exit at J10 on M90, enter town on A912,
cross park & turn L at traffic lights. Park Lane
on R opp park
6 Rooms, S £28-£32 D £46-£52, No smoking,
Closed 1 Dec-20 Jan

RECOMMENDED IN THE AREA

*Scone Palace (2 miles); theatre trips,
shopping and eating out in Perth;
Blair Castle and Pitlochry (30 minute
drive)*

A prime location within easy walking distance of the town centre and the golf club makes this an ideal guest house for anyone visiting the area. Part of an elegant Georgian terrace (Grade II listed) overlooking the South Inch Park, this delightful historic property boasts stylish reception rooms with high ceilings, plaster mouldings and one with marble fireplace. Walls are hung with interesting paintings, some of them by the owner. Bedrooms come in a variety of combinations, including twins, doubles, a single and a family room, and all are en suite, stylishly decorated, and provided with plenty of useful extras. Towel warmers, radio/alarm, television, hairdryer and hospitality trays are standard. Delicious Scottish breakfasts cooked to order from a large menu are served in the dining room, and a popular vegetarian choice is also available. Inside the house is immaculately maintained, and at the front there is a beautiful garden.

Nether Johnstone House ♦♦♦♦♦

A charming house with thoughtfully equipped bedrooms and a peaceful lounge

☎ 01505 322210
📠 01505 324004
✉ bookings@
netherjohnstone.co.uk
www.netherjohnstone.co.uk

Map ref 9 - NS46

Off Barochan Road, Nether Johnstone, JOHNSTONE, Renfrewshire, PA5 8YP
M8, then A737 (Irvine), after Glasgow Airport take Johnstone exit. From A737 turn L towards Johnstone then immediate R into private lane
7 Rooms, S £38-£48 D £66-£76, No smoking

*T*his recently refurbished house nestles in an acre of woodland yet is within easy reach of Glasgow city centre, the airport and the motorways. The well-tended mature gardens are delightful to wander in, while indoors there is a tranquil lounge and an elegant dining room, both furnished and decorated in Edwardian style. Bedrooms are individually decorated and equipped with honesty bar, television and courtesy tray. En suite facilities are spotlessly clean and well lit. Traditional breakfasts are made from the best of local produce with plenty of choice for all tastes, and served at separate tables

RECOMMENDED IN THE AREA

Coats Observatory; Paisley Museum and Art Galleries; West Coast

East Lochhead ♦♦♦♦♦

Renovated 100-year-old farmhouse with loch views

☎ 01505 842610
📠 01505 842610
✉ eastlochhead@aol.com
www.eastlochhead.co.uk

Map ref 9 - NS35

Largs Road, LOCHWINNOCH, Renfrewshire, PA12 4DX
from Glasgow take M8 J28a for A737 Irvine. At Roadhead rdbt turn R on A760. Premises 2m on L
3 Rooms, S £35-£40 D £60-£70, No smoking

*E*nthusiastic and award-winning owner Janet Anderson has made a superb job of renovating the farmhouse, outbuildings and gardens, situated one mile west of Lochwinnoch. The location is convenient for Glasgow Airport - ideal before or after a long flight - and a good base for visiting Glasgow, Ayrshire, the Clyde Coast, the Trossachs and Loch Lomond. There is a relaxed country house atmosphere, and accommodation is offered in an en suite ground floor room, suitable for double/family occupation, and two en suite upstairs bedrooms, one double with shower, one twin with bathroom. Guests can relax in the lounge/dining room, which has magnificent views of Barr Loch. Janet is an enthusiastic cook and her award winning home cooking is served at the communal table. Vegetarian and other diets are catered for. Pets can be brought by prior arrangement.

RECOMMENDED IN THE AREA

Seaside town of Largs; Robert Burns Cottage; Kelvin Art Gallery

$\mathcal{M}$yfarrclan Guest House ♦♦♦♦♦

Delightful bungalow with pretty garden and snug bedrooms

☎ 0141 884 8285
🖷 0141 581 1566
✉ myfarrclan_qwest@
   compuserve.com
www.myfarrclanqwest.co.uk

Map ref 9 - NS46

146 Corsebar Road, PAISLEY, Renfrewshire, PA2 9NA
M8 J29, A726 to Paisley. At BP Garage mini rdbt, turn R and follow Hospital signs. Pass Royal Alexandra Hospital on L, house 0.5m up hill on R, with tall evergreen hedge
3 Rooms, S £50-£60 D £70-£80, No smoking

$\mathcal{A}$ genuine commitment to their guests is evident from the owners of this cosy bungalow. From its setting in the leafy suburbs of Paisley it is no distance to Paisley Abbey and Museum, while Glasgow Airport is only 10 minutes away. Bedrooms though not spacious are very well equipped, and prettily decorated with lovely soft furnishings and quality fittings. A comfortable sitting room and a conservatory lounge looking onto the attractive garden are magnets for guests. Hearty breakfasts and enjoyable dinners (by arrangement) are served in the bright dining room at one large table. Sightseeing tours throughout Scotland are offered.

RECOMMENDED IN THE AREA

Paisley Museum and Art Gallery; Coats Observatory; Glasgow

$\mathcal{T}$he Glenholm Centre ♦♦♦♦

Peace and quiet on an upland farm with superb views

☎ 01899 830408
🖷 01899 830408
✉ glenholm@dircon.co.uk
www.glenholm.dircon.co.uk

Map ref 10 - NT03

BROUGHTON, Biggar, Scottish Borders, ML12 6JF
A701, 1m S of Broughton, turn R signed Glenholm. Follow rd for 1m, centre on R near road, before cattlegrid
4 Rooms, S £25-£28 D £45-£50, No smoking, Closed Jan

$\mathcal{A}$ converted school house set in a peaceful valley, with 1,000 acres of farmland to explore. Situated just 30 miles south of Edinburgh, it makes an excellent stopover on your journey through Scotland, or a base for exploring the upper Tweed Valley. Wholesome cooking is a special feature here and all tastes can be catered for. Home cooked breakfasts and baking are the highlight of any stay. The en suite bedrooms are bright and airy, a family suite is available in an adjacent cottage, sleeping up to four people. In addition to colour televisions, the rooms are equipped with extras such as a fridge, direct dial telephone and video. The Centre is licensed and there is plenty of parking.

A small computer training centre adjoins the guest house and computing activity holidays are available.

RECOMMENDED IN THE AREA

Dawyck Botanic Gardens (15 minute drive); Traquair (30 minute drive); New Lanark (40 minute drive)

313

The Spinney ♦♦♦♦♦

Attractive modern home set in mature landscaped gardens

☎ 01835 863525
🖷 01835 864883
✉ thespinney@btinternet.com

Map ref 10 - NT61

Langlee, JEDBURGH, Scottish
Borders, TD8 6PB
2m S of Jedburgh on A68
3 Rooms, D £44-£46, No smoking,
Closed Dec-Feb

Set picturesquely in the foothills of the Cheviots, this attractive guest house enjoys mature gardens bordered by woodland and open countryside. Guests can choose between smart double or twin en suite rooms. All rooms are tastefully furnished, with colour televisions and courtesy trays. Breakfast makes an excellent start to the day, with a wide choice of dishes available in the very comfortable dining room. There is also a spacious lounge for guests' use, and several acres of gardens to stroll or sit in. Plenty of parking is provided.

RECOMMENDED IN THE AREA

Dozens of golf courses; walking – the St Cuthbert Way or countryside walks; various historic houses

---

Glen Orchy House ♦♦♦♦

Impeccably kept hotel with friendly owners and warm, comfortable accommodation

☎ 01595 692031
🖷 01595 692031
✉ glenorchy.house@virgin.net
www.guesthouselerwick.com

Map ref 13 - HU44

20 Knab Road, LERWICK, Shetland,
ZE1 0AX
adj to coastguard station
22 Rooms, S £40 D £66, No smoking
in dining room or new wing

Once an Episcopalian convent, this smart hotel has swapped its austere past for the sort of modern comforts expected by discerning guests. Renovated and extended within the past 10 years, it offers several new bedrooms in a non-smoking wing which come equipped with satellite television and air conditioning, as well as some older but equally appealing rooms. One of the inviting lounges has an honesty bar, and there are plenty of books and games for wet days. Delicious three-course dinners and substantial breakfasts are served in the dining room. Fax and VCR facilities are available on request.

RECOMMENDED IN THE AREA

Explore Shetland's beautiful and picturesque scenery; visit the 2000 year old Pictish broch on the Island of Mousa; St Nimian's Isle

Craggallan ♦♦♦♦

Fresh, well cared for house with a very hospitable owner

☎ 01292 264998 ✆ 01292 264998
✉ craggallan@aol.com
www.craggallan.com

Map ref 9 - NS32

8 Queens Terrace, AYR, South Ayrshire, KA7 1DU
from A70 or A77 take town centre signs, A19 through Wellington Square to beach, off seafront)
5 Rooms, S £22-£30 D £36-£50, No smoking

tea/coffee tray and television. Guests can use the internet to check onward reservations or keep in touch with home, and special golfing packages can be arranged. Breakfast is served at a large communal dining table, and evening meals are also available. The town centre is an easy walk away.

*I*dyllically set in a conservation area beside the sea, this immaculate house is geared entirely around the well-being of its guests. Owner Margot McLaughlan has been twice nominated for the AA's Landlady of the Year award, and she extends a very special welcome to her home. Most bedrooms are spacious and smart, with en suite facilities,

RECOMMENDED IN THE AREA

Culzean Castle; many golf courses; Glasgow for shopping and sightseeing

Daviot House ♦♦♦♦

Early Victorian terraced house peacefully located close to the shore

☎ 01292 269678
✆ 01292 880567
✉ thedaviot@aol.com
www.daviothouse.com

Map ref 9 - NS32

12 Queens Terrace, AYR, South Ayrshire, KA7 1DU
into Ayr by A71 (N) or A77 (S), take town centre signs, L, R at lights, next L, R at lights, 2nd L, 2nd R
5 Rooms, S £22-£30 D £40-£50, No smoking

*G*uests are assured of a friendly welcome from Ann Vance, an AA Landlady of the Year finalist. The house is just a minute's walk from the beach, and handy for the town centre, with free parking permits provided for residents' cars. Ann prides herself on her home cooking and is happy to provide dinner for guests in addition to the full Scottish breakfast served at individual tables in the dining room.

Bedrooms include a choice of double, family or twin rooms, four with en suite facilities and one with a private bathroom. All are equipped with television, radio alarms, hairdryers and hospitality trays. Pets accommodated by arrangement.

RECOMMENDED IN THE AREA

Culzean Castle and Country Park; Robert Burns Birthplace and Heritage Centre; two championship golf courses, plus many private and municipal courses

Dunduff Farm ♦♦♦♦♦

A stone-built farmhouse with wonderful sea views

☎ 01292 500225
🖷 01292 500222
✉ gemmelldunduff@aol.com

Map ref 9 - NS21

Dunure, DUNURE, South Ayrshire, KA7 4LH
on A719, 400yds past village school on L
3 Rooms, S £35 D £48, No smoking, Closed Nov-Feb

There are panoramic coastal sea views to be enjoyed from all the rooms at this working farm, parts of which date back to the 15th and 17th centuries. From its wonderful position above the Firth of Clyde, the sheep and beef farm looks out towards Arran and the Mull of Kintyre, and over to Ailsa Craig. Thoughtful touches are evident throughout the house, and the comfortable bedrooms are well equipped and modern, with en suite facilities. The genuine Scottish hospitality makes visitors feel at home, and there is a welcoming lounge. Specialities such as locally-smoked kippers are served at breakfast, and guests have a choice of places to eat in nearby Ayr.

RECOMMENDED IN THE AREA

Dunure Castle; Crossragual Abbey; Culzean Castle

The Fairways Private Hotel ♦♦♦♦

Private hotel overlooking the golf links

☎ 01292 470396
🖷 01292 470396
✉ anne@thefairways.co.uk
www.thefairways.co.uk

Map ref 9 - NS32

19 Links Road, PRESTWICK, South Ayrshire, KA9 1QG
turn west off A79 at Prestwick Cross, after 800yds hotel on L overlooking Prestwick Golf Course
5 Rooms, £33 per person, No smoking in bedrooms or dining room

Ideally located for the golfing enthusiast, the Fairways overlooks the world famous links of Prestwick Golf Club. There are over 40 golf courses in the area to suit all abilities, and bookings and transport can be arranged. The building is a handsome Victorian property retaining many original features enhanced by fine antique furniture in the public areas. Splendid views of the links are afforded from the lounge and dining room, and there is a drinks licence for residents and their guests. All the bedrooms have en suite or private facilities, colour television and hospitality tray. The seafront, main shopping area and railway station are just a few minutes' walk away, and Glasgow Prestwick International Airport is five minutes' drive.

RECOMMENDED IN THE AREA

Culzean Castle and Country Park (20 miles); Burns Cottage and National Heritage Park (5 miles); Loudown Castle Family Theme Park (15 miles)

$\mathcal{A}$rden House ♦♦♦♦

Large Victorian house enjoying panoramic views of nearby Ben Ledi

☎ 01877 330235
🖷 01877 330235
📧 ardenhouse@onetel.net.uk
www.smoothhound.co.uk./hotels/arden.html
Map ref 9 - NN60
Bracklinn Road, CALLANDER, Stirling, FK17 8EQ
from A84 in Callander turn R into Bracklinn Rd, signed to golf course & Bracklinn Falls. House 200yds on L
6 Rooms, S £30 D £55-£65, No smoking, Closed Nov-30 Mar

$\mathcal{R}$emember the BBC's Dr. Finlay's Casebook? Well, Arden House was the splendid television home of doctors Finlay and Cameron. Only a short walk from the centre of Callander, in a quiet part of the village, here lies a delightful retreat, an ideal base from which to explore the Highlands and the Loch Lomond and Trossachs National Park. The friendly proprietors pride themselves on their freely-given hospitality and attention to detail, genuinely welcoming you into their home. Comfortable en suite bedrooms, individually refurbished, provide thoughtful extra touches, including tea and coffee making facilities. There is also a stylish lounge and bright, airy dining room where traditional Scottish breakfasts are served. Not suitable for pets or children under 14. Non smoking.

RECOMMENDED IN THE AREA

Stirling Castle and the Old Town (15 miles); boat trips on Loch Katrine (20 minute drive); Loch Lomond and Trossachs National Park

---

$\mathcal{B}$rook Linn Country House ♦♦♦♦

Victorian country house on the edge of Callander

☎ 01877 330103
🖷 01877 330103
📧 derek@blinn.freeserve.co.uk
www.brooklinn-scotland.co.uk
Map ref 9 - NN60
Leny Feus, CALLANDER, Stirling, FK17 8AU
A84 thro Callander from Stirling, R at Pinewood Nursing Home (Leny Feus). R, up hill at 'Brook Linn' sign
6 Rooms, S £25-£27 D £27-£31 (per person), No smoking, Closed Nov-Etr

$\mathcal{F}$iona and Derek House have sympathetically restored their elegant home to provide guests with a comfortable, relaxing and friendly place to stay. Bedrooms are bright and airy with big windows showing off the super views. All rooms are now en suite and are equipped with televisions, radios, hospitality trays, hairdryers and electric blankets. Attractive decor, pretty fabrics and thick duvets are a home from home touch.

Public areas include an inviting sitting room and pleasantly appointed dining room. The house stands in an elevated position ten minutes' walk from town and is set in two acres of mature grounds, with terraced lawns, flowers, shrubs and a kitchen garden.

RECOMMENDED IN THE AREA

Scotland's first National Park; Historic Stirling; The Trossachs

$\mathcal{L}$eny House •••••

Listed country mansion dating from 1513 set in extensive parkland with its own private glen

☎ 01877 331078
📠 01877 331335
📧 res@lenyestate.com
www.lenyestate.com

Map ref 9 - NN60

Leny Estate, CALLANDER, Stirling, FK17 8HA
leave Callander going N on A84, just beyond town outskirts, look R for sign to Leny Estate
3 Rooms, D £100-£110, No smoking, Closed Nov-Etr

$\mathcal{A}$ special property, where quality and good taste are evident in every room, Leny House is a recent winner of our prestigious Guest Accommodation of the Year Award for Scotland. The historic house, which featured in the Jacobite Rebellion of 1745, was originally a small fortress, enlarged in 1691 and again in 1845 to its present form. During 1998-99 it was carefully restored in close consultation with Historic Scotland. Antiques, tapestries and Victorian prints characterise the baronial style of the décor, and comfort is a clear priority in the lounge, where large windows give on to superb views over the lawns towards the Trossachs. An impressive staircase leads up to the guest accommodation. Double and twin rooms are offered including some with four-poster beds. Two rooms have open fires in season, and all have luxurious bathrooms. In the morning a full Scottish breakfast is served house-party style in the elegant dining room. Children under 12 cannot be accommodated and dogs are not accepted.

RECOMMENDED IN THE AREA

Loch Lomond and Trossachs; set in Scotland's first National Park; Stirling and Doune Castles nearby

Rokeby House.....

Edwardian villa in the heart of Perthshire

☎ 01786 824447
📠 01786 821399
📧 rokeby.house@
btconnect.com
www.aboutscotland.co
m/stirling/rokeby.html

Map ref 9 - NN70

Doune Road, DUNBLANE,
Stirling, FK15 9AT
M9 N, Dunblane exit, then
next turn to Doune along
Doune Road. Premises
0.5m on left
3 Rooms, S £65-£75 D £80-
£100, No smoking

RECOMMENDED IN
THE AREA

Stirling Castle; William Wallace Monument; National Trust properties; Edinburgh and Glasgow

*B*uilt in 1907, this delightful property has been sympathetically restored to its former glory by enthusiastic proprietor Richard Beatts. A combination of high standards of accommodation, warm hospitality and gracious surroundings make this a wonderful place to rest and relax. Antique pieces and original paintings are a feature of many of the rooms, and the lovely grounds include a secret garden and an Italian garden with a rustic pergola. All the bedrooms have either en suite or private facilities and look out onto the gardens. They are decorated in period style and are equipped with central heating, colour television, clock radios and tea and coffee making facilities. Elegant guests' lounge. Breakfast is served in the stylish dining room and evening meals are available by prior arrangement. For golfing enthusiasts, Gleneagles is just a few minutes away, and St Andrews and Carnoustie are within easy reach. Licensed establishment.

*T*hornton ◆◆◆◆

Family home quietly located in large secluded gardens

☎ 01506 844693
🖷 01506 844876
✉ inglisthornton@hotmail.com

Map ref 10 - NT07

Edinburgh Road, LINLITHGOW,
West Lothian, EH49 6AA
A803 into Linlithgow High Street. At
rdbt take B9080. Pass garage on L,
turn 2nd R up lane before corner &
lights
2 Rooms, S £25-£30 D £50-£56, No
smoking, Closed mid Dec-mid Jan

*T*hornton is a delightful property dating from the 1870s, situated within easy reach of the centre of historic Linlithgow, birthplace of Mary Queen of Scots. The Millennium Link canal project, with its impressive centrepiece, the world's first rotating boat-lift, is in the vicinity, as are many National Trust and Historic Scotland properties. The house is traditionally furnished to a high standard and, with easy frequent rail links to Glasgow, Edinburgh and Stirling, makes an ideal base for leisure or business. The ground floor bedrooms, both en suite, are comfortably proportioned and offer many thoughtful extras. An award winning, freshly cooked, breakfast is served in the spacious dining room overlooking the garden.

RECOMMENDED IN THE AREA

Linlithgow Palace, town museum and St Michael's Church; Hopetown House, Dalmeny House; Millennium Link Wheel in Falkirk

Eilean Donan Castle, Highland

Wales

A selection of places to eat from the AA Restaurant & AA Pub Guides

Restaurants

◎◎ Ye Olde Bulls Head Inn (Chic, Minimalist)
Castle St, Beaumaris, Isle of Anglesey LL58 8AP
Tel 01248 810329 Fax 01248 811294

◎◎ da Venditto (Modern, Italian)
7-8 Park Place, Cardiff CF10 3DP
Tel 029 2023 0781 Fax 029 2039 9949

◎◎ The Cors Restaurant (Modern, Country-house)
Newbridge Rd, Laugharne, Carmarthenshire
SA32 7NY
Tel 01994 427219

◎ Penbontbren Farm (Traditional, Country-house)
Glynarthen, Aberporth, Ceredigion SA44 6PE
Tel 01239 810248 Fax 01239 811129

◎ Café Niçoise (Modern, French)
124 Abergele Rd, Colwyn Bay, Conwy LL29 7PS
Tel 01492 531555 Fax 01492 531555

◎◎ Bodidris Hall (Traditional, Country-house)
Llandegla, Denbighshire LL1 3AL
Tel 01978 790434 Fax 01978 790335

◎ The Brasserie (Modern, Minimalist)
68 The Highway, Haywarden, Flintshire
CH5 3DH
Tel 01244 536353 Fax 01244 520888

◎◎ Bontddu Hall (Classic)
Bontddu, Gwynedd LL40 2UF
Tel 01341 430661 Fax 01341 430284

◎◎ Plas Bodegroes (Modern, Chic)
Nefyn Road, Pwllheli LL53 5TH
Tel 01758 612363 Fax 01758 701247

◎ Parva Farmhouse (Traditional)
Tintern, Monmouthshire NP16 6SQ
Tel 01291 689411 Fax 01291 689557

◎ The Inn at the Elm Tree (Modern, Minimalist)
St Brides Wentlooge, Newport NP10 8SQ
Tel 01633 680225 Fax 01633 681035

◎◎ Morgan's Brasserie (Traditional, Bistro-style)
20 Nun Street, St David's, Pembrokeshire
SA62 6NT
Tel 01437 720508 Fax 01437 720508

◎ The White Swan (Traditional, Rustic)
Brecon, Powys LD3 7BZ
Tel 01874 665276

◎ The Bricklayers Arms (Traditional, Rustic)
Chirbury Road, Montgomery, Powys SY15 6QQ
Tel 01686 668177

◎◎ Dermott's Restaurant (Modern)
219 High Street, Swansea SA1 1NN
Tel 01792 459050 Fax 01792 459050

Pubs

🍺 The Salutation Inn
Pont-ar-Gothi, Carmarthenshire SA32 7NH
Tel 01267 290336

🍺 The Queens Head
Glanwydden, Llandudno Junction, Conwy
LL31 9JP
Tel 01492 546570 Fax 01492 546487

🍺 White Horse Inn
Hendrerwydd, Ruthin, Denbighshire LL16 4LL
Tel 01824 790218

🍺 Stables Bar Restaurant
Soughton Hall, Northop, Flintshire CH7 6AB
Tel 01352 840577 Fax 01352 840382

🍺 Penhelig Arms Hotel
Terrace Rd, Aberdyfi, Gwynedd LL35 0LT
Tel 01654 767215 Fax 01654 767690

🍺 George III Hotel
Penmaenpool, Dolgellau, Gwynedd LL40 1YD
Tel 01341 422525 Fax 01341 423565

🍺 The Ship Inn
Red Wharf Bay, Isle of Anglesey LL75 8RJ
Tel 01248 852568 Fax 01248 851013

🍺 Walnut Tree Inn
Llandewi Skirrid, Abergavenny, Monmouthshire
NP7 8AW
Tel 01873 852797 Fax 01873 859764

🍺 The Newbridge Inn
Tredunnock, Monmouthshire NP15 1LY
Tel 01633 45100 Fax 01633 541001

🍺 Georges Bar
24 Market St, Haverfordwest, Pembrokeshire
SA61 1NH
Tel 01437 766683 Fax 01437 779090

🍺 White Swan Inn
Llanfrynach, Brecon, Powys LD3 7BZ
Tel 01874 665276

🍺 The Bear
Brecon Road, Crickhowell, Powys NP8 1BW
Tel 01873 810408 Fax 01873 811696

🍺 The Famous Black Lion
Hay-on-Wye, Powys HR3 5AD
Tel 01497 820841

🍺 The Bricklayers Arms
Chirbury Rd, Montgomery, Powys SY15 6QQ
Tel 01686 668177

🍺 Castle Coaching Inn
Trecastle, Powys LD3 8UH
Tel 01874 636354 Fax 01874 636457

🍺 Blue Anchor Inn
East Aberthaw, Vale of Glamorgan CF62 3DD
Tel 01446 750329 Fax 01446 750077

Yr Hendre ◆◆◆◆

A warm welcome to Holyhead, off the West coast of the Isle of Anglesey

☎ / 🖷 01407 762929
✉ rita@
   yr-hendre.freeserve.co.uk
www.yr-hendre.co.uk

Map ref 5 - SH28

Porth-y-Felin Road, HOLYHEAD,
Isle of Anglesey, LL65 1AH
from A5 in centre L at War Memorial.
Next L, up steep hill, straight on x-
roads, house on R facing park
3 Rooms, S £25-£30 D £45-£50, No
smoking

The house and grounds are opposite a park yet are only a few minutes from the Holyhead town centre and ferry terminals. There are many lovely walks to enjoy in the area as well as sandy beaches, a sailing school, watersports, pony trekking and a championship golf course. Boat trips can also be arranged locally giving opportunities for bird watching.

The house itself has been tastefully restored to provide high standards of guest accommodation. The bedrooms are individually designed and furnished, all with en suite bathrooms and nice views. Facilities include colour TV, tea and coffee, radio alarms, hairdryers and many extras. The lounge has TV, video and a selection of books. Wonderful views of the sea and gardens can be appreciated from the dining room.

RECOMMENDED IN THE AREA

South Stack Lighthouse; Nature Reserve at Penrhos; daily ferry trip to Dublin

---

Wern Farm ◆◆◆◆

Farmhouse with landscaped gardens and breathtaking views of Snowdonia

☎ / 🖷 01248 712421
✉ wernfarmanglesey@
   onetel.net.uk
www.angleseyfarms.com/
wern.htm

Map ref 5 - SH57

Pentraeth Road, MENAI BRIDGE, Isle
of Anglesey, LL59 5RR
from A5/A55 take 2nd exit after
crossing Britannia Bridge signed
A5025 Amlwch/Benllech. After rdbt
pass large garage, farm on R
3 Rooms, S £30-£50 D £50-£56, No
smoking, Closed Nov-Feb

Peter and Linda Brayshaw's lovely home has developed over the years from an original two up two down built around 1600. Generations of farmers have built on, and the house now has 20 rooms and two staircases. It is surrounded by 260 acres of grazing and woodland, and from the conservatory breakfast room there are views over the garden and pond to the Snowdonia mountain range beyond. On-site facilities include an all-weather tennis court, nature trails, an antique three-quarter size billiard/snooker table, and games to play by the log fire in the lounge. The en suite bedrooms offer colour televisions, tea/coffee, hairdryers, books and toiletries. Cot and highchair available. Winner AA Best Breakfast for Wales 2001.

RECOMMENDED IN THE AREA

Historic town of Beaumaris; Llanddwyn Island National Nature Reserve; National Trust properties – Plas Newydd, Penrhyn Castle

Glasfryn Guest House & Restaurant ♦♦♦♦

A friendly, well-run house offering good food and cosy bedrooms

☎ 01267 202306
📠 0870 1341770
✉ joyce.glasfryn@clara.co.uk
glasfrynbrechfa.co.uk

Map ref 2 - SN53

BRECHFA, Carmarthen, SA32 7QY
M4 J49, onto A48 to Cross Hands,
towards Carmarthen for approx 1m,
turn 2nd L onto B4310, past gardens
over the A40
3 Rooms, S £25-£30 D £45-£50, No
smoking in bedrooms or dining room

$\mathcal{S}$et in a picturesque valley ideally located for touring the southern part of Wales is this large stone house exuding traditional Welsh hospitality. The late Victorian property has been sympathetically refurbished to retain stone walls and stripped pine, and the accommodation has been extended into a large, bright conservatory. The pretty bedrooms have the benefit of power showers in the en suite bathrooms. In the evening an à la carte menu is available, when imaginative meals are served in the smart dining room overlooking a pretty patio. This homely guest house is only 15 minutes from the National Botanic Gardens.

RECOMMENDED IN THE AREA

Aberglasney Garden (15 minutes); forest walks (1 mile); mountain biking in the forest (1 mile)

Capel Dewi Uchaf Country House ♦♦♦♦

Old world farmhouse in the beautiful Towy Valley

☎ 01267 290799
📠 01267 290003
✉ uchaffarm@aol.com
www.walescottageholidays.uk.com

Map ref 1 - SN43

Capel Dewi, CARMARTHEN,
SA32 8AY
M4 J49, A48 to exit for National
Botanical Garden. B4310 to junct with
B4300. L, premises approx 1m on R
3 Rooms, S £40 D £56, No smoking,
Closed Xmas

$\mathcal{D}$ating from the 16th century, this Grade II listed farmhouse is located in 30 acres by the River Towy with stunning country views. Private fishing and stabling for guests' horses is available. The lovely gardens have a new terrace and, inside, a welcoming log fire and period décor and furnishing schemes enhance the property's original features. Bedrooms are equipped with en suite or private facilities, televisions, hairdryers and hospitality trays. Fresh local produce is a feature of the memorable dinners and generous Welsh breakfasts, including home-grown vegetables. There's a guests' lounge, with a piano, guitar and wind-up gramophone as well as the TV, and the house has a residential license. Winner of AA Best Breakfast Award for Wales.

RECOMMENDED IN THE AREA

National Botanic Gardens; Aberglasney Garden; Newton House and Dinefwr Park (National Trust)

323

Cwmtwrch, Four Seasons Restaurant with Rooms ···· ◉

Good food, wine and leisure facilities in a farmhouse setting with beautiful gardens

☎ 01267 290238
🖷 01267 290808
✉ jen4seasons@aol.com
www.visit-carmarthenshire.co.uk/4seasons

Map ref 1 - SN42

Nantgaredig, CARMARTHEN, SA32 7NY
5m E of Carmarthen, take B4310 at Nantgaredig x-roads towards Brechfa, 0.25m N off A40 on R
6 Rooms, S £40-£70 D £56-£80, No smoking in dining room, Closed 23 Dec-28 Dec

A 200 year old farmhouse and outbuildings converted into a renowned restaurant with rooms and extensive leisure facilities. Surrounded by thirty acres of its own land, there are views of the rolling Towy valley countryside and beyond to the Black Mountains and the Brecon Beacons. The en suite bedrooms are all furnished to match the period of the buildings; three are at ground level in the converted Georgian barn; three are in the farmhouse itself including a small suite. The restaurant, with its relaxed and easygoing atmosphere, is at the hub of things, serving imaginative food, cooked with flair and based on the best of local produce and with a good value wine list. The leisure facilities include an 18m heated indoor pool and a recently built gym with state of the art equipment.

RECOMMENDED IN THE AREA

The National Botanical Gardens of Wales (5 minute drive); restored Aberglasney Gardens (5 minute drive)

$\mathscr{A}$berconwy House ♦♦♦♦

Quietly located house with excellent views of the Conwy Valley from most of the rooms

☎ 01690 710202
🖷 01690 710800
✉ welcome@aberconwy-house.co.uk
www.aberconwy-house.co.uk

Map ref 5 - SH85

Lon Muriau, BETWS-Y-COED, Snowdonia National Park, Conwy LL24 0HD
on A470, 0.5m N from A5/A470 junction
8 Rooms, D £46-£52, No smoking

$\mathscr{A}$berconwy House is a Victorian property just ten minutes walk from Betws-y-Coed, affording lovely views over the Llugwy and Conwy valleys. It is an ideal location from which to explore the glories of Snowdonia. Bedrooms are attractively decorated and comfortably furnished, all with en suite facilities. Colour televisions, tea and coffee making equipment, trouser presses and ironing facilities are provided. Guests are welcome to send and receive e-mails. Public rooms comprise a relaxing residents' lounge and a separate breakfast room. Car parking is provided for guests. Credit cards accepted.

RECOMMENDED IN THE AREA

Bodnant Gardens; Castles of North Wales (Caernarfon, Conwy, Harlech); Mountains (Snowdon, Tryfan)

Henllys ♦♦♦♦

Intriguing conversion of a police station and court house

☎ 01690 710534
✉ henllys@betws-y-coed.co.uk
http://betws-y-coed.co.uk/acc/henllys

Map ref 5 - SH85

Old Church Road, BETWS-Y-COED, Conwy LL24 0AL
A5 into Betws-y-Coed pass two petrol stations on L then turn 1st R into Old Church Rd from south or from north A5 pass Royal Oak Hotel, village green & turning for railway station then turn L into Old Church Rd
9 Rooms, D £54-£60, No smoking

$\mathscr{A}$ccommodation of great charm is provided in this Victorian property, a former police station and magistrates' court, set in a peaceful garden beside the River Conwy. One bedroom was originally a cell, and all the rooms have quirks and features from their time as judges' and magistrates' chambers. Modern comforts are not forgotten, however, with televisions, hospitality trays and en suites in every room, except one with a private bathroom. Breakfast is served in the former courtroom, and in the lounge bar a collection of police badges and hats from around the world is displayed. Henllys is centrally situated for all the attractions of North Wales and Snowdonia.

RECOMMENDED IN THE AREA

Snowdon and Snowdon Mountain Railway (30 minute drive); Caernarfon Castle (scenic drive); Italianate village Portmeirion

Gwern Borter Country Manor ♦♦♦♦

Creeper-clad mansion with plenty to entertain both adults and children

☎ 01492 650360
📠 01492 650360
✉ mail@
snowdoniaholidays.co.uk
www.snowdoniaholidays.co.uk

Map ref 5 - SH77

Barkers Lane, CONWY, LL32 8YL
from Conwy take B5106 for 2.25m,
turn R onto unclass rd towards Rowen
for 0.5m then R (Gwern Borter) 0.5m
on L
3 Rooms, S £30-£35 D £50-£56, No
smoking in dining room

*A*n impressive and historic manor house set in 12 acres of grounds and gardens, amongst the forests, lakes and rivers of Snowdonia, close to the sea. The creeper-clad guest house is an ideal place for children, with its pets' corner, rustic play area, games room and plenty of bikes, skateboards and scooters to play with. Bedrooms are tastefully decorated and equipped with modern facilities and period or antique furniture; one room has an Edwardian four-poster bed. A magnificent oak fireplace distinguishes the Victorian-style dining room, where hearty Welsh breakfasts are served. Also available on site at an extra charge are horse riding, a well-fitted gym and a sauna.

RECOMMENDED IN THE AREA

National Trust properties – Bodnant Garden, Penrhyn Castle and Plas Newydd (within easy driving distance); lots of walks direct from the manor house; Conwy and Caernarfon Castle (easy driving distance)

Bryn Derwen Hotel ♦♦♦♦♦

Beautifully converted Victorian building with tranquil ambience and central location

☎ 01492 876804
📠 01492 876804
✉ brynderwen@fsbdial.co.uk
www.bryn-derwen-hotel.co.uk

Map ref 5 - SH78

34 Abbey Road, LLANDUDNO,
Conwy LL30 2EE
from A55 onto A470, left at
promenade to cenotaph, turn left,
straight on at rdbt, 4th right into York
Rd, hotel at top
10 Rooms, S £50-£60 D £70-88, No
smoking, Closed Nov-Feb

*B*uilt in 1878 as a gentleman's residence, Bryn Derwen has the atmosphere a private town house of considerable charm and elegance, and Stuart and Valerie Langfield welcome you as valued house-guests. The lounge boasts superb stained glass windows and fine period furniture, while in the candle-lit dining room you can be sure of exciting food from the chef. You might try a beauty or relaxation treatment in 'Complexions' salon before taking the impressive pine staircase to your en suite bedroom. Decorated in rich colours and matching fabrics, rooms are equipped with colour television, luxury toiletries and tea and coffee-making facilities. Children cannot be accommodated.

RECOMMENDED IN THE AREA

Snowdonia National Park; Castles of Conwy, Caernarfon and Beaumans; Great Orme Country Park

Abbey Lodge .....

Former gentleman's residence built in 1870, close to town centre and beaches

T 01492 878042
F 01492 878042
E enquiries@
abbeylodgeuk.com
www.abbeylodgeuk.com

Map ref 5 - ST78

14 Abbey Road, LLANDUDNO, Conwy LL30 2EA
from promenade (sea on R) at the t-junct near pier, R, straight on at rdbt, 3rd R into Clement Ave, at top, R into Abbey Rd. Abbey Lodge on L
4 Rooms, S £30-£35 D £55-£60, No smoking, Closed Xmas/New Year

RECOMMENDED IN THE AREA

Bodnant Gardens; Snowdonia; the promenade (one of Europe's finest)

Abbey Lodge has been carefully restored over recent years by Trish and Geoffrey Howard. The atmosphere is welcoming and the luxurious bedrooms are attractively decorated, all have bath and shower, with bathrobes. Hospitality trays, bottled mineral water, colour television, hairdryer, new beds and furnishings all contribute to a very comfortable stay. The charming drawing room with its open fire and elegant furniture is the ideal place to relax. Evening dinner is available by prior arrangement. The country house style dining room is used for breakfast, a choice of continental or traditional cooked breakfast is offered and individual requirements are willingly catered for. The emphasis is very much on relaxation and pampering, and Geoff and Trish will be happy to assist you in planning a tailor-made holiday or just finding your feet in the area. You can board a Victorian tram nearby which will take you to the summit of the Great Orme. Sights and activities include the country park, ancient copper mines ski slope, tobbogan run and cable car.

Powys Country House ◆◆◆◆

Riverside guest house with spectacular mountain views

☎ 01490 412367
✉ powyshouse@aol.com
www.powyscountryhouse.co.uk

Map ref 5 - SJ14

Bonwm, CORWEN, Denbighshire
LL21 9EG
from A5 Corwen to Llangollen rd,
premises approx 1m on L after leaving
Corwen
7 Rooms, S £20 D £50, No smoking
in bedrooms or dining room,
Closed Xmas

The Carnie family extend a warm welcome to guests at their comfortable home, which is set in three acres of gardens next to the River Dee, with views of the Berwyn mountains. In the grounds you'll find a grass tennis court, an ornate fountain and a patio area where you can sit and relax. Spacious en suite bedrooms include televisions, hairdryers and tea and coffee-making facilities. A cosy beamed residents' lounge is also provided. Breakfast is traditional, with alternatives on request, and home-cooked evening meals and packed lunches are offered. The house has a table license and guests can choose from a comprehensive wine list. Three self-catering cottages are also available.

RECOMMENDED IN THE AREA

Snowdonia (60 minutes); Porthmadog and Portmeirion (60 minutes); Llangollen

Erw Feurig Guest House ◆◆◆◆

Superbly located farmhouse overlooking the Berwyn Mountain

☎ 01678 530262
📠 01678 530262
✉ erwfeurig@yahoo.com
www.ukworld.net/erwfeurig

Map ref 5 - SH93

Cefnddwysarn, BALA, Gwynedd,
LL23 7LL
on the A494, Bala to Corwen road,
2nd on L after telephone kiosk at
Cefnddwysarn
4 Rooms, S £22-£25 D £40-£44,
No smoking, Closed Xmas period

A warm Welsh welcome awaits guests at this extended farmhouse, which is set in 200 acres of sheep and cattle grazing land. Gareth and Glenys Jones are the third generation of the family to live at Erw Feurig, where homely accommodation is offered in family, double and twin rooms, all with colour television, hospitality trays and toiletries. Two rooms are en suite and the ground floor twin has private facilities. A cosy lounge is provided for guests and breakfast is served in the pleasant dining room, at separate tables if preferred. Fishing is available on the farm. Sorry no dogs or smoking indoors.

RECOMMENDED IN THE AREA

Ewe-phoria – Agri Theatre and Sheepdog Centre; National White Water Centre; Llyn Tegid Narrow Gauge Steam Railway

Nant y Fedw ◆◆◆◆

Grade II listed country cottage with a lovely atmosphere

☎ 01248 351683
✉ nantyfedw1.fsnet.co.uk

Map ref 5 - SH66

Trefelin, Llanedgai, BANGOR,
Gwynedd, LL57 4LH
take A5122 to Bangor, turn onto road
signed Llandegai/Tal-y-Bont at
Penrhyn Castle, 100mtrs down hill,
turn R to large gates, turn R.
2 Rooms, S -£25 D -£38, No smoking
in bedrooms or dining room

A pair of 150-year-old cottages knocked into one provides a charming base for visiting this part of North Wales. Owner Mrs Davies is a former runner-up in the AA Landlady of the Year Award, an accolade for which she is still well qualified. Her warm friendliness creates a pleasant atmosphere in this beamed cottage, where a lovely garden with an unusual gazebo is an enjoyable spot to wander in. Both bedrooms are comfortable and well furnished, with one at ground floor level and each having either en suite or private facilities. A restful sitting room with open fires and colour television is available for guests.

RECOMMENDED IN THE AREA

Penrhyn Castle (500 yards); Mount Snowdon (9 miles); many local walks bordering the Snowdonia National Park

Hafoty ◆◆◆◆

Snowdonian farmhouse with stunning views of Caernarfon Castle

☎ 01286 830144
🖷 01286 830441
✉ hafoty@btinternet.com
www.hafotyfarmguesthouse.co.uk

Map ref 5 - SH55

Rhostryfan, CAERNARFON,
Gwynedd, LL54 7PH
off A487 2.5m from Caernarfon follow
brown signs for Hafoty
4 Rooms, S £28 D £48-£52, No
smoking in bedrooms or dining room,
Closed Dec-Feb

From its rural situation, the farm enjoys spectacular views of the Menai Straits and Caernarfon Castle. Hafoty has been created over several years from converted farm buildings and provides well-equipped modern accommodation. Mari and Wil Davies are the friendly owners, who create a peaceful and relaxing atmosphere. Bedrooms are spacious and children are especially welcome. There is a play area, and a cot and highchair are available. The main house has comfortable, attractively decorated public areas, where cheery log fires burn in cooler weather. One bedroom is located in nearby outbuildings and several self-catering cottages are also available. Two nearby pubs serve reasonably priced meals, and there's a very good fish and chip shop five minutes' drive away.

RECOMMENDED IN THE AREA

Snowdon (walking or by train); five Welsh castles within easy reach; Portmeirion Italianate village

Llwyndu Farmhouse ••••

Historic farmhouse in a stunning location above the shore overlooking Cardigan Bay and the Lleyn Peninsula

☎ 01341 280144
📠 01341 281236
✉ Intouch@llwyndu-farmhouse.co.uk
www.llwyndu-farmhouse.co.uk

Map ref 2 - SH51

Llanaber, BARMOUTH, Gwynedd, LL42 1RR
A496 towards Harlech. Where street lights end, on outskirts of Barmouth, take next R
7 Rooms, D £60-£68, No smoking, Closed 25-26 Dec

As far back as the 16th century, this farmhouse was known for its 'hospitality, song and good ale'. In that same tradition, Llwyndu today is fully licensed and offers candlelit dinners, a little music and good company. Ancient features add up to a property of considerable character, including a circular stone staircase, large inglenook fireplaces, oak beams and mullioned windows. There are three bedrooms in the main farmhouse - two with four-poster beds - and more rooms in the converted outbuildings, all of them equipped with en suite facilities, colour television, clock radio and hospitality tray. Breakfast specialities are kippers or naturally smoked haddock, Welsh vegetarian breakfast cutlets or local pork and leek sausages, and smoked bacon and laverbread. Freshly prepared dishes from high quality ingredients are also offered at dinner, with vegetarian options and fine wines. This is a great area for walking with easy access from the house to the Rhinog Mountains behind and the nearby Panorama Walk with its wonderful estuary views.

RECOMMENDED IN THE AREA

Cader Idris (15 minute drive); Portmeirion (30 minute drive); Centre for Alternative Technology (40 minute drive)

$\mathcal{P}$engwern Farm ◆◆◆◆

Victorian house with unobstructed views of Snowdonia

☎ 01286 831500
📠 01286 830741
✉ pengwern@talk21.com

Map ref 5 - SH45

Saron, CAERNARFON, Gwynedd,
LL54 5UH
from Caernarfon take A487 S, pass
supermarket on R take 1st R turn after
bridge 2m to Saron, through x-roads,
farm is 1st drive on R
3 Rooms, S £30-£38 D £48-£56,
No smoking, Closed Dec & Jan

$\mathcal{P}$engwern is a delightful farmhouse surrounded by 130 acres of beef and sheep farmland running down to Foryd Bay, noted for its bird life. There are fine views from many bedrooms over to Anglesey, and the top of Snowdon can also be seen on clear days.

Bedrooms are generally spacious and all are well equipped with modern facilities, including en suite bath and shower rooms, colour televisions, and tea and coffee making equipment. A comfortable lounge is provided for guests and good home cooking is served.

The farmhouse is a good base from which to explore the Snowdonia National Park and the historic town of Caernarfon.

RECOMMENDED IN THE AREA

Caernarfon Castle; Segontium Roman Museum; Plas Newydd (National Trust)

$\mathcal{T}$yddynmawr Farmhouse ◆◆◆◆◆

18th-century farmhouse at the foot of Cader Idris

☎ 01341 422331

Map ref 2 - SH71

Islawrdref, DOLGELLAU, Gwynedd,
LL40 1TL
from town centre branch L at top of
square, then turn L at garage into
Cader Rd for approx 3m. 1st farm on
L after Gwernan Lake
3 Rooms, D -£50, No smoking,
Closed Nov-17 Mar

$\mathcal{A}$bout three miles from the historic market town of Dolgellau you will find this 18th century farmhouse, winner of the 2002 AA Guest Accommodation of the Year Award for Wales. It lies at the foot of Cader Idris in breathtaking mountain scenery. Oak beams and log fires give it plenty of character, and bedrooms are spacious, with Welsh oak furniture. One has a balcony, and the ground floor room has a patio area. En suites are large and luxurious. The magnificent surroundings make this a paradise for birdwatchers, ramblers, photographers and artists. Owners Olwen and Alun farm the mountain and guests are welcome to explore the land, with its hidden waterfalls and mountain lakes with private fishing, or even climb to the summit. Pets cannot be accommodated.

RECOMMENDED IN THE AREA

Excellent walking – Cader Idris, Precipice Walk, Torrent Walk, Maddach Estuary Walk, steam railways; Centre for Alternative Technology

Gwrach Ynys Country Guest House ◆◆◆◆

Country house close to the mountains and sea

☎ 01766 780742
📠 01766 781199
✉ aa@gwrachynys.co.uk
www.gwrachynys.co.uk

Map ref 5 - SH53

Talsarnau, HARLECH, Gwynedd, LL47 6TS
2m N of Harlech on A496
7 Rooms, S £20-£25 D £44-£56, No smoking, Closed Nov-Feb

Billed as the ideal house for nature lovers, this impeccably maintained Edwardian property is situated on reclaimed marshland, in a lowland area between Harlech Castle and Cardigan Bay. A National Nature Reserve is close by and Snowdonia is within easy reach. Gwrach Ynys is surrounded by lawns and gardens and the family's ponies graze in the adjoining paddock.

Bedrooms are decorated with pretty wallpapers and six of them are equipped with en suite facilities. Some rooms are suitable for families, and children are especially welcome.

Two comfortably furnished lounges are provided for residents, and hospitality from Deborah and Gwynfor Williams is warm and welcoming. Deborah is an accomplished cook and provides hearty breakfasts. Gwynfor looks after front of house matters and is always happy to offer advice on local attractions.

RECOMMENDED IN THE AREA

Lovely beach at Harlech; Portmeirion; several golf courses including Royal St David's; climbing and walking in Snowdonia

Tŷ Isaf Farmhouse ◆◆◆◆

Peaceful 16th-century longhouse, perfect for the active or the contemplative

☎ 01341 423261
📠 01341 423261
✉ raygear@tyisaf78.freeserve.co.uk
www.tyisaf78.freeserve.co.uk

Map ref 5 - SH72

LLANFACHRETH, Dolgellau, Gwynedd, LL40 2EA
from Dolgellau, cross river & turn R onto A494 towards Bala, pass Kwiksave store on R then next L signed LLanfachreth & up hill
3 Rooms, S £25-£35 D -£50, No smoking, Closed Xmas & New Year

Encircled by hills and meadows, and nestling in a sleepy hamlet, this traditional Welsh longhouse offers homely accommodation in idyllic surroundings. The former farmhouse, built from thick stone walls and exposed oak rafters, exudes a warm and welcoming atmosphere. Three pretty en suite bedrooms are furnished with stripped pine and comfy beds, and there's a delightful TV lounge and a separate study with stacks of books and inspiring views. Wonderful home cooking using authentic Welsh recipes is served in the smart dining room, and breakfast involves eggs from the Tŷ Isaf hens, and home-made sausages and preserves. Two pet llamas wander in the grounds to complete the picture.

RECOMMENDED IN THE AREA

Walking, climbing, birdwatching, riding and fishing in Snowdonia; many golf courses; beautiful scenery to explore

Llanwenarth House ◆◆◆◆

Beautifully-proportioned, light and spacious accommodation in a welcoming manor house

☎ 01873 830289
🖷 01873 832199
✉ info@welsh-hotel.co.uk
www.welsh-hotel.co.uk

Map ref 2 - SO21

Govilon, ABERGAVENNY,
Monmouthshire, NP7 9SF
E of Abergavenny follow A465
towards Merthyr Tydfil for 3.5m to
next rdbt. Take 1st exit to
Govilon, drive 150yds on R 0.5m
long
5 Rooms, S £62-£66 D £82-£86,
No smoking in bedrooms or
dining room

This gracious 16th-century Welsh manor house is open throughout the year, so its many charms can be appreciated in all seasons. From its beautiful setting in tranquil grounds bordering the Brecon and Monmouthshire canal and within the Brecon Beacons National Park, it looks out over the lush countryside of the Usk Valley. The full-length windows in many parts of the house bring light flooding into the spacious rooms, and help to create a sense of elegance. One such room is the large dining room, where candle-lit dinners cooked from local fish and game, and the family's home-produced meat, poultry and garden vegetables, are served with wines from a well-stocked cellar. Interesting, innovative dishes are produced, and dining here is a memorable experience. The bedrooms are delightfully appointed, with quality en suite shower or bathrooms, televisions and hospitality trays, and the same well-proportioned space as the reception rooms. The stylish drawing rooms is just the place to relax in the evening.

RECOMMENDED IN THE AREA

Hill walking, riding and pony trekking; many golf courses; steam railways

Hardwick Farm ◆◆◆◆

Family-run farm with wonderful views of the Black Mountains

☎ 01873 853513
📠 01873 854238
✉ hardwickfarm@
netscapeonline.co.uk
www.downourlane.co.uk/
hardwickfarm.htm

Map ref 2 - SO31
ABERGAVENNY, Monmouthshire,
NP7 9BT
1m from Abergavenny, off A4042,
farm sign on R
2 Rooms, S £27 D £45, No smoking,
Closed Xmas

Set in the Usk Valley surrounded by beautiful scenery, Hardwick Farm provides a peaceful retreat just a mile from Abergavenny. It is the ideal base for outdoor pursuits including walking, fishing, mountain biking, hang gliding/paragliding, water sports and pony trekking. The Blorenge, Sugar Loaf and Skirrid mountains are close by with the Brecon Beacons beyond, and there is a pleasant riverside walk from the house. Two large en suite bedrooms with fabulous views offer televisions, hairdryers and hot drinks trays. For meals you have a good choice of pubs and restaurants in and around Abergavenny. Rates are reduced for children (cot and highchair available) and pets are welcome by arrangement.

RECOMMENDED IN THE AREA

Mountain walks; Monmouthshire Brecon canal; Raglan Castle and Llanthony Abbey

Highfield House ◆◆◆◆◆

Stone-built property affording wonderful country views

☎ 01291 689286
📠 01291 689890
✉ highfieldhouse@callnetuk.com

Map ref 2 - SO50
Chapel Hill, TINTERN,
Monmouthshire, NP16 6TF
after passing Tintern Abbey, next L at
Royal George Hotel, bear L at road
fork & uphill for 0.25m into forest.
Signed on L
4 Rooms, S £30-£35 D £49.50-£65,
No smoking in bedrooms

Perched on the hillside above Tintern Abbey and surrounded by forest, this remarkable house offers glorious views of the surrounding countryside. Bedrooms and public rooms have been imaginatively decorated throughout. All the bedrooms have en suite facilities, and log fires enhance the welcoming atmosphere of the public rooms in cooler weather. Dinner is lovingly prepared by the proprietor, with an emphasis on Mediterranean cuisine. The six acres of land around the house include woodland areas with plenty of scope for lovely walks. There is also a variety of farm animals, including chickens to ensure fresh free-range eggs for your breakfast. For the more adventurous, mountain biking, canoeing and badminton can be arranged.

RECOMMENDED IN THE AREA

Tintern Abbey (0.5 mile walk); Offa's Dyke (0.5 mile approximately); Chepstow Castle and Racecourse (5 miles)

Penylan ....

Elizabethan house in commanding elevated position, combining high levels of character and comfort

☎ 01633 400267
📠 01633 400997

Map ref 2 - ST49

St Brides Netherwent,
CALDICOT, Newport,
Monmouthshire,
NP26 3AS
M4 J23A, turn L just
before village of Magor
into St Brides Rd. North
2m, 100yds past
Carrow Hill turning
3 Rooms, S £25D £50,
No smoking, Closed
Dec-mid-Mar

This splendid Elizabethan farmhouse is set in half an acre of well-kept gardens and enjoys a peaceful location in south east Monmouthshire, amongst open farmland and ancient woodlands. Its hill-top position, overlooking St Brides Valley has much to recommend it. Conveniently situated just three miles from the M4 and Severn Bridge, and 15 minutes from Newport and Chepstow, it will appeal to both business and holiday travellers, who will be warmly welcomed with tea or coffee and cake on arrival. Inside, many original features, including oak beams, and the inglenook fireplace in the lounge, have been retained, adding to the comfort and charm of the property. The bright, attractive conservatory, meanwhile, is a lovely setting for memorable Welsh breakfasts. Bedrooms are filled with homely extras and all have tea/coffee-making facilities. One bedroom has en suite facilities; the other two share a modern, efficient bathroom. As an added benefit, guests have use of the large heated indoor swimming pool. No dogs.

RECOMMENDED IN THE AREA

Millennium Stadium Cardiff (15 miles); Forest of Dean (10 miles); Celtic Manor golf complex (5 miles)

Green Lanterns Guest House ♦♦♦♦♦

Stunning views, tasteful accommodation and pony trekking all within easy reach of the coast

☎ 01639 631884
📠 01639 899550
📧 carenjones@ btinternet.com
www.thegreenlanterns.co.uk

Map ref 2 - SS79

Hawdref Ganol Farm, Cimla, NEATH, Neath Port Talbot, SA12 9SL
M4 J43 towards Neath. Take B4287 signed Cimla & R at x-roads 300yds past school, AA signed
4 Rooms, S £26-£30 D £46-£54, No smoking in bedrooms or dining room

*P*eacefully located in open country yet just 15 minutes from the coast, this 18th-century farmhouse offers an appealing opportunity to escape from outside pressures. The property is part of a 46-acre equestrian and pony-trekking centre, and it nestles on a hillside overlooking the Vale of Neath with superb panoramic views across mountains and valleys. Once used as a reformatory school, it has been tastefully renovated to provide spacious, airy bedrooms, furnished and decorated in the style of the house, and equipped with modern facilities. Guests can relax in the welcoming lounge where an enormous inglenook fireplace is a cosy feature in the winter. Hearty Welsh breakfasts are enjoyed at a communal table in the attractive dining room or in the new restaurant and grill in the adjoining property. Green Lanterns is one hour away from the Severn Bridge, and it boasts three country parks within easy driving distance. Guests are assured of a warm welcome from the hospitable owners.

RECOMMENDED IN THE AREA

Neath canal boat trips (7 miles); Aberdulais Waterfalls (4 miles); Gower Peninsula (14 miles)

Erw-Lon Farm ◆◆◆◆

Working farm in the Pembrokeshire Coast National Park

☎ 01348 881297

Map ref 1 - SN03

Pontfaen, FISHGUARD,
Pembrokeshire, SA65 9TS
on B4313 between Fishguard and
Maenclochog
3 Rooms, S £25 D £50, No smoking,
Closed Dec-Feb

Traditional Welsh hospitality is offered by the friendly McAllister family at their comfortable farmhouse. It is a beef and sheep farm looking over the lovely wooded Gwaun Valley at the foot of the Preseli Hills, with some superb views to be enjoyed. There are three thoughtfully furnished and well equipped bedrooms, two doubles and one twin, all with en suite facilities, colour television, clock radios, hairdryers, shaving points and tea and coffee-making equipment. A relaxing lounge is also provided for residents. Maintenance standards are high throughout and a homely atmosphere prevails. Mrs McAllister serves up some of the finest examples of traditional farmhouse cooking, where the size of the portions matches the warmth of the welcome!

RECOMMENDED IN THE AREA

Fishguard seaside market town and ferry port (10 minute drive); Pembrokeshire Coast National Park

Giltar Grove Country House ◆◆◆◆

Impressive Victorian famhouse close to the Pembrokeshire Coastal Path

☎ 01834 871568
✉ giltarbnb@aol.com
www.gitargrovecountryhouse.
co.uk

Map ref 1 - SN09

Penally, TENBY, Pembrokeshire,
SA70 7RY
from Tenby, take A4139 towards
Manorbier/Pembroke. Pass petrol
station, after 2m reach railway bridge
on bend, 2nd R after bridge
6 Rooms, S £20-£25 D £40-£50, No
smoking, Closed Xmas & New Year

Owner Sarah Diment describes her lovely late-Victorian country house as 'a warm, comfortable and friendly home run by warm, comfortable and friendly people', and as a top twenty finalist in the 2001-2002 AA Landlady of the Year Awards, a really welcoming atmosphere is assured. Giltar Grove enjoys a beautiful, tranquil setting just a five minute stroll from the spectacular coastal path and close to several lovely beaches. Originally a working farm, the house has been beautifully restored and retains many original features. The charming bedrooms are all en suite, and two have four-poster beds. Televisions and tea and coffee making facilities are provided and a full traditional or vegetarian breakfast is served in the magnificent conservatory.

RECOMMENDED IN THE AREA

Pembrokeshire Coastal Path; Manorbier, Carew and Pembroke Castles; unspoilt beaches of Tenby, Penally and Lydstep

WALES

Poyerston Farm ····

Victorian farmhouse on a 400-acre working farm in the heart of South Pembrokeshire

☎ 01646 651347
🖷 01646 651347
✉ poyerstonfarm@ btinternet.com
www.poyerston-farm.co.uk

Map ref 1 - SM00

Cosheston, PEMBROKE, Pembrokeshire, SA72 4SJ from Carmarthen take A40 to St Clears rdbt, then A447 towards Pembroke Dock, drive through Milton. Poyerston 0.75m on L opp Vauxhall garage
5 Rooms, S £30-£35 D £50-£56, No smoking, Closed 20-27 Dec

Relax and enjoy the beauty of South Pembrokeshire, staying in this delightful Victorian farmhouse of character, situated on a working farm on the edge of the village of Milton and approached by a private tarmac drive. Poyerston is in an excellent central location, just two miles from Pembroke with its imposing castle. The wonderful coastline, with its lovely beaches, scenic walks, theme and leisure parks is close by. This sympathetically renovated farmhouse provides very comfortable en suite bedrooms (some ground floor) with many homely extras. There is a guests' lounge, and an elegant dining room extends into the conservatory, a charming setting for breakfast and imaginative dinners, featuring delicious traditional farmhouse cooking using fresh local produce. The conservatory overlooks the attractive gardens. Ample parking is available.

 ## RECOMMENDED IN THE AREA

Pembroke Castle and Carew Castle (2 miles); beautiful walks in Pembrokeshire Coast National Park (4 miles); Oakwood Theme Park (10 minutes drive)

The Usk Inn ····

Village pub transformed into delightful country inn with high quality accommodation and food

☎ 01874 676251
🖷 01874 676392
✉ stay@uskinn.co.uk
www.uskinn.co.uk

Map ref 2 - SO12

Station Road, Talybont-on-Usk, BRECON, Powys, LD3 7JE
just off the A40 6m E of Brecon. 10m W of Abergavenny
11 Rooms, S £29.50-£45
D £50-£85,
No smoking in bedrooms,
Closed 25-27 Dec

Established in the 1840s at the time of the Brecon to Merthyr railway, The Usk is positioned on the edge of the village. Popular with visitors to the Brecon Beacons National Park and handily located for exploring south and mid-Wales, guests might take advantage of activities on offer in the area: walking, fishing, cycling, horse-riding or cruising the Monmouthshire and Brecon canal, which flows through Talybont. The inn is family owned and personally run by Michael and Barbara Taylor in a warm and friendly manner. It has been renovated to a very high standard: public areas have a wealth of charm, whilst the thoughtfully equipped and appointed en suite bedrooms, each individually decorated and furnished with locally-made pine furniture, include some rooms with four-poster beds. An imaginative touch is the naming of each bright and cheerful room after a bird found along the river-bank. The inn has a deserved reputation for food.

RECOMMENDED IN THE AREA

Brecon Beacons National Park; Hay on Wye bookshops (20 minute drive); Museum of Royal Regiment of Wales 24th Foot & the Zulu Experience

Glangrwyney Court •••••

*Well proportioned
Georgian property set in
four acres of gardens
surrounded by
magnificent scenery*

☎ 01873 811288
🖷 01873 810317
✉ glangrwyne@aol.com
www.walescountryhouse
bandb.com

Map ref 2 - SO21

CRICKHOWELL, Powys,
NP8 1ES
3m from Abergavenny on
A40 towards Brecon, first R
after Powys county change
on L
5 Rooms, S £35-£50
D £45-£55, No smoking in
bedrooms or dining room

A Grade II listed country house, Glangrwyney Court is set in the National Park midway between Abergavenny and Crickhowell. The interior is graciously furnished with antiques, porcelain and paintings and log fires welcome guests in winter weather. Breakfast is served at one large table in the elegant dining room and guests can relax in the sumptuous lounge. There is a good choice of bedrooms, including single, twin, double and family rooms, all with en suite or private facilities, televisions, tea and coffee-making equipment, and wonderful views over the garden and surrounding countryside. The Master Suite has the additional luxury of a steam shower and extra deep bath, while the twin room has its own Jacuzzi. Croquet and boules are available in the grounds and activities such as pony trekking, golf, fishing and shooting can be arranged. There are many lovely walks in the area, with the Brecon Beacons and Black Mountains within easy reach. Children and pets welcome.

RECOMMENDED IN THE AREA

Hill walking in the Brecon Beacons; pony trekking; golf

Ffforddfawr Farmhouse ♦♦♦♦

Stone-built 17th-century farmhouse set in lovely gardens

☎ 01497 847332
📠 01497 847003
✉ barbara@ffordd-fawr.co.uk
www.ffordd-fawr.co.uk

Map ref 2 - SO13

GLASBURY, Hay-On-Wye, Powys,
HR3 5PT
from Hay-on-Wye take B4350
towards Brecon, farm 3m on R
3 Rooms, S £30-£32 D £42-£46,
No smoking, Closed Dec-Feb

Ffordd-Fawr Farmhouse offers a unique and captivating combination of 17th century character and the last word in modern amenities. Savour the breathtaking panorama of the Wye Valley, the Black Mountains and the Radnor Hills as you relax in the comfort of one of the en suite bedrooms or enjoy your farmhouse breakfast on the tranquil patio. Whether your pleasure is exploring the rich historical heritage of the Welsh Marches, the rugged magnificence of the mountains, the world-famous Hay-on-Wye bookshops or the quiet enchantment of the farm's nature trail along the banks of the river, Ffordd-Fawr is the perfect holiday venue. Your hosts Barbara and Richard are dedicated to ensuring that your visit will be an unforgettable experience.

RECOMMENDED IN THE AREA

Hay on Wye (3 miles); explore the beautiful Wye Valley; Brecon Beacons

Guidfa House ♦♦♦♦

An elegant setting for Cordon Bleu cooking in the heart of Wales

☎ 01597 851241
📠 01597 851875
✉ guidfa@globalnet.co.uk
www.guidfa-house.co.uk

Map ref 2 - SO06

Crossgates, LLANDRINDOD WELLS,
Powys, LD1 6RF
3m N, at junct of A483/A44
6 Rooms, S £31.50-£37.50 D £53-£58, No smoking in bedrooms or dining room

Tony and Anne Millan are the welcoming proprietors of this long established country guest house in a fine Georgian property. In 1999 Tony's front of house qualities were recognised when he reached the finals of the AA Landlady of the Year award. Bedrooms, including one located at ground floor level, are individually designed and all have en suite facilities. Central heating, colour television, tea and coffee making equipment are provided along with various thoughtful extras. In the comfortable sitting room a cheerful log fire burns in the cooler months, and in the evenings Tony serves drinks to guests at the bar. In fine weather guests may wish to take their drinks out onto the front lawn, or enjoy a stroll in the garden. Food at Guidfa House is rather special. Anne is a qualified chef and serves imaginative dishes using fresh local produce whenever possible

RECOMMENDED IN THE AREA

Elan Valley (10 minutes' drive); RSPB Red Kite feeding station (8 miles); located on the route of one of the AA's '10 great drives of the world' (New Radnor-Aberystwyth)

York House Guest House ◆◆◆◆

Victorian property with a country house aspect, conveniently close to the town centre

☎ 01497 820705
📠 01497 820705
✉ roberts@yorkhouse
59.fsnet.co.uk
www.hay-on-
wye.co.uk/yorkhouse

Map ref 2 - SO24

Hardwick Road, Cusop,
HAY-ON-WYE, Powys,
HR3 5QX
on B4348 0.5m from main
car park in Hay-on-Wye
4 Rooms, S £28-£38 D
£52-£56, No smoking

Visitors to York House are greeted by Basil and Sybil, the resident cats, who are also in charge of the white doves that live out in the garden. Olwen and Peter Roberts are the friendly owners, and they make sure that guests feel at home in this fine house just half a mile from Hay town centre. The interior décor is traditional in style to retain the period feel. Bedrooms are attractively presented and well equipped with en suite facilities, televisions, hairdryers, electronic alarm clocks, books and hospitality trays. On each landing guests can also help themselves from baskets of fruit, herb teas and sweets. Some rooms are suitable for family occupation and all of them face away from the road and overlook the large garden to the hills beyond. The guests' lounge is supplied with books and games, and there is a separate dining room where a full cooked breakfast is served, including a vegetarian option.

RECOMMENDED IN THE AREA

Hay-on-Wye bookshops; Llanthony Abbey ruins; Gospel Path through the Black Mountains

$\mathscr{W}$oodside Guest House ♦♦♦♦

Charming 18th-century converted cottage with homely accommodation

☎ 01792 390791
✉ david@oxwich.fsnet.co.uk
Map ref 2 - SS48
OXWICH, Gower, Swansea, SA3 1LS
from A4118 from Penmaen after 1m
turn left for Oxwich and Slade,
premises atx-rds
5 Rooms, D £38-£64, No smoking in
dining room or lounge, Closed Dec-
Jan

$\mathcal{S}$et close to three miles of magnificent beach in one of the prettiest Gower villages, this charming guest house is a real find. The 200-year-old cottage and an adjoining barn have been sensitively converted to reflect the character of their period. Bedrooms have been tastefully decorated and comfortably furnished to provide all the ease and relaxation of home, and three are at ground floor level for extra convenience. All rooms have en suite facilities, colour television, comfy seating and courtesy tray. A small private bar has a fire burning in winter, and there is also a lounge attached to the spacious conservatory where breakfast is served.

RECOMMENDED IN THE AREA

National Botanic Gardens of Wales

$\mathcal{T}$he Grosvenor House ♦♦♦♦

An elegant property in the fashionable Uplands district

☎ 01792 461522 ☎ 01792 461522
✉ grosvenor@ct6.com
www.ct6.com/grosvenor

Map ref 2 - SS69
Mirador Crescent, Uplands, SWANSEA,
SA2 0QX
off A4118 in the uplands area of Swansea
7 Rooms, S £28-£32 D £46-£54, No smoking,
Closed 23 Dec-3 Jan

$\mathcal{T}$he Grosvenor House provides comfortable accommodation with secure parking a short distance from the city centre and some 20 minutes' drive from Three Cliffs Bay, making it a convenient base for touring the Gower Peninsula and the Mumbles. The house is located in the same road as Dylan Thomas' former school and close to his childhood home. The bedrooms are all en suite, with central heating, colour televisions, radio alarms, hairdryers and tea and coffee making equipment. Family rooms are also available. A freshly cooked breakfast is served in the dining room, and a separate lounge is accessible to guests at all times. Vegetarian and special diets are catered for.

RECOMMENDED IN THE AREA

Explore the Gower Peninsula – walking, fishing, golf, surfing, pony trekking and swimming; various ancient churches, castles and monuments

$\mathcal{M}$ill Farm ◆◆◆◆

A marvellous blend of old and new in an idyllic setting

☎ 01495 774588
📠 01495 774588

Map ref 2 - SO20

Cwmafon, PONTYPOOL, Torfaen, NP4 8XJ
between Pontypool and Blaenavon on A4043, 0.5m S of Cwmafon Village, turn E into Denbridge Rd, after 100 mtrs R over river, 400mtrs to house
4 Rooms, S £25-£30 D £50-£60, No smoking in bedrooms or dining room, Closed 16 Dec-2 Jan

$\mathcal{Q}$uietly located in a picturesque valley, and surrounded by extensive grounds and farmland including an ancient wood. This wonderful old house dates back in part to medieval times with Tudor additions, and retains original features like beams, stone-flagged floors, spiral stone staircases and huge fireplaces. The latest in modern comforts are also evident. One of the lounges houses a full-sized swimming pool next to a roaring inglenook fire in winter, while bedrooms are tasteful and comfortable, with en suite bathrooms; one boasts a four-poster bed. A full 'Flavours of Wales' breakfast can be enjoyed until noon, when garden games like boules and croquet can help to work off the excess.

RECOMMENDED IN THE AREA

World Heritage site Blaenafon and Big Pit Mining Museum (2 miles); Brecon Beacons National Park (2 miles); Caerleon Roman Barracks and amphitheatre (10 minute drive)

Pen-y-Fan and Pentwyn Reservoir, Powys

*C*ounty & Country Index

Permission for the use of the photographs on the back cover was kindly given by the proprietors of Wesley House, Winchcombe
Alderholt Mill, Fordingbridge
The following images are held in the Automobile Association's own photo library (AA PHOTO LIBRARY) and were taken by the following photographers:
M Adelman: page 2, 6; P Baker: page 127; A Besley: page 56; M Birkitt: page 10; I Burgum: page 344, 346; S Day: page 9; D Forss: page 1, 5; J Henderson: page 320; A Lawson: page 4; M Siebert: page 8; T Souter: page 10; D Tarn: page 269; P Trenchard: page 2, 272; V Bates: page 276.